THE COMMON LAW LIBRARY

TORTS

AUSTRALIA
Law Book Co.
Sydney

CANADA and USA
Carswell
Toronto

HONG KONG
Sweet & Maxwell Asia

NEW ZEALAND
Brookers
Wellington

SINGAPORE and MALAYSIA
Sweet & Maxwell
Singapore and Kuala Lumpur

THE COMMON LAW LIBRARY

CLERK & LINDSELL

ON

TORTS

SECOND SUPPLEMENT
TO THE
EIGHTEENTH EDITION

Up-to-date until
August 2002

LONDON
SWEET & MAXWELL
2002

First Edition	(1889)	J. F. Clerk and W. H. B. Lindsell
Second Edition	(1896)	" " " "
Third Edition	(1904)	Wyatt Paine
Fourth Edition	(1906)	" "
Fifth Edition	(1909)	" "
Sixth Edition	(1912)	" "
Seventh Edition	(1921)	" "
Eighth Edition	(1929)	W. A. Macfarlane and G. W. Wrangham
Ninth Edition	(1937)	Under the General Editorship of Harold Potter
Tenth Edition	(1947)	" " " "
Eleventh Edition	(1954)	Under the General Editorship of John Burke and Peter Allsop
Twelfth Edition	(1961)	General Editor: A. L. Armitage
Thirteenth Edition	(1969)	" " " "
Fourteenth Edition	(1975)	General Editor: Sir Arthur L. Armitage and R. W. M. Dias
Fifteenth Edition	(1982)	General Editor: R. W. M. Dias
Sixteenth Edition	(1989)	" " " "
Seventeenth Edition	(1995)	General Editor: Margaret R. Brazier
Second Impression	(1996)	" " " "
Third Impression	(1998)	" " " "
Eighteenth Edition	(2000)	General Editor: Anthony M. Dugdale

Published in 2002 by
Sweet & Maxwell Ltd of
100 Avenue Road, Swiss Cottage,
London NW3 3PF
Computerset by Interactive Sciences Ltd
Gloucester
Printed in Great Britain by Ashford Colour Press ltd, Gosport, Hants
Reprinted 2003
British Cataloguing in Publication Data

Clerk, John Frederic
  Clerk & Lindsell on torts.—(The Common
Law Library)
    1. Torts. Law. England.
    I. Title II. Lindsell, William Henry Barber
    III. Dugdale, Anthony M.
    IIII. Series 344. 2063

ISBN 0421 795 808

All rights reserved. Crown Copyright legislation is reproduced under the terms of Crown Copyright Policy Guidance issued by HMSO. No part of this publication may be reproduced or transmitted in any form or by any means, or stored in any retrieval system of any nature without prior written permission, except for permitted fair dealing under the Copyright, Designs and Patents Act 1988, or in accordance with the terms of a licence issued by the Copyright Licensing Agency in respect of photocopying and/or reprographic reproduction. Application for permission for other use of copyright material including permission to reproduce extracts in other published works shall be made to the publishers. Full acknowledgment of author, publisher and source must be given.

©
Sweet & Maxwell Ltd
2002

GENERAL EDITOR

ANTHONY M. DUGDALE, B.A., B.C.L.

Beachcroft Wansbroughs Professor, Keele University

EDITORS

DANIEL ALEXANDER, B.A., LL.M.

Of the Middle Temple, Barrister

R.A. BUCKLEY, M.A., D. PHIL.

Of Lincoln's Inn, Barrister;
Professor of Law of the University of Reading

ANDREW S. BURROWS, M.A., B.C.L., LL.M. (Harvard)

Of the Middle Temple, Barrister;
Fellow of St Hugh's College and Norton Rose Professor of Commercial Law
in the University of Oxford

HAZEL F. CARTY, M.A.

Of the Middle Temple, Barrister;
Senior Lecturer in Law of the University of Manchester

MICHAEL A. JONES, B.A., LL.M., Ph.D.

Solicitor: Professor of Common Law,
The University of Liverpool

MAUREEN MULHOLLAND, LL.B., LL.M.

Lecturer in Law of the University
of Manchester

JOHN MURPHY

Senior Lecturer in Law of the University of Manchester

ALAN SPRINCE, LL.B.

Lecturer in Law of the University of Liverpool

ANDREW TETTENBORN, M.A., LL.B.

Of Lincoln's Inn, Barrister;
Bracton Professor of Law in the
University of Exeter

LORD WEDDERBURN OF CHARLTON, Q.C., M.A., LL.B., F.B.A.

Of the Middle Temple;
Professor Emeritus of Commercial Law of the University of London
(London School of Economics and Political Science)

How to use this Supplement

This is the Second Supplement to the Eighteenth Edition of *Clerk and Lindsell on Torts*, and has been compiled according to the structure of the main volume.

At the beginning of each chapter of this Supplement a mini table of contents from the main volume has been included. Where a heading in this table of contents has been marked by the symbol ■, there is relevant information included in *this* Supplement to which you should refer.

Within each chapter, updating information is referenced to the relevant paragraph in the main volume.

Introductory paragraphs containing material pertinent to the chapter as a whole and not to a specific paragraph have been identified as *e.g.* 2a. This enables references contained within these paragraphs to be identified in the tables included in this Supplement.

TABLE OF CASES

800 Flowers Trade Mark [2001] EWCA Civ. 721, *The Times*, July 9, 2001, CA ... 25–73
A Fulton Co. Ltd v. Grant Barnett & Co. Ltd [2001] R.P.C. 16 25–51
A v. B (Copyright: Diary pages) [2002] EWCA Civ. 337; [2002] E.M.L.R. 371,
    CA; [2000] E.M.L.R.1007 .... 27–02, 27–03, 27–08, 27–17, 27–36, 27–43
A v. National Blood Authority [2001] 3 All E.R. 289, *The Times*, April 4, 2001 2–28,
    9A, 9–39, 9–41, 9–44, 9–45, 9–62
A. E. Beckett & Sons (Lyndons) Ltd v. Midlands Electricity plc [2001] 1 W.L.R.
    281, *The Times*, January 10, 2001 3–62
AB v. South West Water Services Ltd [1993] Q.B. 507; [1993] 2 W.L.R. 507;
    [1993] 1 All. E.R. 609, CA 13–85, 15–43
Abouzaid v. Mothercare (UK) Ltd [2000] All E. R. (D) 246, *The Times*, February
    20, 2001 9–62
Ackers v. Taylor [1974] 1 W.L.R. 405; [1974] 1 All E.R. 771, DC 13–45
Adams v. Rhymney Valley District Council [2001] P.N.L.R. 68 7–187
Ad-Lib Club v. Granville [1971] 2 All E.R. 300; [1971] F.S.R. 1; [1972] R.P.C.
    673; (1970) 115 S.J. 74; *The Times*, December 15, 1970 [1972] R.P.C.
    673 26–11
AGDA Systems Intl. Ltd v. Valcom Ltd (1999) 168 D.L.R. (4th) 351 (Ont CA) ... 24–44
AK (adult Patient) (Medical Treatment: Consent), Re [2001] 1 F.L.R. 129 ...... 3–106, 8–25
Alcoa Minerals of Jamaica Ltd v. Broderick [2000] 3 W.L.R. 23; *The Times*,
    March 22, 2000 7–149
Alcock v. Wraith 59 B.L.R. 20; [1991] E.G.C.S. 137; [1991] N.P.C. 135; *The
Times*, December 23, 1991, CA 5–53
Alexander v. Arts Council of Wales [2001] EWCA Civ. 514; [2001] 1 W.L.R.
    1840; [2001] 4 All E.R. 205; [2001] E.M.L.R. 27; (2001) 98(22) L.S.G. 35;
    (2001) 145 S.J.L.B. 123; *The Times*, April 27, 2001; *Independent*, April 27,
    2001, CA 22–02, 22–06, 22–159, 22–183
Al-Fagih v. HH Saudi Research and Marketing (U.K.) Ltd [2001] EWCA Civ
    1634; [2002] E.M.L.R. 13, CA 22–08, 22–12, 22–39, 22–79, 22–113, 22–122,
    22–139
Allen v. British Rail Engineering [2001] EWCA Civ 242; [2002] I.C.R. 942;
    [2001] P.I.Q.R. Q10, CA 2–22
Allied Maples Group Ltd v. Simmons & Simmons [1995]1 W.L.R. 1602; [1995]
    4 All E.R.907, CA 8–67, 8–83
American Cyanamid Co. v. Ethicon Ltd [1975] A.C. 396; [1975] 2 W.L.R. 316;
    [1975] 1 All E.R. 504; [1975] F.S.R. 101; [1975] R.P.C. 513; 119 S.J. 136,
    HL 24–142
Anderson v. Newham College for Further Education [2002] EWCA Civ 505 3–22
Aneco Reinsurance Underwriting Ltd (In Liquidation) v. Johnson & Higgins Ltd
    [2001] UKHL 51; [2001] 2 All E.R. (Comm) 929; [2002] 1 Lloyd's Rep.
    157; [2002] C.L.C. 181; [2002] Lloyd's Rep. I.R. 91; [2002] P.N.L.R. 8, HL 2–67,
    7–158
Anglian Water Services v. Crawshaw Robbins & Co. [2001] B.L.R. 173; [2001]
    N.P.C. 32 .... 19–08, 19–10, 20–15, 20–36, 20–65
Antiquest Portfolio.Com plc v. Rodney Fitch & Co. Ltd [2001] F.S.R. 345, *The
Times*, July 21, 2000 25–09

Table of Cases

Anyanwu v. South Bank Student Union [2001] UKHL 14; [2001] 1 W.L.R. 638; [2001] 2 All E.R. 353; [2001] I.C.R. 391; [2001] I.R.L.R. 305; [2001] E.L.R. 511; (2001) 98(21) L.S.G. 39; (2001) 151 N.L.J. 501; (2001) 145 S.J.L.B. 110, *The Times*, March 27, 2001; *Independent*, March 28, 2001, HL 24–102
APQ v. Commonwealth Serum Laboratories Ltd [1999] 3 V.R. 633 9–17
Arab Bank plc v. John D. Wood Commercial Ltd [2000] Lloyd's Rep. P.N. 173 ... 3–56
Arsenal Football Club plc v. Reed [2001] E.T.M.R. 77, *The Times*, April 26, 2001 .... 25–73, 26–09
Ashdown v. Telegraph Group Ltd [2001] EWCA Civ. 1142, *The Times*, August 1, 2001, CA.
Ashingdane v. United Kingdom (A/93) (1985) 7 E.H.R.R. 528, ECHR 1–81
Ashworth Security Hospital v. MGN Ltd [2001] 1 W.L.R. 515; [2001] F.S.R. 559 ...24–61, 27–02, 27–16, 27–28
Asprey and Garrard Ltd v. WRA (Guns) Ltd [2001] EWCA Civ 1499; [2002] E.T.M.R. 47; [2002] F.S.R. 31; (2002) 25(1) I.P.D. 25001, CA 25–74
Associated British Ports v. T.G.W.U. [1989] 1 W.L.R. 939; [1989] 3 All E.R. 822, HL 24–78, 24–142
Att.-Gen. v. Barker (Civil Proceedings Order) [2001] 1 F.L.R. 759 16–51
Att.-Gen. v. Blake [2001] 1 A.C. 268, HL 14–103, 24–97
Att.-Gen. v. Covey and Mathews, *The Times*, March 2, 2001, CA 16–51
Att.-Gen. v. Punch [2001] EWCA Civ 403; [2001] Q.B. 1028; [2001] 2 W.L.R. 1713; [2001] 2 All E.R. 655; [2001] E.M.L.R. 24; (2001) 98(21) L.S.G. 39; (2001) 145 S.J.L.B. 101; *The Times*, March 30, 2001; *Independent*, March 30, 2001; *Daily Telegraph*, April 3, 2001, CA 24–61, 24–139
Att.-Gen. for Hong Kong v. Reid [1994] 1 A.C. 324 28–25
Australian Workers' Union v. BHP Iron-Ore Pty. Ltd [2001] F.C.A. 3 24–126
Aylwen v. Taylor Joynson Garrett [2001] EWCA Civ 1171; [2002] P.N.L.R. 1; (2001) 98(29) L.S.G. 40, CA 8–101

B. v. Croydon Health Authority [1995] Fam. 133; [1995] 1 All E. R. 683; [1995] 2 W.L.R. 294 13–72
B (a child) v. London Borough of Camden [2001] P.I.Q.R. P143 .... 7–171, 10–31
B (a child) v. McDonald's Ltd [2002] EWHC (QB) 409 .... 9–25, 9–44, 10–26
B (adult: refusal of medical treatment) v. NHS Trust [2002] EWHC 429; [2002] 2 All E.R. 449; [2002] 1 F.L.R. 1090; [2002] 2 F.C.R. 1; (2002) 65 B.M.L.R. 149; [2002] Fam. Law 423; (2002) 99(17) L.S.G. 37; (2002) 152 N.L.J. 470; (2002) 146 S.J.L.B. 83; *The Times*, March 26, 2002; *Daily Telegraph*, March 28, 2002 .... 3–106, 8a, 8–25
Bacardi-Martini Beverages Ltd v. Thomas Hardy Packaging Ltd [2002] 1 Lloyd's Rep. 62 .... 9a, 9–20
BACH and BACH Flower Remedies Trade Marks [2000] R.P.C. 513, CA 26–68
Bailey v. Command Security Ltd, unreported, October 25, 2001 10–28
Baker v. Willoughby [1970] A.C. 467; [1970] 2 W.L.R. 50; [1969] 3 All E.R. 1528, HL 2–35
Baldwin v. Rusbridger [2001] E.M.L.R. 47; *The Times*, July 23, 2001 22–121
Bank of China v. NBM (2001) 151 N.L.J.1034 30–43
Bank of Credit and Commerce International S.A. v. Ali [2001] UKHL 8; [2002] 1 A.C. 251; [2001] 2 W.L.R. 735; [2001] 1 All E.R. 961; [2001] I.C.R. 337; [2001] I.R.L.R. 292; (2001) 98(15) L.S.G. 32; (2001) 151 N.L.J. 351; (2001) 145 S.J.L.B. 67; (2001) 145 S.J.L.B. 70; *The Times*, March 6, 2001, HL 24–39
Bank of Scotland v. A Ltd [2001] 1 W.L.R. 751; *The Times*, February 6, 2001, CA 30–50
Bank of Scotland v. Fuller Peiser 2002 S.L.T. 574; 2002 S.C.L.R. 255; [2002] P.N.L.R. 13; 2002 Rep. L.R. 2; 2001 G.W.D. 37–1411, OH 8–111, 8–113

TABLE OF CASES

Banque Bruxelles Lambert SA v. Eagle Star Insurance Co. Ltd [1997] A.C. 191; [1995] Q.B. 375; [1995] 2 W.L.R. 607; [1995] 2 All E.R. 769; [1995] L.R.L.R. 195; [1996] 5 Bank.L.R. 64; 73 B.L.R. 47; [1995] E.C.C. 398; [1996] 5 Re.L.R. 23; [1995] 1 E.G.L.R. 129; [1995] 12 E.G. 144; [1995] E.G.C.S. 31; (1995) 92(12) L.S.G. 34; (1995) 145 N.L.J. 343; (1995) 139 S.J.L.B. 56; [1995] N.P.C. 32; *The Times*, February 21, 1995; *Independent*, February 24, 1995, CA 7–22
Barbara v. Home Office (1984) 134 New L.J. 888 13–85
Barings plc (in liquidation) v. Coopers & Lybrand (No.5) [2002] EWHC 461; [2002] Lloyd's Rep. P.N. 395; [2002] P.N.L.R. 321 ....7–96, 7–97, 8–13, 8–145, 15–10, 15–35
Barrett v. Enfield London Borough Council [2001] 2 A.C. 550; [1999] 3 W.L.R. 79; [1999] 3 All E.R.193; [1999] 2 F.L.R. 426; [1999] 2 F.C.R. 434; (1999) 1 L.G.L.R. 829; [1999] B.L.G.R. 473; (1999) 11 Admin.L.R. 839; [1999] Ed.C.R. 833; (1999) 2 C.C.L. Rep. 203; [1999] P.I.Q.R. P272; (1999) 49 B.M.L.R. 1; [1999] Fam. Law 622; (1999) 96(28) L.S.G. 27; (1999) 143 S.J.L.B. 183; *The Times*, June 18, 1999, HL 11–33, 12–61, 12–62, 12–63
Baxall Securities Ltd v. Sheard Walshaw Partnership [2001] P.N.L.R. 257 .....7–23, 7–123, 8–133
Bazley v. Curry (1999) 174 D.L.R. (4th) 45 .... 5A
BBMB Finance v. Eda Holdings Ltd [1990] 1 W.L.R. 409 14–103
BCCI v. Akindele [2000] *The Times*, June 22, 2000 24–39
BCCI v. Ali [2001] 2 W.L.R. 735, HL 24–39
Beck v. United Closures & Plastics Ltd 2001 S.L.T. 1299; 2002 S.C.L.R. 154; 2001 Rep.L.R. 91; 2001 G.W.D. 22–842, OH 11–15
Bellefield Computer Services Ltd v. Turner & Sons Ltd (No.2), November 9, 2001 8–137
Berezovsky v. Michaels [2000] 1 W.L.R. 1004; [2000] 2 All E.R. 986 22–01
Berry v. British Transport Commission [1962] 1 Q.B. 306; [1961] 3 W.L.R. 450; [1961] 3 All E.R. 65; 105 S.J. 587, CA 29–115
Best v. Charter Medical of England Ltd [2001] EWCA Civ 1588; [2002] E.M.L.R. 18; (2001) 98(47) L.S.G. 27; *The Times*, November 19, 2001, CA 22–14
Bibby v. Chief Constable of Essex Police (2000) 164 J.P. 297 13–43
Biggs v. Sotnicks (a firm) [2002] EWCA Civ 272 15–02
Birse Construction Ltd v. Haiste [1996] 1 W.L.R. 675; [1996] 2 All E.R. 1; [1996] C.L.C. 577; 76 B.L.R. 31; 47 Con.L.R. 162; [1996] P.N.L.R. 8; (1996) 93(2) L.S.G. 29; (1996) 140 S.J.L.B. 25; *The Times*, December 12, 1995, CA 8–133
Bladet Tromso v. Norway (2000) 29 E.H.R.R. 125; 6 B.H.R.C. 599, ECHR 22–01, 22–12
Blue Circle v. TGWU, unreported, July 7, 1989 24–176
Boehringer Ingelheim KG v. Swingward Ltd (C–143/00) [2002] 2 C.M.L.R. 26; [2002] C.E.C. 378; (2002) 65 B.M.L.R. 177; [2002] E.T.M.R. 898; *The Times*, May 23, 2002, ECJ 25–74
Bolam v. Friern Hospital Management Committee [1957] 1 W.L.R. 582; [1957] 2 All E. R. 118 11–33
Bond v. Livingstone & Co. [2001] P.N.L.R. 286 8–93
Bonnington Castings Ltd v. Wardlaw [1956] A.C. 613; [1956] 2 W.L.R. 707; [1956] 1 All E.R. 615; 1956 S.C. (H.L.) 26; 1956 S.L.T. 135; 54 L.G.R. 153; 100 S.J. 207, HL 2–13A, 2–13E, 2–13J, 2–16
Bordin v. St Mary's NHS Trust [2000] Lloyd's L.R. Med. 287 29–96
Boyle v. Kodak Ltd [1969] 1 W.L.R. 661; [1969] 2 All E.R. 439; 6 K.I.R. 427; 113 S.J. 382, HL 3–22
BP Amoco v. John Kelly Ltd [2001] N.I. 25; [2002] F.S.R. 5; [2001] E.T.M.R. CN14, CA (NI) 26–18

TABLE OF CASES

Bradford & Bingley plc v. Hayes, unreported, July 25, 2001 .... 8–06A
Bradford Building Society v. Borders [1941] 2 All E.R. 205 15–27
Bradley v. Wingnut Films Ltd [1992] 1 N.Z.L.R. 415 1–76
Brandeis Goldschmidt Ltd v. Western Transport Ltd [1981] Q.B. 864; [1981] 3
  W.L.R. 181; [1982] 1 All E.R. 28; [1981] F.S.R. 481; 125 S.J. 395, CA 14–103
Branson v. Bower (No.2) [2001] EWCA 791; [2002] 2 W.L.R. 452; [2001]
  E.M.L.R. 33; *The Times*, July 23, 2001 .... 22–159, 22–162, 22–164, 22–165, 22–168,
  22–171, 22–183
BRB (Residuary) Ltd v. Cully 2001 W.I. 1476357 18–65
Briody v. St Helens Health Authority and Knowsley AHA (Claim for Damages
  and Costs) [2001] EWCA Civ 1010; [2002] 2 W.L.R. 394; [2001] 2 F.L.R.
  1094; [2001] 2 F.C.R. 481; (2001) 62 B.M.L.R. 1; [2001] Fam. Law 796;
  (2001) 98(33) L.S.G. 32; *The Times*, August 14, 2001; *Independent*, July 3,
  2001, CA 8–69, 29–19, 29–20
Bristol and West Building Society v. Mothew [1998] Ch. 1; [1997] 2 W.L.R.
  436; [1996] 4 All E.R. 698; [1997] P.N.L.R. 11; (1998) 75 P. & C.R. 241;
  [1996] E.G.C.S. 136;. (1996) 146 N.L.J. 1273; (1996) 140 S.J.L.B. 206;
  [1996] N.P.C. 126; *The Times*, August 2, 1996, CA 2–09
Bristol and West Building Society v. Richard Grosse & Co. [1999] Lloyd's Rep.
  P.N. 348 28–23
British Airways plc v. Ryanair Ltd [2001] F.S.R.541; [2001] E.T.M.R. 24 .... 23–19, 23–22
British Horseracing Board Ltd v. William Hill Organisation Ltd, unreported
  judgment of CA, dated July 31, 2001 on appeal from a decision of Mr
  Justice Laddie reported at [2001] R.P.C. 612 25–08
British Telecommunications plc v. One in a Million Ltd [1999] 1 W.L.R. 903;
  [1998] 4 All E.R. 476; [1999] E.T.M.R. 61; [1997–98] Info. T.L.R. 423;
  [1998] I.T.C.L.R. 146; [2001] E.B.L.R. 2; [1999] F.S.R. 1; [1998] Masons
  C.L.R. 165; (1998) 95(37) L.S.G. 37; (1998) 148 N.L.J. 1179; *The Times*,
  July 29, 1998; *Independent*, July 31, 1998, CA 26–08
British Waterways Board v. Severn Trent Water Ltd [2001] EWCA Civ. 276;
  [2002] Ch. 25; [2001] 3 W.L.R. 613; [2001] 3 All E.R. 673; [2001]
  Env.L.R. 45; [2002] E.H.L.R. 1; (2001) 98(16) L.S.G. 34; (2001) 98(13)
  L.S.G. 43; [2001] N.P.C. 53; *The Times*, March 23, 2001; *Independent*,
  March 14, 2001, CA 18A, 18–08, 18–37, 18–53, 19–84
Britvic Soft Drinks Ltd v. Messer UK Ltd [2002] Lloyd's Rep. 20 .... 9a, 9–20
Broklesby v. Armitage and Guest [2001] 1 All E.R.172, CA 33–25
Bromiley v. United Kingdom (App. No. 33747/96) (2000) 29 E.H.R.R. CD111,
  ECHR 12–73
Brooks v. Home Office [1999] 2 F.L.R. 33; (1999) 48 B.M.L.R. 109; *The Times*,
  February 17, 1999 13–28
Brown v. Bennett (Wasted Costs Orders) (No.2) [2002] 1 W.L.R. 713; [2002]
  Lloyd's Rep. P.N. 242; (2002) 98(8) L.S.G. 35; *The Times*, January 4,
  2002 8–83
Buchanan v. Alba Diagnostics Ltd [2000] R.P.C. 367; 2001 S.C.L.R. 307 (Ct. of
  Session) 27–28
Buchanan v. Jennings [2001] N.Z.L.R. 71 22–99
Burdis v. Livsey [2002] EWCA 510 29–110
Burge v. Haycock [2001] EWCA Civ. 900; [2002] R.P.C. 28 26–12
Burrows v. Azadani [1995] 1 W.L.R. 1372 13–17
Burrows v. Brent London Borough Council [1966] 1 W.L.R. 1448 19–42
Burstein v. Times Newspapers [2001] 1 W.L.R. 579; [2001] E.M.L.R.14, CA 22–05,
  22–159
Byebrook Barn Centre v. Kent County Council [2000] B.L.G.R.302, *The Times*,
  January 5, 2001, CA A19, 19–21, 19–82, A20, 20–39

TABLE OF CASES

Byrne v. Sefton Health Authority [2001] EWCA Civ 1904; [2002] 1 W.L.R. 775; (2002) 99(1) L.S.G. 19; (2001) 145 S.J.L.B. 268; *The Times*, November 28, 2001, CA 8–83

C (a child) v. W School [2002] P.I.Q.R. P134; [2001] E.L.R. 285; (2000) 97(45) L.S.G. 40; *The Times*, November 14, 2000 7–231
C Inc. plc v. L (2001) 151 N.L.J. 535 30–40
Cable & Wireless plc v. BT [1998] F.S.R. 383; (1998) 21(4) I.P.D. 21042, Ch. D 23–22
Cachia v. Faluyi [2001] EWCA Civ 998; [2001] 1 W.L.R. 1966; [2002] 1 All E.R. 192; [2001] C.P. Rep. 102; [2002] P.I.Q.R. P5; (2001) 98(29) L.S.G. 39; (2001) 145 S.J.L.B. 167; *The Times*, July 11, 2001; *Daily Telegraph*, July 3, 2001, CA 29–73
Cadbury Schweppes Inc. v. FBI Foods Ltd [2000] F.S.R. 491 ...... 27–02, 27–11, 27–12, 27–44, 27–45
Cala Homes (South) Ltd v. Alfred McAlpine Homes East Ltd [1995] F.S.R. 818 25–21
Calderdale Metropolitan Borough Council v. Gorringe [2002] EWCA Civ 595; (2002) 99(22) L.S.G. 36; *The Times*, May 16, 2002 11–09
Caldwell v. Maguire and Fitzgerald [2001] EWCA Civ 1054; [2002] P.I.Q.R. P45 7–167
Calver v. Westwood Veterinary Group [2001] Lloyd's Rep. Med. 20; [2001] Lloyd's Rep. P.N.102 8–37
Cambridge Water Co. Ltd v. Eastern Counties Leather Plc [1994] 2 A.C. 264; [1994] 2 W.L.R. 53; [1994] 1 All E.R. 53; [1994] 1 Lloyd's Rep. 261; [1994] Env.L.R. 105; [1993] E.G.C.S. 211; (1994) 144 N.L.J. 15; (1994) 138 S.J.L.B. 24; *The Times*, December 10, 1993; *Independent*, December 10, 1993, HL 20–12
Campbell v. Frisbee [2002] EWHC 328; [2002] E.M.L.R. 31 .... 27–03, 27–37
Campbell v. MGN [2002] EWHC 499; [2002] E.M.L.R. 617 .... 22–90, 27–03, 27–19
Caparo Industries plc v. Dickman [1990] 2 A.C. 605; [1990] 2 W.L.R. 358; [1990] 1 All E.R. 568; [1990] B.C.C. 164; [1990] B.C.L.C. 273; [1990] E.C.C. 313; [1955–95] P.N.L.R. 523; (1990) 87(12) L.S.G. 42; (1990) 140 N.L.J. 248; (1990) 134 S.J. 494; *The Times*, February 12, 1990, HL 3–11A, 7–22
Capital and Counties v. Hampshire CC [1997] Q.B. 1004 7–52
Cardile v. LED Builders Pty Ltd [1999] HCA 18 30–40
Carlton Communications v. News Group; Cook v. News Group, [2001] EWCA Civ 1644; [2002] E.M.L.R. 16, CA 22–49, 22–222
Carmichael v. Bearsdon & District Rifle and Pistol Club [2001] S.L.T. 49 (Sh Ct) 5–19
Carmichael v. National Power plc [1999] 1 W.L.R. 2042; [1999] 4 All E.R. 897, HL 5–10
Cartonneries de Thulin S.A. v. CTP White Knight Ltd [2001] R.P.C. 107 25–85
Casey v. Morane Ltd [2001] I.C.R. 316; [2001] I.R.L.R. 166; (2000) 97(21) L.S.G. 38; *The Times*, May 10, 2000, CA 2–54A
Caslo Computer Ltd v. Sayo, *The Times*, February 2, 2001 24–39
Casson v. Ostley PJ Ltd [2001] B.L.R. 126 8–14
Cavanagh v. Bristol and Weston Health Authority [1992] 3 Med. L.R. 49 2–10
Center Optical (Hong Kong) Ltd v. Jardine Transport Services (China) Ltd [2001] 2 Lloyd's Rep. 678 14–104
Channon v. Lindley Johnstone (a firm) [2002] EWCA Civ 353; [2002] P.N.L.R. 884 8–107
Chappell v. Hart [1998] H.C.A. 55; (1998) 156 A.L.R. 517 .... 2–08, 8–43
Charles v. Hugh James Jones & Jenkins (A Firm) [2000] 1 W.L.R. 1278; [2000] 1 All E.R. 289; [2001] P.I.Q.R. P1; [2000] Lloyd's Rep. P.N. 207; *The Times*, December 22, 1999, CA 2–28

[xi]

Table of Cases

Chartered Trust plc v. King, unreported, February 23, 2001 14–122
Chase v. Newsgroup [2002] EWHC 1101 ....22–39, 22–49, 22–78, 22–79
Cheng v. Tse Wai Chun [2000] 3 H.K.L.R.D. 418 22–159
Chester v. Afshar [2002] EWCA Civ 724; [2002] 3 All E.R. 552; *The Times*,
    June 13, 2002 .... 2–08, 8–43
Chief Constable of Humberside Police v. McQuade [2001] EWCA Civ 1330;
    [2002] 1 W.L.R. 1347 13–45
Cia. De Seguros Imperio v. Heat (REBX) Ltd [2001] 1 W.L.R. 112, CA 24–37
Clark v. University of Lincolnshire and Humberside [2001] 1 W.L.R. 1988;
    [2000] 3 All E.R. 752, CA 33–04
Clarke v. Barber [2002] C.L. 70 21–04
Coflexip S.A. v. Stolt Comex Seaway MS Ltd [2001] R.P.C. 182 25–95
Colbeck v. Diamanta (U.K.) Ltd [2002] EWHC 616 14–109
Collins v. Brebner [2000] Lloyd's Rep. P.N. 587, CA 28–25
Collins v. Mid-Western Health Board [2000] 1 I.R. 154 8–47
Commission v. UK [1997] 3 C.M.L.R. 923 .... 9–39, 9–62
Compagnhia de Soguras Imperio v. Heath (R.E.B.X.) Ltd [2001] 1 W.L.R. 112,
    CA 28–05
Connex S.E. Ltd v. R.M.T. [1999] I.R.L.R. 249, CA 24–171
Consul Development Pty Ltd v. D.P.C. Estates Pty Ltd [1975] 132 C.L.R. 373 28–25
Cook v. Lewis [1952] 1 D.L.R. 1 ....2–13D, 2–13I, 2–30
Cook v. News Group, December 18, 2000 .... 22–49, 22–222
Cookson v. Knowles [1979] A.C. 556; [1978] 2 W.L.R. 978; [1978] 2 All E.R.
    604; [1978] 2 Lloyd's Rep. 315; 122 S.J. 386, HL 29–90
Corbett v. Bond Pearce [2001] Lloyd's Rep. P.N. 501 .... 7–100, 8–78
Corbin v. Penfold Metallising Co. Ltd [2000] Lloyd's Rep. Med. 247; *The Times*,
    May 2, 2000, CA 33–46
Cornelius v. De Taranto [2002] E.M.L.R. 6, CA; [2001] E.M.L.R. 12; [2001]
    E.M.L.R. 329 ....22–44, 22–90, 27–16, 27–45
Cornwall Gardens Pte Ltd v. Garrard & Co. Ltd [2001] EWCA Civ. 699; *The
Times*, June 19, 2001 .... 15–02, 23–09
Cossey v. Lonnkvist [2000] Lloyd's Rep. P.N. 885, CA 7–102, 7–155
Costello v. Chief Constable of Derbyshire [2001] EWCA Civ. 381; [2001] 1
    W.L.R. 1437 .... 3–07, 14A, 14–53
Cottingham v. Attey Bower [2000] P.N.L.R. 557, *The Times*, April 19, 2000 8–99,
    8–102
Cowan v. Chief Constable of Avon and Somerset, *The Times*, December 11,
    2001; *Independent*, November 21, 2001, CA 12–36, 12–65
Crane v. Premier Prison Services Ltd [2001] C.L.Y. 3298 11–15
Creutzfeldt–Jacob Disease Litigation, Groups A and C Plaintiffs v. Secretary of
    State for Health (1998) 54 B.M.L.R.100 .... 2–23, 2–28
Cross v. Highlands and Islands Enterprise 2001 S.L.T. 1060; 2001 S.C.L.R. 547;
    [2001] Eu.L.R. 256; [2001] I.R.L.R. 336; 2001 Rep.L.R. 26; 2000 G.W.D.
    40–1506, OH 2–16, 11–15
Crosse & Crosse v. Lloyds Bank plc [2001] EWCA Civ. 366; [2001] Lloyd's
    Rep. P.N. 452; [2001] P.N.L.R. 34; [2001] 12 E.G.C.S. 167; [2001] N.P.C.
    59, CA 8–102

D.P.P. v. Moseley (Joanna), *The Times*, June 23, 1999, QBD 13–18
D.P.P. v. Orum [1989] 1W.L.R. 88; [1988] Crim.L.R. 848, DC 13–46, 13–47
Daido Asia Japan Co. Ltd v. Rothen 2001 WL 825034; [2002] B.C.C. 589 ....4–89, 4–108,
    15–25
Daniels v. Griffiths [2001] EWCA Civ 1376 22–06
Daniels v. Whetstone Entertainments Ltd , 106 S.J. 284; [1962] 2 Lloyd's Rep.
    1 5–37

Table of Cases

Darby v. National Trust [2001] E.W.C.A. Civ. 189; (2001) 3 L.G.L.R. 29; [2001] P.I.Q.R. P27; *The Times*, February 23, 1001, CA 9a, 2–66, 3–82, 7–144,10A, 10–14, 10–27, 10–28, 10–36

Das v. Ganju [1999] P.I.Q.R. P260; [1999] Lloyd's Rep. Med. 198, CA 33–46

Davies v. Ilieff, unreported, December 21, 2000 .... 18A, 18–66

Davis and Docherty v. Balfour Kilpatrick Ltd [2002] EWCA Civ 736 2–05

Dawnday & Co. Ltd v. Cantor Fitzgerald Int. [2000] R.P.C. 669, CA 26–11

Day v. Cook [2001] EWCA Civ 592; [2002] 1 B.C.L.C. 1; [2001] Lloyd's Rep. P.N. 551; [2001] P.N.L.R. 32, CA 8–13

De Beers Abrasive Products v. International General Electric [1975] 1 W.L.R. 972; [1975] 2 All E.R. 599 23–20

De Haes v. Belgium (1997) 25 E.H.R.R. 445 22–01

Dean v. Allin & Watts [2001] E.W.C.A. Civ. 758; [2000] P.N.L.R. 690 ...... 7–21, 7–43, 7–99, 7–116, 8–80, 8–87

Delaware Mansions Ltd v. Westminster City Council [2001] UKHL 55; [2002] 1 A.C. 321; [2001] 3 W.L.R. 1007; [2001] 4 All E.R. 737; [2002] B.L.R. 25; 79 Con.L.R. 39; [2002] B.L.G.R. 1; [2001] 44 E.G.C.S. 150; (2001) 98(45) L.S.G. 26; (2001) 151 N.L.J. 1611; (2001) 145 S.J.L.B. 259; [2001] N.P.C. 151; *The Times*, October 26, 2001; *Independent*, December 17, 2001 (C.S.), HL 1–37, 7–01, 7–126, 19a, 19–23, 19–42

Den Norske Bank A.S.A. v. Antonators [1999] Q.B.271; [1998] 3 W.L.R. 711, CA 30–44

Department of Natural Resources v. Harper [2000] 1 V.R. 1 .... 1–28, 10–28

Derbyshire C.C. v. Times Newspapers [1993] A.C. 534; [1993] 2 W.L.R. 449; [1993] 1 All E.R. 1011; 91 L.G.R. 179; (1993) 143 N.L.J. 283; (1993) 137 S.J.L.B. 52; *The Times*, February 19, 1993; *Independent*, February 19, 1993; *Guardian*, February 19, 1993, HL 22–60

Designers Guild Ltd v. Russell Williams (Textiles) Ltd [2000] 1 W.L.R. 2416; [2001] F.S.R. 113 25–22

Devine v. Jeffreys & Anor [2001] P.N.L.R. 407 8–126

Dhesi v. Chief Constable of West Midlands Police, *The Times*, May 9, 2000, CA 13–56

Dingley v. Chief Contable of Strathclyde Police (2000) 55 B.M.L.R. 1, HL 2–14

Disley v. Levine [2001] P.I.Q.R. P159; [2001] P.I.Q.R. P10 7–214

Docker v. Chief Constable of West Midlands Police [2001] 1 A.C. 435 .... 7–37, 16–53, 17–137

Donaldson v. Brighton District Council [2002] 4 C.L. 344 11–15

Douglas v. Hello! Ltd [2001] 2 W.L.R. 992; *The Times*, January 16, 2001 ....1–34, 1–76, 1–77, 22–90, 24–41, 27–03, 27–21, 27–37, 27–43

Drage v. Grassroots Ltd [2001] 11 C.L. 298 11–16

DSG Retail Ltd v. Comet Group plc [2002] EWHC 116 23–19

DSM NV's Patent [2001] R.P.C. 675 25–87

Duke of Brunswick and Luneberg v. Harmer (1849) 14 Q.B. 185 22–07

Dyson Appliances Ltd v. Hoover Ltd [2001] R.P.C. 26 25–87

East Hertfordshire District Council v. Isobel Hospice Trading Ltd [2001] J.P.L. 597 19–106

Easy Jet Airline Co. Ltd v. Dainty [2002] F.S.R. 6 26–19

Eden v. West & Co. [2002] EWCA Civ 991 10–32

Edgson v. Vickers plc [1994] I.C.R. 510; *The Times*, April 8, 1994 2–29

Elliot v. Bickerstaff [1999] 2 N.S.W.L.R. 214 8–64

Emaco v. Dyson Appliances Ltd [1999] E.T.M.R. 903; (1999) 22(6) I.P.D. 22056 23–22

Emeh v. Kensington Area Health Authority [1985] Q.B. 1012; [1985] 2 W.L.R. 233, CA 29–53

Table of Cases

Environment Agency v. Empress Car Co. (Abertillery) Ltd [1999] 2 A.C. 22; [1998] 2 W.L.R. 350; [1998] 1 All E.R. 481; [1998] Env.L.R. 396; [1998] E.H.L.R. 3; [1998] E.G.C.S. 16; (1998) 95(8) L.S.G. 32; (1998) 148 N.L.J. 206; (1998) 142 S.J.L.B. 69; [1998] N.P.C. 16; *The Times*, February 9, 1998, HL 2–08

Esanda Finance Corporation v. Peat Marwick Hungerfords [2000] Lloyd's Rep. P.N. 684 7–90

Estill v. Cowling, Swift & Kitchen [2000] Lloyd's Rep. P.N. 378 8–93

Euromarket Designs Inc. v. Peters and Crate & Barrel Ltd [2001] F.S.R.288; [2000] E.T.M.R. 1025 25–73

Express and Echo Publications Ltd v. Tanton [1999] I.C.R. 693; [1999] I.R.L.R. 367, CA 5–10

Fairchild v. Glenhaven Funeral Services Ltd [2002] UKHL 22; [2002] 3 W.L.R. 89; [2002] 3 All E.R. 305; (2002) 152 N.L.J. 998; *The Times*, June 21, 2002; *Independent*, June 25, 2002; *Daily Telegraph*, June 27, 2002, HL ...2–08, 2–13, 2–13D, 2–13E, 2–13F, 2–13H, 2–13J, 2–23, 2–29, 2–30, 10–32

Fairline Shipping Corp. v. Adamson [1975] Q.B. 180; [1974] 2 W.L.R. 824; [1974] 2 All E.R. 967 .... 8–06A

Farley v. Skinner (No.2) [2001] UKHL 49; [2001] 3 W.L.R. 899; [2001] 4 All E.R. 801; [2002] B.L.R. 1; [2002] T.C.L.R. 6; 79 Con.L.R. 1; [2002] H.L.R. 5; [2002] P.N.L.R. 2; [2001] 49 E.G. 120; [2001] 48 E.G. 131; [2001] 42 E.G.C.S. 139; (2001) 98(40) L.S.G. 41; (2001) 145 S.J.L.B. 230; [2001] N.P.C. 146, *The Times*, October 15, 2001; *Independent*, November 26, 2001 (C.S.); *Daily Telegraph*, October 16, 2001, HL; reversing 73 Con.L.R. 70; [2000] Lloyd's Rep. P.N. 516; [2000] P.N.L.R. 441; [2000] 2 E.G.L.R. 125; [2000] E.G.C.S. 52; (2000) 97(15) L.S.G. 41; [2000] N.P.C. 40; [2001] 3 W.L.R. 899 .... 1–32, 7–62, 8a, 8–126, 8–130

Farrell v. Avon Health Authority [2001] Lloyd's Rep. Med. 458 .... 7a, 7–64, 7–68, 7–81, 8–69

Farrell v. Merton, Sutton and Wandsworth Health Authority (2000) 57 B.M.L.R. 158 2–16

Fashion Brokers Ltd v. Clarke Hayes (a firm) [2000] Lloyd's Rep. P.N. 398 ... 7–115

Fennelly v. Connex S. Eastern Ltd [2001] I.R.L.R. 390, CA 5–37

Ferguson v. Associated Newspapers Ltd, unreported, December 3, 2001 .. 23–11, 23–17

Fitzgerald v. Lane [1987] Q.B. 781; [1987] 3 W.L.R. 249; [1987] 2 All E.R. 455; (1987) 84 L.S.G. 1334; (1987) 137 N.L.J. 316; (1987) 132 S.J. 976, CA 2–13J, 2–29

Flack v. Hudson [2001] 2 W.L.R. 982, CA 21–04, 21–06, 21–07, 21–08

Flack v. Pattinson, unreported, December 19, 2001 15–40

Fleming v. Stirling Council, 2001 S.L.T. 123 11–15

Foster v. Biosil Ltd (2001) 59 B.M.L.R. 178 9–44

Fraser v. Winchester Health Authority (2000) 55 B.M.L.R. 122 3–82

Friend v. Civil Aviation Authority (No.2) [2001] EWCA Civ 1204; [2001] 4 All E.R. 385; [2002] I.C.R. 525; [2001] I.R.L.R. 819; [2001] Emp.L.R. 1141; *Independent*, November 26, 2001 (C.S.), CA 32–24

Friends Provident Life Office v. Hilier, Parker, May and Rowden [1997] Q.B. 85 4–119

Froom v. Butcher [1976] Q.B. 286; [1975] 3 W.L.R. 379; [1975] 3 All E.R. 520, CA 3–46

Frost v. Chief Constable of West Yorkshire Police [1999] 2 A.C. 455; [1998] 3 W.L.R. 1509; [1999] 1 All E.R. 1; [1999] I.C.R. 216; [1999] I.R.L.R. 110; (1999) 45 B.M.L.R. 1; (1999) 96(2) L.S.G. 28; (1998) 148 N.L.J. 1844; (1999) 143 S.J.L.B. 51; *The Times*, December 4, 1998; *Independent*, December 9, 1998, HL 7–22

Table of Cases

Fyffes Group Ltd v. Templeman [2000] 2 Lloyd's Rep. 643; (2000) 97(25) L.S.G. 40; *The Times*, June 14, 2000 .... 28–12, 28–25

Gainers Inc. v. Pockington Holdings Inc. (2001) 194 D.L.R. (4th) 109 (Alberta CA) 24–63
Gangway Ltd v. Caledonian Park Investments (Jersey) Ltd [2001] 2 Lloyd's Rep. 715 30–42
Gapper v. Chief Constable of the Avon and Somerset Constabulary [2000] 1 Q.B. 29; [1999] 2 W.L.R. 928, CA 3–121, 13–50
Gbaja-Biamila v. DHL International (UK) Ltd [2000] I.C.R.730 29–121
General Hospital Corp's European Patent (UK) [2000] F.S.R.633, CA 25–82
Gibbons v. Nelsons [2000] P.N.L.R. 734, *The Times*, April 21, 2000 8–78
Gilbert (James) Ltd v. MGN [2000] E.M.L.R. 680, QBD 22–05
GKR Karate v. Yorkshire Post [2000] 2 All E.R. 931 ...22–06, 22–78, 22–122, 22–139, 22–183
Gloster v. Chief Constable of Greater Manchester [2000] P.I.Q.R. P114 21–04
Goddard v. Day 194 DLR (4th) 559 2001 22–122
Goode v. Martin [2001] EWCA Civ 1899; [2002] 1 W.L.R. 1828; [2002] 1 All E.R. 620; [2002] C.P. Rep. 16; [2002] C.L.C. 420; [2002] P.I.Q.R. P24; (2002) 152 N.L.J. 109; *The Times*, January 24, 2002; *Independent*, January 16, 2002, CA 33–01
Gooden v. Northamptonshire County Council [2001] EWCA Civ 1744; [2002] P.N.L.R. 18; [2001] 49 E.G.C.S. 116; [2001] N.P.C. 167, CA 7–96, 7–97
Goose v. Wilson Sandford & Co. (No.2) [2001] Lloyd's Rep. P.N. 189, CA ... 15–27
Gorham v. British Telecommunications plc [2000] 1 W.L.R. 2129, *The Times*, August 16, 2000 .... 3–46, 3–50, 7–99
Governor and Company of the Bank of Scotland v. Fuller Peiser [2002] P.N.L.R. 289 .... 3–66, 7–118
Graham v. Dodds [1983] 1 W.L.R. 808; [1983] 2 All E.R. 953; (1983) 147 J.P. 746, HL 29–90
Grant v. Langley 2001 W.L. 513090 .... 4–100A
Gray v. Southampton & SW Hampshire HA (2001) 57 B.M.L.R. 148 8–52
Greatorex v. Greatorex [2000] 1 W.L.R. 1970; *The Times*, June 6, 2000 .... 7–66, 7–76
Green v. Berry [2001] Qd. R. 605 8–104
Green v. Collyer-Bristow [1999] Lloyd's Rep. P.N. 798; [1999] N.P.C. 56, QBD 8–93
Green v. Hancock [2001] P.N.L.R. 286; [2001] Lloyd's Rep. P.N. 212 8–93
Greenfield v. Flather; Greenfield v. Irwin [2001] EWCA Civ 113; [2001] 1 W.L.R. 1279; [2001] 1 F.L.R. 899; [2001] P.I.Q.R. Q7; [2001] Lloyd's Rep. Med. 143; (2001) 59 B.M.L.R. 43; *The Times*, February 6, 2001, CA 8–58
Gregory v. Portsmouth City Council [2000] 1 A.C. 419, *The Times*, February 2, 2000 .... 1A, 1–33, 16–03
Gregory v. Shepherds [2000] P.N.L.R. 769; *The Times*, June 28, 2000 8–75
Greville v. Sprake [2001] EWCA Civ. 234, CA 17–145
Grice v. Stourport Tennis, Hockey and Squash Club [1997] 9 C.L. 592, CA ... 5–19
Griffith v. Brown and Lindsay [1999] P.I.Q.R. P131; *The Times*, October 23, 1998, QBD 3–54
Griffiths v. British Coal Corp [2001] 1 W.L.R. 1493; *The Times*, March 13, 2001, CA 29–34
Griffiths v. Brown and Lindsay [1999] P.I.Q.R. P131 3–54
Grobbelaar v. News Group Newspapers [2001] 2 All E.R. 437, CA 22–02, 22–78, 22–122
Groom v. Selby [2001] EWCA Civ 1522; [2002] P.I.Q.R. P18; [2002] Lloyd's Rep. Med. 1; (2002) 64 B.M.L.R. 47, CA; affirming [2001] Lloyd's Rep. Med. 39 .... 2–56, 8–58, 29–53

Table of Cases

Groves v. Lord Wimborne [1898] 2 Q.B. 402, CA 11–15

H v. Associated Newspapers; H v. N (a health authority) [2002] EWCA Civ 195;
[2002] E.M.L.R. 23, CA; [2002] E.M.L.R. 425 .... 27–03, 27–37
H v. C [2001] 1 W.L.R. 2386 6–11
H v. S, *The Times*, July 3, 2002, CA 29–96
Halewood International Ltd v. Addleshaw Booth & Co. [2000] P.N.L.R. 788 8–91
Hall v. Bank of England [2000] Lloyd's Rep. Bank 186 17–145
Hall v. Woolston Hall Leisure Ltd [2001] 1 W.L.R. 225 ; [2000] 4 All E. R. 787,
CA 3–13, 3–16, 24–132
Hamilton v. Al Fayed [2000] 2 W.L.R. 609; [2000] 2 All E.R. 224, HL 22–100, 22–101,
22–229
Hamilton v. Papakura District Council [2002] UKPC 9; (2002) 146 S.J.L.B. 75;
The Times, March 5, 2002, PC 19–36, 20–17
Hanina v. Morland (2000) 97 (47) L.S. Gaz. 41 .... 18–35, 18–49, 18–65
Hannah v. Scottish Daily Record 2000 S.L.T. 673 (OH) 22–20
Hardaker v. Newcastle Health Authority & The Chief Constable of Northumbria
[2001] Lloyd's Rep. Med. 512 .... 2–20, 2–28, 8–62
Hardman v. Amin [2000] Lloyd's Med. Rep. 498; [2001] P.N.L.R. 303 ...... 7–26, 8–58,
29–53
Harley v. McDonald [2001] UKPC 18; [2001] 2 A.C. 678; [2001] 2 W.L.R.
1749; [2001] Lloyd's Rep. P.N. 584; *The Times*, May 15, 2001, PC (NZ) 8–83
Harper (Ross) & Murphy v. Scott Banks [2000] Lloyd's Rep. P.N. 631 7–42
Harris v. Leech (2000) 16 Const. L.J. 1 8–137
Harris v. Lewisham and Guy's Mental Health NHS Trust [2000] 3 All E.R. 769,
CA 29–65
Harrison v. Bloom Camillin [2001] P.N.L.R. 195 8–104
Harry Winton Investments Ltd v. CIBC Development Corp. (2001) 199 D.L.R.
(4th) 709 (Ont. CA) 24–49
Hatton v. Sutherland [2002] EWCA Civ 76; [2001] 2 All E.R. 1; [2002] I.C.R.
613; [2002] I.R.L.R. 263; [2002] Emp.L.R. 288; [2002] P.I.Q.R. P21;
(2002) 99(12) L.S.G. 34; (2002) 146 S.J.L.B. 43; *The Times*, February 12,
2002; *Independent*, February 13, 2002; *Daily Telegraph*, February 14, 2002,
CA 2–16, 7a, 7–82, 7–171, 7–224
Hatton v. United Kingdom [2002] 1 F.C.R. 732; (2002) 34 E.H.R.R. 1; 11
B.H.R.C. 634; *The Times*, October 8, 2001, ECHR 19–23
Haystead v. Chief Constable of Derbyshire [2000] 3 All E. R. 890; [2000] 2 Cr.
App. R. 339 .... 13–02, 13–05
Hedley Byrne v. Heller [1964] A.C. 465; [1963] 3 W.L.R. 101; [1963] 2 All E.R.
575; [1963] 1 Lloyd's Rep. 485; 107 S.J. 454, HL 8–06A
Heil v. Rankin [2000] Q.B.272; [2001] P.I.Q.R. Q16 2–35
Henderson v. Chief Constable of Cleveland [2001] EWCA Civ. 335; [2001] 1
W.L.R. 1103 13–54
Henderson v. Jaouen [2002] EWCA Civ 75; [2002] 2 All E.R. 705; [2002]
C.L.C. 708; (2002) 99(12) L.S.G. 32; *The Times*, March 7, 2002; *Independent*, February 8, 2002 6–02
Henderson v. Merrett Syndicates Ltd [1995] A.C. 145; [1994] 3 W.L.R. 761;
[1994] 3 All E.R. 506; [1994] 2 Lloyd's Rep. 468; (1994) 144 N.L.J. 1204;
The Times, July 26, 1994; *Independent*, August 3, 1994, HL 7–22
Henderson v. Radio Corporation Pty Ltd [1969] R.P.C. 218 26–08
Henry v. London General Transport Services [2001] I.R.L.R. 132 24–27
Hewlett Packard v. O'Murphy [2002] I.R.L.R. 4; [2002] Emp.L.R. 54, EAT ... 5–12
Hilton v. Barker Booth & Eastwood [2002] EWCA Civ 723; (2002) 146 S.J.L.B.
152; [2002] N.P.C. 74; *The Times*, June 6, 2002; *Independent*, May 29,
2002 8–98
Hoadley v. Edwards [2001] P.N.L.R. 41; [2001] 14 E.G.C.S. 148 8–130

TABLE OF CASES

Holbeck Building Society v. Arthur Cole [2001] Lloyd's Rep. P.N. 649; [2002] P.N.L.R. 4 28–23
Holbeck Hall Hotel Ltd v. Scarborough Council [2001] Q.B. 836 1–52
Holden v. Chief Constable of Lancashire [1987] Q.B. 380; [1987] 3 W.L.R. 1107, CA 13–85
Holden v. Express Newspapers, unreported, June 7, 2001 27–03
Holtyerhoff v. Freiesleben (C–2/00) [2002] E.T.M.R. 917, ECJ 25–73
Holtby v. Brigham & Cowan (Hull) Ltd [2000] 3 All E.R. 421; [2000] I.C.R. 1086; [2000] P.I.Q.R. Q293; [2000] Lloyd's Rep. Med. 254; (2000) 97(19) L.S.G. 44; (2000) 150 N.L.J. 544; (2000) 144 S.J.L.B. 212; *The Times*, April 12, 2000, CA 2–13, 2–16
Home Brewery plc v. William Davis & Co. (Loughborough) Ltd [1987] Q.B. 339; [1987] 2 W.L.R. 117 .... 19–86, 20–30
Home Office v. Dorset Yacht [1970] A.C. 1004; [1970] 2 W.L.R. 1140; [1970] 2 All E.R. 294; [1970] 1 Lloyd's Rep. 453; 114 S.J. 375, HL 12–58
Home Office v. W (2002) 99(9) L.S.G. 31 1–77
Horne-Roberts v. SmithKline Beecham plc [2001] EWCA Civ 2006; [2002] 1 W.L.R. 1662; [2002] C.P. Rep. 20; (2002) 65 B.M.L.R. 79; (2002) 99(8) L.S.G. 35; (2002) 146 S.J.L.B. 19; *The Times*, January 10, 2002, CA 33–01
Hotson v. East Berkshire Area Health Authority [1987] A.C. 750; [1987] 3 W.L.R. 232; [1987] 2 All E.R. 909, HL 2–28, 8–67
Hough v. Chief Constable of Staffordshire [2001] E.W.C.A. Civ. 39; *The Times*, February 14, 2001 13–53
Howes v. Crombie 2001 S.C.L.R. 921; [2002] P.N.L.R. 3; 2001 Rep.L.R. 98; 2001 G.W.D. 23–873, OH 8–111, 8–133
Hulse v. Chambers, [2000] W.L. 415623 6–11
Hunter v. Butler [1996] R.T.R. 396, CA 3–16
Hunter v. Canary Wharf [1997] A.C. 655; [1997] C.L.Y. 3865; [1997] A.C. 655 ..... 13–17, 19a, 19–08, 19–22, 19–42
Hunter v. Earnshaw [2001] P.N.L.R. 982 8–104
Hunter BNZ Finance v. ANZ Banking Group [1990] V.R. 41 14–129
Hyde Park Residence Ltd v. Yelland [2000] 3 W.L.R. 215; [2000] E.M.L.R. 363, CA 25–26, 27–37

I v. DPP [2001] UKHL 10; [2002] 1 A.C. 285; [2001] 2 W.L.R. 765; [2001] 2 All E.R. 583; [2001] 2 Cr.App.R. 14; (2001) 165 J.P. 437; [2001] Crim.L.R. 491; (2001) 165 J.P.N. 506; (2001) 98(20) L.S.G. 40; (2001) 151 N.L.J. 385; (2001) 145 S.J.L.B. 101; *The Times*, March 9, 2001; *Independent*, March 13, 2001, HL 24–67
Imutran Ltd v. Uncaged Campaigns Ltd [2001] 2 All E.R. 385; [2001] C.P. Rep. 28; [2001] E.C.D.R. 16; [2001] E.M.L.R. 21; [2001] H.R.L.R. 31; [2002] F.S.R. 2; (2001) 24(5) I.P.D. 24031; (2001) 98(14) L.S.G. 40; *The Times*, January 30, 2001 .... 24–190, 27–37, 27–43, 30–20
In Gainers Inc. v. Pocklingtons Holiday Inc. (2001) 194 D.L.R. 109 24–21
Instance v. CCI Label Inc. [2002] F.S.R. 27 25–89
Interlink Express Parcels Ltd v. Night Truckers Ltd [2001] E.W.C.A. Civ. 360; [2001] R.T.R. 23; (2001) 98 (20) L.S.G. 43 5–21
Invergui Investments Ltd v. Hackett [1995] 1 W.L.R. 713; [1995] 3 All E.R. 841 .... 18A
Irvine v. Talksport Ltd [2002] EWHC 367; [2002] 2 All E.R. 414; [2002] E.M.L.R. 32; (2002) 25(6) I.P.D. 25039; (2002) 99(18) L.S.G. 38; (2002) 152 N.L.J. 553; (2002) 146 S.J.L.B. 85 .... 26–01, 26–09, 26–12, 26–14

J v. North Lincolnshire County Council [2000] P.I.Q.R. 84 .... 7–192, 7–230
J(A Child) v. Wilkins [2001] P.I.Q.R. P179; *The Times*, February 6, 2001, CA 3–46
Jacobi v. Griffith (1999) 174 D.L.R. (4th) 71 .... 5A

[xvii]

TABLE OF CASES

Jaffray v. Society of Lloyd's [2002] EWCA Civ 1101 15–10
James Gilbert Ltd v. MGN [2000] E.M.L.R. 680 22–03
Jan de Nul (UK) v. NV Royal Belge [2000] 2 Lloyd's Rep. 700 .... 19–04, 19–27, 19–36, 19–42, 19–106
Janvier v. Sweeney [1919] 2 K.B. 316 13–16
Jaroo v. Att.-Gen. of Trinidad [2002] UKPC 5; [2002] 1 A.C. 871; [2002] 2 W.L.R. 705; (2002) 146 S.J.L.B. 44; *The Times*, February 6, 2002, PC (Trin) 14–53
Jarvis v. Hampshire County Council [2000] 2 F.C.R. 310; (2000) 2 L.G.L.R. 636; [2000] Ed. C.R. 1; [2000] E.L.R. 36; *The Times*, November 23, 1999, CA 17–141
Jarvis & Sons Ltd v. Castle Wharf Developments Ltd [2001] E.W.C.A. 19; [2001] Lloyd's Rep. P.N. 308, CA 7–105, 8–06A
Jayes v. IMI (Kynoch) Ltd [1985] I.C.R. 155; (1984) 81 L.S.G. 3180, CA 3–22, 3–38
JD Williams & Co. Ltd v. Michael Hyde & Associates Ltd [2001] B.L.R. 99; (2001) 3 T.C.L.R. 1; [2000] Lloyd's Rep. P.N. 823; [2001] P.N.L.R. 8; [2000] N.P.C. 78; *The Times*, August 4, 2000, CA 7–187
Jebson v. Ministry of Defence [2000] 1 W.L.R. 2055;*The Times*, June 28, 2000 ...3–54, 7–144
Jenmain Builders Ltd v. Steed & Steed [2000] P.N.L.R. 616 8–94
Jeromson v. Shell Tankers (U.K.) Ltd [2001] EWCA Civ 100; [2001] I.C.R. 1223; [2001] P.I.Q.R. P19; *The Times*, March 2, 2001; *Daily Telegraph*, February 27, 2001, CA 2–64, 11–45
Jobling v. Associated Dairies Ltd [1982] A.C. 794; [1981] 3 W.L.R. 155; [1981] 2 All E.R. 752, HL 2–35, 2–54A
John Laing Construction v. Ince [2001] C.L.Y. 4543 5–69
Johnson v. BJW Property Developments Ltd [2002] N.P.C. 17 ...5–35, 5–56, 5–59, 19–52, 20–46, 20–55
Johnson v. Gore Wood & Co. [2001] 2 W.L.R. 72; *The Times*, December 22, 2000 ....1–32, 7–62, 8–13, 8–107, 32–24
Jolly v. Sutton LBC [2000] 1 W.L.R. 1082 .... 7–144, 10–28
Jones v. London Borough of Tower Hamlets [2001] R.P.C. 407 25–21
Joy v. Newell (t/a Copper Room) [2000] N.I. 91 (NICA) 3–54
Jupiter Unit Trust Managers Ltd v. Johnson Fry Asset Managers plc, unreported, April 19, 2000 .... 23–19, 23–20

K v. Secretary of State for the Home Department [2002] EWCA Civ 983; (2002) 152 N.L.J. 917; *Daily Telegraph*, June 13, 2002, CA 7–57
Kane v. New Forest District Council [2001] EWCA Civ 878; [2002] 1 W.L.R. 312; [2001] 3 All E.R. 914; [2002] J.P.L. 409; [2001] 27 E.G.C.S. 132; [2001] N.P.C. 100; *Independent*, July 23, 2001 (C.S.), CA ...7–210, 12–26, 12–32, 19–122
Kay Aviation BV v. Rofe (2002) 202 D.L.R. (4th) 683 (Pr. Ed. Is. Sup. Ct. App. Div.) 24–44
KBC Bank v. Industrial Steels (UK) Ltd [2001] 1 Lloyd's Rep. 320 15–42
Keating v. Bromley London Borough Council. *See* Phelps v. Hillingdon London Borough Council.
Keenan v. UK (Application No. 27229/95), (2001) 10 B.H.R.C. 319, *The Times*, April 18, 2001, ECHR 2–58, 3–31, 13–28
Kenny & Good Pty Ltd v. M.G.I.C.A. (1992) Ltd [2000] Lloyd's Rep. P.N. 25 28–26
Kent v. Griffiths [2001] Q.B. 36; [2000] 2 W.L.R. 1158; *The Times*, February 10, 2000 .... 7–51 – 7–53, 12–51
Kent v. London Ambulance Service [2001] Q.B. 36 11–34
Kerry O'Shea v. MGN [2001] 1 All E.R.(D) 65, CA 22–08, 22–09, 22–12, 22–60
Khodaparast v. Shad [2000] 1 W.L.R. 618; [2000] All E.R. 545, CA 23–18

TABLE OF CASES

Khorasandjian v. Bush [1993] Q.B. 727; [1993] 3 W.L.R. 476; [1993] 3 All E.R. 669; [1993] 2 F.L.R. 66; (1993) 25 H.L.R. 392; [1993] Fam. Law 679; (1993) 137 S.J.L.B. 88; *The Times*, February 18, 1993; *Independent*, March 16, 1993, CA 13–17

Kiam v. MGN [2002] EWCA Civ 43; [2002] 2 All E.R. 219; [2002] E.M.L.R. 25; (2002) 99(11) L.S.G. 35; *The Times*, February 11, 2002, CA ... 22–02, 22–207, 22–227, 29–135

Killick v. PriceWaterhouseCoopers [2001] 1 B.C.L.C. 65; [2001] Lloyd's Rep. P.N. 17; [2001] P.N.L.R. 1; [2001] W.T.L.R. 699 .... 3–68, 7–117, 8–14, 8–145

Kimberly Clark Worldwide Inc. v. Procter & Gamble Ltd (No.2) [2001] F.S.R. 22; [2000] R.P.C. 422, CA 25–89

King v. RCO Support Services Ltd and Yorkshire Traction Company Ltd [2001] P.I.Q.R. P206; *The Times*, February 7, 2001 11–15

Kooltrade Ltd v. XTS Ltd [2001] F.S.R. 158 25–100

Koonjal v. Thamelink Healthcare Services [2000] P.I.Q.R. P123 11–15

Kuddus v. Chief Constable of Leicestershire Contabulary [2001] UKHL 29; [2001] 2W.L.R. 1789; *The Times,* June 13, 2001 .. 1A, 1–14, 5–01, 13–85, 15–43, 17–146, 22–211

Kuwait Airways Corp. v. Iraq Airways Co. (No.6) [2002] UKHL 19; [2002] 2 W.L.R. 1353; [2002] 3 All E.R. 209; [2002] 1 All E.R. (Comm) 843; *The Times*, May 21, 2002, HL; affirming [2001] 3 W.L.R. 1117; [2001] 1 All E.R. (Comm) 557; [2001] 1 Lloyd's Rep. 161; [2001] C.L.C. 262; (2000) 97(48) L.S.G. 37; (2001) 145 S.J.L.B. 5; *The Times*, November 21, 2000; *Daily Telegraph*, November 21, 2000, CA 2–06, 2–08, 2–34, 2–63, 2–68, 14A, 14–09, 14–10, 14–12, 14–14, 14–32, 14–36, 14–99, 14–103, 14–104, 14–114

Kuwait Airways Corp. v. Iraqi Airways Co. (No.7), unreported, April 7, 2000 14–114

Kuwait Oil Tanker SAK v. Al Bader [2000] 2 All E.R. Comm. 271, CA 24–14, 24–127

L v. Robinson [2000] 3 N.Z.L.R. 499 8–44
L and P v. Reading Borough Council [2001] P.I.Q.R. P387 7–37
L v. Tower Hamlets L.B.C. [2001] 2 W.L.R. 909 .... 12–61, 12–62, 12–63
L. (S.) (Sterilisation) Re, [2000] 1 Lloyd's Rep. Med. 339 8–33
Lacroix (Guardian) v. Dominique (2001) 202 D.L.R. (4th) 121 8–57
Lambeth L.B.C. v. Blackburn [2001] EWCA Civ 912; (2001) 33 H.L.R. 74; (2001) 82 P. & C.R. 39; (2001) 98(26) L.S.G. 46, CA 18–83
Lange v. Atkinson (No.2) [2000] 3 N.Z.L.R. 385, CA (NZ) 22–08, 22–122
Langford v. Hebran [2001] EWCA Civ 361; [2001] P.I.Q.R. Q160 2–28
Larner v. Solihull Metropolitan Borough Council [2001] P.I.Q.R. P 17; [2001] P.I.Q.R. P248, CA 7–208, 12–58
Lau v. D.P.P. [2000] 1 F.L.R. 799, *The Times*, March 29, 2000 13–18
Law Society v. KPMG Peat Marwick [2000] P.N.L.R. 831, *The Times*, July 6, 2000, CA 7–97, 8–145
Leakey v. National Trust [1980] Q.B. 485; [1980] 2 W.L.R. 65, CA 19–21, 19–82, 19–95
Leebody v. Ministry of Defence [2001] C.L.Y. 4544 5–37
Leeds & Holbeck Building Society v. Alex Morison & Co. 2001 S.C.L.R. 41; [2001] P.N.L.R. 346 8–102
Leeds & Holbeck Building Society v. Arthur & Cole [2002] P.N.L.R. 78 8–21
Levi Strauss & Co. v. Tesco Stores Ltd [2000] EWHC 1556 25–74
Lindley v. Rutter [1981] Q.B.128; [1980] 3 W.L.R. 660, DC 13–62
Lister v. Hesley Hall Ltd [2001] U.K.H.L. 22; [2002] 1 A.C. 215, HL; [2001] 2 W.L.R. 1311, HL 5A, 5–24, 5–38, 24–14
Liverpool Roman Catholic Archdiocese Trustees Inc. v. Goldberg [2001] 1 All E.R.182 33–25
Lloyd v. Grace Smith & Co. [1912] A.C. 716, HL 5A

[xix]

TABLE OF CASES

Lloyds Bank plc v. Burd Pearse (a firm) [2001] EWCA Civ. 366; [2001] Lloyd's
  Rep. P.N. 452; [2001] P.N.L.R. 34; [2001] 12 E.G.C.S. 167; [2001] N.P.C.
  59, CA 2–67
Lloyds Bank plc v. Rogers [1999] 3 E.G.L.R. 83; [1999] 38 E.G.187, CA 33–01
London Underground Ltd v. RMT [2001] EWCA Civ 211; [2001] I.C.R. 647;
  [2001] I.R.L.R. 228; *The Times*, March 7, 2001; *Independent*, February 20,
  2001, CA 24–118, 24–173, 24–178
Long v. Tolchard & Sons Ltd [2001] P.I.Q.R. P18, CA 33–48
Longstaff v. Birtles [2001] EWCA Civ 1219; [2002] 1 W.L.R. 470; [2001] 34
  E.G.C.S. 98; (2001) 98(34) L.S.G. 43; (2001) 145 S.J.L.B. 210; [2001]
  N.P.C. 128; *The Times*, September 18, 2001, CA 8–21, 28–09
L'Oreal (UK) Ltd v. Johnson & Johnson [2000] F.S.R. 686 .... 25–78, 25–100
Loutchansky v. Times Newspapers (No.1) [2001] EWCA Civ. 536; [2002] Q.B.
  321; [2001] 3 W.L.R. 404; [2001] 4 All E.R. 115; [2001] E.M.L.R. 26;
  (2001) 151 N.L.J. 643; *The Times*, April 26, 2001; *Independent*, May 1,
  2001, CA 22–01, 22–05, 22–07, 22–12, 22–14, 22–110, 22–122, 22–139
Loutchansky v. Times Newspapers (No.2) [2001] EWCA Civ 1805; [2002] 2
  W.L.R. 640; [2002] 1 All E.R. 652; [2002] E.M.L.R. 14; (2002) 99(6)
  L.S.G. 30; (2001) 145 S.J.L.B. 277; *The Times*, December 7, 2001; *Independent*, December 11, 2001, CA 22–110, 22–113, 22–121, 22–122, 22–139
Lowe v. Guise [2002] EWCA Civ 197; [2002] 3 All E.R. 454; (2002) 99(15)
  L.S.G. 33; (2002) 146 S.J.L.B. 74; *The Times*, March 25, 2002; *Daily
  Telegraph*, March 7, 2002, CA 29–19, 29–20
Lubbe v. Cape Plc [2000] 1 W.L.R. 1545; [2000] 4 All E.R. 268, HL 6–03
Lukowiak v. Unidad Editorial S.A. [2001] E.M.L.R. 46; *The Times*, July 23,
  2001 .... 22–01, 22–05, 22–08, 22–12, 22–39, 22–49, 22–79

M (A Minor) v. Newham LBC. *See* X (Minors) v. Bedfordshire C.C.
MCA Records Inc. v. Charly Records Ltd (No.5) [2002] E.M.L.R. 1 ...... 4–108, 24–03,
                                                                                                                25–31
McCartan Turkington Breen v. Times Newspapers Ltd [2001] 2 A.C. 277; [2000]
  3 W.L.R. 1670; [2000] 4 All E.R. 913; [2000] N.I. 410; [2001] E.M.L.R. 1;
  [2001] U.K.H.R.R. 184; 9 B.H.R.C. 497; (2000) 97(47) L.S.G. 40; (2000)
  150 N.L.J. 1657; (2000) 144 S.J.L.B. 287; *The Times*, November 3, 2000;
  Independent, November 7, 2000, HL (NI) .. 22–09, 22–122, 22–152, 22–153, 22–156
McConnell v. Police Authority for Northern Ireland [1997] I.R.L.R. 625; [1997]
  N.I. 224, CA (N.I.) 29–121
McCue v. Scottish Daily Record Mail Ltd (No.4) 2000 Rep. L.R. 133 (OH) ... 22–20
McCulloch v. Lewis A May [1947] 5 R.P.C. 58 26–09
McFarlane v. Glasgow CC [2001] I.R.L.R. 7, EAT (Scot) 5–10
McFarlane v. Tayside Health Board [2000] 2 A.C. 59 .... 2–56, 2–67, 7–26, 8A, 8–58
McGhee v. National Board [1973] 1 W.L.R. 1; [1972] 3 All E.R. 1008; 1973 S.C.
  (H.L.) 37; 1973 S.L.T. 14; 13 K.I.R. 471; 116 S.J. 967, HL 2–13, 2–13A, 2–13C
                                                               2–13D, 2–13E, 2–13F, 2–13G, 2–13I, 2–29
McIlgorm v. Bell Lamb [2001] P.N.L.R. 642 8–89
McIlkenny v. Chief Constable of the West Midlands [1980] Q.B. 283; [1980] 2
  W.L.R. 689, CA 13–15
McIntyre v. Chief Constable of Kent [2002] All E.R. (D) 338 22–122
McKenna v. British Aluminium Ltd, *The Times*, April 25, 2002 .... 1–67, 19a, 19–22,
                                                                                                    19–42, 20a, 20–14
McKew v. Holland & Hannen & Cubitts (Scotland) Ltd [1969] 3 All E.R.
  1621 .... 2–54A
McLoughlin v. Grovers (a firm) [2001] EWCA Civ 1743; [2002] 2 W.L.R. 1279;
  [2002] P.I.Q.R. P20; [2002] P.N.L.R. 21, CA 1–25, 7a, 7–22, 7–64, 7–68, 7–78,
                                                                                              7–83, 7–95, 8–107
Macmahon v. Doran & Co. [2002] Lloyd's Rep. P.N. 93; [2001] P.N.L.R. 35 8–100

TABLE OF CASES

McMeechan v. S/S for Employment[1997] I.C.R. 549; [1997] I.R.L.R. 353, CA ...5–10, 5–12
McVicar v. United Kingdom (App. No. 46311/99) (2002) 152 N.L.J. 759, ECHR ...22–03, 22–10
Maddocks v. Clifton [2001] EWCA Civ 1837 10–08
Mahon v. Rahn (No.2) [2000] 1 W.L.R. 2150; [2000] 4 All E.R. 41; [2000] 2 All E.R. (Comm) 1; [2000] E.M.L.R. 873; (2000) 97(26) L.S.G. 38; (2000) 150 N.L.J. 899; *The Times*, June 14, 2000, CA 22–103
Marc Rich v. Agrimex Ltd [2000] 1 All E.R. (Comm) 951 7–23
Marcic v. Thames Water Utilities [2002] EWCA Civ 64 [2002] 2 W.L.R. 932; [2002] 2 All E.R. 55; [2002] B.L.R. 174; 81 Con.L.R. 193; [2002] H.R.L.R. 22; (2002) 18 Const.L.J. 152; [2002] 7 E.G.C.S. 122; (2002) 99(12) L.S.G. 34; (2002) 146 S.J.L.B. 51; [2002] N.P.C. 20; *The Times*, February 14, 2002; *Independent*, February 12, 2002, CA 1–52, 19a, 19–22, 19–32, 19–54, 19–65, 19–127, 19–129, 19–134, 20a, 20–38
Marcic v. Thames Water Utilities (No.2) [2002] 2 W.L.R. 1000 .... 29–117, 29–119
Marks and Spencer plc v. Customs and Excise Commissioners [2000] S.T.C. 16; [2000] 1 C.M.L.R. 256; [2000] Eu.L.R. 293; [2000] B.T.C. 5003; [2000] B.V.C. 35; [2000] S.T.I. 22; *The Times*, January 19, 2000, CA 12–87
Mars v. Techknowledge [2000] E.C.D.R. 99 27–05
Marshall v. Business Blueprints Ltd, unreported, December 18, 2000 5–38
Martin v. Childs [2002] EWCA Civ 283 18–49
Matthews v. Ministry of Defence [2002] EWCA Civ 773; [2002] 3 All E.R. 513; (2002) 152 N.L.J. 879; (2002) 146 S.J.L.B. 144; *The Times*, May 31, 2001, CA 1–81, 4–17A, 8–62
Mattocks v. Mann [1993] R.T.R. 13; *The Times*, June 19, 1992, CA 7–150
Medcalf v. Mardell [2002] UKHL 27; [2002] 3 All E.R. 721, HL; [2001] P.N.L.R. 372 .... 8–83, 8–84, 15–02
MedGen Inc. v. Passion for Life Products Ltd [2001] F.S.R.30 26–11
Melluish v. BMI (No.3) Ltd [1996] A.C. 454; [1995] 3 W.L.R. 630; [1995] 4 All E.R. 453; [1995] S.T.C. 964; 68 T.C. 1; [1995] E.G.C.S. 150; (1995) 92(40) L.S.G. 22; (1995) 139 S.J.L.B. 220; *The Times*, October 16, 1995; *Independent*, November 6, 1995 (C.S.), HL 21–104
Melvin v. Reid (1931) 297 P.91 1–76
Memory Corp Plc v. Sidhu (No.2) [2001] 1 W.L.R. 1443, CA 30–46
Merrett v. Babb [2001] 3 W.L.R. 1; [2001] E.G.C.S. 24, CA 7–43, 7–116, 8A, 8–06A, 8–109
Michaels v. Taylor Woodrow Developments Ltd [2001] Ch. 493; [2001] 2 W.L.R. 224; [2000] 4 All E.R. 645; (2001) 81 P. & C.R. 23; (2000) 97(20) L.S.G. 47; [2000] N.P.C. 53 ..... 24–06, 24–11, 24–56, 24–78, 24–91, 24–94, 24–105, 24–106, 24–127, 24–129, 24–199
Midland Mainline Ltd v. RMT [2001] EWCA Civ 1206; [2001] I.R.L.R. 813; [2001] Emp. L.R. 1097; (2001) 98(38) LS.G. 37; *The Times*, August 7, 2001, CA 24–173
Milne v. Telegraph Group [2001] E.M.L.R. 30 22–05
Mirhavedy v. Henley [2002] 2 W.L.R. 566 .... 21–04, 21–06, 21–08
Modbury Triangle Shopping Centre Ltd v. Anzil (2000) 175 A.L.R. 164 10–28
Monsanto plc v. Tilly [1999] E.G.C.S.143; [2000] Env. L.R. 313 3–103
Monsoon v. India Imports [1993] F.S.R. 486 25–19
Montgomery v. Johnson Underwood [2001] E.W.C.A. 318; [2001] I.R.L.R. 269, CA 5–06, 5–10, 5–12
Moore v. Zerfahs [1999] Lloyd's Rep. P.N. 144, CA 2–32
Moores v. Bude-Stratton T.C. [2001] I.C.R. 271; [2000] I.R.L.R. 676; (2001) 3 L.G.L.R. 17; [2001] B.L.G.R. 129, EAT 24–14
Morris v. Beardmore [1981] A.C. 446; [1980] 3 W.L.R. 283, DC 13–65

TABLE OF CASES

Morris v. C.W. Martin & Sons Ltd [1966] 1 Q.B. 716; [1965] 3 W.L.R. 276; [1965] 2 All E. R. 725, CA 5A,5–38
Morris v. KLM Royal Dutch Airlines [2001] EWCA Civ 790; [2002] Q.B. 100; [2001] 3 W.L.R. 351; [2001] 3 All E.R. 126; [2001] 2 All E.R. (Comm) 153; [2001] C.L.C. 1460; (2001) 98(26) L.S.G. 43; (2001) 151 N.L.J. 851; (2001) 145 S.J.L.B. 142; *The Times*, June 15, 2001; *Independent*, May 23, 2001; *Daily Telegraph*, May 22, 2001, CA 7–214
Motor Crown Petroleum Ltd v. S.J. Berwin & Co. (A Firm) [2001] Lloyd's Rep. P.N. 438 2–28
Motorola Credit Corporation v. Uzan [2002] EWCA Civ 989; *The Times*, July 10, 2002, CA 30–44
Motorola Ltd v. Davidson [2001] I.R.L.R. 4, EAT (Scot) 5–10, 5–12
Mulcahy v. Chief Constable of West Midlands, *Independent*, July 9, 2001, CA ... 12–71
Mulkerrins v. Pricewaterhouse Coopers (2001) 98(5) L.S. Gaz. 36, *The Times*, January 12, 2001 4–52
Mullaney v. CC of West Midlands [2001] EWCA Civ. 700; *The Daily Telegraph*, May 22, 2001 5–62
Multigroup Bulgaria Ltd v. Oxford Analytical, unreported, February 1, 2001 22–01

N.U.R.M.T. v. London Underground [2001] I.R.L.R.228, CA 24–118, 24–178
N.U.R.M.T. v. Midland Mainline Ltd, July 25, 2001, CA 24–178
National Home Loans Corp. plc v. Giffen Couch & Arthur [1998] 1 W.L.R. 207; [1997] 3 All E.R. 808; [1998] P.N.L.R. 111; [1997] N.P.C. 100; *The Times*, October 9, 1997, CA 8–98
Nationwide Building Society v. Balmer Radmore [1999] Lloyd's Rep. P.N. 241; [1999] Lloyd's Rep. P.N. 558 28–23
Nationwide Building Society v. Richard Grosse & Co. [1999] Lloyd's Rep. P.N. 348 28–23
Nelson v. Nicholson, *The Independent*, January 22, 2001, CA .. 18A, 18–09, 18–17, 18–65
Nethermere (St.Neots) Ltd v. Taverna and Gardiner [1984] I.C.R. 612; [1984] I.R.L.R. 240, CA 5–10
New Islington & Hackney HA v. Pollard Thomas & Edwards [2001] B.L.R. 74; (2001) 3 T.C.L.R. 25; [2001] Lloyd's Rep. P.N. 243; [2001] P.N.L.R. 20; (2001) 17 Const.L.J. 55 8–137
Newcastle Building Society v. Paterson Robertson & Graham 2001 S.C. 734; 2002 S.L.T. 747; 2001 S.C.L.R. 737; [2002] Lloyd's Rep. P.N. 223; [2001] P.N.L.R. 36; [2001] N.P.C. 63; 2001 G.W.D. 12–446, OH 8–102
Newman v. Folkes and Dunlop Tyres Ltd [2002] P.I.Q.R. Q2 3–16
Newspaper Licensing Agency Ltd v. Marks & Spencer plc [2001] UKHL 38; [2001] 3 W.L.R. 290 25–07
Nichols TM, Re [2002] EWHC 1424 25–74
Nicol v. D.P.P. [1996] Crim L.R. 318; (1996) 160 J.P. 155 13–45
Noel v. Poland [2001] 2 B.C.L.R. 645; [2002] Lloyd's Rep. IR 30 15–25
Nordic Holdings Ltd v. Mott McDonald Ltd (2001) 77 Con.L.R. 88 8–142
Nottinghamshire Healthcare National Health Service Trust v. News Group Newspapers Ltd [2002] EWHC 409; [2002] E.M.L.R. 33; (2002) 99(18) L.S.G. 36; (2002) 146 S.J.L.B. 92; [2002] E.C.D.R. CN5; *The Times*, April 1, 2002 25–31
NWL Ltd v. Woods [1979] 3 All E.R. 614; [1979] I.C.R. 867, HL 27–43

O v. Surrey Social Services [2001] W.L. 1560834 12–73
Oakes v. Hopcroft (2000) 56 B.M.L.R. 136, CA 33–58
Ogle v. Chief Constable of Thames Valley Police [2001] EWCA Civ 598 4–106
O'Hara v. Chief Constable of the Royal Ulster Constabulary [1997] A.C. 286; [1997] 2 W.L.R. 1, HL 13–53
O'K. (E.) v. K. (D.) [2001] 1 I.R. 636 8–20

TABLE OF CASES

On Demand Information plc (in administrative Receivership) v. Michael Gerson (Finance) plc [2002] UKHL 13; [2002] 2 W.L.R. 919; [2002] 2 All E.R. 949; [2002] 1 All E.R. (Comm) 641; (2002) 99(21) L.S.G. 31; (2002) 146 S.J.L.B. 110; *The Times*, May 2, 2002, HL; reversing [2001] 1 W.L.R. 155; [2000] 4 All E.R. 734; [2000] 2 All E.R. (Comm) 513; [2002] B.C.C. 122; (2000) 150 N.L.J. 1300; *The Times*, September 19, 2000, CA 14–48, 14–50

Ontario Ltd v. Magna International Inc. (2001) 200 D.L.R. (4th) 521 (Ont. CA) 24–44

Orange v. Chief Constable of West Yorkshire Police [2001] EWCA Civ 611; [2002] Q.B. 347; [2001] 3 W.L.R. 736; (2001) 98(24) L.S.G. 44; (2001) 145 S.J.L.B. 125; *The Times*, June 5, 2001; *Independent*, May 9, 2001, CA 2–58, 3–11A, 3–31, 13–63

Oren v. Red Box Toy Factory Ltd [1999] F.S.R. 785; (1999) 22(4) I.P.D. 22038, Pat.Ct. 24–20

Osman v. United Kingdom [1999] 1 F.L.R. 193; (2000) 29 E.H.R.R. 245; 5 B.H.R.C. 293; (1999) 1 L.G.L.R. 431; (1999) 11 Admin.L.R. 200; [1999] Crim.L.R. 82; [1998] H.R.C.D. 966; [1999] Fam. Law 86; (1999) 163 J.P.N. 297; *The Times*, November 5, 1998, ECHR 1–79, 1–81, 8–62, 12–70, 12–74

Owner of Dredger Liesbosch v. Owners of SS Edison; Liesbosch Dredger v. SS Edison [1933] A.C. 449; [1933] All E.R. Rep. 144; (1933) 45 Ll.L.Rep. 123, HL 7–149, 29–08

P v. NAS/UWT [2001] I.C.R. 1241, CA 24–141, 24–173, 24–181, 24–197

Pacific Associates Inc. v. Baxter [1990] 1 Q.B. 993; [1989] 3 W.L.R. 1150; [1989] 2 All E.R. 159; 44 B.L.R. 33; 16 Con.L.R. 90; (1989) 139 N.L.J. 41; (1989) 133 S.J. 123; *The Times*, December 28, 1988; *Independent*, January 6, 1989, CA 3–68, 7–105

Palmer v. Bowman [2000] 1 W.L.R. 842, CA 19A, 19–86, 19–124, A20, 20–12, 20–30

Papamichael v. National Westminster Bank plc [2002] 2 All E.R. (Comm) 60; [2002] 1 Lloyd's Rep. 332 30–39

Paragon Finance plc v. Thakerar & Co. [1999] 1 All E.R. 400; (1998) 95(35) L.S.G. 36; (1998) 142 S.J.L.B. 243; *The Times*, August 7, 1998, CA 15–02

Parfums Chrsitian Dior v. Evora (Case C–53/96) [1998] E.C.R. I–3603 27–01

Parker v. PFC Flooring Supplies Ltd [2001] EWCA Civ 1533; [2001] P.I.Q.R. P7; [2001] P.I.Q.R. P115 ....7–225, 11–16, 11–58

Parkinson v. St James and Seacroft University Hospital NHS Trust [2001] EWCA Civ 530; [2001] 3 All E.R. 97; [2001] W.L.R. 376, CA 1–25, 2–56, 7a, 7–26, 7–95, 8–58, 29–53

Parry v. Edwards Geldard [2001] P.N.L.R. 1032 8–105

Patel v. (Smith) W.H. (Eziot) Ltd [1987] 1 W.L.R. 853; [1987] 2 All E. R. 569, CA 18–65

Patel v. Daybells [2000] Lloyd's Rep. P.N. 844; [2001] P.N.L.R. 195 .... 7–187, 8–88

Patel v. W.H. Smith (Eziot) Ltd [1987] 1 W.L.R. 853; [1987] 2 All E.R. 569; (1987) 84 L.S.G. 2049; (1987) 131 S.J. 888, CA 18–65

Payne v. John Setchell Ltd [2002] P.N.L.R. 146 ... 7–121, 7–123, 7–124, 8–133, 8–137, 8–140, 8–141

Pemberton v. Southwark London Borough Council [2000] 1 W.L.R. 1672; [2000] 21 E.G. 135, CA A19, 19–36, 19–42

Penny, Palmer and Cannon v. East Kent Health Authority [2001] Lloyd's Rep. Med. 41 2–10

Pensher Security Doors Co. Ltd v. Sunderland CC [2000] R.P.C. 249 25–19

Pepper v. Hart [1993] A.C. 593; [1992] 3 W.L.R. 1032; [1993] 1 All E.R. 42; [1992] S.T.C. 898; [1993] I.C.R. 291; [1993] I.R.L.R. 33; [1993] R.V.R. 127; (1993) 142 N.L.J. 17; [1992] N.P.C. 154; *The Times*, November 30, 1992; *Independent*, November 26, 1992, HL 21–04

Percy v. D.P.P. [1995] 1 W.L.R. 1382; [1995] 3 All E.R. 124, DC 13–45

Table of Cases

Percy v. Hall [1997] Q.B. 924; [1997] 3 W.L.R. 573; [1996] 4 All E. R. 523, CA 13–22

Pfizer Ltd v. Eurofood Link (UK) Ltd [2000] E.T.M.R. 896; [2001] F.S.R. 17 25–73

Phelps v. Hillingdon London Borough Council; Anderton v. Clwyd C.C.; Re G (a Minor) v. Bromley LBC and Jarvis v. Hampshire C.C. [2000] 3 W.L.R. 776, HL 7–43, 7–116, 7–230, 11–14, 11–24, 11–26, 11–30, 11–31, 11–33, 12–42, 12–42A, 12–62, 12–72, 17–141

Phipps v. Pears [1965] 1 Q.B. 76; [1964] 2 W.L.R. 996; [1964] 2 All E.R. 35; 108 S.J. 236, CA 19–95

Photo Production Ltd v. Securicor Transport [1980] A.C. 827; [1980] 2 W.L.R. 283, HL 5A, 5–38

Pidgeon v. Doncaster Health Authority [2002] Lloyd's Rep. Med. 130 2–56

Pilmer v. Duke Group Ltd (2001) 75 A.L.J.R. 1067 8–151

Pitts v. Hunt [1991] 1 Q.B. 24; [1990] 3 W.L.R. 542; [1990] 3 All E.R. 344; [1990] R.T.R. 290; (1990) 134 S.J. 834; *The Times*, April 13, 1990; *Independent*, May 11, 1990, CA 3–11A

Platform Home Loans v. Oyston Shipways Ltd [2000] 2 A.C. 190 3–56

Poeton (A.T.) (Gloucester Plating) Ltd v. Horton (Michael Ikem) [2001] F.S.R. 169; [2000] I.C.R. 1208 .... 27–09, 27–14

Pollard v. Chief Constable of the West Yorkshire Police [1999] P.I.Q.R. P219, CA 13–41

Popi M, The. See Rhesa Shipping Co. SA v. Edmunds (The Popi M).

Poplar Housing and Regeneration Community Association Ltd v. Donoghue [2001] EWCA Civ. 595; [2002] Q.B. 48; [2001] 3 W.L.R. 183; [2001] 4 All E.R. 604; [2001] 2 F.L.R. 284; [2001] 3 F.C.R. 74; [2001] U.K.H.R.R. 693; (2001) 33 H.L.R. 73; (2001) 3 L.G.L.R. 41; [2001] B.L.G.R. 489; [2001] A.C.D. 76; [2001] Fam. Law 588; [2001] 19 E.G.C.S. 141; (2001) 98(19) L.S.G. 38; (2001) 98(23) L.S.G. 38; (2001) 145 S.J.L.B. 122; [2001] N.P.C. 84; *The Times*, June 21, 2001; *Independent*, May 2, 2001; *Daily Telegraph*, May 8, 2001, CA 12–01, 12–02, 12–78

Portman Building Society v. Bevan Ashford [2000] Lloyd's Rep. Bank. 96; [2000] Lloyd's Rep. P.N. 354; [2000] P.N.L.R. 344; (2000) 80 P. & C.R. 239; [2000] 1 E.G.L.R. 81; [2000] 07 E.G. 131; [2000] E.G.C.S. 2; (2000) 79 P. & C.R. D25, CA 8–102

Postle v. Norfolk & Norwich NHS Healthcare Trust [2000] 12 C.L. 280 11–15

Prentice v. Hereward Housing Association, unreported, March 22, 2001 10–10

Price v. U.K. (App. No. 33394/96) (2002) 34 E.H.R.R. 53; 11 B.H.R.C. 401; [2001] Crim.L.R. 916; *The Times*, August 13, 2001, ECHR 13–28

Price Waterhouse v. Kwan [2000] 3 N.Z.L.R. 39 8–145

Primark Stores Ltd v. Lollypop Clothing Ltd [2001] E.T.M.R. 30 26–09

Queen Elizabeth's School Blackburn Ltd v. Banks Wilson [2001] EWCA Civ 1360; [2002] P.N.L.R. 300 8–99

Queensland v. Pioneer Concrete Ltd [1999] FCA (F.C. Aus) 24–127

Quinland v. Governor of Belmarsh Prison [2002] EWCA Civ 174 4–19

R. v. Bedfordshire County Council, ex p. Piggott [2002] EWHC 77; (2002) 99(10) L.S.G. 31 .... 1–77A

R. v. BHB Community Healthcare NHS Trust, ex p. Barker [1999] Lloyd's Rep. Med. 101; [1999] 1 F.L.R. 106; (1999) 47 B.M.L.R. 112 13–69

R. v. Bournewood Community and Mental Health NHS Trust, ex p. L [1999] 1 A.C. 458; [1998] 3 W.L.R. 107, HL 13–12, 13–23, 13–67

R. v. Burns [2001] F.S.R. 423 25–76

R. v. Camden and Islington Health Authority [2001] Lloyd's Rep. Med. 152, *The Times*, March 15, 2001, CA 13–70

TABLE OF CASES

R. v. Canons Park Mental Health Review Tribunal, ex p. A [1995] Q.B. 60; [1994] 2 All E. R. 659; [1994] 3 W.L.R. 630 13–69
R. v. Chalkley [1998] Q.B.848; [1998] 3 W.L.R. 146, CA 13–56
R. v. Chappell (1985) 80 Cr. App. R. 31; (1984) 6 Cr. App. R. (S.) 214 13–86
R. v. Chief Constable of Dorset, ex p. Fuller [2001] EWHC Admin 1057; [2002] 3 All E.R. 57; [2001] N.P.C. 186; *Independent*, February 4, 2002 .... 1–77A
R. v. Collins and Ashworth Hospital Authority, ex p. Brady [2000] Lloyd's Rep. Med. 355 .... 3–106, 13–63, 13–72
R. v. Colohan; *sub nom.* R. v. C (Sean Peter) [2001] EWCA Crim 1251; [2001] 2 F.L.R. 757, CA 13–18
R. v. Constanza [1997] 2 Cr. App. R. 492; [1997] Crim.L.R. 576, CA 13–13
R. v. Department of Health, ex p. Source Informatics Ltd [2001] F.S.R. 74 .... 27–02, 27–11, 27–21
R. v. DPP, *The Times,* February 20, 2001 24–67
R. v. Galbraith [1981] 1 W.L.R. 1039; [1981] 2 All E.R. 1060; (1981) 73 Cr. App. R. 124; [1981] Crim.L.R. 648; 125 S.J. 442, CA 22–159
R. v. Governor of Brockhill Prison, ex p. Evans (No.2) [2001] 2 A.C. 19; [2000] 3 W.L.R. 843; [2000] 4 All E.R. 15; [2000] U.K.H.R.R. 836; (2000) 97(32) L.S.G. 38; (2000) 144 S.J.L.B. 241; *The Times*, August 2, 2000; *Independent*, November 6, 2000 (C.S.), HL 1–26, 1–28, 1–64, 11–17, 11–21, 13–22, 13–25
R. v. H (Reasonable Chastisement) [2001] 2 F.L.R. 431; *The Times,* May 17, 2001, CA 13–81
R. v. Hallstrom, ex p. W. (No.2) [1986] Q.B.1090, [1986] 2 W.L.R. 883 13–69
R. v. Ireland [1998] A.C. 147; [1997] 3 W.L.R. 534, HL 13–13
R. v. Keane [2001] F.S.R.63 25–76
R. v. Lee [2001] 1 Cr. App. R. 293; [2001] 1 Cr.App.R.(S.) 1, CA 13–57
R. v. London South and South West Region Mental Health Review Tribunal, ex p. Moyle [2000] Lloyd's Rep. Med. 143; *The Times*, February 10, 2000 13–69
R. v. McKoy [2002] EWCA Crim 1628; *The Times*, June 17, 2002, CA 13–21
R. v. Mental Health Review Tribunal, ex p. Hall [2000] 1 W.L.R. 1323; [1999] 4 All E.R. 883; [1999] 2 C.C.L. Rep. 383; [1999] Lloyd's Rep. Med. 417; (2000) 51 B.M.L.R. 117; [1999] C.O.D. 429; (1999) 96(33) L.S.G. 31; (1999) 149 N.L.J. 1368; *The Times*, October 5, 1999, CA 13–70
R. v. Ministry of Defence, ex p. Smith [1996] Q.B. 517; [1996] 2 W.L.R. 305; [1996] 1 All E.R. 257; [1996] I.C.R. 740; [1996] I.R.L.R. 100; (1996) 8 Admin. L.R. 29; [1996] C.O.D. 237; (1995) 145 N.L.J. 1689; *The Times*, November 6, 1995; *Independent*, November 7, 1995, CA 13–78
R. v. Reid [1973] Q.B. 299; [1972] 3 W.L.R. 395, CA 13–19
R. v. Richardson [1999] Q.B.444 13–10
R. v. Secretary of State for Health, ex p. Imperial Tobacco [2001] 1 W.L.R. 127; [2001] 1 All E.R.50, HL 24–12, 30–21
R. v. Secretary of State for Transport, ex p. Factortame Ltd (No.5) [2000] 1 A.C. 524; [1999] 3 W.L.R. 1062; [1999] 4 All E.R. 906; [1999] 3 C.M.L.R. 597; [2000] Eu.L.R. 40; (1999) 96(43) L.S.G. 32; [1999] N.P.C. 126; *The Times*, November 3, 1999, HL 11–39, 24–127
R. v. Secretary of State for Transport, ex p. Factortame Ltd (No.6) [2001] 1 W.L.R. 942, *The Times*, January 10, 2001 24–127
R. v. Tabassum [2000] Lloyd's Rep. Med. 404; *The Times*, May 26, 2000, CA 13–10
R. v. Thomson Holidays Ltd [1974] Q.B. 592; [1974] 2 W.L.R. 371, CA 13–86
R. v. Vivian [1979] 1 W.L.R. 291; [1979] 1 All E.R.48, CA 13–86
R. v. Wilson [1997] Q.B.47; [1996] 3 W.L.R. 125, CA 13–08
R. (on the application of C) v. Mental Health Review Tribunal, London and South West Region [2001] EWCA Civ 1110; [2002] 1 W.L.R. 176; [2002] 2 F.C.R. 181; [2001] Lloyd's Rep. Med. 450; (2001) 98(29) L.S.G. 39; (2001) 145 S.J.L.B. 167; *The Times*, July 11, 2001; *Independent*, July 10, 2001, CA 13–70

TABLE OF CASES

R. (on the application of Ford) v. Press Complaints Commission [2001] EWHC Admin 683; [2002] E.M.L.R. 5; *Daily Telegraph*, September 4, 2001 27–21

R. (on the application of H) v. Mental Health Review Tribunal for North and East London Region [2001] EWCA Civ 415; [2002] Q.B. 1; [2001] 3 W.L.R. 512; [2001] H.R.L.R. 36; [2001] U.K.H.R.R. 717; [2001] Lloyd's Rep. Med. 302; (2001) 61 B.M.L.R. 163; [2001] A.C.D. 78; (2001) 98 (21) L.S.G. 40; (2001) 145 S.J.L.B. 108; *The Times*, April 2, 2001; *Independent*, April 3, 2001, CA 13–69, 13–70

R (on the application of Heather) v. Leonard Cheshire Foundation [2002] EWCA Civ 366; [2002] 2 All E.R. 936; [2002] A.C.D. 43; *The Times*, April 8, 2002, CA; affirming [2001] EWHC Admin 429; [2001] A.C.D. 75; *Daily Telegraph*, June 26, 2001; [2002] EWCA Civ 366 12–01

R. (on the application of K) v. Mental Health Review Tribunal [2002] EWHC 639 (Admin); (2002) 152 N.L.J. 672 13–70

R. (on the application of Rottman) v. Commissioner of Police for the Metropolis [2002] UKHL 20; [2002] 2 All E.R. 865 13–52

R. (on the application of W) v. Broadmoor Hospital [2001] EWCA Civ 1545; [2002] 1 W.L.R. 419; [2002] U.K.H.R.R. 390; [2002] Lloyd's Rep. Med. 41; (2002) 65 B.M.L.R. 15; (2001) 98(44) L.S.G. 36; (2001) 145 S.J.L.B. 247; *The Times*, November 2, 2001; *Independent*, December 10, 2001 (C.S.); *Daily Telegraph*, October 30, 2001, CA 13–74, 13–78, 13–78

Racz v. Home Office [1994] 2 A.C. 45; [1994] 2 W.L.R. 23, HL 13–27, 13–28

Radstock Co-operative and Industrial Society v. Norton-Radstock UDC [1968] Ch. 605; [1968] 2 W.L.R. 1214; [1968] 2 All E.R. 59; 132 J.P. 238; 66 L.G.R. 457; 112 S.J. 135, CA 19–82

Rahman v. Arearose Ltd [2001] Q.B. 351; [2000] 3 W.L.R. 1184, CA 2–16, 2–35, 2–55, 24–127

Raiss v. Palmano [2001] Lloyd's Rep. P.N. 341; [2001] P.N.L.R. 540 7–37

Rand v. East Dorset Health Authority [2000] Lloyd's Rep. Med. 181; (2000) 56 B.M.L.R. 39 .... 7–26, 29–53

Ready Mixed Concrete (South East) Ltd v. Minister of Pensions and National Insurance [1968] 2 Q.B. 497; [1968] 2 W.L.R. 775 5–10

Reality Group Ltd v. Chance [2002] F.S.R. 13 26–08

Reavey v. Century Newspapers [2001] N.I. 187 .... 22–11, 22–106

Reckitt & Coleman Products Ltd v. Borden Inc. [1990] R.P.C. 341 26–18

Reeman v. Department of Transport [1997] 2 Lloyd's Rep. 648; [1997] P.N.L.R. 618, CA 7–96

Rees v. Darlington NHS Trust [2002] EWCA Civ 88; [2002] 2 W.L.R. 1483; [2002] 2 All E.R. 177; [2002] 1 F.L.R. 799; [2002] 1 F.C.R. 695; [2002] P.I.Q.R. P26; (2002) 65 B.M.L.R. 117; [2002] Fam. Law 348; (2002) 99(12) L.S.G. 32; (2002) 152 N.L.J. 281; (2002) 146 S.J.L.B. 53; *The Times*, February 20, 2002; *Independent*, February 19, 2002, CA 7a, 7–26, 8–58, 29–53

Rees v. Skerrett [2001] EWCA Civ 760; [2001] 1 W.L.R. 1541; (2001) 3 T.C.L.R. 27; [2001] 24 E.G.C.S. 162, *The Times*, June 18, 2001, CA [2001] 1 W.L.R. 1541 19–95

Reeves v. Commissioner of Police for the Metropolis [2000] 1 A.C. 360; [1999] 3 W.L.R. 363; [1999] 3 All E.R. 897; (2000) 51 B.M.L.R. 155; (1999) 96(31) L.S.G. 41; (1999) 143 S.J.L.B. 213; *The Times*, July 16, 1999; *Independent*, July 21, 1999, HL .. 2–37, 2–58, 3–10, 3–11A, 3–16, 3–21, 3–31, 3–33, 3–54, 3–81, 7–32, 13–63

Regan v. Taylor NLJR March 9, 2000 Vol. 150, p.392 22–67

Reid v. Secretary of State for Scotland [1999] 2 A.C. 512 13–69

Renaissance Leisure Inc. v. Frazer (2001) 197 D.L.R. (4th) 336 10–26

Revill v. Newberry [1996] Q.B.567; [1996] 2 W.L.R. 239; [1996] 1 All E.R. 291, CA 13–02

TABLE OF CASES

Reynolds v. Times Newspapers [1999] 3 W.L.R. 1010; [1999] 4 All E.R. 609, HL 22–121, 22–122
Rhesa Shipping Co. SA v. Edmunds (The Popi M); Rhesa Shipping Co. SA v. Fenton Insurance Co. Ltd [1985] 1 W.L.R. 948; [1985] 2 All E.R. 712; [1985] 2 Lloyd's Rep. 1; (1985) 82 L.S.G. 2995; (1985) 129 S.J. 503, HL ... 2–05
Ribee v. Norrie, *The Times*, November 22, 2000 .... A20, 20–60
Richardson v. London Rubber & Co. Ltd [2000] Lloyd's Rep. Med. 280 .... 9–62, 9–63
Roadtech Computer Systems Ltd v. Mandata Ltd [2000] E.T.M.R. 970 25–75
Roberts v. Chief Constable of the Cheshire Constabulary [1999] 1 W.L.R. 662; [1999] 2 All E.R. 236, CA 13–21, 13–25, 13–61
Roerig v. Valiant Trawlers Ltd [2002] EWCA Civ 21; [2002] 1 All E.R. 961; [2002] 1 Lloyd's Rep. 681; [2002] C.L.C. 629; [2002] P.I.Q.R. Q8; (2002) 152 N.L.J. 171, CA 6–10A, 6–11
Rohm and Haas Co. v. Collag Ltd [2001] EWCA Civ 1589; [2002] F.S.R. 28; (2002) 25(2) I.P.D. 25007, CA 25–85
Rookes v. Bernard [1964] A.C. 1129; [1964] 2 W.L.R. 269, HL 13–85, 15–43
Ross Harper & Murphy v. Scott Banks [2000] Lloyd's Rep. P.N. 631 7–42
Rowland v. Gulfpac Ltd [1999] 1 Lloyd's Rep. Bank 86 30–39
Royal Brompton Hospital NHS Trust v. Hammond (No.3) [2002] UKHL 14; [2002] 1 W.L.R. 1397; [2002] 2 All E.R. 801; [2002] 1 All E.R. (Comm) 897; 81 Con. L.R. 1; *The Times*, April 26, 2002, HL 4–119
Royal Brunei Airlines Sdn. Bhd v. Tan [1995] 2 A.C. 378; [1995] 3 W.L.R. 64; [1995] 3 All E.R. 97; [1995] B.C.C. 899; (1995) 92(27) L.S.G. 33; (1995) 145 N.L.J. 888; [1995] 139 S.J.L.B. 146; *The Times*, May 29, 1995; *Independent*, June 22, 1995, PC (Bru) 28–25
Royscot v. Rogerson [1991] 2 Q.B. 297; [1991] 3 W.L.R. 57; [1991] 3 All E.R. 294 15–47
Rugby Football Union v. Cotton Traders Ltd [2002] EWHC 467; [2002] E.T.M.R. 76 25–73
Rylands v. Fletcher (1868) L.R. 3 H.L. 330 ...... 1–67, 5–56, 20a, 20–12, 20–14, 20–34, 20–46

S. v. Gloucestershire County Council [2001] 2 W.L.R. 90; [2001] Fam. 313, CA 11–33, 12–61, 12–62, 12–63, 12–73
SA Societe LTJ v. SA Sadas (C–291/00) [2002] E.T.M.R. 441 25–73
S (Adult Patient: Sterilisation), Re [2001] Fam. 15; [2000] 3 W.L.R. 1288; [2000] 2 F.L.R. 389; [2000] 2 F.C.R. 452; [2000] Lloyd's Rep. Med. 339; (2000) 55 B.M.L.R. 105; [2000] Fam. Law 711; (2000) 97(24) L.S.G. 40; *The Times*, May 26, 2000, CA 3–105
Sabri-Tabrizi v. Lothian Health Board and McKew v. Holland and Cubitts (Scotland) Ltd 1998 S.C. 373; 1998 S.L.T. 607; (1998) 43 B.M.L.R. 190; 1998 Rep. L.R. 37; 1998 G.W.D. 5–247, OH 2–56
Sacco v. Chief Constable of the South Wales Constabulary, unreported, May 15, 1998 .... 3–11A
Saddington v. Colleys Professional Services (1995) [1999] Lloyd's Rep. P.N. 140; [1995] E.G.C.S. 109, CA 2–32
Safeway Stores v. Tate [2001] 2 W.L.R. 1377; [2001] E.M.L.R. 13 .... 22–02, 22–06
Sallows v. Griffiths [2001] F.S.R. 15, CA 16–02, 16–03
Sanwa Australia Finance Ltd v. Finchill Pty Ltd [2001] N.S.W.C.A. 446 14–129
Savill v. Roberts (1698) 12 Mod. 208 16–02
Savings and Investment Bank Ltd v. Fincken, *The Times*, March 2, 2001 33–01
SBJ Stephenson Ltd v. Mandy [2000] F.S.R. 286; [2000] I.R.L.R. 233 ... 27–07, 27–09, 27–12
Scandecor Development AB v. Scandecor Marketing AB [2001] UKHL 21; [2001] 2 C.M.L.R. 30; [2001] E.T.M.R. 74; [2002] F.S.R. 7; (2001) 24(9) I.P.D. 24056, HL 25–74

[xxvii]

Table of Cases

Scholes Windows Ltd v. Magnet Ltd [2001] EWCA Civ 532; [2002] E.C.D.R. 20; [2002] F.S.R. 10; (2001) 24(6) I.P.D. 24036; *The Times*, June 5, 2001, CA 25–51
Scott v. Associated British Ports Ltd, unreported , November 22, 2000 ... 10–60, 10–69, 10–75
Secretary of State for the Home Department v. Robb [1995] Fam. 127; [1995] 2 W.L.R. 722, Fam. Div. 13–63
Sefton M.B. v. UNISON and Flanagan, July 2, 2001 24–178
Sellars Arenascene Ltd v. Connolly [2001] E.W.C.A. Civ. 184; [2001] I.R.L.R. 223, CA 5–03
Shade v. Compton Partnership [2000] P.N.L.R. 218, [2000] Lloyd's Rep. P.N. 81, CA 33–01
Shah v. Standard Chartered Bank [1999] Q.B. 241; [1998] 3 W.L.R. 592; [1998] 4 All E.R. 155; [1998] E.M.L.R. 597; (1998) 142 S.J.L.B. 164; *The Times*, May 13, 1998, CA 22–39, 22–79
Shakoor v. Kang Situ [2001] 1 W.L.R. 410 8–35
Sharif v. Garrett & Co. (a firm) [2001] EWCA Civ 1269; [2002] 3 All E.R. 195; [2002] Lloyd's Rep. I.R. 11; (2001) 151 N.L.J. 1371, CA 2–28, 29–12
Shendish Manor Ltd v. Coleman [2001] EWCA Civ 913 4–78
Simpson v. Al Dairies Ltd [2001] EWCA Civ. 13 10–32
Skinner v. Aberdeen City Council 2001 Rep. L.R. 118; 2001 G.W.D. 16–657, OH 11–15
Skrine & Co. v. Euromoney Publications plc [2001] EWCA Civ 1479; [2002] E.M.L.R. 15 22–20
Smith v. Eric S. Bush [1990] 1 A.C. 831; [1989] 2 W.L.R. 790; [1989] 2 All E.R. 514; (1989) 21 H.L.R. 424; 87 L.G.R. 685; [1955–95] P.N.L.R. 467; [1989] 18 E.G. 99; [1989] 17 E.G. 68; (1990) 9 Tr. L.R. 1; (1989) 153 L.G. Rev. 984; (1989) 139 N.L.J. 576; (1989) 133 S.J. 597, HL 8–113
Smith v. Lloyds TSB plc [2000] 2 All E.R. Comm. 293; *The Times*, September 6, 2000 .... 14–41, 14–111
Smith v. National Health Service Litigation Authority [2001] Lloyd's Rep. Med. 90 .... 2–28, 8–65, 8–67
Smith v. Peter North & Partners [2001] EWCA Civ 1533; [2002] Lloyd's Rep. P.N. 111; [2002] P.N.L.R. 12; [2002] 1 P. & C.R. 37; [2001] 42 E.G.C.S. 138; (2001) 98(41) L.S.G. 35, CA 8–126
Smith v. Secretary of State for Health, *The Times*, March 11, 2002 9–14
Smith v. Stemler [2001] C.L.Y. 2309 23–18
Smith v. White Knight Laundry Ltd [2001] EWCA Civ 660; [2002] 1 W.L.R. 616; [2001] 3 All E.R. 862; [2001] C.P. Rep. 88; [2001] 2 B.C.L.C. 206; [2001] P.I.Q.R. P30; *Independent*, July 2, 2001 (C.S.), CA 33–16
Smith (Administrator of Cosslett Contractors) Ltd v. Bridgend C.C. [2001] UKHL 58; [2002] 1 A.C. 336; [2001] 3 W.L.R. 1347; [2002] 1 All E.R. 292; [2001] B.C.C. 740; [2002] 1 B.C.L.C. 77; [2002] B.L.R. 160; [2002] T.C.L.R. 7; 80 Con. L.R. 172; [2001] N.P.C. 161, HL 14–18, 14–48
Smith New Court Securities Ltd v. Scrimgeour Vickers (Asset Management) Ltd [1997] A.C. 254; [1996] 3 W.L.R. 1051; [1996] 4 All E.R. 769; [1997] 1 B.C.L.C. 350; (1996) 93(46) L.S.G. 28; (1996) 146 N.L.J. 1722; (1997) 141 S.J.L.B. 5; *The Times*, November 22, 1996; *Independent*, November 27, 1996, HL 15–40
Sniezek v. Bundy (Letchworth) Ltd [2000] P.I.Q.R. P213, CA 33–33
Snowden v. Ministry of Defence [2001] EWCA Civ 1524 8–83
Solloway v. McLoughlin [1938] A.C. 247 14–103
South Australia Asset Management Corp. v. York Montague [1997] A.C.191; [1996] 3 W.L.R. 87; [1996] 3 All E.R. 365, HL 2–67, 8A
South Australia Asset Management Corp. v. York Montague Ltd [1995] N.P.C. 66; [1995] E.G.C.S. 71, QBD 2–66

[xxviii]

Table of Cases

South West Trains Ltd v. N.U.R.M.T., October 25, 1999	24–193
Spice Girls v. Aprilla World Service BV (Damages) [2001] E.M.L.R. 8	15–45
Spicer v. Smee [1946] 1 All E.R. 489	5–58
St Georges Healthcare NHS Trust v. S [1999] Fam.26; (1998) 1 C.C.L.Rep. 578, CA	13–69
Standard Chartered Bank v. Pakistan National Shipping Corporation (No.2) [2000] 1 Lloyd's Rep. 218	7–116, 15–35
Standard Chartered Bank v. Pakistan National Shipping Corporation (No.4) (Reduction of Damages) [2001] Q.B. 167	3–28, 3–33, 15–35
Standard Chartered Bank v. Pakistan National Shipping Corporation (Assessment of Damages) [2001] E.W.C.A. Civ. 55, CA	15–40
Staples v. West Dorset District Council [1995] P.I.Q.R. P439; (1995) 92(18) L.S.Gaz. 36, CA	10–27
Stark v. The Post Office [2000] P.I.Q.R. P105; *The Times*, March 29, 2000	7–227
Steeds v. Peverel Management Services Ltd, *The Times*, May 16, 2001	33–46
Steliou v. Compton [2002] 2 All E.R. 737	32–24
Stern v. Piper [1997] Q.B. 123; [1996] 3 W.L.R. 715; [1996] 3 All E.R. 385; [1996] E.M.L.R. 413; (1996) 93(22) L.S.G. 27; (1996) 140 S.J.L.B. 175; *The Times*, May 30, 1996; *Independent*, June 17, 1996 (C.S.), CA	22–39
Stewart v. Engel [2000] 1 W.L.R. 2268; *The Times*, May 26, 2000, CA	33–01
Stockport Metropolitan Borough Council v. British Gas plc [2001] All E.R.(D) 190, CA	A20, 20–12, 20–33, 20–34
Stoke-on-Trent City Council v. B & Q Retail; Nottingham City Council v. Z [2002] 1 W.L.R. 607	19–48
Stovin v. Wise [1996] A.C. 923; [1996] 3 W.L.R. 388; [1996] 3 All E.R. 801; [1996] R.T.R. 354; (1996) 93(35) L.S.G. 33; (1996) 146 N.L.J. 1185; (1996) 140 S.J.L.B. 201; *The Times*, July 26, 1996; *Independent*, July 31, 1996, HL	12–32
Stubbing v. Webb [1993] A.C. 498; [1993] 2 W.L.R. 120; [1993] 1 All E.R. 322, CA	13–02
Sugar v. Associated Newspapers, unreported, February 6, 2001	22–159
Summers v. Tice 199 P. 2d 1 (1948)	2–13D
Sun Valley Foods Ltd v. John Philip Vincent [2000] F.S.R. 825	27–44, 27–46
Surface Technology plc v. Young [2002] F.S.R. 387	27–08
Surrey Asset Finance Ltd v. National Westminster Bank plc, *The Times*, November 30, 2000	14–46
Surrey County Council v. M [2001] EWCA Civ 691	12–37
Sutherland v. V2 Music Ltd [2002] EWHC 14; [2002] E.M.L.R. 28	26–11
Swain v. Denso Marston Ltd [2000] P.I.Q.R. P129; *The Times*, April 24, 2000	11–15
Swain v. Hillman [2001] 1 All E.R. 91; [2001] C.P. Rep. 16; [1999] C.P.L.R. 779; [2000] P.I.Q.R. P51; *The Times*, November 4, 1999; *Independent*, November 10, 1999, CA	22–06
Swallows v. Griffiths [2001] F.S.R. 15	23–20
Sweeney v. Macmillan Publishers Ltd [2002] R.P.C. 35	25–07
Sykes v. Harry [2001] EWCA Civ 167; [2001] Q.B. 1014; [2001] 3 W.L.R. 62; (2001) 33 H.L.R. 80; (2001) 82 P. & C.R. 35; [2001] L. & T.R. 40; [2001] 1 E.G.L.R. 53; [2001] 17 E.G. 221; (2001) 98(14) L.S.G. 39; (2001) 145 S.J.L.B. 61; [2001] N.P.C. 26; (2001) 82 P. & C.R. D9; *The Times*, February 27, 2001; *Independent*, February 7, 2001, CA	10–60
Symbian Ltd v. Chritiansen [2001] I.R.L.R. 77	24–37
T, Re [1988] Fam.52; [1988] 2 W.L.R. 189	13–70, 13–72
T. (Adult: Refusal of Medical Treatment) Re, [1993] Fam. 95; [1992] 3 W.L.R. 782	13–63
Ta Ho Ma Pty Ltd v. Allen (1999) 47 N.S.W.L.R. 1	8–111
Tasci v. Pekalp of London Ltd [2001] I.C.R. 633; *The Times*, January 17, 2001	11–45

TABLE OF CASES

Taunton and Somerset NHS Trust [2001] 1 F.L.R. 419 29–53
Taylor v. Shropshire Health Authority [2000] Lloyd's Rep. Med. 96 7–26
Teleworks Ltd v. Telework Group plc [2002] R.P.C. 27 26–11
Theakston v. MGN Ltd [2002] EWHC 137; [2002] E.M.L.R. 22 ....27–03, 27–21, 27–43
Thomas v. Chief Constable of Cleveland [2001] EWCA Civ 1552 17–145
Thomas v. N.U.M. [1986] Ch.20; [1985] 2 W.L.R. 1081 13–13
Thomas v. News Group Newspapers [2001] EWCA Civ 1233; [2001] E.M.L.R. 4; *The Times*, July 25, 2001, CA 13–18, 24–67
Thomas (Susan) v. Pearce (Elizabeth) [2000] F.S.R. 718 .... 27–08, 27–23
Thompson v. Commissioner of Police for the Metropolis [1998] Q.B. 498; [1997] 3 W.L.R. 403, CA 13–84
Thompson and Venables v. News Group Newspapers [2001] Fam. 430; [2001] 2 W.L.R. 1038; [2001] 1 All E.R. 908; [2001] E.M.L.R. 10; [2001] 1 F.L.R. 791; [2002] 1 F.C.R. 333; [2001] H.R.L.R. 19; [2001] U.K.H.R.R. 628; 9 B.H.R.C. 587; [2001] Fam. Law 258; (2001) 98(12) L.S.G. 41; (2001) 151 N.L.J. 57; (2001) 145 S.J.L.B. 43; *The Times*, January 16, 2001; *Independent*, January 17, 2001, *Daily Telegraph*, January 16, 2001 1–77
Thorgeirson v. Iceland (A/239) (1992) 14 E.H.R.R. 843 22–01
Thornberry v. Coleman [2001] EWCA Civ 1858 22–207
Three Rivers District Council v. Bank of England (No.3) [2000] 2 W.L.R. 15, CA ; [2001] 2 W.L.R. 1220; [2001] 2 All E.R. 513, HL 1–59, 12–87, 17–145, 24–127
Todd v. Adams and Chope (t/a Trelawney Fishing Co.) (The Maragetha Maria) [2002] EWCA Civ 509; [2002] 2 Lloyd's Rep. 293; (2002) 99(21) L.S.G. 32; (2002) 146 S.J.L.B. 118; *The Times*, May 3, 2002 ....11–02, 11–12, 11–15, 11–36
Tomlinson v. Congleton Borough Council [2002] EWCA Civ 309; [2002] 12 E.G.C.S. 136; (2002) 99(18) L.S.G. 38; (2002) 146 S.J.L.B. 92; [2002] N.P.C. 42; *The Times*, March 22, 2002; *Independent*, March 21, 2002 ..... 3–82, 9a, 10–70, 10–75
Toole v. Bolton Metropolitan Borough Council [2002] EWCA Civ 588 .... 3–29, 3–38
Toshiba Europe GmbH v. Katun Germany GmbH (C–112/99) [2002] All E.R. (EC) 325; [2001] E.C.R. I–7945; [2002] E.T.M.R. 26; [2002] F.S.R. 39, ECJ 25–74
Totalise PLC v. Motley Fool [2002] 1 W.L.R. 1233; *The Times*, March 15, 2001 22–07
TP and KM v. United Kingdom (2002) 34 E.H.R.R. 42; *The Times*, May 31, 2001 ....1A, 1–77, 1–79, 1–80, 1–84, 8–62, 11–24, 11–30, 12–08, 12–09A, 12–70, 12–74
Triomed (Proprietary) Ltd v. Beecham Group Plc [2001] F.S.R. 583 .... 27–07, 27–44, 27–46
Trotman v. North Yorkshire County Council [1999] LCR 584 .... 5A, 5–24, 5–38
Trustees Executors & Agency Co of NZ v. Price Waterhouse [2000] P.N.L.R. 673 8–145
Trustor AB v. Smallbone (No.3) [2001] 1 W.L.R. 1177; [2001] 3 All E.R. 987; [2001] 2 B.C.L.C. 436; (2001) 98(20) L.S.G. 40; (2001) 151 N.L.J. 457; (2001) 145 S.J.L.B. 99; *The Times*, March 30, 2001 24–39
Tucker v. News Media Ownership Ltd [1986] 2 N.Z.L.R. 716 1–76
Turkington v. Breen [2001] 3 W.L.R. 1670 .... 22–152, 22–153, 22–156
Turton & Co. v. Kerslake & Partners [2000] Lloyd's Rep. P.N. 967 .... 7–105, 8–133
Twinsectra Ltd v. Yardley [2002] UKHL 12; [2002] 2 W.L.R. 802; [2002] 2 All E.R. 377; [2002] W.T.L.R. 423; (2002) 99(19) L.S.G. 32; (2002) 152 N.L.J. 469; (2002) 146 S.J.L.B. 84; [2002] N.P.C. 47; *The Times*, March 25, 2002, HL 28–25

UCB Bank plc v. Hephard Winstanley & Pugh (a Firm) [1999] Lloyd's Rep. P.N. 963; (1999) 96(34) L.S.G. 34, CA 3–34

[xxx]

TABLE OF CASES

UCB Corporate Services Ltd v. Clyde & Co. [2000] P.N.L.R. 841, CA ...3–56, 8–85, 8–94
UCB Home Loans v. Carr [2000] Lloyd's P.N.L.R. 754 15–02
Unilever plc v. Frisa N.V. [2002] F.S.R. 708; (2000) 23(4) I.P.D. 23028 25–82
Unilever v. Gillette [1989] R.P.C. 583; *Financial Times*, June 28, 1989, CA ... 24–03
Unilever plc v. Procter & Gamble Co. [2000] F.S.R. 344 25–100
Union Discount Co. Ltd v. Zoller [2001] EWCA Civ 1755; [2002] 1 W.L.R. 1517; [2002] 1 All E.R. 693; [2002] C.L.C. 314; (2002) 99(3) L.S.G. 25; (2001) 151 N.L.J. 1769; (2001) 145 S.J.L.B. 276; *The Times*, December 10, 2001; *Independent*, November 29, 2001, CA 29–115
United Wire Ltd v. Screen Repair Services (Scotland) Ltd [2001] F.S.R. 365, HL 25–90

Vellino v. Chief Constable of the Greater Manchester Police [2001] EWCA Civ 1249; [2002] 1 W.L.R. 218; [2002] 3 All E.R. 78; [2002] P.I.Q.R. P10; (2001) 151 N.L.J. 1441; *The Times*, August 9, 2001, CA ...3–05, 3–11A, 3–13, 3–19, 7–31
Venables v. News Group Newspapers [2001] 2 W.L.R. 1038; *The Times*, January 16, 2001 24–41
Vermaat and Powell v. Boncrest Ltd [2001] F.S.R. 43 25–09
Vernon v. Bosley (No.1) [1997] 1 All E.R. 577; [1997] R.T.R. 1; [1998] 1 F.L.R. 297; [1997] P.I.Q.R. P255; (1997) 35 B.M.L.R. 135; [1997] Fam. Law 476; (1996) 146 N.L.J. 589; *The Times*, April 4, 1996, CA 2–16
Verrecchia v. Metropolitan Police Commissioner, unreported, March 15, 2001 14–53
Vine v. Waltham Forest London Borough Council [2000] 1 W.L.R. 2383 3–58
Vodden v. Gayton [2001] P.I.Q.R. P27 .... 10–08, 10–20, 10–77
VOF Schieving-Nijstad v. Robert Groenveld (Case C–89/99) [2001] E.T.M.R. 630 27–01

W v. Essex County Council [2001] 2 A.C. 592; [2000] 2 W.L.R. 601; [2000] 2 All E.R. 237; [2000] 1 F.L.R. 657; [2000] 1 F.C.R. 568; [2000] B.L.G.R. 281; (2000) 53 B.M.L.R. 1; [2000] Fam. Law 476; (2000) 164 J.P.N. 464; (2000) 97(13) L.S.G. 44; (2000) 144 S.J.L.B. 147; *The Times*, March 17, 2000, HL 7–64, 11–33, 12–37, 12–61, 12–63, 12–73
W v. Home Office [2001] EWCA Civ 2081; [2002] 3 W.L.R. 405; *The Times*, January 4, 2002 .... 13–16, 13–17
W v. L. (Mental Health Patient) [1974] Q.B. 711; [1973] 3 W.L.R. 859, CA 13–70
WB v. H Bauer Publishing [2002] E.M.L.R. 145 27–08
Waldron, Re [1986] Q.B. 824; [1985] 3 W.L.R. 1090, CA 13–78
Walker v. Stones [2001] 2 W.L.R. 623, CA 24–39
Wandsworth London Borough Council v. Railtrack plc [2001] EWCA Civ 1236; [2002] 2 W.L.R. 512; [2002] Env. L.R. 9; [2002] E.H.L.R. 5; [2001] B.L.G.R. 544; [2001] 32 E.G.C.S. 88; (2001) 98(37) L.S.G. 38; (2001) 145 S.J.L.B. 219; [2001] N.P.C. 131; *The Times*, August 2, 2001; *Daily Telegraph*, September 4, 2001, CA 19–111
Ward v. Chief Constable of the Royal Ulster Constabulary [2000] N.I. 543 ..... 3–31, 13–08
Warriner v. Warriner [2002] EWCA Civ 81; [2002] 1 W.L.R. 1703; [2002] P.I.Q.R. Q7; (2002) 99(14) L.S.G. 25; *The Times*, March 28, 2002, CA ... 29–28
Waters v. Commissioner of Police of the Metropolis [2000] 1 W.L.R. 1607, HL 7–218, 12–44, 12–66, 12–68, 12–72, 24–67
Watson v. British Boxing Board of Control [2002] Q.B. 1134; [2001] 2 W.L.R. 1256; [2001] P.I.Q.R. P16; (2001) 98(12) L.S.G. 44; (2001) 145 S.J.L.B. 31; *The Times*, February 2, 2001; *Independent*, January 11, 2001; *Daily Telegraph*, January 16, 2001, CA 3–97, 7A, 7–22, 7–51, 7–52, 7–53, 7–231
Webb v. Barclays Bank plc and Portsmouth Hospitals NHS Trust [2001] EWCA Civ 1141; [2001] Lloyd's Rep. Med. 500 .... 2–55, 2–08

[xxxi]

TABLE OF CASES

Webb v. Chief Constable of Merseyside Police [2000] Q.B. 427; [2000] 2 W.L.R. 546; [2000] 1 All E.R. 209; (1999) 96(47) L.S.G. 33; (2000) 144 S.J.L.B. 9; *The Times*, December 1, 1999 3–07
Westminster City Council (Lord Mayor and Citizens) v. UNISON [2001] I.C.R. 1046, CA 24–178, 24–198
Wheatley (Davina) v. Drillsafe Ltd [2001] R.P.C.133 25–85
White v. ESAB Group (U.K.) Ltd [2002] P.I.Q.R. Q6 29–90
White v. Jones [1995] 2 A.C. 207; [1995] 2 W.L.R. 187, HL 3–46, 3–50, 7–21
Whitehead v. Alexander [2000] 5 C.L.Y. 205 21–06
Wilkinson v. Downton [1897] 2 Q.B. 57 .... 13–16, 13–17
William (G) v. W. Harts. HA [2002] EWCA Civ 1041 10–54
Williams (J.D.) & Co. Ltd v. Michael Hyde & Associates Ltd [2001] P.N.L.R. 8 7–187
Williams v. Natural Life Health Foods Ltd [1998] 1 W.L.R. 830; [1998] 2 All E.R. 577, HL 7–43, 7–116, 8–06A, 15–25
Wilsher v. Essex Area Health Authority [1988] A.C. 1074; [1988] 2 W.L.R. 557; [1988] 1 All E.R. 871; (1988) 138 N.L.J. Rep. 78; (1988) 132 S.J. 418, HL 2–13A, 2–13C, 2–13D, 2–13E, 2–13I, 2–13J
Wilson v. Pringle [1987] Q.B. 237; [1986] 3 W.L.R. 1, CA 13–05, 13–06
Winch v. Jones [1986] Q.B. 296; [1985] 3 W.L.R. 729, CA 13–78
Windsor v. Boycott [2001] EWCA Civ 1321 22–49
Wong v. Parkside Health NHS Trust [2001] EWCA Civ 1721; (2002) 99(2) L.S.G. 28; (2001) 145 S.J.L.B. 276; *The Times*, December 7, 2001; *Independent*, November 27, 2001, CA 13–16, 13–17
Worby v. Rosser [2000] P.N.L.R. 140 8–78
WWF World Wide Fund for Nature v. World Wrestling Federation Entertainment Inc. [2002] EWCA Civ 196; [2002] U.K.C.L.R. 388; [2002] E.T.M.R. 53; [2002] F.S.R. 33; (2002) 25(4) I.P.D. 25023; (2002) 99(15) L.S.G. 33; (2002) 152 N.L.J. 363; (2002) 146 S.J.L.B. 70; *The Times*, March 12, 2002, CA 25–73

X (Minors) v. Bedfordshire County Council [1995] A.C. 633; [1995] 3 W.L.R. 152; [1995] 3 All E.R. 353; [1995] 2 F.L.R. 276; [1995] 3 F.C.R. 337; 94 L.G.R. 313; (1995) 7 Admin. L.R. 705; [1995] Fam. Law 537; (1996) 160 L.G. Rev. 123; (1995) 145 N.L.J. 993; *The Times*, June 30, 1995; *Independent*, June 30, 1995, HL 1–79, 1–80, 8–62, 11–12, 11–24, 11–30, 11–31, 11–33, 12–09A, 12–42, 12–61, 12–70, 12–71, 12–74

Yukong Line Ltd v. Rendsburg Investments Corporation [2001] 2 Lloyd's Rep. 113, CA 30–40

Z v. United Kingdom [2001] 2 F.C.R. 612; [2001] 2 F.C.R. 246; (2002) 34 E.H.R.R. 3; 10 B.H.R.C. 384; (2001) 3 L.G.L.R. 51; [2001] Fam. Law 583; *The Times*, May 31, 2001, ECHR 1A, 1–73, 1–79, 1–80, 1–81, 1–84, 8–62, 11–12, 11–24, 11–30, 12–08, 12–09A,12–70, 12–71, 12–74
Zino Davidoff SA v. A&G Imports Ltd (C–414/99 to C–416/99) [2002] Ch. 109; [2002] 2 W.L.R. 321; [2002] All E.R. (EC) 55; [2001] E.C.R. I–8691; [2002] 1 C.M.L.R. 1; [2002] C.E.C. 154; [2002] E.T.M.R. 9; [2002] R.P.C. 20; *The Times*, November 23, 2001; *Daily Telegraph*, November 27, 2001, ECJ 24–41, 25–74, 27–02, 27–36, 27–43

TABLE OF STATUTES

1861	Offences against the Person Act (24 & 25 Vict. c.100)			1972	Defective Premises Act —cont.	
	s.38	13–57			s.1(6)	10–60
1882	Bills of Exchange Act (45 & 46 Vict., c.61)	14–111			s.2(3)(b)	10–32
					s.4	10–31
1890	Partnership Act (53 & 54 Vict., c.39)			1976	Fatal Accidents Act (c.30)	3–16
	s.1	4–100A, 4–110A		1976	Race Relations Act (c.74)	29–65
1925	Law of Property Act (15 & 16 Geo.5, c.20)			1977	Patents Act (c.37)	
	s.62	18–35			s.48A	25–98
1934	Law Reform (Miscellaneous Provisions) Act (24 & 25 Geo.5, c.41)			1977	Protection from Eviction Act (c.43)	12–65
					s.1	12–36
				1978	Civil Liability (Contribution) Act (c.47)	3–46
	s.1(1)	29–65			s.1(1)	4–119
1944	Education Act (7 & 8 Geo.6, c.31)	11–30, 11–31		1980	Limitation Act (c.58)	21–04, 28–05
1945	Law Reform (Contributory Negligence) Act (8 & 9 Geo.6, c.28)	3–11A, 3–33, 3–46			s.2	33–01
					s.32(1)(b)	33–25
					s.33(3)(f)	33–47
	s.1(1)	3–28, 3–46, 3–50		1981	Supreme Court Act (c.54)	
1947	Crown Proceedings Act (10 & 11 Geo. 6, c.44)				s.69	22–02, 22–159
					(1)	22–02
				1981	Education Act (c.60)	11–30, 11–31
	s.10	1–81, 4–17A		1983	Mental Health Act (c.20)	
1952	Defamation Act (15 & 16 Geo. 6 & 1 Eliz. 2, c.66)				s.3	13–69
					s.57	13–78
					s.58	13–78
	s.7	22–153			s.72	13–69
1955	Defamation Act (Northern Ireland) (c.55)	22–122			(1)(b)	13–69
					s.73	13–70
	s.7	22–153			s.117	13–70
1957	Occupiers' Liability Act 1957 (5 & 6 Eliz. 2, c.31)				s.139	13–78
					(1)	13–70
					(2)	13–78
	s.2(4)	10–18			(4)	13–78
1961	Carriage by Air Act (9 & 10 Eliz., c.27)	7–214		1984	Occupiers Liability Act (c.3)	3–82, 10–18, 10–20, 10–77
1971	Animals Act (c.22)				s.1(6)	10–69
	s.2	21–04			(6A)(a)	10–77
	(2)	21–04, 21–06			(b)	10–77
	(b)	21–04, 21–06			(6B)	10–77
	(c)	21–08			(6C)	10–77
1972	Defective Premises Act (c.35)	7–125, 8–141, 10–60			(7)	10–77

[xxxiii]

Table of Statutes

1984 Police and Criminal Evidence Act (c.60)
    s.40 13–61
1985 Companies Act (c.6)
    s.395 14–48
    s.651(1) 33–16
1985 Sexual Offences Act (c.44)
    s.1 13–52
1985 Housing Act (c.68)
    Pt IV 19–42
1985 Sex Discrimination Act (c.65) 29–65
1986 Latent Damage Act (c.37) 7–124
    ss1, 2 33–58
    s.3 7–124
1987 Consumer Protection Act (c.43) A9
    s.1 2–28
    (2) 9–41
    s.2(4) 0–43
    s.3 2–28
    (2) 9–44
    s.4(1)(e) 9–39, 9–62
    s.8 9–43
1988 Road Traffic Act (c.52)
    s.39 .... 7–208, 12–58
    s.170(4) 13–52
1989 Electricity Act (c.29)
    s.21 3–62
1989 Law of Property (Miscellaneous Provisions) Act (c.34) 8–93
1990 Courts and Legal Services Act (c.41)
    s.8 22–227
1991 Water Industry Act (c.56) 18A
    s.159 .... 18–37, 19–84
    s.209(1) 20–36
1992 Trade Union and Labour Relations (Consolidation) Act (c.52)
    s.10(2) 24–118
    s.226C 24–175
    s.227(1) 24–173
    s.229(2A) 24–171, 24–177
    s.235A 24–141
    (b) 24–142
    (6) 24–142
    s.246 24–171
1993 Trade Union Reform and Employment Rights Act (c.19)
    s.22 24–141

1994 Trade Marks Act (c.26) ... 23–22
1995 Merchant Shipping Act (c.21)
    Pt V 11–12
    s.121 .... 11–15, 11–36
1995 Goods Vehicles (Licensing of Operators) Act (c.23)
    s.58(2) 5–21
1995 Private International Law (Miscellaneous Provisions) Act (c.42)
    s.12(1)(b) 6–10A
    s.14(3)(b) 6–11
1995 Disability Discrimination Act (c.50) 29–65
1996 Defamation Act (c.31) 22–153
    ss8, 9 .... 22–05, 22–06
    s.13 .... 22–100, 22–101
    s.15 22–153
    Sched.1, para.12 22–153
1996 Damages Act (c.48)
    s.1(1) 29–28
1997 Protection from Harassment Act (c.40) 13–17
    s.1(1) 13–18
    (2) 13–18
    (3)(c) 13–18
1998 Data Protection Act (c.29)
    s.13 .... 27–03, 27–19
1998 Human Rights Act (c.42) 1–67, 1–76, 1–77, 3–106, 4–17A, 12–09A, 19a, 19–22, 19–42, 22–01, 22–09, 24–190, 27–03, 29–74
    s.2 .... 12–09A
    s.3 .... 22–122, 27–43
    (1) 29–73
    s.6 .... 1–77, 1–77A
    (1) 1–67, 29–73
    s.7(1) 1–67
    s.8 .... 1–67, 29–117–29–119
    (1) 1–67
    s.12 27–43
    (3) 27–43
    (4) 30–22
1999 Contracts (Rights of Third Parties) Act (c.3) 3–71
1999 Employment Relations Act (c.26)
    Sched. 3, para. 6 ....24–171, 24–176

[xxxiv]

Table of Statutes

2000	Countryside and Rights of Way Act (c.37) .. 10A, 10–18, 10–77	2001	Criminal Justice and Police Act (c.16)	
	s.12(1) 10–77		s.71	13–52
	s.13 .... 10–18, 10–77			
2001	Private Security Industry Act (c.12)			
	s.3(2)(j) 14–147			

TABLE OF STATUTORY INSTRUMENTS

1931	Asbestos Industry Regulations (SR & O 1931 No. 1140)	11–45
1967	Carriage by Air Acts (Application of Provisions) Order (S.I. 1967 No. 480)	7–214
1974	Woodworking Machine Regulations (S.I. 1974 No. 903)	11–45
	reg.13(2)	11–45
1975	Fishing Vessels (Safety Provisions) Rules (S.I. 1975 No. 330)	11–15, 11–36
1983	Education (Special Needs) Regulations (S.I. 1983 No. 29)	11–31
1992	Manual Handling Operations Regulations (S.I.1992 No.2793)	11–15
1992	Workplace (Health, Safety and Welfare) Regulations (S.I.1992 No. 3004)	11–16
1998	Provision and Use of Work Equipment Regulations (S.I.1998 No. 2306)	11–15
1998	Civil Procedure Rules (S.I.1998 No.3132)	
	Pt 20	3–34
	r. 24 22–02,	22–06
	Pt 54	11–27
2000	Consumer Protection Act 1987 (Product Liability) (Modification) Order (S.I. 1987 No. 2771)	9–43
2001	Unfair Terms in Consumer Contracts (Amendment) Regulations (S.I. 2001 No.1186)	3–62
2001	Damages (Personal Injury) Order (S.I.2001 No. 2301)	29–28

CHAPTER 1

PRINCIPLES OF LIABILITY IN TORT

	PARA.
2. The boundaries of tort	1–05
(e) Tort and crime	1–14
■ 3. The functions of tortious liability	1–16
■ 4. The framework of tortious liability	1–21
(a) Interests protected by the law of torts	1–22
(b) Elements of wrongdoing	1–46
(c) Impact of the Human Rights Act 1998	1–67

The most significant consideration of the principles of liability in tort since the last edition has come in the House of Lords decisions in *Gregory v. Portsmouth City Council* and *Kuddus v. Chief Constable of Leicestershire Constabulary*. The decisions of the European Court of Human Rights in *Z v. United Kingdom* and *TP and KM v. United Kingdom* are also of considerable significance and are discussed both here and in the supplement to Chapter 12.

2. THE BOUNDARIES OF TORT

(e) *Tort and Crime*

NOTE 57. See now the discussion of exemplary damages in *Kuddus v. Chief Constable of Leicestershire Constabulary* [2001] 2 W.L.R. 1289.   **1–14**

3. THE FUNCTIONS OF TORTIOUS LIABILITY

Functions of the law of torts. In the John Maurice Kelly Memorial Lecture **1–16** published by University College Dublin and entitled *Perspectives of Corrective and Distributive Justice in Tort Law*, Lord Steyn reflected both on the perspectives of justice and the functions of tort law. To the proposition that the tort system "is becoming too expansive and wasteful", he insisted on "hearing further argument".

4. THE FRAMEWORK OF TORTIOUS LIABILITY

(a) *Interests protected by the Law of Torts*

(i) *Personal interests*

Bodily integrity. In *Parkinson v. St James and Seacroft University Hospital* **1–25** *N.H.S. Trust* [2001] 3 All E.R. 97, 114, Hale L.J. citing this paragraph, said: "The right to bodily integrity is the first and most important of the interests protected

1-25 CHAPTER 1—PRINCIPLES OF LIABILITY IN TORT

by the law of tort.... Included within that right are two others. One is the right to physical autonomy: to make one's own choices about what will happen to one's own body. Another is the right not to be subjected to bodily injury or harm. These interests are regarded as so important that redress is given both against intentional and negligent interference with them. In contrast, economic interests come very much lower in the list, and for obvious reasons ... The object of much commercial activity is deliberately to harm the economic interests of competitors: only in very special situations, therefore, does the law recognise a liability to compensate those whose economic interests have been damaged." See also the comment of the same judge in *McLoughlin v. Grovers (a firm)* [2002] P.N.L.R. 516, 535, [2002] P.I.Q.R. P222, 238, that "Loss of liberty is just as much an interference in bodily integrity as loss of a limb." See further para. **7–68.**

1-26 **Personal liberty.** See *R v. Governor of Brockhill Prison, ex p. Evans (No. 2)* [2000] 3 W.L.R. 843, for an illustration of the importance attached by tort law to the liberty of the subject.

1-32 **Bereavement, distress and anxiety.** See *Farley v. Skinner* [2001] 4 All E.R. 801, in which the House of Lords held that damages in contract could be awarded for distress where a major object of the contract is to give "pleasure, relaxation or peace of mind": *per* Lord Steyn at p. 812. There was no consideration whether the same principle would apply to a tortious claim where a major object of the relationship between the parties was to provide pleasure, relaxation or peace of mind for the claimant.

1-33 **Reputation.** See *Gregory v. Portsmouth City Council* [2000] 1 A.C. 419, in which the House of Lords refused to extend the tort of malicious prosecution to cover allegedly malicious disciplinary proceedings which had damaged the claimant's reputation. Lord Steyn suggested that remdy should be found by an extension of torts such as defamation, malicious falsehood and conspiracy rather than by extension of malicious prosecution in which the distinctive feature was an abuse of the coercive powers of the state.

1-34 **Privacy.** See now the recognition of the protection of privacy by the Court of Appeal in *Douglas v. Hello Ltd* [2001] 2 W.L.R. 992. See further para. **1–76.**

1-37 **Physical damage to property.** For an illustration of the wider recovery in nuisance as opposed to negligence, see *Delaware Mansions Ltd v. Westminster City Council* [2001] 4 All E.R. 737, and see *post* paras **7–126** and **19–23.**

(b) *Elements of wrongdoing*

1-52 **Acts and Omissions.** NOTE 59. See further *Holbeck Hall Hotel Ltd v. Scarborough Borough Council* [2000] Q.B. 836, and *Marcic v. Thames Water Utilities* [2002] 2 All E.R. 55. See *post* para. **19–54.**

(ii) *Intention*

1-59 **Recklessness.** See *Three Rivers District Council v. Bank of England (No. 3)* [2000] 2 W.L.R. 1220, where the House of Lords held that subjective recklessness *i.e.* with a state of mind of reckless indifference to the illegality of the act, was sufficient to ground liability for the tort of misfeasance in a public office.

(iv) Strict liability

Role of strict liability at common law. See *R v. Governor of Brockhill Prison, ex p. Evans (No. 2)* [2000] 3 W.L.R. 843, where the House of Lords held that as false imprisonment was a strict liability tort, liability could not be escaped even by showing that a defendant had acted in accordance with a view of the law relating to detention which, at the time, was accepted by the courts to be correct. 1–64

(c) *Impact of Human Rights Act 1998*

(i) *Horizontal impact of Convention rights*

Horizontal and vertical impact. Replace text following note 93 with: In *McKenna v. British Aluminium Ltd, The Times,* April 25, 2002, for example, Neuberger J. refused to strike out an action in nuisance and the rule in *Rylands v. Fletcher* brought by over thirty claimants on the basis that some of the claimants had no proprietary interest in the land affected. It was recognised that this restrictive aspect of the common law may need to be abandoned in the light of the Human Rights Act 1998 which imported an equal respect to the private lives of all citizens, not merely those with proprietary interests. This pressure to develop the common law in line with Convention standards is likely to be particularly strong where the liability of public authorities is in issue and claimants have formerly found it difficult to obtain satisfaction through the law of torts. On the other hand, under section 7(1) of the Act, an alternative cause of action will now lie where "a public authority has acted (or proposes to act) in a way which is made unlawful by section 6(1)". In respect of such statutory actions, the courts will have wide remedial powers under section 8 of the Act.[93a] Secondly, one of the Convention Rights, that of Fair Trial under Article 6, impacts directly on the courts. This "vertical effect" has already had a significant (albeit indirect) impact on the way the courts approach immunities from liability and the handling of policy arguments.[93b] 1–67

NOTE 93a: Section 8(1) provides that "In relation to any act (or proposed act) of a public authority which the court finds is (or would be) unlawful, it may grant such relief or remedy, or make such order, within its powers as it considers just and appropriate". For detailed discussion see Wright, *Tort Law & Human Rights* (2001) pp. 35–45.

NOTE 93b: See Wright, *loc. cit.*, ch. 4; Gearty, "*Osman* Unravels" (2002) 65 M.L.R. 87.

Article 8: right to respect for private and family life

Privacy. Replace existing paragraph with: 1–76
Prior to the entry into force of the Human Rights Act 1998, the right to privacy was never firmly established at common law in this country.[22] Such protection as did exist was achieved piecemeal, chiefly via the laws of defamation, confidentiality, nuisance and trespass to land. In *Douglas v. Hello Ltd*,[23] however, Sedley L.J. took the first bold step in the direction of recognising such a right. The case concerned the allegedly wrongful publication of wedding photographs taken of two famous film stars. According to his Lordship, section 6 of the Human Rights Act could be invoked where there was no existing cause of action to protect an invasion of privacy. Under this provision, he said *obiter*, the court's obligation to

adjudicate consistently with a claimant's Article 8 right to respect for private life would enable it to develop the common law so as to give full and proper protection to the Convention right to privacy.[24]

NOTE 22: In the United States, the right not to have facts concerning the claimant's private life made public against his will has existed since *Melvin v. Reid* (1931) 297 P. 91. The parallel right to privacy under New Zealand law is of much more recent vintage: see *Tucker v. News Media Ownership Ltd* [1986] 2 N.Z.L.R. 716 and (less equivocally) *Bradley v. Wingnut Films Ltd* [1993] 1 N.Z.L.R.

NOTE 23: [2001] Q.B. 967.

NOTE 24: *Ibid.*, at para. 129. For an element of doubt in the case, however, see *per* Keene L.J., at para. 88.

1–77   **Family life.** Replace existing paragraph with:

Very shortly after the decision in *Douglas v. Hello Ltd* followed a decision of Butler-Sloss L.J. in the High Court in *Thompson and Venables v. News Group Newspapers*.[25] While her ladyship recognised the section 6 obligation of the courts to act compatibly with Convention rights, she nonetheless felt that they could only do so within the confines of extant common law causes of action. She did not feel that section 6 provided *carte blanche* to create *new* causes of action. Read against the background of *Douglas v. Hello Ltd*, this judgment left matters rather uncertain. Yet, it was an uncertainty with which the Court of Appeal elected to grapple very shortly afterwards in *Home Office v. W*,[26] the latest case in which the question of a right to privacy has surfaced. What was said there, however, was also purely *obiter*. For the Court of Appeal was able to dispose of the instant case on the basis that the 1998 Act did not empower the courts to introduce a retrospective right to privacy at common law (which would have been necessary given that the material facts occurred prior to the 1998 Act). On the privacy question, however, Buxton L.J. offered this:

> "I have no doubt that in being invited to recognise the existence of a tort of breach of privacy we are indeed being invited to make the law, and not merely to apply it. Diffidence in the face of such an invitation is not, in my view, an abdication of our responsibility, but rather a recognition that, in areas involving extremely contested and strongly conflicting social interests, the judges are extremely ill-equipped to undertake the detailed investigations necessary before the proper shape of the law can be decided. It is only by enquiry outside the narrow boundaries of a particular case that the proper ambit of such a tort can be determined. The interests of democracy demand that such enquiry should be conducted in order to inform, and the appropriate conclusions should be drawn from the enquiry by, Parliament and not the courts. It is thus for Parliament to remove, if it thinks fit, the barrier to the recognition of a tort of breach of privacy."[27]

NOTE 25: [2001] Fam. 430.
NOTE 26: (2002) 99(9) L.S.G. 31.
NOTE 27: *Ibid.*, at para. 112.

1–77A   In *R. v. Bedfordshire County Council, ex p. Piggott*,[28] Burton J. acknowledged (*obiter*) that the Article 8 right to respect for private life could be relevant in the context of trespass to land where a lawful owner seeks to recover vacant possession of land unlawfully occupied by a trespasser. This may be of particular significance in respect of local authorities which, like the authority in the present case, have to deal with travellers who encamp themselves unlawfully on local authority land. On the other hand, the judge in *Ex parte Piggott* also made it clear that where a local authority seeks to evict such travellers, its right to do so will not be unduly emasculated by Article 8(1). Rather, "by virtue of Article 8(2), there must always be an interplay, particularly where the possession or occupation by the traveller is unauthorised, of the other interests of the community".[29] In other words, although the section 6 duty will require such authorities to act consistently with travellers' Convention rights, the Article 8 right to respect for private life will not be interpreted as a general licence to Gypsies to camp unlawfully.[30]

NOTE 28: (2002) 99(10) L.S.G. 31.

NOTE 29: *Ibid.*, at para. 26.

NOTE 30: For an endorsement of this point, see *R v. Chief Constable of Dorset, ex p. Fuller* 2001 W.L. 1479755.

Article 6: Right to a fair trial

Replace existing paragraphs with the following: 1–79—
                                                   1–84

Z v. United Kingdom In a sharp about-turn on its own earlier decision in   1–79
Osman v. United Kingdom[35] the European Court of Human Rights, in *Z v. United Kingdom*[36] held that Article 6 affected neither the striking out procedure nor the English law of negligence in so far as a duty of care could be denied on the basis of it not being "fair, just and reasonable" to impose such a duty. The applicants in the Z case were siblings who had been mistreated and subjected to unsanitary conditions at their parents' home. Despite having been made aware of these circumstances, the local authority failed to act expeditiously or effectively to ameliorate their condition. Acting as the siblings' next friend, the Official Solicitor brought an action for damages under the law of negligence. This action was struck out at first instance in a ruling that was subsequently upheld both by the Court of Appeal and the House of Lords in *X v. Bedfordshire County Council*.[37] The crux of their Lordships' decision was that the action could be struck out on the basis that a direct duty of care was not owed to the children since it was not "fair, just and reasonable" to impose such a duty on the local authority.

NOTE 35: (1998) 5 B.H.R.C. 293.

NOTE 36: (2002) 34 E.H.R.R. 97. See also *TP and KM v. United Kingdom* (2002) 34 E.H.R.R. 42.

NOTE 37: [1995] A.C. 633.

Subsequent to the decision of the House of Lords in *X v. Bedfordshire County*   1–80
Council, the siblings began proceedings against the United Kingdom on the basis, inter alia, of a breach of Article 6 of the European Convention on Human Rights: *viz*, that they had been denied a right to a fair and public hearing in determination of their civil rights. The Strasbourg court held by twelve votes to five that there had been no such violation of Article 6. Under the domestic proceedings, the strike out had not occurred without a serious and full hearing of the applicants' argument that they had a legitimate cause of action. Indeed, the applicants had argued their case vigorously, all the way up to the House of Lords. As such, they had perfectly well enjoyed the right to a fair hearing.

The significance of the Z decision for English tort law lies in its explanation   1–81
of the operation of Article 6 (this being relevant to both the striking out procedure

[5]

and the general law of negligence). According to the court, Article 6 is essentially a procedural safeguard. It ensures only that court hearings be themselves fair and public. It does not offer any substantive guarantees so that principles of liability B such as the familiar just, fair and reasonableness test in negligence B will normally be beyond the review of the court.[38] In other words, it is firmly a matter for the English courts to settle what is and is not actionable. As the Strasbourg court put it "Article 6(1) extends only to contestations (disputes) over (civil) rights and obligations which can be said, at least on arguable grounds, to be recognised under domestic law; it does not in itself guarantee any particular content for (civil) rights and obligations in the substantive law of the Contracting States".[39] As such, all that Article 6 offers in these circumstances is a procedural guarantee in respect of the claimant's endeavour to demonstrate in court that his or her claim is actionable. And this, the siblings in Z had clearly been afforded. The point that Article 6 does not offer any substantive guarantees has since been endorsed by the English Court of Appeal in *Matthews v. Ministry of Defence*.[40] In this case, the claimant had sought a declaration of incompatibility between Article 6 and the immunity from suit granted to the Crown by section 10 of the Crown Proceedings Act 1947.[41] The Court of Appeal dismissed this argument, making it clear that Article 6 did not arise for consideration in that case, given that the immunity granted by section 10 meant that there was no substantive right of action in the first place to which Article 6's procedural guarantees could be applied.

NOTE 38: This is subject only to the Strasbourg Court's "fallback" jurisdiction to scrutinise immunities and exclusionary rules in terms of "legitimate aim" and "proportionality": see *Ashingdane v. United Kingdom*, Series A No. 93 (1985). See also, Gearty, "Unravelling *Osman*" (2001) 64 M.L.R. 159 and "*Osman* Unravels" (2002) 65 M.L.R. 87. *Cf.* Wright, *Tort Law & Human Rights* (2001) ppxxxii–xxxiii.

NOTE 39: (2002) 34 E.H.R.R. 97, para. 91.

NOTE 40: *The Times*, May 31, 2002.

NOTE 41: See paras 4–13 B 4–17.

Chapter 2

CAUSATION IN TORT: GENERAL PRINCIPLES

		PARA.
■	1. Introduction	2–01
■	2. Factual causation	2–06
■	3. *Novus actus interveniens*	2–36
■	4. Remoteness of damage	2–60

1. INTRODUCTION

General Principles. NOTE 1. Add: *Stauch* (2001) 64 M.L.R. 191. 2–01

The burden of proof. If the judge is unable, on the evidence, to resolve the 2–05 causation issue, but concludes simply that he is not persuaded that the claimant's symptoms were caused by the defendant's breach of duty, he is not required to go further and make a positive diagnosis of the cause of the claimant's symptoms. In these circumstances the action fails on the burden of proof: *Davis and Docherty v. Balfour Kilpatrick Ltd* [2002] EWCA Civ 736, applying *The Popi M* [1985] 1 W.L.R. 948.

2. FACTUAL CAUSATION

The "but for" test. There are also some circumstances, and some torts, where 2–06 the "but for" test is not satisfied, but nonetheless the court considers it appropriate to attribute responsibility to the defendant's conduct (see the example at paragraph 2–34, note 5). In *Kuwait Airways Corp. v. Iraq Airways Co.* [2002] UKHL 19; [2002] 3 All E.R. 209; *The Times*, May 21, 2002 the claimants sought damages in respect of the loss of 10 airplanes taken by the Iraqi government following the invasion of Kuwait and subsequently handed over to the defendants for their use. The defendants argued that there was a general rule of liability in tort that the tortious act must have been at least a necessary condition of the damage, and that a claimant will fail if he cannot prove that the damage would not have happened but for the tort. On the facts, the claimants could not show that but for the defendants' tortious acts of conversion they would not have been kept out of possession of their airplanes, because the Iraqi government would have retained them or given them to some other state institution. The House of Lords held that the claimants did not have to satisfy the "but for" causation test in these circumstances. Lord Nicholls pointed out (at [74]) that in cases involving multiple wrongdoers, "the court may treat wrongful conduct as having sufficient causal connection with the loss for the purpose of attracting responsibility even though the simple 'but for' test is not satisfied. In so deciding the court is primarily making a value judgment on responsibility. In making this judgment the court will have regard to the purpose sought to be achieved by the relevant tort, as applied to the particular circumstances." Lord Hoffmann commented (at

[7]

[127] to [128]) that it would be an irrational system of tort liability which did not insist upon there being *some* causal connection between the tortious act and the damage, but there is "no uniform causal requirement for liability in tort. Instead, there are varying causal requirements, depending upon the basis and purpose of liability. One cannot separate questions of liability from questions of causation. They are inextricably connected. One is never simply liable; one is always liable *for* something and the rules which determine what one is liable for are as much part of the substantive law as the rules which determine which acts give rise to liability." In the case of conversion, a tort of strict liability, the causal requirements followed from the nature of the tort, which exists to protect proprietary or possessory rights in property, and is committed by an act inconsistent with those rights. It followed that it was irrelevant that if the defendants had not taken possession of the airplanes, someone else would have done so (*i.e.* the traditional "but for" test was not satisfied), and it was also irrelevant that, having taken possession, the defendants would have been prevented from restoring the aircraft (even if it had wished to do so) by circumstances beyond their control: "The liability is strict. Thus the causal questions are answered by reference to the nature of the liability." (*ibid.* at [129]).

2–08   Add: In many cases resolution of the hypothetical question of what the claimant would have done had the defendant discharged his duty to advise about the risks associated with treatment, although dependant upon the credibility of evidence, is relatively straightforward. Thus, if on the evidence the claimant would have proceeded with the treatment even if given a warning, the defendant's breach of duty is not the cause of the damage. On the other hand, if the claimant would never have accepted the treatment had she known about the risks then the non-disclosure has caused the damage in the sense that the claimant would not have had that particular treatment and therefore the risk associated with the procedure would not have had an "opportunity to materialise". Where, however, the evidence is not that the claimant would never have undergone the treatment, but if informed of the relevant risks, would at least have postponed the treatment in order to obtain a second or third opinion about treatment options, the causation issue is more complex. On one view, if, on the balance of probabilities, the claimant would have undergone the procedure at some stage in the future then she would have faced the same inherent risks associated with it, and therefore the defendant's negligent failure to inform her of those risks would have been of no causative effect. The alternative view is that the materialisation of a small random risk inherent in a medical treatment producing injury to the claimant is the result of the particular time and circumstances in which the treatment was given (assuming that there is nothing which predisposes the particular patient to this risk), and therefore if treatment had been delayed to another occasion the probability is that the small inherent risk would not have materialised *on that occasion*, and thus the materialisation of the risk is causally linked to the negligent non-disclosure of risk. In *Chester v. Afshar* [2002] EWCA Civ 724; [2002] 3 All E.R. 552, the Court of Appeal held that the latter approach was correct (applying *Chappell v. Hart* [1998] H.C.A. 55; (1998) 156 A.L.R. 517). The claimant's damage consisted not in being exposed to the inherent risks of the procedure, since the risks were always the same and the defendant did not increase them, but in causing the claimant to have an operation which she would not otherwise have had "then and there". Thus the correct comparison of risk would be between "having that operation on that occasion and not having it" (at

[40]). Citing the observations of Lord Hoffmann in *Environment Agency v. Empress Car Co. (Abertillery) Ltd* [1999] 2 A.C. 22 at 31 that one cannot give a commonsense answer to a question of causation for the purpose of attributing responsibility under some rule without knowing the purpose and scope of the rule (see paragraph 2–46 in the main text) the Court of Appeal held, at [47], that: "The purpose of the rule requiring doctors to give appropriate information to their patients is to enable the patient to exercise her right to choose whether or not to have the particular operation to which she is asked to give her consent ... The object is to enable the patient to decide whether or not to run the risks of having that operation at that time. If the doctor's failure to take that care results in her consenting to an operation to which she would not otherwise have given her consent, the purpose of that rule would be thwarted if he were not to be held responsible when the very risk about which he failed to warn her materialises and causes her an injury which she would not have suffered then and there." It is respectfully submitted that the analysis of the Court of Appeal in *Chester v. Afshar* is correct. It provides another illustration of the limits of the "but for" test, even as an exclusionary test of causation (which can be particularly difficult to apply in cases involving multiple causes: see, *e.g.* paragraph 2–34, note 5 of the main text, and *Fairchild v. Glenhaven Funeral Services Ltd* [2002] UKHL 22, discussed at paragraph 2–13 of this *Supplement*) and of the importance of considering the specific "liability context" in which the causation question arises (see, *e.g. Kuwait Airways Corp. v. Iraq Airways Co.* [2002] UKHL 19; [2002] 3 All E.R. 209, paragraph 2–06 of this *Supplement*). Even questions of "factual causation" involve elements of judgment about the appropriate standard of responsibility that ought to be applied to a defendant's conduct.

NOTE 23. Add. There is no rule of law that a patient must give evidence personally about what would or would not have happened if she had been properly informed of the facts before making a decision: *Webb v. Barclays Bank plc and Portsmouth Hospitals NHS Trust* [2001] EWCA Civ 1141; [2001] Lloyd's Rep. Med. 500 at [42].

Misrepresentation. For a helpful analysis of *Bristol and West Building Society v. Mothew* see O'Sullivan (2001) 17 P.N. 272.

2–09

Defendant's conduct. NOTE 31. Add. Note that the *Bolam* test does not apply where what the judge is required to do is to make findings of fact. This is so, even where those findings of fact are subject to conflicting expert evidence. If there is a dispute amongst the experts about a question of fact (such as what was visible on a laboratory slide) the judge is entitled to prefer one group of experts over the other: *Penney, Palmer and Cannon v. East Kent Health Authority* [2000] Lloyd's Rep. Med. 41, 46. This will frequently be the case on questions of causation. For example, where the issue is whether the claimant's medical condition would or would not have deteriorated with appropriate treatment, it is not simply a question of opting for the view of the majority of experts or of a reasonable body of medical opinion, since "that would be to import the well-known *Bolam* test into the issue of causation, where it has no proper place": *Cavanagh v. Bristol and Weston Health Authority* [1992] 3 Med. L.R. 49, 56, *per* Macpherson J.

2–10

Causation and industrial disease. Statements appearing in the main text in paragraphs 2–13 to 2–19 should be read in the light of the decision of the House of Lords in *Fairchild v. Glenhaven Funeral Services Ltd* [2002] UKHL 22, [2002] 3 All E.R. 305, which applied *McGhee v. National Coal Board* [1973] 1

2–13

2–13 CHAPTER 2—CAUSATION IN TORT: GENERAL PRINCIPLES

W.L.R. 1 to three cases where workers had developed mesothelioma following exposure to asbestos at work. All of the employees had worked for a number of employers and at a number of sites where they had negligently been exposed to asbestos fibres. They contracted mesothelioma, a form of cancer which is always fatal, with death usually occurring within two years of its appearance. The disease can be latent for up to 40 years, but may develop within 10 years. The precise mechanics of the disease are unknown, but the vast majority of cases of mesothelioma result from exposure to asbestos. In the United Kingdom 50 or 60 people suffer mesothelioma each year where there has been no history of exposure to asbestos dust, in contrast to 1,500 where there is a history of exposure to asbestos. Thus, the overwhelming probability was that the employees' mesothelioma was caused by their occupation. The problem, however, was that on the current level of scientific knowledge about the disease the claimants could not identify which employer was responsible because, unlike asbestosis (and pneumoconiosis) which is also caused by exposure to asbestos dust, mesothelioma is not a "cumulative disease". With asbestosis there is a minimum dose of asbestos below which there is no risk that asbestosis will develop, and above that minimum dose the severity of the condition, if it develops, increases in relation to the total dose of asbestos inhaled. In the case of a cumulative disease, where the severity of the condition is related to the period of exposure, each negligent employer is responsible for a proportionate part of the damage (see *Holtby v. Brigham & Cowan (Hull) Ltd* [2000] 3 All E.R. 421, CA, at paragraph 2–22 of the main text). In contrast, mesothelioma arises when one of the mesothelial cells in the pleura of the lung is damaged and undergoes malignant transformation. A tumour develops from the single malignant mesothelial cell. The *risk* that mesothelioma will occur increases in relation to the total dose of asbestos received, but the severity of the condition and the resulting disability do not vary with the dose. It may be caused by a single fibre, a few fibres, or many fibres. Further exposure to asbestos, once the malignancy has developed does not exacerbate the condition. The problem for a claimant that this creates was explained by Lord Bingham at [7]:

> "So if C is employed successively by A and B and is exposed to asbestos dust and fibres during each employment and develops a mesothelioma, the very strong probability is that this will have been caused by inhalation of asbestos dust containing fibres. But C could have inhaled a single fibre giving rise to his condition during employment by A, in which case his exposure by B will have had no effect on his condition; or he could have inhaled a single fibre giving rise to his condition during his employment by B, in which case his exposure by A will have had no effect on his condition; or he could have inhaled fibres during his employment by A and B which together gave rise to his condition; but medical science cannot support the suggestion that any of these possibilities is to be regarded as more probable than any other. There is no way of identifying, even on a balance of probabilities, the source of the fibre or fibres which initiated the genetic process which culminated in the malignant tumour."

2–13A On these facts, the Court of Appeal ([2001] EWCA Civ 1881; [2002] 1 W.L.R. 1052) held that the claimants had failed to establish causation, because they could not prove on a balance of probabilities that the "guilty" fibres were the result of any particular defendant's breach of duty. There was an "evidential gap" over which the Court refused to leap because it "defied logic." *McGhee*, said the Court, did not assist, because in that case there was only one causative agent (brick dust) and only one possible tortfeasor, and therefore in the light of

[10]

Wilsher v. Essex Area Health Authority [1988] A.C. 1074 (which held that an inference of causation could not be drawn where there was more than one causative agent), it was not possible to rely on *McGhee* where there was more than one tortfeasor, unless the evidence established that the disease was caused by a cumulative exposure (*ibid.* at [104]). Moreover, a "leap over the evidential gap" was "also susceptible of unjust results" because it could impose liability for the whole of an insidious disease on an employer with whom the claimant was employed for quite a short time in a long working life, when the claimant was unable to prove on the balance of probabilities that that period of employment had any causative relationship with the inception of the disease. Accepting the claimants' argument would be to accept that all claimants who had suffered injury after being exposed to a risk of that injury from which someone else should have protected them should be able to recover compensation even if they were unable to prove who was the culprit (*ibid.* at [103]).

Of course, the Court of Appeal's conclusion was equally susceptible of unjust results. An employee negligently exposed to asbestos who worked for the same employer throughout his working life would be able to prove causation in respect of contracting mesothelioma. There is only one defendant and only one probable cause. If, on the other hand, he worked for two or more employers (which is the more common employment pattern) it would be impossible to say from which employer he inhaled the ultimately fatal fibre, and therefore neither would be held liable for the disease, notwithstanding that both were in breach of duty and that it is possible to say almost beyond reasonable doubt, let alone on the balance of probabilities, that the claimant contracted the disease at work. The injustice to the claimant in these circumstances is even more stark than the situation in *Bonnington Castings Ltd v. Wardlaw* [1956] A.C. 613 or in *McGhee*, where at least there was some exposure to the risk which could be categorised as "innocent" (or at least not in breach of duty). In *Fairchild*, *none* of the exposure was "innocent" in this sense. All the defendants were in breach in duty. It was simply that the claimants could not identify which breach of duty had produced the fatal fibre.

The House of Lords reversed the decision of the Court of Appeal, on the basis that in the special circumstances of this type of case, there should be a relaxation of the normal rule that a claimant must prove that but for the defendant's breach of duty he would not have suffered the damage. Following a review of how courts in many other jurisdictions have approached this type of problem, Lord Bingham noted that most jurisdictions would afford a remedy to the plaintiff, whether by treating an increase in risk as equivalent to a material contribution to the damage, or by placing the burden of proof on the defendant, or by enlarging the ordinary approach to tortfeasors acting in concert, or on more general grounds influenced by policy considerations (at [32]). Moreover, said their Lordships, the policy considerations which influenced the decision of Court of Appeal (the injustice to defendants of imposing liability on a defendant who has not been proved to have caused the claimants' damage) had to be weighed against the injustice to claimants. Thus, Lord Nicholls commented (at [36]): "these appeals should be allowed. Any other outcome would be deeply offensive to instinctive notions of what justice requires and fairness demands." Lord Hoffmann indicated that "as between the employer in breach of duty and the employee who has lost his life in consequence of a period of exposure to risk to which that employer has contributed, I think it would be both inconsistent with the policy of the law imposing the duty and morally wrong for your Lordships to

2–13B   CHAPTER 2—CAUSATION IN TORT: GENERAL PRINCIPLES

impose causal requirements which exclude liability" (at [63]). And Lord Bingham said (at [33]): "... there is a strong policy argument in favour of compensating those who have suffered grave harm, at the expense of their employers who owed them a duty to protect them against that very harm and failed to do so, when the harm can only have been caused by breach of that duty and when science does not permit the victim accurately to attribute, as between several employers, the precise responsibility for the harm he has suffered. I am of opinion that such injustice as may be involved in imposing liability on a duty-breaking employer in these circumstances is heavily outweighed by the injustice of denying redress to a victim."

2–13C   Contrary to the view expressed by Lord Bridge in *Wilsher v. Essex Area Health Authority* [1988] A.C. 1074, 1088, the decision of the House of Lords in *McGhee v. National Coal Board* [1973] 1 W.L.R. 1 did not rest upon a "robust and pragmatic" approach to the drawing of an inference of fact (see *per* Lord Bingham at [22]; Lord Nicholls at [45]; Lord Hoffmann at [70]; Lord Rodger at [142], [144] and [150]; *cf.* the speech of Lord Hutton). Rather, *McGhee* decided a question of law which was "whether, on the facts of the case as found, a pursuer who could not show that the defender's breach had probably caused the damage of which he complained could nonetheless succeed" (*per* Lord Bingham at [21]). The *ratio* of *McGhee*, said Lord Bingham (at [21]), was "that in the circumstances no distinction was to be drawn between making a material contribution to causing the disease and materially increasing the risk of the pursuer contracting it". This was not, said Lord Hoffmann (at [65]), because the burden of proof was reversed. It would be artificial to treat the employer as having a burden of proof in a case in which *ex hypothesi* the state of medical knowledge is such that the burden cannot be discharged. Nor was materially increasing the risk equivalent to materially contributing to the damage, because that was precisely what the expert witnesses were not prepared to say in *McGhee*. Thus, what their Lordships meant in *McGhee* was that, "in the particular circumstances, a breach of duty which materially increased the risk should be treated *as if* it had materially contributed to the disease."

2–13D   *Wilsher*, however, was correctly decided on its facts (*per* Lord Bingham at [22], Lord Hoffmann at [70], Lord Hutton at [118], Lord Rodger at [149]). It is one thing, said Lord Bingham, "to treat an increase of risk as equivalent to the making of a material contribution where a single noxious agent is involved, but quite another where any one of a number of noxious agents may equally probably have caused the damage." It is questionable, however, whether the point of distinction between *Wilsher* and *Fairchild* (or *McGhee*) is that there was only one type of noxious agent in *Fairchild* but several in *Wilsher*. For example, what if C in *Fairchild* had been exposed to asbestos dust by employer A but to a different cancer-producing agent by employer B? Assume that both agents are capable of producing mesothelioma; does C fall within *Wilsher* or *Fairchild*? If the relaxation of the causal test is limited, as Lord Bingham limited it, to exposure to asbestos dust (see below), then the answer is he fails, applying *Wilsher*. The injustice that *Fairchild* seeks to address is not, however, that which is specifically limited to a particular noxious agent (though this is the agent that highlights the problem most acutely). This is apparent from their Lordships' survey of the jurisprudence from other jurisdictions, which reveal a similar conceptual problem arising in very different factual circumstances, the most obvious being the "hunting cases" where the claimant is simultaneously shot by two or more negligent hunters but cannot identify which one shot him (here, courts have usually reversed the burden of proof: see *Summers v. Tice* 199 P. 2d 1 (1948), Supreme Court of California; *Cook v. Lewis* [1952] 1 D.L.R. 1, Supreme Court of Canada). There is no need to limit the relaxation of the "but for" test to cases specifically involving the inhalation of asbestos. As Lord Hoffmann commented the distinction between a case involving a single agent and number of different agents is not a principled distinction: "What if [the claimant] had been exposed to two different agents—asbestos dust and some other dust—both of which created a material risk of the same cancer and it was equally impossible to say which had caused the fatal cell mutation? I cannot see why this should make a difference" (*per* Lord Hoffmann at [71–72]).

Of course, it is true, as Sir Nicolas Browne-Wilkinson V.-C. observed in his judgment (approved by the House of Lords) in *Wilsher*, that: "A failure to take preventative measures against one out of five possible causes is no evidence as to which of those five caused the injury." But it is also true that a failure by employer A to take precautions against the risk to employees of mesothelioma caused by exposure to asbestos, where other defendants have also failed to take such precautions, is not evidence that the mesothelioma was caused by employer A's breach of duty. It cannot matter whether there was only one other employer or several. *Fairchild* applies where there are multiple defendants in breach of a similar duty, because it is unfair or unjust as a matter of policy to deprive a claimant of compensation because he is unable to prove the impossible. In *Wilsher* the plaintiff was also faced with having to prove the impossible on the then state of medical knowledge. Why is it less unjust in *Wilsher* than in *Fairchild*, so that in the latter case the normal rules on causation may be relaxed, but not in the former? The only obvious difference was that the other potential causes of the damage were "innocent" causes (though there were policy questions at stake, such as the potential burden of increased liability upon the NHS: see Lord Hoffmann at [69]). The defendant, if found liable, would have had no other defendant(s) from whom to seek contribution. But there is no guarantee that a defendant found liable for the whole of the claimant's damage in a *Fairchild* situation will have solvent defendants with whom to share the loss through contribution proceedings. Moreover, what if the only other defendant(s) were found not to be in breach of duty, despite having exposed the claimant to asbestos (recall that in both *Bonnington Castings* and *McGhee* there were both "innocent" and "guilty" exposures)? Does *Fairchild* apply? According to Lord Bingham's test (see below) the answer is "no" (since his Lordship requires that both employers, A and B, were in breach of duty). Lord Rodger, however, reserved his opinion (at [170]) on the question of what the position would be if defendant A was in breach of duty but defendant B was held to be "innocent".

The circumstances in which the *Fairchild* principle will apply. In order to limit the situations in which the normal requirements of the "but for" test could be dispensed with, their Lordships were careful to specify the precise circumstances in which the *McGhee/Fairchild* test would apply. Unfortunately, the "precise" circumstances identified by Lords Bingham, Hoffmann and Rodger are not identical. Lord Bingham specified (at [2]) six conditions:

"(1) C was employed at different times and for differing periods by both A and B; and

(2) A and B were both subject to a duty to take reasonable care or to take all practicable measures to prevent C inhaling asbestos dust because of the known risk that asbestos dust (if inhaled) might cause a mesothelioma; and

2–13F CHAPTER 2—CAUSATION IN TORT: GENERAL PRINCIPLES

> (3) both A and B were in breach of that duty in relation to C during the periods of C's employment by each of them with the result that during both periods C inhaled excessive quantities of asbestos dust; and
> (4) C is found to be suffering from a mesothelioma; and
> (5) any cause of C's mesothelioma other than the inhalation of asbestos dust at work can be effectively discounted; but
> (6) C cannot (because of the current limits of human science) prove, on the balance of probabilities, that his mesothelioma was the result of his inhaling asbestos dust during his employment by A or during his employment by B or during his employment by A and B taken together".

If each of these conditions is satisfied (and in "no other case") then his Lordship considered that it was "just and in accordance with common sense" to treat the conduct of A and B in exposing C to a risk to which he should not have been exposed as making a material contribution to the contracting by C of a condition against which it was the duty of A and B to protect him (at [34]). This conclusion followed even if either A or B was not before the court.

Lord Hoffmann expressed the test (at [61]) at slightly higher level of generality. There must be:

> (1) a duty specifically intended to protect employees against being unnecessarily exposed to the risk of (among other things) a particular disease;
> (2) the duty is one intended to create a civil right to compensation for injury relevantly connected with its breach;
> (3) it is established that the greater the exposure to asbestos, the greater the risk of contracting that disease;
> (4) except in the case in which there has been only one significant exposure to asbestos, medical science cannot prove whose asbestos is more likely than not to have produced the cell mutation which caused the disease;
> (5) the employee has contracted the disease against which he should have been protected.

In these circumstances, said his Lordship, a rule requiring proof of a link between the defendant's asbestos and the claimant's disease would, with the arbitrary exception of single-employer cases, empty the duty of content. If liability depended upon proof that the conduct of the defendant was a necessary condition of the injury, it could not effectively exist. Thus, "it is sufficient, both on principle and authority, that the breach of duty contributed substantially to the risk that the claimant would contract the disease" (at [47]).

2–13G Lord Rodger suggested (at [169] to [170]) that certain conditions were necessary, but may not always be sufficient, for applying the principle. These conditions are clearly at a higher level of generality than those indicated by Lord Bingham or Lord Hoffmann:

> "(1) the principle is designed to resolve the difficulty that arises where it is inherently impossible for the claimant to prove exactly how his injury was caused. It applies, therefore, where the claimant has proved all that he possibly can, but the causal link could only ever be established by scientific investigation and the current state of the relevant science leaves it uncertain exactly how the injury was caused and, so, who caused it. *McGhee* and the present cases are examples.
> (2) part of the underlying rationale of the principle is that the defendant's wrongdoing has materially increased the risk that the claimant will suffer injury. It is therefore

essential not just that the defendant's conduct created a material risk of injury to a class of persons but that it actually created a material risk of injury to the claimant himself.

(3) it follows that the defendant's conduct must have been capable of causing the claimant's injury.

(4) the claimant must prove that his injury was caused by the eventuation of the kind of risk created by the defendant's wrongdoing. In *McGhee*, for instance, the risk created by the defenders' failure was that the pursuer would develop dermatitis due to brick dust on his skin and he proved that he had developed dermatitis due to brick dust on his skin. By contrast, the principle does not apply where the claimant has merely proved that his injury could have been caused by a number of different events, only one of which is the eventuation of the risk created by the defendant's wrongful act or omission. *Wilsher* is an example.

(5) this will usually mean that the claimant must prove that his injury was caused, if not by exactly the same agency as was involved in the defendant's wrongdoing, at least by an agency that operated in substantially the same way. A possible example would be where a workman suffered injury from exposure to dusts coming from two sources, the dusts being particles of different substances each of which, however, could have caused his injury in the same way . . .

(6) the principle applies where the other possible source of the claimant's injury is a similar wrongful act or omission of another person, but it can also apply where, as in *McGhee*, the other possible source of the injury is a similar, but lawful, act or omission of the same defendant. I reserve my opinion as to whether the principle applies where the other possible source of injury is a similar but lawful act or omission of someone else or a natural occurrence."

2–13H All of their Lordships were clear that in applying *Fairchild* to future cases caution will be essential. There are dangers in over-generalising the principle, which will not apply merely because the claimant has difficulty in discharging the burden of proof (*per* Lord Nicholls at [43]). Both Lord Bingham and Lord Hoffmann emphasised that it should be limited to the specific conditions that they laid down, but with the greatest respect it is difficult to see how, or indeed why, it should be so severely restricted. For example, there is no obvious reason to limit *Fairchild* to the relationship between employer and employee, still less to the specifics of mesothelioma caused by exposure to asbestos. In this respect Lord Rodger's conditions probably reflect a more principled approach. In any event, both Lord Bingham and Lord Hoffmann acknowledged that the principle could be developed to apply in new situations. As Lord Nicholls expressed it (at [43]): "Policy questions will loom large when a court has to decide whether the difficulties of proof confronting the plaintiff justify taking this exceptional course. It is impossible to be more specific."

2–13I **Summary.** (1) Where the relevant conditions for the application of the principle are present (though these are different in the speeches of Lords Bingham, Hoffmann and Rodger) then a material increase in the risk of harm to the claimant can be treated as if it were a material contribution to the damage; (2) this is based on a policy judgment or principle that in these circumstances it is more unfair to claimants to deny liability than it is to defendants to impose liability; (3) *McGhee v. National Coal Board* is good law. It did not involve either reversing the burden of proof or the drawing of an inference of fact, based on robust and pragmatic view of the evidence, to overcome an evidential gap; (4) *Wilsher v. Essex Area Health Authority* is also good law, thus *McGhee* can apply where

2–13I CHAPTER 2—CAUSATION IN TORT: GENERAL PRINCIPLES

there are multiple tortfeasors, but probably not where there are multiple causation factors (*sed quaere*, see Lord Rodger's speech); (5) the principle can apply even if other potential defendants are not before the court; (6) the claimant is entitled to full compensation from the negligent defendant; there is no question of apportioning the loss; (7) the defendant remains entitled to seek contribution against any other defendant liable in respect of the same damage; (8) the principle may be extended to other factual circumstances in future cases, but only with considerable caution so as not to undermine the basic rule that in order to establish the defendant's *responsibility* in law to compensate the for the claimant's loss the claimant must prove, on a balance of probabilities, that the defendant's breach of duty was at least a necessary condition for that loss. It would seem likely that if a "hunting case" (such as *Cook v. Lewis*) were to occur, the principle would be extended to cover that situation, despite the restrictive approach of Lords Bingham and Hoffmann.

2–13J A number of issues remain unresolved: (1) what constitutes "multiple" causation factors is unclear. Certainly, where there are four "innocent" possible causes of C's damage, and D adds a fifth "guilty" possible cause, the increase in overall risk cannot be equated with a material contribution to the damage (*Wilsher*); (2) where there are multiple tortfeasors and they all add to the risk of damage caused by the *same* noxious agent then the principle applies. But query whether the principle applies where there are multiple tortfeasors and they add to the risk of damage caused by *different* noxious agents, but by the same, or broadly the same, mechanism? (according to Lord Bingham, no, but according to Lord Hoffmann and Lord Rodger, possibly yes); (3) query whether the principle applies where there is a single tortfeasor and he adds to the risk of damage caused by the *same* noxious agent, where there is another party who also contributes to the risk by the same mechanism, but that party is "innocent", *i.e.* not in breach of duty? (applying Lord Bingham's criteria, no, but Lord Rodger specifically reserved his opinion on this point); (4) it is not obvious why the relaxation of the ordinary rules of causation (namely that the defendant's breach of duty must least be a necessary condition of the claimant's damage) applies only to the employer-employee relationship (Lord Bingham's and Lord Hoffmann's first condition) or why it should only apply to the inhalation of asbestos dust causing mesothelioma (Lord Bingham's third and fourth condition, and Lord Hoffmann's third condition which refers to asbestos dust but not to a specific disease). Given the recognition that the principle could be extended to other factual circumstances in future cases, these conditions are unlikely to be regarded as crucial; (5) the exposure to asbestos dust (and hence the risk of developing the cancer) must be "not insignificant" (*per* Lord Nicholls at [42]), or the breach of duty must have "contributed substantially to the risk" that the claimant would contract the disease (*per* Lord Hoffmann at [47]). Their Lordships did not indicate what a *substantial* contribution meant, perhaps not surprisingly given that on any view of the facts in *Fairchild* the defendants' contribution clearly was substantial. Other cases may arise, however, where the only solvent or traceable defendant exposed the claimant to the risk for a relatively short period of the claimant's working life, where the issue will be important. It will be recalled that in *Bonnington Castings Ltd v. Wardlaw* the House of Lords held that anything that did not fall within the principle *de minimis non curat lex* would constitute a material contribution to the claimant's damage, and it would seem that a similar test is appropriate where the breach of duty contributes to the *risk of* damage; (6) it is not obvious why the principle should be confined to *scientific* uncertainty

[16]

about causation (*cf. Fitzgerald v. Lane* [1987] Q.B. 781, paragraph 2–29 of the main text).

NOTE 42. Add: *Dingley v. Chief Constable of Strathclyde Police* (2000) 55 B.M.L.R. 1, HL—if there is insufficient evidence to establish whether as a general proposition multiple sclerosis can ever be triggered by trauma, the claimant will be unable to establish the specific issue that there was a connection between his injury in an accident and the subsequent onset of multiple sclerosis.

2–14

Add: In cases involving traumatic events which precipitate a psychiatric reaction (typically, the traditional "nervous shock" cases producing "post-traumatic stress disorder") the temporal sequence makes it generally easier to persuade the court to draw an inference that there must be a causal link between the defendant's negligence and the claimant's psychiatric state. In cases involving allegations of occupational stress, however, where an employee alleges that the employer's negligent system of work has so overstressed him that he has suffered permanent psychiatric damage, the causal link is more difficult to establish. In *Hatton v. Sutherland* [2002] EWCA Civ 76; [2002] 2 All E.R. 1 the Court of Appeal said that there are no occupations which are inherently dangerous to mental health since it is not the job, but the interaction between the individual and the job which causes the harm. All occupations involve some element of stress and it can be difficult to anticipate which employees are foreseeably likely to succumb. Moreover, there many other stressful factors in ordinary life which can affect an individual employee's mental health (*e.g.* illness, divorce, bereavement) and can contribute to mental breakdown. The claimant must demonstrate that the psychiatric illness is not due simply to stress at work but that it was the employer's specific breach of duty that caused the damage. Thus: "Where there are several different possible causes, as will often be the case with stress related illness of any kind, the claimant may have difficulty proving that the employer's fault was one of them" (at [35]; on which see *Cross v. Highlands and Islands Enterprise* [2001] I.R.L.R. 336 (Court of Session, OH), where the pursuer failed to prove that the cause of his illness was work-related). In other words, proof of a psychiatric condition together with a "stressful" working environment is not sufficient to establish a causal link, though the employee does not have to prove that the employer's breach of duty was the sole cause, merely that it made a material contribution to his mental illness (*ibid.*, applying *Bonnington Castings*). On the other hand, it is arguable that, in the light of the Court of Appeal decision *Holtby v. Brigham & Cowan (Hull) Ltd* [2000] 3 All E.R. 421 (see below at paragraph 2–22), where it is possible to identify the extent of the contribution made by the defendant's negligence to the claimant's psychiatric damage, then the defendant is only liable to that extent (see the discussion of this point in *Hatton v. Sutherland* [2002] EWCA Civ 76; [2002] 2 All E.R. 1 at [36] to [41]; and *Rahman v. Arearose Ltd* [2001] Q.B. 351, paragraph 2–55 in this *Supplement*). This would suggest that unless the psychiatric harm was considered to be "indivisible" in *Vernon v. Bosley (No. 1)*, the outcome in that case (damages awarded for the plaintiff's mental illness caused partly by the defendant's negligence and partly by pathological grief attributable to the death of his children, with no discount for the consequences of the grief although the mental illness was partly caused by grief) was incorrect.

2–16

2–16   CHAPTER 2—CAUSATION IN TORT: GENERAL PRINCIPLES

NOTE 45. Add: *Farrell v. Merton, Sutton and Wandsworth Health Authority* (2000) 57 B.M.L.R. 158.

2–20   NOTE 56. Add: See also *Hardaker v. Newcastle Health Authority & the Chief Constable of Northumbria* [2001] Lloyd's Rep. Med. 512, at [69].

2–22   NOTE 60. Add: *Owen* [2000] J.P.I.L. 82; *Gullifer* (2001) 117 L.Q.R. 403.

Add: The difficulty of quantifying that part of the damage which is attributable to the defendant's negligence should not preclude a court from seeking to do so, even if this involves adopting a "broad brush" approach. In *Allen v. British Rail Engineering* [2001] EWCA Civ 242; [2001] I.C.R. 942 the claimant sought damages from his employer in respect of damage to his hands caused by the use of hand-held vibratory tools ("vibration white finger"). The damage is cumulative depending upon the length and intensity of use of such tools. The judge assessed the overall level of the claimant's disability and then deducted from the award damages: (1) a sum in respect of the damage sustained prior to the point at which the defendants were in breach of duty; (2) a sum in respect of the damage caused after the claimant ceased to be employed by the defendants (the claimant having continued to work with vibrating tools); and (3) a sum (50 per cent of the remaining damage) to take account of the fact that, on the evidence, the exercise of reasonable care by the defendants would only have reduced the claimant's exposure by about half. The claimant appealed on the question of this last deduction. The Court of Appeal upheld the judge's approach, on the basis that the employer's liability is limited to the extent of the contribution which his tortious conduct made to the employee's disability, even though the remaining damage was caused by the defendant's innocent conduct and the extent of the harm has been aggravated by his tortious conduct. Moreover, the judge was entitled to take a "broad brush" approach to assessing the extent of the defendant's contribution. The difficulty of undertaking that assessment was not a basis for saying that it should not occur, otherwise the conclusion would have to be either that the claimant's action failed because he could not prove the precise amount of damage attributable to the defendant's negligence, or that the defendants were liable for all of the damage, including that part attributable to exposure for which they were not responsible. There was greater injustice in either of these of options than the middle course, which was to attempt a "broad brush" assessment of the contribution. The court should not be astute to deny the claimant relief on the basis that he could not establish with demonstrable accuracy precisely what proportion of his injury was attributable to the defendant's tortious conduct (*ibid.* at [20]).

2–23   Add: In a case where the damage is not cumulative but is attributable to a single event, but it is not possible to identify which event, then a mathematical approach to determining the balance of probabilities may be applied. In *The Creutzfeldt-Jacob Disease Litigation, Groups A and C Plaintiffs* (1998) 54 B.M.L.R. 100 the claimants had all developed Creutzfeldt-Jacob Disease (CJD) as a consequence of receiving human growth hormone (HGH) treatment contaminated with the CJD virus. The treatment, consisting of an injection, was given on a regular basis over a period of time. Although there was some uncertainty, the accepted scientific view was that the CJD was caused by a single injection or dose containing a sufficient titre of the CJD agent. There was no issue of a cumulative cause nor that some individuals are more susceptible to developing CJD. The defendants were found to have been in breach of duty from July 1,

1977 by failing to give appropriate information to clinicians treating the claimants about the risks of transmitting CJD. The claimants had received injections of HGH both before and after July 1, 1977, but it was not scientifically possible to identify whether they had received a contaminated dose before or after that date. The defendants were only liable if it could be proved that the claimants received the contaminated dose after that date. The claimants argued that if a victim received more doses after the cut-off date than before it then it was more likely than not that the contaminated dose was received after the cut-off date. For example, if a pack of cards was divided into two piles containing 27 and 25 cards respectively there is a higher probability that the pile of 27 cards contains the ace of spades. The defendants argued that this was a simplistic, mechanistic approach. There was a likelihood or possibility that a victim received a number of contaminated doses, although only one would prove fatal. If there were a number of potential aces of spades in the pack then the analogy of the pack of cards was inappropriate. Morland J. rejected the defendants' argument that causation was only established if the preponderance of doses were given after the cut-off date, and that a preponderance should be substantial (possibly three-quarters or two-thirds). That argument, said his Lordship, would alter the civil standard of proof from the balance of probabilities to a standard of substantially probable or very probable. Thus, any straddler victim would succeed on causation if it was proved that he received the majority of doses after the cut-off date.

See also the discussion of *Fairchild v. Glenhaven Funeral Services Ltd* [2002] UKHL 22 at paragraph 2–13 of this *Supplement*.

Loss of a chance. Add: In *A. v. The National Blood Authority* [2001] 3 All E.R. 289 Burton J. held that a claim based on loss of a chance is not appropriate in the context of an action for breach of section 3 of the Consumer Protection Act 1987. The Act, and the European Union Product Liability Directive 1985 (Council Directive (EEC) 85/374) upon which the Act is based, imposes strict liability. The question is whether the product was defective, and if so what damage was caused by that defect. It is not what damage was caused by any conduct, whether wrongful or otherwise, or breach of duty. Questions of what would or might have happened in hypothetical circumstances are not relevant. See [176]–[180], *per* Burton J. For general comment on *A v. The National Blood Authority* see Howells and Mildred (2002) 65 M.L.R. 95; Hodges (2001) 117 L.Q.R. 528.

2–28

In *Smith v. National Health Service Litigation Authority* [2001] Lloyd's Rep. Med. 90, 101, Andrew Smith J. indicated that the approach adopted by the Court of Appeal in *Allied Maples* can apply to cases of clinical negligence, though in *Hardaker v. Newcastle Health Authority & Chief Constable of Northumbria* [2001] Lloyd's Rep. Med. 512, at [70] Burnton J. made it clear that this could only be the case where causation depends upon the actions of a third party. Where causation does not depend on the actions of third parties: "the claimant must establish what injury has been caused, or what aggravation to his injuries has been caused, on the balance of probabilities, by the defendants' negligence. If he succeeds on a probability of 51 per cent, he recovers 100 per cent of the appropriate compensation for his injury (or aggravation of his injuries); if he establishes only a 49 per cent probability, he recovers nothing."

Where, however, the conduct of a third party is an essential link in the causal chain from the defendant's breach of duty to the claimant's damage, that issue should be resolved on the balance of probabilities. Thus in *The Creutzfeldt-Jacob*

Disease Litigation, Straddlers Groups A and C v. Secretary of State for Health (1998) 54 B.M.L.R. 104 the claimants had all developed Creutzfeldt-Jacob Disease (CJD) as a consequence of receiving human growth hormone (HGH) treatment contaminated with the CJD virus. The defendants were found to have been in breach of duty from July 1, 1977 on the basis of their failure to inform clinicians treating the patients that there was a risk of transmitting the CJD virus in this manner. The claimants had received injections of HGH both before and after July 1, 1977 (hence they "straddled" the relevant date). The question was whether the doctors would have stopped the treatment had they been informed about the risk by the defendants. The defendants argued that this should be dealt with on the basis of the chances that individual clinicians would have stopped treatment of individual patients in light of the low risk and the benefits of treatment. Morland J. rejected this argument, commenting, at p. 107, that: "In order to maintain the chain of causation, it must be proved in relation to a straddler CJD victim on the balance of probabilities that his clinician would have stopped the therapy after receipt of the letter. Once that is established, no discount arises in the quantification of damages in respect of any percentage chance that the clinician might not have stopped treatment. Damages for CJD are then awarded without discount for that chance. Discounts for chance arise only at the quantification stage . . . " The evidence accepted by Morland J. was that, on the balance of probabilities, treatment for all non-hypoglycaemic patients would have ceased. Thus, the case was similar to *Hotson v. East Berkshire Area Health Authority*, the difference being that on the evidence the claimants were not already "doomed" to suffer the damage when the defendants' breach of duty occurred. [For discussion of how to determine whether the claimants received an injection of infected HGH before or after July 1, 1977 see *The Creutzfeldt-Jacob Disease Litigation, Groups A and C Plaintiffs* (1998) 54 B.M.L.R. 100, discussed at para. 2–23 in this *Supplement*]

NOTE 82. Add: *Sharif v. Garrett & Co. (a firm)* [2001] EWCA Civ 1269; [2001] Lloyd's Rep. P.N. 751 at [18] to [22] discussing the appropriate approach where the original claim was struck out because a fair trial of the issues was no longer possible as a result of delay by the solicitors: the judge should not attempt to try the original claim in the action against the negligent solicitors, but should make a realistic assessment of the claimant's prospects of success in the original claim, tending towards a generous assessment given that it was the defendant's negligence which lost the claimant the opportunity of succeeding in full; *Motor Crown Petroleum Ltd v. S.J. Berwin & Co. (A Firm)* [2000] Lloyd's Rep. P.N. 438; *Charles v. Hugh James Jones & Jenkins (A Firm)* [2000] 1 W.L.R. 1278, CA. For discussion of how to approach the assessment where there are multiple contingencies, each with its own probability see *Langford v. Hebran* [2001] EWCA Civ 361, [2001] P.I.Q.R. Q160.

Statements appearing in the main text in these paragraphs should be read in the light of the decision of the House of Lords in *Fairchild v. Glenhaven Funeral Services Ltd* [2002] UKHL 22. See the discussion at paragraph 2–13 of this *Supplement*.

2–29 **Multiple tortfeasors.** Note that in *Fairchild v. Glenhaven Funeral Services Ltd* [2002] UKHL 22 at [170] Lord Rodger "incline[d] to the view" that in *Fitzgerald v. Lane* [1987] Q.B. 781 the Court of Appeal was correct to apply the principle of *McGhee v. National Coal Board* [1973] 1 W.L.R. 1. Note also that, in the light of *Fairchild*, *Edgson v. Vickers plc*, which was not referred to in their Lordships' speeches, must nonetheless be correct.

Note that the statement in the main text that "it seems unlikely that the English courts would follow *Cook v. Lewis*" is probably incorrect in the light of *Fairchild v. Glenhaven Funeral Services Ltd* [2002] UKHL 22, though this would not necessarily involve a reversal of the burden of proof, as opposed to a relaxation of the normal rule concerning the proof of causation on the balance of probabilities.

2–30

Selection of the predominant cause. NOTE 95. Add: *Saddington v. Colleys Professional Services* [1999] Lloyd's Rep. P.N. 140, CA—an overvaluation of a property resulting in a mortgage advance did not cause a loss to the borrower when the money was invested in a business which subsequently failed. It merely provided the opportunity for the loss to occur. *Saddington* was applied in *Moore v. Zerfahs and others* [1999] Lloyd's Rep. P.N. 144, CA.

2–32

NOTE 5. Add: See *Kuwait Airways Corp. v. Iraq Airways Co.* [2002] UKHL 19; *The Times*, May 21, 2002 at [74] *per* Lord Nicholls: "In this type of case, involving multiple wrongdoers, the court may treat wrongful conduct as having sufficient causal connection with the loss for the purpose of attracting responsibility even though the simple 'but for' test is not satisfied. In so deciding the court is primarily making a value judgment on responsibility."

2–34

Vicissitudes of life. NOTE 10. *Heil v. Rankin* is now reported at [2001] P.I.Q.R. Q16

Add: See, however, the comments of Laws L.J. in *Rahman v. Arearose Ltd* [2001] Q.B. 351 at [32]–[33] commenting on *Baker v. Willoughby* and *Jobling v. Associated Diaries Ltd*: "Although the reasoning in *Jobling's* case involved the raising of some judicial eyebrows as to the approach taken by the House in *Baker's* case, with great respect I see no inconsistency whatever between the two cases. Once it is recognised that the first principle is that every tortfeasor should compensate the injured claimant in respect of that loss and damage for which he should justly be held responsible, the metaphysics of causation can be kept in their proper place: of themselves they offered in any event no hope of a solution of the problems which confront the courts in this and other areas. The law has dug no deeper in the philosophical thickets of causation than to distinguish between a *causa sine qua non* and a *causa causans*. The latter is an empty tautology. The former proves everything, and therefore nothing: if A kills B by stabbing him, the birth of either of them 30 years before is as much a *causa sine qua non* of the death as is the wielding of the knife. So the law makes appeal to the notion of a proximate cause; but how proximate does it have to be? As a concept, it tells one nothing. So in all these cases the real question is, what is the damage for which the defendant under consideration should be held responsible."

2–35

3. NOVUS ACTUS INTERVENIENS

Definition. NOTE 14. *Reeves v. Commissioner of Police for the Metropolis* now reported at [2000] 1 A.C. 360.

2–37

Intervening disciplinary proceedings. Where, following an accident at work, an employee has been disciplined, demoted and suffered a loss of earnings, but his employers subsequently settle a claim in respect of the employee's injuries on

2–54A

the basis that they are liable for 85 per cent of the damage (the employee being 15 per cent contributorily negligent), the admission of liability is inconsistent with the argument that that the loss of earnings was entirely attributable to the disciplinary proceedings, and not the employer's breach of duty. Accordingly, the claimant was entitled to recover the loss of earnings caused by the demotion, subject to a deduction of 15 per cent in respect of his contributory negligence: *Casey v. Morane Ltd* [2001] I.C.R. 316, CA. Mance L.J. suggested that, ordinarily, where an employee was justifiably disciplined after an accident, following an objective review of his conduct, and lost income as a result, "the law would be likely to select as the relevant cause of that loss his own conduct and nothing else, and that this would be so even though another person's negligence also contributed to the occurrence of the accident" (at [27]. See also *per* Peter Gibson L.J. at [37]: "In such a case the disciplinary proceedings might be thought to be an intervening event breaking the chain of causation"). In his Lordship's view this would still be the case even if the other negligent party was also disciplined: "That other person might, of course, also be disciplined and lose income as a result of his part. Where that other person was his employer the law would not treat any breach by the employer as a relevant cause" (at [27]). The Court drew an analogy with a road traffic accident caused by the negligence of two drivers where, following a prosecution, the claimant is disqualified from driving and loses income as a result. The loss of income would be due to the independent decision of the court having adjudicated on the claimant's own conduct, and therefore the loss of earnings would be attributable to the claimant's conduct and not the other driver's negligence (*ibid.* at [28] *per* Mance L.J. and [37] *per* Peter Gibson L.J.). (Though, query what the position would be if the claimant was also injured in the accident and was unable to work due his injuries—would *Jobling v. Associated Dairies Ltd* [1982] A.C. 794, paragraph 2–35, above, apply?) With respect, there is a difference between a court imposing a penalty for criminal conduct which results in financial loss to the claimant, which would rightly be treated as an intervening cause, and the potential defendant to a tort action imposing a financial penalty following disciplinary proceedings. The decision of the court is an intervening event of an independent "third party", whereas the decision of the employer to institute disciplinary proceedings is the subsequent conduct of the defendant himself. In conducting disciplinary proceedings the employer is far more likely to concentrate on the employee's culpability than his own (as would appear to have occurred in *Casey v. Morane Ltd* itself). Clearly, if the claimant is wholly responsible for his own inappropriate conduct leading to the accident and is then disciplined, the resulting loss of earnings can be attributed to the claimant's conduct rather than the defendants' breach of duty. But if the claimant is wholly responsible for the accident the claim for injuries and loss resulting from the accident would in any event fail on grounds of causation. Whether the employer has taken disciplinary proceedings would be irrelevant to the causation issue. Moreover, the fact that an employer has disciplined an employee is clearly not binding on a court in assessing the respective responsibilities of employer and employee for the consequences of an industrial accident. In *Casey v. Morane Ltd* the apportionment of responsibility was agreed between the parties, but even if the apportionment was contested, it must remain a question of fact for the court whether the loss of earnings is partly attributable to the employer's breach of duty, otherwise employers might be tempted to discipline careless employees in order to avoid compensation claims, and thereby avoid the consequences if their own carelessness.

Add: In *Rahman v. Arearose Ltd* [2001] Q.B. 351 the claimant was seriously 2–55 assaulted by two black youths, causing an injury to his right eye. His employers were held liable in negligence for failing to take reasonable care to reduce the risk of such assaults. Subsequently, as a result of the negligence of a surgeon who conducted a bone graft, he was rendered blind in the right eye. In addition to the physical injuries, the claimant developed severe psychiatric consequences, including post traumatic stress disorder, a severe depressive disorder, a specific phobia of Afro-Caribbean people, and enduring personality change. The psychiatric reaction was partly due to the assault and partly due to the loss of his eye, and the psychiatric evidence indicated that the post traumatic stress disorder was due to the loss of the eye; the phobia was due to the assault and subsequent events; and the personality change was due to the synergistic interaction between the depression and the post traumatic stress disorder. The Court of Appeal held that a second act of negligence did not necessarily break the causal link between an initial act of negligence and the subsequent damage. Laws L.J. commented at [29] that: "it does not seem to me to be established as a rule of law that later negligence always extinguishes the causative potency of an earlier tort. Nor should it be. The law is that every tortfeasor should compensate the injured claimant in respect of that loss and damage for which he should justly be held responsible. To make that principle good, it is important that the elusive conception of causation should not be frozen into constricting rules. It is true that the idea of a supervening cause—*novus actus interveniens*—is generally deployed in cases where it is suggested that the first tortfeasor should bear responsibility for the effects of the second tort, and this is not such a case: Mr Livesey accepts that the second defendants are solely responsible for the loss of the eye. However the spirit of *novus actus* rattles its chains at the suggestion that the first defendants should bear some responsibility, given that this is not a case of concurrent torts, for the continuing effects of the claimant's psychological damage after the loss of vision in the right eye." Nonetheless, once one had left behind "the dogmas of *novus actus* and eggshell skulls, there is nothing in the way of a sensible finding that while the second defendants obviously (and exclusively) caused the right-eye blindness, thereafter each tort had its part to play in the claimant's suffering" (at [34]). For criticism of the court's approach in *Rahman v. Arearose Ltd* see *Weir* [2001] C.L.J. 237.

Similarly, in *Webb v. Barclays Bank plc and Portsmouth Hospitals NHS Trust* [2001] EWCA Civ 1141; [2001] Lloyd's Rep. Med. 500 the claimant injured an already vulnerable knee in a fall at work for which her employers were responsible. The Court of Appeal held that the subsequent negligence of a surgeon in advising the claimant to undergo an above the knee amputation of her leg "did not eclipse the original wrongdoing". The employers were held liable for all the damage attributable to the fall, and 25 per cent of the damage attributable to the amputation. Thus, if the claimant acts reasonably in seeking or accepting treatment, negligence in carrying out the treatment is not necessarily a *novus actus interveniens* relieving the first tortfeasor from liability for the claimant's subsequent condition. The original injury can be regarded as carrying some risk that medical treatment might be negligently given.

The statement in the text of the main work preceding footnote 66 was approved by the Court of Appeal in *Webb v. Barclays Bank plc and Portsmouth Hospitals NHS Trust* at [55].

NOTE 66. Add: Amend the reference to Smith & Hogan, *Criminal Law*, to: (9th ed., 1999), pp. 342–344.

2–56 *McFarlane v. Tayside Health Board* now reported at [2000] 2 A.C. 59.

NOTE 71. Add: Note that in *Parkinson v. St. James and Seacroft University Hospital NHS Trust* [2001] EWCA Civ 530; [2001] 3 All E.R. 97 the Court of Appeal held that *McFarlane* did not apply where the child was born disabled. The parents of a disabled child born following a negligently performed sterilisation operation were entitled to the additional costs of raising that child (*i.e.* those costs over and above the costs of raising a healthy child, not the full costs of maintenance). Brooke L.J., at [53], was careful to emphasise, however, that if the child's disabilities were brought about between conception and birth "by some ultroneous cause", the negligent surgeon should not, without more, be held liable for the economic consequences of the child's disabilities [though note that supervening negligence does not necessarily break the causal link: see para. 2–55]. The fact that the child's disabilities were not present at birth will not necessarily break the causal link. Thus, in *Groom v. Selby* [2001] EWCA Civ 1522; [2002] Lloyd's Rep. Med. 1 there was a negligent failure to conduct a pregnancy test with the result that the claimant was unaware that she was pregnant until 15 weeks. Had she been informed sooner she would have undergone a termination of the pregnancy. The child was born apparently healthy, but quite by chance, the child developed meningitis within three to four weeks of the birth as a result of an infection which was probably contracted during the course of the birth. The Court of Appeal rejected the defendant's argument that this was an intervening cause. The child's condition was a rare, but a natural and foreseeable consequence of childbirth. The fact that it was mere chance that the child happened to have a disability or that the disability developed after the birth was irrelevant. It is arguable, on the other hand, that disabilities due to an infection arising after the perinatal period would break the causal link. The risk of disablement to an otherwise healthy child is then simply one of the vicissitudes of life.

NOTE 72. Add: *cf. Pidgeon v. Doncaster Health Authority* [2002] Lloyd's Rep. Med. 130 (County Court) where the judge distinguished *Sabri-Tabrizi v. Lothian Health Board* and *McKew v. Holland and Hannen and Cubitts (Scotland) Ltd* (paragraph 2–51 above). The claimant was negligently advised in 1988 that a smear test for cervical cancer was normal, when it showed pre-cancerous abnormalities. A further test in 1997 resulted in a diagnosis of cervical cancer. In the intervening period the claimant had been spoken to on no less than seven occasions about the need to have smear test, and had received four letters from the defendants' cervical cancer screening programme about the need to have a smear test. The claimant had not undergone the test because she found it painful and embarrassing, although she was aware that she could develop cervical cancer. It was held that the claimant's failure to undergo a smear test did not break the causal link between the original negligence and the development of cancer. The difference between this and the cases of *Sabri-Tabrizi* and *McKew* was that in those cases the claimants knew about their particular condition (not being sterile and weakness in the leg), whereas the claimant did not know of her condition, and had been reassured by the reported result of the 1988 test. There was "an important difference between a claimant indulging in behaviour against a background of known vulnerability, whether it be weakness of the leg or ability to conceive, and a claimant failing to take steps which may well reveal a condition, if in fact present, having previously been reassured that it was not present" (at [23]). The claimant may have been unwise or unreasonable, but her failure was not "so utterly unreasonable" as to break the chain of causation. She was, however, assessed to be two-thirds contributorily negligent.

[24]

Suicide. *Reeves v. Commissioner of Police for the Metropolis* now reported at [2000] 1 A.C. 360.

NOTE 82. Add: On the duty of care owed by the police and prison authorities to prisoners who are foreseeably at risk of committing suicide see also: *Orange v. Chief Constable of West Yorkshire Police* [2001] EWCA Civ 611; [2001] 3 W.L.R. 736, CA; *Keenan v. UK (Application No. 27229/95)* (2001) 10 B.H.R.C. 319, where the European Court of Human Rights held that inadequate medical treatment and a lack of effective monitoring of a prisoner who was an identified suicide risk could constitute a breach of Article 3 of the European Convention for the Protection of Human Rights.

4. REMOTENESS OF DAMAGE

Unintended consequences. NOTE 97. Add: Though note that in *Kuwait Airways Corp. v. Iraq Airways Co.* [2002] UKHL 19; *The Times*, May 21, 2002 the House of Lords held that the test of remoteness in the tort of wrongful interference with goods should be directness of consequence where the defendant has acted dishonestly, but where the defendant can prove that he was "innocent" (although strictly liable to the defendant in conversion) the test of remoteness is the more restrictive one of foreseeability (*per* Lord Nicholls at [103] to [104]).

Foreseeable kind of damage. NOTE 2. Add: In the case of occupational disease, foreseeability of the risk of injury of the same type is sufficient; the defendant does not have to foresee the precise disease that the employee is likely to contract. Thus, if it was known that exposure to asbestos dust could produce lung disease it is irrelevant that the causal link between asbestos and mesothelioma was not established until a later date: *Jeromson v. Shell Tankers (UK) Ltd* [2001] EWCA Civ 100; [2001] I.C.R. 1223.

Add: In *Darby v. National Trust* [2001] EWCA Civ 189, [2001] P.I.Q.R. P372, CA, the deceased drowned while swimming in a pond on the defendant's land. His widow argued, *inter alia*, that the failure to post a sign warning about the risk of contracting Weil's disease was a cause of the death since had he seen the sign he would not have swum in the pond. The Court of Appeal held that the risk of contracting Weil's disease and the risk of drowning were fundamentally different. An alleged duty to take reasonable care to warn against the risk contracting a disease could not form the basis of a claim for damages attributable to a different cause (*i.e.* drowning) (applying *South Australia Asset Management Corp. v. York Montague Ltd*).

NOTE 12. *McFarlane v. Tayside Health Board* now reported at [2000] 2 A.C. 59.

NOTE 13. Add: The House of Lords affirmed the Court of Appeal's decision in *Aneco Reinsurance Underwriting Ltd (In Liquidation) v. Johnson & Higgins Ltd* [2001] UKHL 51; [2002] 1 Lloyd's Rep. 157 on the basis that the defendants undertook to advise about the transaction, not merely to provide information. This was because the judgment about the market assessment of the reinsurance risks was central to Aneco's decision to undertake those risks. In *South Australia Asset Management Corp. v. York Montague Ltd* (*SAAMCO*) the lender's assessment of the risk was only partly influenced by the value of the security it was expecting to obtain (other factors included, for example, the value of the borrower's covenant to repay the loan, and the lender's own policy on the percentage of the value of the security it was prepared to lend, which in turn would be affected by its own judgment as to the commercial risk involved and the expected return which was reflected in the interest rate charged to the borrower). Their Lordship's made it clear that the *SAAMCO* principle creates a sub-rule that valuers are not generally liable for all the foreseeable consequences of their negligence, but only for the consequences of the valuation being wrong. This sub-rule is an exception to the more general rule that professionals are normally liable for the foreseeable consequences of their negligence. *SAAMCO*, said Lord Lloyd, at [13], is "an example of a special class of case—typically that of a valuer, but not confined to valuers—where a scope of the defendant's duty is confined to the giving of specific information." Contrast *Lloyds Bank plc v. Burd Pearse (a firm)* [2001] EWCA Civ 366; [2001] Lloyd's Rep. P.N. 452 where it was held that in a conveyancing transaction the failure of solicitors to draw to the lender's attention matters, such as restrictive covenants, which might affect the value of the property being taken as security for a loan constituted the provision of information rather than advice; and therefore their liability was limited to the difference in the value of the property with and without the restrictive covenants as at the date of the conveyance.

2–68   NOTE 14. Add: Delete the reference to the High Court decision in *Kuwait Airways Corp. v. Iraq Airways Co.* and the following text, and substitute:

In *Kuwait Airways Corp. v. Iraq Airways Co.* [2002] UKHL 19; [2002] 3 All E.R. 209; *The Times*, 21 May, 2002 the House of Lords held that the test of remoteness in the tort of wrongful interference with goods could be either foreseeability or directness of consequence depending on the nature of the defendant's conduct. Lord Nicholls pointed out (at [103] to [104]) that the tort of conversion can be committed innocently, and for a person "who can prove he acted in the genuine belief the goods were his" the test should be foreseeability—the defendant is liable for the losses the true owner can be expected to have suffered as a result of the defendant's misappropriation of the claimant's goods. Where, however, the defendant has knowingly converted the claimant's goods he acts dishonestly, and there was no good reason why the remoteness test of "directly and naturally" applied in cases of deceit should not apply in such cases. See also *per* Lord Hope at [169].

CHAPTER 3

GENERAL DEFENCES

	PARA.
■ 2. Conduct of the claimant	3–02
(a) Claimant's wrongdoing	3–02
(b) Contributory negligence	3–22
■ 3. Assumption of risk and exclusion of liability	3–57
(a) Consent	3–57
(b) Exclusion of liability	3–62
(c) *Volenti non fit injuria*	3–72
■ 4. Miscellaneous defences	3–100
(a) Necessity and private defence	3–100
(b) Authorisation	3–112

2. CONDUCT OF THE CLAIMANT

(a) *Claimant's Wrongdoing*

The conceptual foundation of *ex turpi causa* in tort. Note that the Law 3–04
Commission has published a Consultation Paper, *The Illegality Defence in Tort*, No. 160, 2001, which provisionally proposes that the present law should be replaced with a structured discretion to bar a claim when the claim arises from or is connected to an illegal act on the part of the claimant.

Impossible to determine the standard of care. NOTE 16. Add: Of course, the 3–05
court may simply decide that the circumstances are such that no duty of care is owed, irrespective of how "difficult" it might be to set a *standard* of care: see *Vellino v. Chief Constable of the Greater Manchester Police* [2001] EWCA Civ 1249; [2002] 1 W.L.R. 218, discussed at paragraph 3–11A, below.

Reliance on the illegality. It may be that actions concerned with the exercise 3–07
of rights over property are in a different category from claims based on the infliction of loss. Thus, the fact that property has been acquired illegally does not confer a common law power on the police to confiscate that property by refusing to return it. In the absence of a statutory power to confiscate the property the police must return cash belonging to the claimant which is believed to be the proceeds of drug trafficking (*Webb v. Chief Constable of Merseyside Police* [2000] Q.B. 427, CA) and must return a stolen vehicle to the thief if there is no one with a better title to the vehicle (*Costello v. Chief Constable of Derbyshire Constabulary* [2001] 1 W.L.R. 1437, CA; see Getzler (2001) 117 L.Q.R. 565). The Court's concern was to avoid establishing a mechanism of non-statutory expropriation by means of a defence to a civil claim where property had been seized from persons who were not subsequently convicted of a criminal offence. This is an example of the need for certainty in rights of property overriding otherwise legitimate policy concerns in the law of torts.

3–10 **Which test?** NOTE 42. *Reeves v. Commissioner of Police for the Metropolis* in the House of Lords is now reported at [2000] 1 A.C. 360.

3–11A Add: The diversity of view in the Court of Appeal on the appropriate conceptual basis for dealing with claims where the claimant was engaged in illegality at the time of sustaining damage has continued. It is apparent that in some circumstances the claimant's illegal conduct will prevent a duty of care from ever arising, in which case there is no need to consider the illegality to be a *defence* to an "accrued" liability. In *Vellino v. Chief Constable of the Greater Manchester Police* [2001] EWCA Civ 1249; [2002] 1 W.L.R. 218 the claimant was injured when he jumped from a second floor window to evade arrest by the police. He alleged that the police were under a duty of care not negligently to let him escape once they had arrested him. It is clear that the police must come under some duty of care to persons they have arrested, since the fact of detention prevents a prisoner from avoiding certain dangers (*e.g.* if a prisoner fell ill, the police would undoubtedly have a duty to seek medical treatment for him). Similarly, it is well-established that the police may owe a duty of care to a prisoner known to be suicidal to take reasonable precautions to prevent suicide attempts (as was conceded in *Reeves v. Commissioner of Police for the Metropolis* [2000] 1 A.C. 360; and see *Orange v. Chief Constable of West Yorkshire Police* [2001] EWCA Civ 611; [2001] 3 W.L.R. 736). However, by a majority, in *Vellino* the Court of Appeal held there was no duty of care owed to a prisoner who was attempting to escape from custody. Schiemann L.J. commented (at [19]) that: "To suggest that the police owe a criminal the duty to prevent the criminal from escaping, and that the criminal who hurts himself while escaping can sue the police for the breach of that duty, seems to me self-evidently absurd." The claimant was the author of his own misfortune and by breaking away from an officer arresting him he was committing a criminal offence. His Lordship accepted that there was an overlap between the considerations which had to be taken into account in determining whether a duty of care existed and whether the defence of *ex turpi causa* applied, but based his decision on the absence of a duty of care rather than the defence. Sir Murray Stuart-Smith agreed that "if the facts are such that the maxim *ex turpi causa non oritur actio* is applicable, it does not matter whether the correct legal analysis is that the defendants owed no duty of care, because the third limb of the test in *Caparo Industries plc v. Dickman* [1990] 2 A.C. 605, namely that it is just fair and reasonable to impose a duty of care, is not satisfied, or that the maxim affords a freestanding reason for holding that the cause of action does not arise or cannot be pursued" (*ibid.* at [62]). *Vellino* followed and applied *Sacco v. Chief Constable of the South Wales Constabulary* (unreported) May 15, 1998, where the Court of Appeal held that the police were not liable to a prisoner who, while being transported in the back of a police van, kicked open the rear doors of the van in an attempt to escape and was injured when he fell out of the vehicle. In *Sacco* Schiemann L.J. said:

> "Second, he was engaged in a criminal act, namely attempting to escape from lawful custody. As a matter of legal policy, I see no reason to permit a man to recover damages against the police if he hurts himself as part of that illegal enterprise. The basis of such recovery must be either an allegation of a breach of a duty owed to him not to let him escape, or of a duty owed to him to take care that he does not hurt himself if he tries to escape. I see no reason to create such duties owed to him. It is common ground that the policy of the law is not to permit one criminal to recover damages from a fellow criminal who fails to take care of him whilst they are both engaged on a criminal

enterprise. The reason for that rule is not the law's tenderness towards the criminal defendant, but the law's unwillingness to afford a criminal plaintiff a remedy in such circumstances. I see no reason why that unwillingness should be any the less because the defendant is a policeman and not engaged in any crime."

Sedley L.J. dissented in *Vellino*, concluding that arresting officers owe a prisoner a duty not to afford both a temptation to escape and an opportunity of doing so when there is a known risk that the prisoner will do himself real harm, even if much of the blame for hurting himself will ultimately come to rest on the prisoner himself. The power to apportion responsibility under the Law Reform (Contributory Negligence) Act 1945 "afforded a far more appropriate tool for doing justice than the blunt instrument of turpitude. In many cases, classically where both parties have been involved in a single criminal enterprise, the outcome would be the same" (*ibid.* at [55]). With respect, this argument proves rather too much, since it is an argument for abolishing all tort defences except contributory negligence. Moreover, it is not necessarily correct to suggest that in the case of a joint criminal enterprise the result would be the same, since it is not appropriate to apportion 100 per cent contributory fault to a claimant (see *Pitts v. Hunt* [1991] 1 Q.B. 24). The argument that the claimant is 100 per cent at fault for damage is an argument that, as a question of causation, he is wholly responsible for his own injuries, which is not that different from Schiemann L.J.'s view that the claimant was the author of his own misfortune. Nor is it clear why a claimant engaged in a joint criminal enterprise should be regarded as wholly responsible for his own injuries when he sues his fellow criminal, but not when he sues the police.

Seriousness of the claimant's conduct. In *Vellino v. Chief Constable of the Greater Manchester Police* [2001] EWCA Civ 1249; [2002] 1 W.L.R. 218 Sir Murray Stuart-Smith said at [70] that: "In the case of criminal conduct this has to be sufficiently serious to merit the application of the principle. Generally speaking a crime punishable with imprisonment could be expected to qualify. If the offence is criminal but relatively trivial, it is in any event difficult to see how it could be integral to the claim." 3–13

Connection with the claimant's injury. NOTE 63. Add: In *Hall v. Woolston Hall Leisure Ltd* [2001] 1 W.L.R. 225 the Court of Appeal held that an employee's acquiescence in the employer's failure to deduct tax and national insurance contributions from wages, did not bar the employee from bringing a complaint of sex discrimination against the employer. The complaint of sex discrimination was not so closely bound up or linked with the unlawful conduct that the court would be seen to be condoning unlawful conduct by the employee. Mance L.J. commented at [79]: "While the underlying test therefore remains one of public policy, the test evolved in this court for its application in a tortious context thus requires an inextricable link between the facts giving rise to the claim and the illegality, before any question arises of the court refusing relief on the grounds of illegality. In practice, as is evident, it requires quite extreme circumstances before the test will exclude a tort claim." Similarly, in *Newman v. Folkes and Dunlop Tyres Ltd* [2002] P.I.Q.R. Q2, QBD, it was held that where earnings are from a lawful source, collateral illegality in the performance of the contract, such as the deliberate failure to pay tax or national insurance contributions, does not preclude a claimant recovering in respect of lost earnings; *cf. Hunter v. Butler* [1996] R.T.R. 396, CA—the deceased's earnings were obtained from "moonlighting", 3–16

3–16 whereby he did not disclose his earnings while drawing social security benefits at the full rate, and the Court of Appeal held that his widow was not entitled to claim for loss of dependency under the Fatal Accidents Act 1976.

NOTE 66. *Reeves v. Commissioner of Police for the Metropolis* in the House of Lords is now reported at [2000] 1 A.C. 360.

3–19 Add: See also *Vellino v. Chief Constable of the Greater Manchester Police* [2001] EWCA Civ 1249; [2002] 1 W.L.R. 218 where Sir Murray Stuart-Smith said, at [70], that: "The principle is one of public policy; it is not for the benefit of the defendant. Since if the principle applies, the cause of action does not arise, the defendant's conduct is irrelevant. There is no question of proportionality between the conduct of the claimant and defendant."

3–21 *Ex turpi, volenti* **and contributory negligence.** NOTE 88. *Reeves v. Commissioner of Police for the Metropolis* in the House of Lords is now reported at [2000] 1 A.C. 360.

(b) *Contributory Negligence*

3–22 NOTE 94. Add: In *Anderson v. Newham College of Further Education* [2002] EWCA Civ 505 a two-judge Court of Appeal suggested that the decision in *Jayes v. IMI (Kynoch) Ltd* had been reached *per incuriam*, since the decision of the House of Lords in *Boyle v. Kodak Ltd* [1969] 1 W.L.R. 661 was not cited. In *Boyle* the House of Lords held that to escape liability for injury to an employee caused by a breach of statutory duty, the employer must prove that the breach was both coextensive with a breach of the same statutory duty by the injured employee, and that the employer had done all he reasonably could to ensure compliance by the employee [see paragraph 11–58 of the main work]. Sedley L.J. said that *Boyle v. Kodak* demonstrated how high is the standard of proof that is required to shift the entire blame for a breach of statutory duty to the injured employee, but that if the defendant employer manages to satisfy this standard, then there is no liability capable of apportionment and the claimant fails altogether. Thus, concluded his Lordship at [1.18]: " ... *Jayes* should, in my respectful view, not be followed by judges of first instance and should not be relied upon by advocates in argument. The relevant principles are straightforward. Whether the claim is in negligence or for breach of statutory duty, if the evidence, once it has been appraised as the law requires, shows the entire fault to lie with the claimant there is no liability on the defendant. If not, then the court will consider to what extent, if any, the claimant's share in the responsibility for the damage makes it just and equitable to reduce his damages. The phrase '100 per cent contributory negligence', while expressive, is unhelpful, because it invites the court to treat a statutory qualification of the measure of damages as if it were a secondary or surrogate approach to liability, which it is not. If there is liability, contributory negligence can reduce its monetary quantification, but it cannot legally or logically nullify it."

3–28 **Scope of contributory negligence.** NOTE 24. See also the discussion of the meaning of the word "fault" in s. 1(1) of the 1945 Act in *Standard Chartered Bank v. Pakistan National Shipping Corporation (No. 4)* [2001] Q.B. 167, particularly in the judgment of Ward L.J.

Breach of statutory duty. NOTE 26. Add: *Toole v. Bolton Metropolitan Borough Council* [2002] EWCA Civ 588 at [14].   3–29

Intentional injury to the person. *Reeves v. Commissioner of Police for the Metropolis* is now reported at [2000] 1 A.C. 360.   3–31

NOTE 29. Add: *Ward v. Chief Constable of the Royal Ulster Constabulary* [2000] N.I. 543—contributory negligence applied to a claim for assault and battery.

NOTE 32. Add: Such a duty is not owed where there is no foreseeable risk of suicide by the prisoner: *Orange v. Chief Constable of West Yorkshire Police* [2001] EWCA Civ 611; [2001] 3 W.L.R. 736, CA.

Note that the failure to provide appropriate medical supervision to a prisoner who is a known suicide risk may constitute a breach of Article 3 of the European Convention for the Protection of Human Rights: *Keenan v. U.K. (Application No. 27229/95)* (2001) 10 B.H.R.C. 319, ECHR.

Contributory negligence excluded. NOTE 41. The issue referred to in this note was not addressed when further argument was presented in *Standard Chartered Bank v. Pakistan National Shipping Corporation (No. 4)* [2001] Q.B. 167. Rather the point that the Court of Appeal resolved was whether the Law Reform (Contributory Negligence) Act 1945 could be relied upon by a defendant found liable in deceit where the claimant's own conduct amounted to an attempted deceit of a third party. By a majority (Evans L.J. dissenting) the Court of Appeal held that a defendant found liable in deceit could not rely on the Act to reduce the damages. Aldous L.J. stated, at [61], that "it has always been the law that a defendant who has been found liable in deceit cannot establish a defence based upon the contributory fault of the plaintiff." Ward L.J. accepted that deceit by a claimant can constitute contributory "fault" on the part of the claimant (relying on *Reeves v. Commissioner of Police for the Metropolis* [2000] 1 A.C. 360, HL, that "fault" can include intentional acts by the claimant, as well as negligence). However the question remained whether apart from the Act, the claimant's negligence and/or attempted deception would have given rise to the defence of contributory negligence at common law. The common law applied a causation test, namely whether the claimant's negligence could be said to have contributed to his loss (and if so, the contributory negligence was a complete defence, the fact that the defendant's negligence also contributed to the loss being irrelevant). However, the common law applied special rules of causation to the tort of deceit. So long as the defendant's fraudulent misrepresentation was *a* cause of the loss suffered by the claimant, the claimant recovered in full even though there were other factors causing the claimant's loss. Thus, "In cases of deceit the authorities show that the deceit is held to be the only cause of the loss." *per* Ward L.J. at [115]. Moreover: "As a matter of law it seems to me the sole cause of the damage is the defendant's deceit and any reason operating on the plaintiff's mind which causes him to act as he did pales into legal irrelevance. If that analysis is right then the claimant's own fault has no causative effect upon his suffering his loss. Thus the defendant fails to establish that the claimant is a person who 'suffers damage as the result partly of his own fault'." *per* Ward L.J. at [121]. This interpretation of the Act was reinforced by Ward L.J.'s perspective on the policy issues that fraudulent conduct raises, expressed, at [126], in the context of an appropriate apportionment of responsibility between the parties: "Nevertheless it is necessary to focus on the extent to which [the claimants'] loss   3–33 suffered as it was by the defendants' deceit should be apportioned for their share in the responsibility for the damage. In my judgment the responsibility for the damage is wholly that of the defendants. It was the defendants who set out to deceive and succeeded in deceiving. The mixed motives of the claimants do not mitigate that dishonesty. Commercial fraud must be condemned. It can only be properly condemned by an award of the whole of the damage which the defendants intended to cause. Highwaymen in commerce forfeit the right to just and equitable treatment. In my judgment in the law of deceit there is to be no apportionment. If the parties were in *pari delicto* then the claimants would fail to recover anything. In this field it is all or nothing."

3–34 **Contributory negligence and contract.** NOTE 47. *UCB Bank plc v. Hepherd Winstanley & Pugh (a Firm)* is reported at [1999] Lloyd's Rep. P.N. 963.

3–38 **Breach of statutory duty.** NOTE 60. Add: Contributory negligence is not a defence where even if the employee had taken the precautions suggested by the defendant employer, the defendant would still have been in breach of statutory duty: *Toole v. Bolton Metropolitan Borough Council* [2002] EWCA Civ 588— employee failed to wear gloves provided by the employer, but the gloves would probably not have prevented the injury even if used.

NOTE 61. Add: See, however, the discussion of *Jayes v. IMI (Kynoch) Ltd* at paragraph 3–22, note 94, above.

3–46 **Seat belts and crash helmets.** NOTE 95. Add: In *J. (A Child) v. Wilkins* [2001] P.I.Q.R. P179 the Court of Appeal held that the same principles of apportionment as apply to contributory negligence should apply to a case involving contribution under the Civil Liability (Contribution) Act 1978 when there was a failure to wear a seat belt. The claimant was a two year old child who was held on her mother's knee in the front passenger seat of a car being driven by her aunt. The defendant negligently collided with the car, causing serious injuries to the claimant which could have been wholly avoided if she had been restrained in an approved child seat. The defendant joined the claimant's mother and aunt as CPR Part 20 defendants. The Court of Appeal upheld the judge's assessment that liability should be apportioned 75 per cent to the defendant and 25 per cent to the Part 20 defendants applying the approach adopted in *Froom v. Butcher*.

3–50 **Doctrine of identification.** Add: The issue of identification at common law arose, but was not resolved, in *Gorham v. British Telecommunications plc* [2000] 1 W.L.R. 2129. The claimants were the spouse and children of the deceased who was a customer of an insurance company which gave negligent advice to the deceased about pensions and life cover. The Court of Appeal held that, by analogy with the wills cases (see *White v. Jones* [1995] 2 A.C. 207), the insurance company owed a duty of care to the customer's dependant spouse and children where it was clear that he intended to create a benefit for them on his death. It was found that in relation to part of the loss the deceased himself had been negligent in failing to take steps to remedy the situation brought about by the defendants' negligence. Pill and Schiemann L.JJ. held that this broke the causal link between the defendants' negligence and the relevant financial loss, and neither considered it appropriate to comment on the question of contributory negligence. Sir Murray Stuart-Smith, dissented on the causation issue, and then considered whether the deceased's contributory negligence should be taken into account to reduce the claimants' award of damages. The Law Reform (Contributory Negligence) Act 1945, s.1(1) provides that the damages " ... shall be reduced to such extent as the court thinks just and equitable having regard to *the claimant's share* in the responsibility for the damage" (emphasis added). Read literally this would appear to preclude reducing the claimants' award in *Gorham*, since it was not their negligence which contributed to the loss. Sir Murray Stuart-Smith suggested that this problem could be overcome because it was acknowledged in *White v. Jones* that the court was fashioning a remedy to meet an apparent injustice. The duty of care owed to the beneficiaries in *White* was said to be subject to any contractual terms between the testator and the solicitor to which the dependants were not party, which might exclude or restrict the solicitor's liability to the testator. There was, said his Lordship, no reason why the same principle should not apply to contributory negligence on the part of the testator, and in *Gorham* on the part of the deceased customer. Fashioning a remedy to meet the justice of the case also required justice for the defendants which would be achieved by reducing the award of damages to the dependants to reflect the deceased's negligence. It remains to be seen whether, in a case where the customer's negligence is not regarded as being so potent as to break the causal link, a court would adopt Sir Murray Stuart-Smith's approach or apply the literal wording of the 1945 Act.

Apportionment. NOTE 25. Add: See also *Jebson v. Ministry of Defence* [2000] 1 W.L.R. 2055, where the Court of Appeal held that the defendants were liable for injury to a soldier injured when, in a drunken state, he fell off an army truck after a night out organised by the defendants. The claimant was held 75 per cent contributorily negligent. *cf. Joy v. Newell (t/a Copper Room)* [2000] N.I. 91 (NICA) where the claimant went into defendant's bar in an intoxicated condition and ordered a drink. After a couple of sips he fell off his stool and sustained serious injury. The NICA held that despite it being a criminal offence to serve alcohol to someone who is obviously intoxicated, it did not follow that a licensee assumes a positive duty of care to an intoxicated customer. Moreover, there was no evidence that either the defendant or his barman knew of the extent of the claimant's intoxication. See also *Griffiths v. Brown and Lindsay* [1999] P.I.Q.R. P131 where it was held that a taxi driver was not liable to a drunken passenger who was dropped off on the opposite side of the road from a bank and was injured by a negligent motorist as he was crossing the road. A taxi driver does not undertake an additional duty for the safety of a passenger simply because the passenger was known to be inebriated.

NOTE 27. *Reeves v. Commissioner of Police for the Metropolis* is now reported at [2000] 1 A.C. 360.

Apportionment and the *SAAMCO* "Cap". NOTE 36. Add: There is no necessary reason why a lender's share of responsibility should be limited to a share of the amount of the imprudent excess lending. The excess lending may be the immediate reason for the additional loss, but without the excess lending it may be that there would have been no transaction and no loss at all. Thus, it may be appropriate to arrive at a share of the overall loss which the lender should be required to bear: *Arab Bank plc v. John D. Wood Commercial Ltd* [2000] Lloyd's Rep. P.N. 173, 204, *per* Mance L.J. at [109].

NOTE 41. Add: Howarth (2000) 8 Tort L. Rev. 85.

3–56

Add: The negligence of a firm of solicitors in failing to procure from company directors personal guarantees of a commercial loan to a company gives rise to a loss of opportunity by the lender to recover under the guarantees the monies owed by the company. Thus, the release by the lender of a security over an additional property owned by the directors did not contribute to that loss and therefore did not constitute contributory negligence: *UCB Corporate Services Ltd v. Clyde & Co.* [2000] P.N.L.R. 841, CA.

Platform Home Loans v. Oyston Shipways Ltd now reported at [2000] 2 A.C. 190.

3. Assumption of Risk and Exclusion of Liability

(a) Consent

3–58 **Consent and the intentional torts.** NOTE 44. *Vine v. Waltham Forest London Borough Council* now reported at [2000] 1 W.L.R. 2383.

(b) Exclusion of Liability

3–62 **At common law.** NOTE 61. Add: See also the Unfair Terms in Consumer Contracts (Amendment) Regulations 2001, S.I. 2001 No. 1186.

Add: Note that other statutory provisions may permit the exclusion of liability for negligence in the context of the specific service covered by the statute. Thus, the Electricity Act 1989, s.21 provides that a public electricity supplier may require any person who requires a supply of electricity to accept, in respect of the supply, any terms restricting any liability of the supplier for economic loss resulting from negligence which it is reasonable in all the circumstances for that person to be required to accept. In *A.E. Beckett & Sons (Lyndons) Ltd v. Midlands Electricity plc* [2001] 1 W.L.R. 281 the Court of Appeal held that this section permitted terms which restricted liability in economic loss only in relation to such loss caused by the interruption or variation of the supply of electricity. An exclusion clause did not extend to the negligent installation of electrical equipment.

3–66 **The reasonableness test.** See also *Governor and Company of the Bank of Scotland v. Fuller Peiser* [2002] P.N.L.R. 289 where the lender relied on a valuation report prepared by the defendant for the purchaser of a hotel. It was reasonable to allow the defendant to rely on a clause excluding liability to anyone other than the purchaser client because the lender was a large commercial organisation and the transaction was entirely commercial in nature

3–68 **Third parties.** NOTE 80. Add: See *Pacific Associates Inc v. Baxter* [1990] 1 Q.B. 993, 1022–3 *per* Purchas L.J. and the discussion of this issue by Neuberger J. in *Killick v. PricewaterhouseCoopers* [2001] Lloyd's Rep. P.N. 17, 21–24.

3–71 **Contracts (Rights of Third Parties) Act 1999.** For comment on the Contracts (Rights of Third Parties) Act 1999 see: MacMillan, C., "A birthday present for Lord Denning: the Contracts (Rights of Third Parties) Act 1999" (2000) 63 M.L.R. 721; Roe, T., "Contractual intention under section 1(1)(b) and 1(2) of the Contracts (Rights of Third Parties) Act 1999" (2000) 63 M.L.R. 887; Burrows,

MISCELLANEOUS DEFENCES   3–106

A., "The Contracts (Rights of Third Parties) Act 1999 and its implications for commercial contracts" [2000] L.M.C.L.Q. 540; Andrews, N., "Strangers to Justice No Longer: The Reversal of the Privity Rule Under the Contracts (Rights of Third Parties) Act 1999" [2001] C.L.J. 352.

(c) *Volenti Non Fit Injuria*

Freely and voluntarily. NOTE 27. *Reeves v. Commissioner of Police for the Metropolis* is now reported at [2000] 1 A.C. 360.   3–81

Knowledge of danger. NOTE 36. Add: In *Darby v. National Trust* [2001] E.W.C.A. Civ. 189, [2001] P.I.Q.R. P372, CA, the deceased drowned while swimming in a pond on the defendant's land. The Court of Appeal held that the defendants were not liable because the risks to competent swimmers of swimming the pond were "perfectly obvious." *cf. Tomlinson v. Congleton Borough Council* [2002] EWCA Civ 309; *The Independent*, March 21, 2002, a case decided under the Occupiers' Liability Act 1984, where a warning sign against the "obvious risk" of swimming in a lake which was known to be ineffective was held to be insufficient.   3–82

NOTE 36a. *Fraser v. Winchester Health Authority* is now reported at (2000) 55 B.M.L.R. 122.

Consent, *volenti* and sport. NOTE 84. *Watson v. British Boxing Board of Control* affirmed at [2001] Q.B. 1134, CA; and is discussed by George, J., "Negligent Rule-Making in the Court of Appeal" (2002) 65 M.L.R. 106.   3–97

See generally Yeo, "Accepted Inherent Risks Among Sporting Participants" (2001) 9 Tort L. Rev. 114.

4. MISCELLANEOUS DEFENCES

(a) *Necessity and Private Defence*

Acting in the public interest. NOTE 2. *Monsanto plc v. Tilly* is now reported at [2000] Env. L.R. 313.   3–103

Acting in the claimant's interest. NOTE 7. Where, however, the question of appropriate medical treatment comes before a court for decision, while there may be a number of different options which might be lawful in any particular case (since there can be more than one responsible practice), logically there is only one best option, and the court must choose that option in making decisions in the patient's best interests rather than leaving the doctors to choose from the lawful options: *Re S (Adult Patient: Sterilisation)* [2001] Fam. 15, CA.   3–105

Acting in the claimant's interest. NOTE 10. Add: *Re AK (Adult Patient) (Medical Treatment: Consent)* [2001] 1 F.L.R. 129—a competent adult patient's refusal to consent to medical treatment must be observed. Such a refusal, given in advance of the circumstances in which it was to take effect should also be observed provided it remains the wish of the patient. The termination of invasive treatment is not unlawful in these circumstances; rather it is unlawful to continue to treat a patient who has expressed a clear and competent wish not to be treated.   3–106

3–106

The Human Rights Act 1998 does not support an alternative view. Thus, a mentally competent patient being kept alive by a respirator is entitled to demand that the respirator be removed even if this will inevitably result in her death: *Re B (adult: refusal of medical treatment)* [2002] EWHC Fam 429; [2002] 2 All E.R. 449.

NOTE 13. Add: Where, however, the prisoner is not competent necessity may justify force-deeding: *R. v. Collins and Ashworth Hospital Authority, ex p. Brady* [2000] Lloyd's Rep. Med. 355.

(b) *Authorisation*

3–121 **Power and trespass.** NOTE 61. *Gapper v. Chief Constable of the Avon and Somerset Constabulary* is now reported at [2000] 1 Q.B. 29.

CHAPTER 4

CAPACITY AND PARTIES

	PARA.
■ 2. The Crown	4–02
6. Bankrupts	4–50
■ 11. Corporations	4–78
13. Partners	4–100
■ 14. Joint and Several Torts	4–101

2. THE CROWN

Insert new paragraph after para. 4–17:

4–17A In relation to the fact that section 10 of the Crown Proceedings Act continues to apply in respect of death and personal injury suffered prior to May 15 1987, it is noteworthy that in *Matthews v. Ministry of Defence* (NOTE 43a) the Court of Appeal held that provision not to be incompatible with the right to a fair trial enshrined in Article 6(1) of the European Convention on Human Rights (which was imported into English Law by virtue of the Human rights Act 1998). Section 10, the court said, governed a substantive right. Thus, the procedural right afforded by Article 6 was unaffected. On facts substantially similar to those in *Quinn*, the serviceman in this case had no cause of action by virtue of section 10. Thus his Article 6 right to a fair and public court hearing did not arise because there was no cause of action to which Article 6 could apply. As such, it followed that it was inconceivable that there was any incompatibility between section 10 and Article 6. (NOTE 43b)

NOTE 43a: *The Times*, May 31, 2002.
NOTE 43b: On the construction of Art 6, see further paras 1–79 *et seq.*

4–19 **Judicial acts.** Insert as penultimate sentence: Furthermore, it is clear that the phrase "execution of judicial process" is to receive a wide interpretation so that the purely administrative errors of a Registrar will be caught. (NOTE 44a)

NOTE 44a: *Quinland v. Governor of Belmarsh Prison* [2002] EWCA Civ 174.

6. BANKRUPTS

4–52 **Bankrupt and trustee.** NOTE 49. Add: Twin losses may also be caused by negligence that results in the claimant's bankruptcy. These are (i) economic loss (in the shape of loss of future earnings that would have accrued but for the bankruptcy), and (ii) loss of status and reputation (synonymous with bankruptcy). In such cases, the former loss vests in the trustee while the latter, being of a personal nature, vests in the bankrupt: *Mulkerrins v. Pricewaterhouse Coopers* (2001) 98(5) L.S. Gaz 36.

11. CORPORATIONS

4–78 **Capacity to sue.** Insert immediately prior to final sentence in para. 4–78: Thus, slanderous words describing the sole owner of a company as a "bloody crook" and someone in respect of whom "I have to count my fingers after shaking hands with him" have been regarded as peculiarly applicable to an individual, and thus incapable of application to a corporate body. (NOTE 56a)

NOTE 56a: *Shendish Manor Ltd v. Coleman* [2001] EWCA Civ 913.

4–89 NOTE 78: Add: Watts (2000) 116 L.Q.R. 525.

Immediately after "becomes a joint tortfeasor" in exception (3) insert: (NOTE 80a)

NOTE 80a: See, *e.g.*, *Daido Asia Japan Co. Ltd v. Rothen* 2001 W.L. 825034.

13. PARTNERS

Insert new paragraph after para. 4–100:

4–100A Not always will the defendant partnership hold itself out as being a partnership. In such a case the court is entitled to infer the existence of a partnership from an agreement, express or implied, that the persons concerned intend to carry on a business in common. (NOTE 13a) Thus, in *Grant v. Langley* (NOTE 13b), despite "an almost total lack of the paperwork which is normally retained for accounting purposes in businesses keeping proper books" the court was nonetheless prepared to infer a partnership based on the fact that the defendants were carrying on a family business together with a view to profit. As such, the normal principles of joint and several liability could be invoked to attach liability to two brothers in the family partnership after their (senior partner) father had been made bankrupt two years prior to the issue of the writ.

NOTE 13a: Partnership Act 1980, s.1.
NOTE 13b: 2001 W.L. 513090.

14. JOINT AND SEVERAL TORTS

4–106 NOTE 34: Add: and *Ogle v. Chief Constable of Thames Valley Police* [2001] EWCA Civ 598.

4–108 NOTE 40: Add: *Daido Asia Japan Co. Ltd v. Rothen* 2001 W.L. 825034; *MCA Records Inc v. Charly Records Ltd (No. 5)* [2002] E.M.L.R. 1.

NOTE 41: Add: *MCA Records Inc. v. Charly Records Ltd (No. 5)* [2002] E.M.L.R. 1.

Replace paragraph 4–119 with:

4–119 **What constitutes the "same damage"?** By section 1(1) of the Civil Liability (Contribution) Act 1978 contribution is recoverable from any person liable in respect of the same damage as the party seeking contribution. At one time, the courts gave a broad interpretation to this phrase so as to include substantially or materially similar damage. (NOTE 75) But in *Royal Brompton Hospital NHS Trust v. Hammond (No. 3)* (NOTE 76) the House of Lords overruled this approach stating that the words "liable in respect of the same damage" were to receive their ordinary and natural meaning. A firm of architects had negligently issued extension certificates to contractors in respect of certain construction work commissioned by a developer. The building work was delayed and the developer sued the architects in respect of their negligence. The architects were unable to claim a contribution from the contractors who actually performed the delayed construction. The contractors were responsible for delayed construction *per se*, whereas the architects (by issuing the extension certificates) had caused the developer to lose the opportunity to sue the contractors for liquidated damages in respect of that delay. The loss of opportunity to sue for liquidated damages was not the same damage as the delay, *per se*.

NOTE 75: *Friends Provident Life Office v. Hilier, Parker, May and Rowden* [1997] Q.B. 85.

NOTE 76: [2002] UKHL 14.

CHAPTER 5

VICARIOUS LIABILITY

	PARA.
1. Introduction	5–01
2. Employer and employee	5–03
■ 3. Liability of the employer	5–23
4. Independent contractors	5–48
■ 5. Loan of chattel	5–67

The most important case to be reported on vicarious liability is the House of **5a** Lords' decision in *Lister v. Hesley Hall Ltd* [2001] UKHL 22, [2001] 2 W.L.R. 1311. The issue for the House was whether the employers of a warden of a school boarding house could be vicariously liable for the torts involved in the acts of sexual abuse perpetrated by that warden on boys in his care. In a similar case, *Trotman v. North Yorkshire County Council* [1999] I.R.L.R. 98 [see main text 5–23 n. 94; 5–24 n. 2] the Court of Appeal had held that such activity would be outside the scope of such an employee's employment so that the employer would not be vicariously liable. However the House of Lords in *Hesley Hall* held that *Trotman v. North Yorkshire County Council* was wrongly decided. Essentially the House found an application of Salmond's unauthorised conduct/unauthorised mode distinction unhelpful in cases of intentional wrongdoing particularly where the employee sets out to benefit himself. Rather the court looked to the close connection between the acts in question and the employment. In *Hesley Hall* rather than the employment merely furnishing an opportunity to commit the sexual abuse, the connection between the employment and the torts was very strong. The sexual abuse was "inextricably interwoven" with the carrying out by the warden of his duties. Lord Steyn noted (p. 1322) "the reality was that the County Council were responsible for the care of the vulnerable children and employed [the warden] . . . to carry out that duty on its behalf. And the sexual abuse took place while the employee was engaged in duties at the very time and place demanded by his employment". Particular assistance was derived from the Court of Appeal decision in *Morris v. C W Martin & Sons Ltd* [1966] 1 Q.B. 716, which, though a case involving bailment (and the conversion by the employee of the bailed goods), is authority for a wider principle of vicarious liability—namely is the tort closely connected to the nature of the employment. (Lord Hobhouse, in reviewing cases such as *Morris v. C W Martin & Sons Ltd*, *Lloyd v. Grace Smith & Co.* [1912] A.C. 716, HL and *Photo Production Ltd v. Securicor Transport* [1980] A.C. 827, HL, preferred the following as representing the general rule: "where the defendant has assumed a relationship to the plaintiff which carries with it a special duty towards the plaintiff, the defendant is vicariously liable in tort if his servant, to whom the performance of that duty has been entrusted, breaches that duty" at p. 1334). In coming to this decision reference was made to the "landmark decisions" of the Canadian Supreme Court in *Bazley v. Curry* (1999) 174 D.L.R. (4th) 45 and *Jacobi v. Griffiths* (1999) 174 D.L.R. (4th) 71 where the Supreme Court, in determining the vicarious liability of employers in cases of sexual abuse of children by employees, enunciated a principle of "close connection". The House of Lords also referred with approval to the article by Peter Cane, "Vicarious Liability for Sexual Abuse" (2000) 116 L.Q.R. 21. This approach based on close connection and essentially "fairness" is likely to colour the approach to vicarious liability in cases where the employee is liable for assault, damage/conversion to goods bailed or entrusted to the employer, theft or fraud (See the views of Laddie J. in *Balfon Trustees Ltd v. Peterson* [2001] I.R.L.R. 758). It may also be the better approach where the tort is committed by the employee contrary to the employer's express prohibition.

1. INTRODUCTION

5–01   **Scope of chapter.** Note that the issue of whether exemplary damages are available where the liability of the defendant is vicarious was debated by the House of Lords in *Kuddus v. Chief Constable of Leicester* [2001] UKHL 29, [2001] 2 W.L.R. 1789. Lord Scott believed that as a matter of principle exemplary damages should not be available in a vicarious liability claim.

2. EMPLOYER AND EMPLOYEE

5–03   **Relationship of employer and employee.** NOTE 11. *Sellars Arenascene Ltd v. Connolly* [2001] EWCA Civ 184, [2001] I.R.L.R. 223, CA: controlling shareholder may still be an employee. The service agreement had not been a sham and the shareholder had "behaved as an employee".

5–06   **Control.** See *Montgomery v. Johnson Underwood* [2001] EWCA Civ 318, [2001] I.R.L.R. 269, CA (below).

5–10   **The "multiple test".** NOTE 38: *McFarlane v. Glasgow CC* [2001] I.R.L.R. 7, EAT (Scot): a limited ability to delegate was not necessarily fatal to a finding of employee status, as indeed was noted by MacKenna J. in *Ready Mixed Concrete (South East) Ltd v. Minister of Pensions and National Insurance* [1968] 2 Q.B. 497. The Court of Appeal decision in *Express & Echo Publications Ltd v. Tanton* [1999] I.R.L.R. 367 was distinguished on the basis that in *McFarlane* (unlike in *Tanton*) the ability to delegate was dependent on the worker being unable to attend, the worker had to provide a replacement from the employer's own register and such substitute would be paid directly by the employer.

NOTE 39: *Montgomery v. Johnson Underwood* [2001] EWCA Civ 318, [2001] I.R.L.R. 269, CA. The issue was whether M was the employee of the employment agency with which he had registered and which had assigned him to work for a client company for two years. The employment agency had paid the worker on the basis of time sheets approved by the client company and the agency had terminated the assignment when requested to do so by the client company. Overturning the EAT, the Court of Appeal held that the worker was not the employee of the agency. There had been a clear finding by the industrial tribunal that there was no control by the agency of the worker. The court noted that mutuality of obligations and control over the worker were the minimum legal requirements for the existence of a contract of employment. The Court of Appeal decision in *McMeechan v. S/S for Employment* [1997] I.R.L.R. 353 was distinguished on the basis that in that case there were review/grievance procedures as between the agency and the worker. However Buckley J. did note (p. 273) that if Waite L.J. in *McMeechan* intended to reduce the criteria of mutual obligations and control to no more than matters to be weighed up with other factors such an approach would be contrary to the CA decision in *Nethermere (St Neots) Ltd v. Taverna and Gardiner* [1984] I.R.L.R. 240 and the House of Lords' decision in *Carmichael v. National Power plc* [1999] 1 W.L.R. 2042. He also noted the considerable uncertainty concerning the status of workers who find work through employment agencies. *cf. Motorola Ltd v. Davidson* [2001] I.R.L.R. 4, EAT (Scot), below.

The issue of mutuality. Add *Stevedoring and Haulage Services Ltd v. Fuller* [2001] I.R.L.R. 627, CA. Workers were self-employed where their contracts expressly provided that they were to be engaged on an "ad hoc and casual basis" with no obligation on the employer to provide work and no obligation on the worker to accept work. 5–12

NOTE 51: On the difficult issue of the employment status of agency workers, *McMeechan v. S/S for Employment* [1997] I.R.L.R. 353 was discussed by Buckley J. in *Montgomery v. Johnson Underwood* [2001] EWCA Civ 318, [2001] I.R.L.R. 269, CA, above. In *Motorola Ltd v. Davidson* [2001] I.R.L.R. 4, Scot EAT the worker had been recruited by an agency on behalf of Motorola Ltd. The contract with the agency stipulated that the worker should comply with the instructions of Motorola Ltd. The worker was trained by Motorola Ltd, wore their uniform and had to arrange any absences with Motorola Ltd. His assignment was terminated by Motorola Ltd, following a disciplinary hearing held by one of their managers. The "practical aspects of control" were sufficient for the EAT (in a claim for unfair dismissal) to find Motorola Ltd to be the employer of the worker. In *Hewlett Packard v. O'Murphy* [2002] I.R.L.R. 4, EAT the employment status of an agency worker hired to a third party employer was discussed, the EAT stressing the need to find a contract between the worker and the third party employer before considering his employment status.

Club Servants. Though there have been indications in English cases that officials or members of unincorporated club committees may be vicariously liable for the torts of employees of the club (see especially *Grice v. Stourport Tennis, Hockey and Squash Club* [1997] 9 C.L. 592, CA), it would appear that such is not the case in Scots law: *Carmichael v. Bearsdon & District Rifle and Pistol Club* [2000] S.L.T. 49 (Sh. Ct.) at least where the claimant is a club member. 5–19

Borrowed employees. *Interlink Express Parcels Ltd v. Night Truckers Ltd* [2001] EWCA Civ 360, [2001] R.T.R. 23. Night Truckers supplied drivers to Interlink Express for use in the delivery of parcels to Interlink Express's depots. The case concerned section 58(2) of the Goods Vehicles (Licensing of Operators) Act 1995 and whether the drivers so supplied were the servants of Interlink Express or Night Truckers (and therefore who needed to hold an operator's licence under the Act). Held that the word servant in the 1995 Act includes a person for whom an employer is vicariously liable under the *Mersey Docks* principle. With temporary deemed employment the paramount test is that of control. Interlink Express specified the drivers' routes and hours and could start disciplinary proceedings. They were the temporary employers of the drivers. 5–21

5–24　　　　　　　　Chapter 5—Vicarious Liability

3. Liability of the Employer

5–24　　**Course of Employment.** Salmond's test for vicarious liability was discussed by the House of Lords in *Lister v. Hesley Hall Ltd* [2001] UKHL 22, [2001] 2 W.L.R. 1311, see above. In cases of intentional wrongdoing the court drew attention to the inadequacy of the test, focussing rather on the need to analyse the connection between the torts and the nature of the employment.

> Note 2: Note that *Trotman v. North Yorkshire County Council* [1999] I.R.L.R. 98 was overruled by the House of Lords in *Lister v. Hesley Hall Ltd* [2001] UKHL 22, [2001] 2 W.L.R. 1311.

5–37　　**Assault by employee.** *Fennelly v. Connex S.Eastern Ltd* [2001] I.R.L.R. 390, CA. The employer was vicariously liable for an assault by their ticket inspector on a passenger, carried out in response to the employee's ticket duties. There was nothing to suggest that the employee carried out the assault for his own purposes. *Daniels v. Whetstone Entertainments Ltd* [1962] 2 Lloyd's Rep. 1 distinguished. *Leebody v Ministry of Defence* [2001] C.L.Y. 4544: personal injury to the claimant resulted from a negligent/illegal tackle in a football tournament organised by Royal Navy. The claimant had been representing his ship and playing in a match against a team from another ship. The Ministry of Defence was vicariously liable for the negligent tackle of the opposing player. See also the discussion of *Lister v. Hesley Hall Ltd* [2001] UKHL 22, [2001] 2 W.L.R. 1311, above.

5–38　　**Damage to goods bailed to the employer.** The decision in *Morris v. CW Martin & Sons Ltd* [1966] 1 Q.B. 716 was applied by McKinnon J. in *Marshall v. Business Blueprints Ltd* December 18, 2000 (unreported) to render the employer liable where their employee's arson over the property she had been employed to protect and which the employer had leased from the claimant led to damage to both that property and the claimant's flat situated within that property. It was held that the employer's duty as tenant to act with due and proper regard to the safety and security of the premises had been delegated to their employee and that having delegated that duty they were vicariously liable for their employee failing to take reasonable care of the premises. That duty to take reasonable care extended indirectly to the claimant's flat (*Photo Production Ltd v. Securicor Transport Ltd* [1980] A.C. 827 also applied). In *Lister v. Hesley Hall Ltd* [2001] U.K.H.L. 22, [2001] 2 W.L.R. 1311, HL, Lord Steyn noted that the Court of Appeal in *Trotman v. North Yorkshire County Council* [1999] 98 erred in treating *Morris v. CW Martin & Sons Ltd* as reflecting a special rule for application in bailment cases only.

4. Independent Contractors

5–50　　**Statutory duty.** *Quaquah v. Group 4 Securities Co. (No. 2), The Times*, June 27, 2001; [2001] 7 C.L. 523, Wright J. Having regard to the statutory powers which governed the detention of the claimant, the Home Office held not vicariously liable for torts committed by the employees of a private company that was running a detention centre under contract with the Home Office. Furthermore, all reasonable care had been taken by the Home Office in the selection of their private company so no liability arose from the torts of that company's employees.

Withdrawal of support from neighbouring land. This principle was extended in *Alcock v. Wraith* (1991) 59 B.L.R. 16, CA [see main text] to include vicarious liability for the negligence of independent contractors, employed to undertake party-wall work of a risky kind. In *Johnson (t/a Johnson Butchers) v. BJW Property Developments Ltd* [2002] N.P.C. 17, HH Judge Thornton Q.C., Technology and Construction Court applied this extended principle. Here the parties occupied adjoining premises and the claimants' premises were damaged by a fire caused by the negligence of independent contractors employed by the defendants. The independent contractors had been employed to work on the defendants' chimney breast and surround of a fire grate. As the relevant work related to a party wall and involved a particular risk of damage to adjoining premises the defendants were vicariously liable. 5–53

The rule in *Rylands v. Fletcher*. See the discussion in *Johnson (t/a Johnson Butchers) v. BJW Property Developments Ltd* [2002] N.P.C. 17, HH Judge Thornton Q.C., Technology and Construction Court. 5–56

Escape of fire. See the discussion in *Johnson (t/a Johnson Butchers) v. BJW Property Developments Ltd* [2002] N.P.C. 17, HH Judge Thornton Q.C., Technology and Construction Court. 5–57

Nuisance. See the discussion in *Johnson (t/a Johnson Butchers) v. BJW Property Developments Ltd* [2002] N.P.C. 17, by HH Judge Thornton Q.C., Technology and Construction Court, of the decision in *Spicer v. Smee* [1946] 1 All E.R. 489. 5–58

Extra-hazardous acts. See the discussion in *Johnson (t/a Johnson Butchers) v. BJW Property Developments Ltd* [2002] N.P.C. 17, HH Judge Thornton Q.C., Technology and Construction Court. 5–59

Employer's common law duty to employee. *Mullaney v. CC of West Midlands* [2001] EWCA Civ 700, *Daily Telegraph*, May 22, 2001. The non-delegable duty of employers to employees is owed by a Chief Constable, subject to considerations of public policy. 5–62

5. Loan of Chattel

Essentials of liability. *John Laing Construction v. Ince* [2001] C.L.Y. 4543, District Judge Collier. The defendant was vicariously liable for the negligence of a subcontractor, driving the defendant's vehicle, given at the time of the accident the subcontractor was driving the vehicle as the defendant's agent. 5–69

CHAPTER 6

FOREIGN TORTS

	PARA.
■ Jurisdiction: Brussels and Lugano Conventions	6–02
■ Jurisdiction: common law	6–03
■ Private International Law (Miscellaneous Provisions) Act 1995	6–09

Jurisdiction: The Lugano Convention and the European Council Regulation. NOTE 3. Replace with: Lugano Convention, Art. 2; Regulation on Jurisdiction and the Recognition of and Enforcement of Judgments in Civil and Commercial Matters (Council Regulation (EC) No. 44/2001) Art. 2(1) (the primary jurisdiction).   **6–02**

NOTE 4. Replace with: Art 5(3) of both the Lugano Convention and the Council Regulation (the alternative jurisdiction).

Immediately prior to final sentence in paragraph 6–02 insert: On the other hand, the option to sue either where the wrongdoing occurred or where the resulting damage ensued will not be available to forum shopping claimants. Thus, in *Henderson v. Jaouen*, (NOTE 6a) the claimant was not permitted to sue in the English courts in respect of a deterioration in his health that occurred in England following a motoring accident in France caused by the defendant. Despite the fact that the (applicable) law of France permits aggravation cases of this kind, it was nonetheless held that the claimant's return to England prior to that deterioration was irrelevant for the purposes of determining under Article 5(3) the place where the harmful event—the road accident—took place.

NOTE 6a: [2002] EWCA Civ 75.

Replace final sentence of 6–02 with:
Whether or not there is an arguable case under the Convention or the Regulation that a tort has been committed is to be referred exclusively to English law. [RETAIN EXISTING FOOTNOTE]

Jurisdiction: Common Law. NOTE 9. Add: A lack of financial assistance in the appropriate forum which means that the claimant will be unable to afford not only professional legal representation but also necessary expert evidence does amount to a denial of justice that justifies refusing a stay of proceedings: *Lubbe v. Cape Plc* [2000] 4 All E.R. 268 (group action involving over 3000 claimants claiming personal injury caused by exposure to asbestos).   **6–03**

Insert new paragraph immediately after note 35:
The Court of Appeal, however, has made it clear in *Roerig v. Valiant Trawlers Ltd* that "the word substantially [in section 12(1)(b)] is the key word" and that "[t]he general rule is not to be dislodged easily". (NOTE 37a) In that case, the claimant was a Dutch woman. She was claiming bereavement damages on behalf of herself and her children (all living in Holland) following her Dutch partner's death for which the defendant admitted tortious liability. Despite the fact that the   **6–10A**

6–10A

consequences of the defendant's tort were felt in Holland, the Court of Appeal did not accept that these were sufficiently *substantial* factors to dislodge the applicability of English law where the defendant was English and the incident had occurred in England.

NOTE 37a: [2002] 1 All E.R. 961, at para. 12 (*per* Waller L.J.).

6–11 NOTE 42. Replace existing note with: *ibid.*, s.14(3)(b). In *H v. C* [2001] 1 W.L.R. 2386, Holland J. held that even where liability is admitted, the assessment of damages in a personal injury action remains a procedural matter that it is apt for the English courts to resolve. The same approach was taken in *Roerig v. Valiant Trawlers Ltd* [2002] 1 All E.R. 961.

CHAPTER 7

NEGLIGENCE

	PARA.
■ 1. The tort of negligence	7–01
■ 2. Duty of care	7–05
(1) The general criteria	7–05
(2) Restricted duties	7–24
■ 3. Foreseeability and Remoteness	7–133
■ 4. Breach of duty	7–159
(b) The criteria of reasonableness	7–162
(c) Proof of carelessness	7–190
■ 5. Particular situations of negligence liability	7–197
(a) Highway accidents	7–198
(b) Transport accidents	7–211
(c) Employment accidents	7–215
(d) Responsibility for children	7–228

The most important developments since the last edition include the decisions in *Watson v. British Boxing Board of Control Limited* on application of duty principles to novel situations, those in *Parkinson v. St James and Seacroft University Hospital NHS Trust* and *Rees v. Darlington NHS Trust* on unwanted birth, those in *McLoughlin v. Grovers (a firm)*, *Farrell v. Avon Health Authority* and *Hatton v. Sutherland* on psychiatric injury, the latter dealing with work stress. Other significant developments have concerned liability for economic loss, the liability of employed professionals, the application of the remoteness test and of the *Bolam* test for breach of duty. **7a**

1. THE TORT OF NEGLIGENCE

The nature of negligence liability. NOTE 5. Commenting on *Goldman* in *Delaware Mansions Ltd v. Westminster City Council* [2001] 4 All E.R. 737 at 748, Lord Steyn said: "The label nuisance or negligence is treated as of no significance. In this field . . . the concern of the common law lies in working out the fair and just content and incidents of a neighbour's duty rather than affixing a label and inferring the extent of the duty from it." See further para. **19–23**. **7–01**

(1) The general criteria   7–21

Pragmatism and principle. In *Dean v. Allin & Watts (a firm)* [2001] P.N.L.R 921, 947, Sedley L.J. reflected on the challenge for the law in these terms: "It is from an objective appraisal of actors' specific relationship with one another that the law will either deduce or decline to deduce the duty. Inevitably, since no two cases are alike, this gives rise to criticism that law is being rendered uncertain. The criticism may wound when applied to cases such as *White v. Jones* . . . as to suggest that these are decisions driven as much by merits as by law. If so, the wounds are honourable, for they represent the constant endeavour to do justice according to law. After a century and a half of development of the law of negligence, we know there is no universal legal formula by which the presence or absence of liability can be determined and policy has correspondingly come to fill some of the spaces. What is not always understood in this context is that the 'fair, just and reasonable' test is not a gate opening on to a limitless terrain of liability but a filter by which otherwise tenable cases of liability in negligence may be excluded."

7–22   **Application of the three-fold test.** See *Watson v. British Boxing Board of Control Limited* [2001] 2 W.L.R. 1256, where Lord Phillips giving the judgment of the Court of Appeal, held that the Board owed a duty to its members, professional boxers, to take reasonable care in making regulations imposing on others a duty to ensure that personal injuries sustained in a fight are properly treated. As the nature of the duty was novel and there were "no stepping stones" for an incremental extension of liability, Lord Phillips applied the three stage test rather than the more limited analysis applied by Hobhouse L.J. in *Perrett*. He found that by making provision in its rules for the provision of medical facilities, the Board had arrogated the task of determining what medical facilities would be provided at a contest and coupled with the specific reliance of the boxers on this provision, this gave rise to proximity. He considered that a duty would be just, fair and reasonable in the light of the following factors: the claimant was one of a defined number of boxing members; the primary object of the Board was to look after its members' safety; it encouraged members in the pursuit of an activity which involved inevitable physical injury and the need for medical precautions; it controlled the medical assistance that would be provided; it had access to specialist expertise; its assumption of responsibility for medical care relieved the fight promoter of responsibility leaving the boxer with a remedy only against the Board; the boxing members could reasonably rely on the Board to look after their safety. Under the head of "policy considerations", Lord Phillips dismissed as irrelevant the fact that the Board was non-profit making and rejected the argument that this would be the "thin end of the wedge" for other sporting regulatory bodies.

See also *McLoughlin v. Grovers (a firm)* [2002] P.N.L.R 516, [2002] P.I.Q.R. P222, where dealing with a novel issue in relation to psychiatric damage (see *post* para. 7–68) Brooke L.J. said that to answer the duty question "one must go once more to the battery of tests which the House of Lords has taught us to use ... the 'purpose' test (*Banque Bruxelles Lambert SA v. Eagle Star Insurance Co. Ltd* [1997] A.C. 191); the 'assumption of responsibility' test (*Henderson v. Merrett Syndicates Ltd* [1995] A.C. 145); the 'principles of distributive justice' test (*Frost v. Chief Constable of South Yorkshire Police* [1999] 2 A.C. 455); and the 'three-pronged' test (*Caparo Industries plc v. Dickman* [1990] 2 A.C. 605). The fact that these tests are usually deployed in cases involving pure financial loss does not mean that they are inappropriate for use when the only damage in question is psychiatric damage."

7–23   See *Baxall Securities Ltd v. Sheard Walshaw Partnership* [2001] P.N.L.R. 257, where Judge Bowsher Q.C. citing *Marc Rich* and Lord Keith's suggestion in *Murphy* that a builder might owe a duty to a subsequent occupier, took the "51st step" and held that an architect might owe a duty to a subsequent occupier in relation to physical damage caused by design defects which could not reasonably have been detected by inspection. See below, para. **8–133**.

(2) Restricted duties

(a) *Parties*

(i) *Claimant's status*

Unwanted birth. NOTE 18. *McFarlane* now reported at [2000] 1 A.C. 59. NOTE 19. In *Parkinson v. St James and Seacroft University Hospital NHS Trust* [2001] 3 W.L.R. 376, the Court of Appeal held that the policy argument against recovery for a healthy child was not applicable in the case of a disabled child. While the basic costs of the child's maintenance were not recoverable, there was no valid reason, moral or legal, not to compensate the mother for the extra costs associated with the child's disability. *Parkinson* was followed by the Court of Appeal in *Rees v. Darlington NHS Trust* [2002] 2 All E.R. 177, where it was held that a disabled mother could recover the costs of bringing up an unwanted child to the extent that those costs were attributable to her disability. See below, para. **8–58** and above para. **2–56**.

7–26

Wrongdoers. See *Vellino v. Chief Constable of Greater Manchester* [2002] 1 W.L.R. 218, where the Court of Appeal held that the police did not owe a duty of care to a claimant injured in a foreseeable attempt to escape police custody. The Court held that escaping from custody was a sufficiently serious criminal offence to attract the operation of the *ex turpi* principle and hence, it would not be unjust to deny the claimant a right to damages. See further para. 3–11A.

7–31

Suicide. NOTE 49. *Reeves* is now reported at [2000] 1 A.C. 360.

7–32

(ii) *Defendant's status*

Participants in legal proceedings. NOTE 74. In *Docker v. Chief Constable of West Midlands Police* [2001] 1 A.C. 435, the House of Lords held that the immunity would not extend to the deliberate fabrication of evidence by a witness. In *Raiss v. Palmano* [2001] P.N.L.R. 540, Eady J. held that it still extended to dishonest statements made by an expert witness in his report, for example, as to his qualifications. In *L and P v. Reading Borough Council* [2001] P.I.Q.R. P387, the Court of Appeal following *Docker* refused to strike out a claim against the police on the ground of witness immunity. Sir Philp Otton said: "there is no distinction in principle between the situation whether it is fair just and reasonable to impose a duty of care and whether it is proportionate to defeat a claim on the ground of witness immunity. In both situations each case must be determined on its own facts. It is arguable [in this case that] the immunity should not be used to shield the police from suit while acting as law enforcers or investigators and if decided to the contrary, the immunity might be disproportionate to the public interest both under the common law and under the jurisprudence arising out of the [HR] Convention".

7–37

(iii) *Special relationships*

Risky activities. In a rather different context, Lord Hamilton giving the judgment of the Court of Session (Outer House) in *Ross Harper & Murphy v. Scott Banks* [2000] Lloyd's Rep. P.N. 631, held that the standard of care to be expected of a partner in fulfilling his duty of care to fellow partners, depended upon such factors as the risks attendant upon the partnership business, the

7–42

7–42 CHAPTER 7—NEGLIGENCE

practices adopted by the partnership and the mutual tolerance of error which might be imported in the relationship.

7–43 **Relationship with employer.** In *Phelps v. Hillingdon London Borough Council* [2000] 3 W.L.R. 776, the House of Lords reversed the decision of the Court of Appeal and held that an educational psychologist employed by a local authority could owe a duty of care to a child who had been referred to the psychologist. In *Merrett v. Babb* [2001] 3 W.L.R. 1, the Court of Appeal relied on *Phelps* in concluding that an employed surveyor could owe a duty of care to a client of his employer despite the absence of personal dealings between the parties. Aldous L.J. dissented on the ground that in *Williams v. Natural Life Health Foods Ltd* [1998] 1 W.L.R. 830, the House of Lords held that in the absence of personal dealings, a director could not owe a duty of care to a client of his company. The majority in *Merrett* distinguished *Williams* on the ground that normally a director of a limited liability company is not personally liable for the actions of the company. See also *Dean v. Allin & Watts (a firm)* [2001] P.N.L.R. 921, where the Court of Appeal applied *Phelps* in holding that a solicitor could owe a duty to a party on the other side of the transaction from his employing client. See below paras **7–116** and **8–06A**.

(b) *Omissions*

(i) *Special relationship*

7–52 **Assumption of responsibility.** See *Watson v. British Boxing Board of Control Limited* [2001] 1 W.L.R. 1256, where Lord Phillips discussed at length the distinction between general reliance on public services as in *Capital and Counties* and *Alexandrou*, which gave rise to no duty and specific reliance or undertakings as in *Barrett* and *Kent* which could give rise to a duty. The facts of the case fell on the specific reliance side: see *ante* para. **7–22**.

Kent v. Griffiths is now reported at [2001] Q.B. 36.

7–57 **Custody.** NOTE 84. *Palmer* has been followed by the Court of Appeal in *K v. Secretary of State for the Home Department* (2002) N.L.J. 917.

(c) *Psychiatric Illness*

7–62 **Distress.** NOTE 17. *Watts* has been followed in *Johnson v. Gore Wood & Co.* [2001] 2 W.L.R. 72, and *Farley v. Skinner* [2000] P.N.L.R. 441, by the House of Lords and Court of Appeal respectively.

(i) *Primary Victims*

7–64 In *W v. Essex C.C.* [2000] 2 W.L.R. 601 at 607, Lord Slynn, considering the case of psychiatric injury suffered by parents as a result of their feeling that they were responsible for introducing an abuser to their children, commented that "the categorisation of those claiming to be included as primary ... victims is not ... finally closed' and that there was nothing in the cases which 'conclusively' showed that these parents were 'prevented from being primary victims'." In *Farrell v. Avon Health Authority* [2001] Lloyd's Rep. Med. 458, Bursell J. treated the claimant who suffered psychiatric illness as a result of being told negligently and wrongly that his new born baby had died, as a primary victim following the

[52]

views expressed in *Essex*. In *McLoughlin v. Grovers (a firm)* [2002] P.N.L.R. 516, [2002] P.I.Q.R. P222, Hale L.J. regarded the claimant who allegedly suffered psychiatric illness as a result of imprisonment following the alleged negligence of the defendant solicitor, as a being a primary victim.

NOTE 46. See also *Greatorex v. Greatorex* [2000] 1 W.L.R. 1970.

7–66

Reasonably foreseeable psychiatric illness. NOTE 63. In *McLoughlin v. Grovers (a firm)* [2002] P.N.L.R. 516, 532, [2002] P.I.Q.R. P222, 235, Brooke L.J. held that where there was a contractual relationship between the parties, the test of foreseeability was; "damages can only be recovered if it is foreseeable that psychiatric illness would have been suffered by the claimant, given all those features of his personal life and disposition of which the defendants were aware." He held that the Trial Judge had been wrong to strike out the claim on the basis of the "person of reasonably fortitude test". Hale L.J. held that the "ordinary phlegm" test did not apply as the claimant could be regarded as a primary victim and hence, "foreseeability must be considered in relation to this particular claimant, and what the defendants knew or ought to have known about him". See para. **7–64** *ante*.

7–68

NOTE 65. In *Farrell v. Avon Health Authority* [2001] Lloyd's Rep. Med. 458, 472, Bursell J. stated that: "[E]ven if the court's decision is made *ex post facto*, logic dictates that foreseeability depends on the facts known to the defendant at the relevant time". The case concerned an unmarried father who had suffered psychiatric illness as a result of being told negligently and wrongly by the defendant's medical staff that his new born baby had died. Bursell J. applied the principle to the facts as follows: "If in the medical notes in their possession at the time the defence were aware of the father's lack of relationship [with the mother and baby] that fact would be properly in their contemplation. On the other hand, where that fact only surfaced later it must be left out of the equation. Thus, in this case the defendants' foreseeability of risk must be on the basis of an ordinary paternal relationship with the unborn child."

(ii) *Secondary victims*

Defendant as immediate victim. In *Greatorex v. Greatorex* [2000] 1 W.L.R. 1970, after extensive consideration of the policy arguments, Cazalet J. held that a primary victim did not owe a duty of care to a third party in circumstances where his self-inflicted injuries had caused that third party psychiatric injury. Imposition of a duty in such circumstances would be a significant limitation on an individual's freedom of action.

7–76

Common law development and legislative reform. See now the judgment of a past Chair of the Law Commission, Brooke L.J. in *McLoughlin v. Grovers (a firm)* [2002] P.N.L.R. 516, [2002] P.I.Q.R. P222. Rather than narrowly focussing on psychiatric damage cases, Brooke L.J. set the duty question in the context of the tests applicable to duty issues generally. See para. **7–22** *ante*.

7–78

(iii) *Illness resulting from factors other than personal injury or imperilment*

Psychiatric illness as a result of distressing news. See also *Farrell v. Avon Health Authority* [2001] Lloyd's Rep. Med. 458, where the claimant who suffered psychiatric illness as a result of being told negligently and wrongly that his new born baby had died, recovered.

7–81

7–82 **Psychiatric illness through stress at work.** In *Hatton v. Sutherland* [2002] 2 All E.R. 1, Hale L.J. giving the judgment of the Court of Appeal, reviewed the area of law and set out the factors to be considered in work stress claims. The threshold question was whether a harmful reaction to the pressures of the workplace was reasonably foreseeable in the individual employee concerned. Crucially, she suggested that unless "he knows of some particular problem or vulnerability, an employer is entitled to assume that his employee is up to the normal pressures of the job."

7–83 **Psychiatric illness arising from other relationships.** See *McLoughlin v. Grovers (a firm)* [2002] P.I.Q.R. P222, in which the Court of Appeal held that a solicitor whose alleged negligence led to his client's wrongful conviction and imprisonment, owed a duty of care to the client in respect of the psychiatric illness suffered as a consequence of the imprisonment. Brooke L.J. cited his own judgment in *Leech* and Hale L.J. treated the claimant as a primary victim.

(d) *Pure Economic Loss*

(i) *The Hedley Byrne Principle*

7–90 **Threefold test.** *Esanda Finance Corporation v. Peat Marwick Hungerfords* is now also reported at [2000] Lloyd's Rep. P.N. 684.

7–95 **The combined approach.** This paragraph was cited by Brooke L.J. in *Parkinson v. St James NHS Trust* [2001] 3 W.L.R. 376, as "a thoughtful passage... which draws a lot of threads together in a helpful way." See also the views of the same judge in *McLoughlin v. Grovers (a firm)* [2002] P.N.L.R. 516, [2002] P.I.Q.R. P222, and see *ante* para. **7–22**.

7–96 **The relevant factors.** Neill L.J.'s summary of the relevant factors continues to be much cited but courts are also finding the approach of Lord Bingham in *Reeman v. Department of Transport* [1997] P.N.L.R. 618, 639 to be helpful. Lord Bingham said: "The cases show that before a plaintiff can recover compensation for financial loss caused by negligent misstatement his claim must meet a number of conditions. Among these are three particularly relevant here. The statement... must be plaintiff-specific: that is, it must be given to the actual plaintiff or to a member of a group, identifiable at the time the statement is made, to which the actual plaintiff belongs. Secondly, the statement must be purpose-specific: the statement must be made for the very purpose for which the actual plaintiff has used it. Thirdly, and perhaps overlapping with the second condition, the statement must be transaction-specific: the statement must be made with reference to the very transaction into which the plaintiff has entered in reliance on it." See *Barings Plc v. Coopers & Lybrand (a firm)* [2002] P.N.L.R. 321, 339, and *Gooden v. Northamptonshire County Council* [2002] P.N.L.R. 440, 453, for recent citations of this passage.

(ii) *The McNaughton criteria*

(1) The purpose of the statement or service

7–97 **Purpose of information.** See the lengthy discussion of the purpose test and the relevant case law in *Barings Plc v. Coopers & Lybrand (a firm)* [2002]

P.N.L.R. 321. The decision in *Law Society v. KPMG Peat Marwick* has been affirmed by the Court of Appeal: [2000] P.N.L.R. 831. See below para. **8–145**.

NOTE 7. See the disagreement in *Gooden v. Northamptonshire County Council* [2002] P.N.L.R. 440, as to the purpose of a local authority response to an enquirer about frontager liability.

Purpose of service. The *White* principle was applied in *Gorham v. British Telcommunications Plc* [2000] 1 W.L.R. 2129, to impose a duty on a pension adviser to the dependents of its client, and both *White* and *Gorham* were followed in *Dean v. Allin & Watts (a firm)* [2001] P.N.L.R. 921, to impose a duty on a solicitor to a party on the other side of his client's transaction. 7–99

In *Corbett v. Bond Pearce* [2001] 3 All E.R. 769, the Court of Appeal held that a solicitor did not owe a duty to the default beneficiary (*i.e.* the person taking in lieu of the disappointed beneficiary) in relation to probate costs incurred as a result of his negligence, as it was the wish of the client that the disappointed beneficiary and not the default beneficiary should benefit from the instructions to the solicitor. 7–100

(2) Purpose of Communication

Services. In *Cossey v. Lonnkvist* [2000] Lloyd's Rep. P.N. 885, the Court of Appeal held by a majority that the purpose of the accountant's service was to advise the claimant on the financing and not the wisdom of a business purchase and hence, there was no liability. 7–102

(3) Relationship between parties

Contractual matrix. In *Turton & Co. v. Kerslake & Partners* [2000] Lloyd's Rep. P.N. 967, the majority of the New Zealand Court of Appeal followed *Pacific Associates* and distinguished *Edgeworth* as resting on its particular contractual context. In *Jarvis & Sons Ltd v. Castle Wharf Developments Ltd* [2001] Lloyd's Rep. P.N. 308, the Court of Appeal held that a professional employed by a developer to issue tender documents could owe a duty to potential contractors who relied on the documents. *Pacific Associates* was distinguished on the ground that in *Jarvis* "there was no contract between the employer and the contractor at the relevant times of the alleged misstatements". 7–105

Reasonable Reliance

Informal or social context. NOTE 69. See also *Fashion Brokers Ltd v. Clarke Hayes (a firm)* [2000] Lloyd's Rep. P.N. 398: telephone response to planning enquiry by a local authority employee did not give rise to a duty. 7–115

Status of defendant. The reasoning in *Williams* was applied by the Court of Appeal in *Standard Chartered Bank v. Pakistan National Shipping Corporation (No. 2)* [2000] 1 Lloyd's Rep. 218, where a director was held not to have assumed personal responsibility for fraudulent representations made by the company. However, In *Phelps v. Hillingdon London Borough Council* [2000] 3 W.L.R. 776, the House of Lords held that an educational psychologist employed by a local authority could owe a duty of care to a child who had been referred to the psychologist. The damage in *Phelps* was categorised as "personal injury" but 7–116 in *Merrett v. Babb* [2001] 3 W.L.R. 1, the Court of Appeal relied on *Phelps* in concluding that an employed surveyor could owe a duty of care in respect of economic loss to a client of his employer despite the absence of personal dealings between the parties. Aldous L.J. dissented on the basis of *Williams* but the majority in *Merrett* distinguished *Williams* as being concerned with the status of directors and not employees. See also *Dean v. Allin & Watts (a firm)* [2001] P.N.L.R. 921, and see above para. **7–43** and below para. **8–06A**.

(iii) *Disclaimers*

7–117 **Effect of disclaimers.** In *Killick v. PriceWaterhouseCoopers* [2001] P.N.L.R. 1, where it was suggested that a limitation of liability clause in a contract between the defendant and its contractual employer, might limit the extent of the defendants liability to a third party claimant arising from performance of its contractual duties.

7–118 **Statutory control of disclaimers.** See *The Governor and Company of the Bank of Scotland v. Fuller Peiser* [2002] P.N.L.R. 289, where a disclaimer of third party liability in a survey report was held reasonable given that the third party pursuer was a commercial bank engaged in a commercial transaction.

(iv) *Defective property*

7–121 **Dangerous defects and economic loss.** NOTE 6. In *Payne v. John Setchell Ltd* [2002] P.N.L.R. 146, 176, Humphrey Lloyd H.H.J. after extensive consideration of the authorities held that nothing in the speeches in *Murphy* "which on their Lordships' reasoning justifies a distinction being made between the 'designer' and the 'builder', nor is there any operational, practical or social reason to do so." Hence a structural engineer did not owe a tort duty to his contractual client in respect of the allegedly negligent design of foundations which it was claimed led to the eventual subsidence of the client's house.

7–123 **Damage to other property and the complex structure theory.** An illustration of liability for damage to other property resulting from a design defect is provided by *Baxall Securities Ltd v. Sheard Walshaw Partnership* [2001] P.N.L.R. 257, where an architect was held liable for water damage to property inside a building resulting from an inadequate roof design which could not reasonably have been detected by inspection. See above para. **7–23** and below, para. **8–133**.

NOTE 16. See *Payne v. John Setchell Ltd* [2002] P.N.L.R. 146, 183, where Humphrey Lloyd H.H.J. held that in the light of Lord Bridge's comments, the "complex structure theory exception is no longer tenable".

7–124 **Statutory consequences: Latent Damage Act 1986.** *Payne v. John Setchell Ltd* [2002] P.N.L.R. 146, 186, confirms that section 3 can only apply where the transferee of the property had a cause of action in tort at the time of transfer. Having a cause of action in contract is of no relevance.

7–125 **Statutory consequences: Defective Premises Act 1972.** *Payne v. John Setchell Ltd* [2002] P.N.L.R. 146, illustrates a situation in which subsequent acquirers of homes could have recovered under the Act against an engineer allegedly responsible for negligent design of the foundations but for the claim being barred by the 6 year period from completion.

(v) *Economic loss following physical damage to another's property*

The exclusionary rule. Note that an action in nuisance for the continuing impact of interference which commenced prior to the claimants acquisition of the property, is not precluded by this rule. See *Delaware Mansions Ltd v. Westminster City Council* [2001] 4 All E.R. 737. 7–126

3. Foreseeability and Remoteness

(b) *Remoteness: physical damage*

Kind of accident. NOTE 98. In *Jebson v. Ministry of Defence* [2000] 1 W.L.R 2055., the Court of Appeal applied *Jolley* in concluding that injury resulting from reckless activity rather than just stumbling, fell within the risk created by the defendant's failure to supervise drunken passengers. However, note the decision in *Darby v. National Trust* [2001] P.I.Q.R. P372, in which it was held that where there has been negligence in failing to warn of one danger on land but the visitor succumbs to a completely different one, the defendant may still escape liability on causation grounds. See above para. **2–66** and para. **3–54**; below para. **10–14** and para. **10–28**. 7–144

Impecuniosity. In *Alcoa Minerals of Jamaica Ltd v. Broderick* [2000] 3 W.L.R. 23, the Privy Council did not apply *Liesbosch* in a case where the plaintiff did not have the money to repair damage done by the defendant immediately, and steep inflation then put up the repair costs. *Liesbosch* was distinguished on the ground that in *Alcoa* there was only one head of damage, the cost of repair, whereas in *Liesbosch* the cost of hiring the replacement dredger was a separate head of damage from its replacement. See *Jones* (2000) P.N. 165. 7–149

NOTE 22. *Mattocks v. Mann* reported at [1993] R.T.R. 13. 7–150

(c) *Remoteness: pure economic loss*

Remoteness and the scope of the duty. Note 39. In *Cossey v. Lonnkvist* [2000] Lloyd's Rep. P.N. 885 at 888, Evans L.J. followed the view of Lord Hobhouse and treated the *Banque Bruxelles* rule as analogous to remoteness. 7–155

Non-recoverable and recoverable economic loss. The line between these two categories is illustrated by several recent professional negligence cases: see *post* para. **8–102**. 7–156— 7–157

Loss attributable to advice. The House of Lords in *Aneco Reinsurance Underwriting Ltd v. Johnson & Higgins Ltd* [2002] 1 Lloyd's Rep. 157, affirmed the decision of the Court of Appeal. Lord Millett at p. 190 said of Lord Hoffmann's distinction between information and advice: "This has been widely misunderstood. Lord Hoffmann was not distinguishing between a duty to provide information and a duty to give advice. That is a distinction without a difference, for the terms are interchangeable. He was distinguishing between a duty to provide particular information or advice on request and a duty to advise generally when it is left to the adviser to decide what matters he should consider. Even 7–158 where the defendant assumes responsibility for advising generally 'whether or not a course of action should be taken' it is still necessary to identify the particular course of action in question. Where the question is whether to enter into a particular transaction, it is necessary to identify the relevant transaction, for the defendant is not responsible for loss arising from any other transaction." The majority considered that the defendant brokers were responsible for failing to advising the claimants against entering the primary reinsurance transaction. Lord Millett dissented on the ground that the brokers duty was limited to securing secondary reinsurance for the claimants and did not extend to advising as to the merits of the primary transaction.

4. Breach of Duty

(b) *The criteria of reasonableness*

(i) *Objectivity*

7–167 **Sporting activity.** In *Caldwell v. Maguire and Fitzgerald* [2002] P.I.Q.R. P45, the Court of Appeal upheld the dismissal of a claim by a jockey that he had been injured in a race incident due to the careless riding of the defendants who had been found guilty of careless riding by the Jockey Club. The Court found that the trial judge had not applied a test of recklessness but what he had properly said was that *in practice*, given the circumstances, the threshold for liability was high. There would be no liability for errors of judgment, oversights or lapses of which any participant might be guilty in the context of a fast-moving contest. It was not possible to characterise momentary carelessness as negligence. The Jockey Club's finding of "careless riding" was relevant but not determinative of negligence.

(ii) *Balancing cost and benefit*

7–171 **The relevant factors.** *B (a child) v. London Borough of Camden* [2001] P.I.Q.R. P143, provides a good illustration of the weighing of the relevant factors. Nelson J. held the defendants not to be negligent in failing to lag central heating pipes against which a nine month old baby had become trapped with resulting burns. The cost of protection would have been substantial, the risk of such accidents was slight, and the primary responsibility for protecting the child rested with the parents.

In *Hatton v. Sutherland* [2002] 2 All E.R. 1, Hale L.J. considered the factors relevant to work stress cases (see *ante* para. **7–82**). These included the size and scope of the employer's operation, its resources, whether or not it is in the public sector and the demands of other employees.

(iii) *Community values*

7–187 **Common practice.** Note 70. *Adams v. Rhymney Valley District Council* is now reported at [2001] P.N.L.R. 68. Note that in *Adams* the Court of Appeal held that where a defendant followed one to two alternative common practices, it was not liable if the chosen practice resulted in injury. Sir Christopher Staughton noted that the particular defendant did not have professional qualifications but held that the *Bolam* test which protected professionals choosing between alternative courses of action, was "not the monopoly of the expert". Sedley L.J.

dissented on the ground that the defendant was negligent in not reflecting on the alternative courses and making a conscious choice. For Sedley L.J. the issue was simply one of causation: if the defendant had reflected would it have chosen the course that led to the injury? On the balance of probabilities, it would not have chosen this course and hence, it was liable. See the similar approach of Sedley L.J. in *J D Williams & Co. Ltd v. Michael Hyde & Associates Ltd* [2001] P.N.L.R. 8.

Note that in *Patel v. Daybells (a firm)* [2002] P.N.L.R. 125, Robert Walker L.J. giving the judgment of the Court of Appeal on facts somewhat similar to those in *Wong*, acknowledged that it established the principle that if "the profession exposes clients or patients to a foreseeable and avoidable risk, the practice may not be capable of being defended on rational grounds, and in those circumstances the fact that it is commonly followed will not exclude liability in negligence. However, he held the defendants not liable as they had shown 'the practice now routinely followed by English solicitors is one on which 'the experts have directed their minds to the question of comparative risks and benefits and have reached a defensible conclusion on the matter'."

(c) *Proof of carelessness*

Doctrine of *Res Ipsa loquitur*. In *J v. North Lincolnshire County Council* [2000] P.I.Q.R. 84, Henry L.J. described the maxim as "merely describing the state of the evidence from which it was proper to draw an inference of negligence". The Court of Appeal held that the inference could be drawn from the fact that a retarded eight year old had escaped from the defendant's primary school. The child was injured in a road accident some 1,000 metres from the school.

7–192

5. PARTICULAR SITUATIONS OF NEGLIGENCE LIABILITY

(a) *Highway accidents*

In *Larner v. Solihull Metropolitan Borough Council* [2001] P.I.Q.R. P248, Lord Woolf C.J. giving the judgment of the Court of Appeal, held that common law liability for failure to take safety measures, *e.g.* by providing warning signs, could only arise where an authority acted outside its discretion under section 39 of the Road Traffic Act 1988 to take appropriate measures to prevent accidents. This would be the case where an authority acted wholly unreasonably. On the facts, the failure to provided warning signs additional to the two "Give Way" signs at the mouth of a junction, was not unreasonable.

7–208

Dangers. See *Kane v. New Forest District Council* [2002] 3 All E.R. 914, where *Stovin* was distinguished on the ground that the defendant planning authority in *Kane* had created the source of danger since it had required the construction of the footpath and knew that the sightlines to the road made it dangerous to use.

7–210

(b) *Transport accidents*

Ships and aircraft. In *Disley v. Levine* [2001] P.I.Q.R. P159, Hunt J. held that a paraglider was not an "aircraft" within the meaning of the Carriage of Air Acts

7–214

7–214

(Application of Provisions) Order 1967 and hence, a trainee's claim resulting from a crash allegedly caused by the negligence of the instructor, was not subject to the two year limitation period imposed by that order. Alternatively, Henry J. considered that the claimant had a common law claim in her capacity as a trainee rather than a passenger.

Note that the carrier's liability for bodily injury or death sustained in international air carriage is governed by the Carriage by Air Act 1961. See further para. **29–99**. In *Morris v. KLM Royal Dutch Airlines* [2002] 1 All E.R. (Comm) 385, the House of Lords held that psychiatric injury itself was not a bodily injury within the terms of the Act.

(c) *Employment accidents*

7–218 **Safe fellow employees.** See *Waters v. Commissioner of Police of the Metropolis* [2000] 1 W.L.R. 1607, where the House of Lords treating a police officer's status as analogous to an employee, considered it arguable that there was a breach of duty where an employer knew that acts done by employees during their employment might cause physical or mental harm to a particular fellow employee and did nothing to supervise or prevent such acts when he had the power to do so.

7–224 **Risks.** In *Hatton v. Sutherland* [2002] 2 All E.R. 1, Hale L.J. giving the judgment of the Court of Appeal, reviewed the area of law and the nature of the risk against which it was reasonable to expect the employer to guard. See *ante* para. **7–171** and **7–82**.

7–225 **Supervision.** See *Parker v. PFC Flooring Supplies Ltd* [2001] P.I.Q.R. P115, where the small size of the employer's operation was a factor in leading the court to conclude that it could have reasonably foreseen employees making inspections of the roof and should have warned employees not to do this.

7–227 **Statutory duties.** Statutory duties may well be construed as imposing absolute obligations: see *Stark v. The Post Office* [2000] P.I.Q.R. P105.

(d) *Responsibility for children*

7–230 **Schools.** See *Phelps v. Hillingdon London Borough Council* [2000] 3 W.L.R. 776, where the House of Lords held that an educational psychologist employed by a local authority could owe a duty of care to a child who had been referred to the psychologist. The reduction of a child's level of achievement as a result of failure to diagnose dyslexia and to take appropriate action, was regarded as a form of "personal injury".

NOTE 44. See also *J v. North Lincolnshire County Council* [2000] P.I.Q.R. 84.

7–231 **Sports supervision.** See *C (a child) v. W. School* [2002] P.I.Q.R. P134, where Leveson J. held a school liable for failing to take care to prevent a child skiing off-piste and suffering injury. The child had merely been reprimanded when previously seen off-piste. The child's conduct showed he could not be trusted and in failing to impose a substantial sanction, the teacher had failed in his duty of care.

See also *Watson v. British Boxing Board of Control Limited* [2001] 2 W.L.R. 1256, where Lord Phillips held that a sports regulatory body could owe a duty of care to its members who relied on it for provision of appropriate medical facilities. See further para. **7–22**.

CHAPTER 8

PROFESSIONAL LIABILITY

	PARA.
■ 1. General considerations	8–01
■ 2. Medicine and allied professions	8–24
(a) Consent to treatment	8–25
(b) Medical negligence	8–35
■ 3. Law	8–70
■ 4. Surveyors	8–109
■ 5. Architects and consulting engineers	8–132
■ 6. Finance	8–143

Major developments since the last edition include (a) a series of decisions setting the precise limits to *McFarlane v. Tayside Health Board* [2000] 2 A.C. 59 as it affects the recovery of damages for failing to prevent pregnancy (or diagnose it once it is a fact); (b) *Re B* [2002] 2 All E.R. 449 on the capacity of a sane patient to refuse treatment; (c) *Merrett v. Babb* [2001] 3 W.L.R. on the personal liability of the employed professional; (d) *Farley v. Skinner (No. 2)* [2001] 3 W.L.R. 899 on the recovery of damages for disappointment and vexation; and (e) further decisions on the measure of damages available against negligent solicitors since the *South Australia Asset Management* case [1997] A.C. 191. **8a**

1. GENERAL CONSIDERATIONS

Add new paragraph after **8–06**:

Duty of care: personal liability of employed professional. Normally the victim of negligence on the part of an employed professional will sue the latter's employer: he has the deeper pocket, and in addition is more likely to be covered by insurance. But if this is not possible (for example, where the employer is bankrupt or the employee acted outside the scope of his employment), how far is it possible to sue the employee personally? **8–06A**

There is little doubt that an employed professional will be liable when he causes physical damage or injury in the course of his employment.[27a] With economic loss, such as that arising from negligent advice, the point is more difficult. As a general rule, the courts have been disinclined to make an employee personally liable under the rule in *Hedley Byrne & Co. Ltd v. Heller & Partners Ltd*,[27b] saying that normally such a person is not to be regarded as accepting responsibility for what he says.[27c] In *Merrett v. Babb*,[27d] an employed valuer who

---

[27a] *e.g., Fairline Shipping Corp. v. Adamson* [1975] Q.B. 180.
[27b] [1964] A.C. 465.
[27c] *Williams v. Natural Life Health Foods Ltd* [1998] 1 W.L.R. 830.
[27d] [2001] 3 W.L.R. 1. See too *Jarvis & Sons Ltd v. Castle Wharf Developments Ltd* [2001] EWCA 19.

negligently over-valued a house was held personally liable to the client, his employer having in the meanwhile became bankrupt and failed to maintain the firm's professional indemnity cover. The valuer had undertaken the appraisal as a qualified professional: he well knew that the client would rely on what he said: and this, said a majority of the Court of Appeal, was sufficient to engender an acceptance of responsibility.

On the other hand, *Merrett v. Babb* is very much the exception rather than the rule. In *Bradford & Bingley plc v. Hayes*[27e] the facts were similar, save that the claimants were mortgage lenders and the employer was a not a firm, but a limited company of which the defendant was a director. These factors, it was held, sufficed to tip the balance against liability, particularly since to allow the defendant to be sued personally would (it was felt) indirectly defeat the whole idea of limited liability.

8–13 **Duties to clients and others.** *Johnson v. Gore Wood* has been upheld on the point in the text by the HL: see [2001] 2 W.L.R. 72. See too *Barings plc & Anor v. Coopers & Lybrand* [2002] P.N.L.R. 321.

Day v. Cook has been upheld in the CA: [2001] P.N.L.R. 755.

8–14 **Excluding a duty of care.** On excluding professional liability, see too *Killick v. PriceWaterhouseCoopers* [2001] P.N.L.R. 1 (validity of accountants' limitation clause discussed), and also *Casson v. Ostley PJ Ltd* [2001] B.L.R. 126.

8–20 **Immunities from suit: public policy.** On the immunity of witnesses in court, see too the Irish decision in *O'K. (E.) v. K. (D.)* [2001] 1 I.R. 636 (plaintiff's marriage declared null on basis of opinion of psychiatrist as to her mental state when marriage celebrated: no action against psychiatrist).

8–21 **Equitable obligations: breach of fiduciary duty.** A professional may be liable for breach of fiduciary duty in respect of a transaction entered into after the other party ceased to be his client. See *Longstaff v. Birtles* [2002] 1 W.L.R. 470 (solicitor guilty of breach of duty in persuading ex-client, whom he knew well, to enter into disastrous business in which he was involved).

On breach of fiduciary duty, see too *Leeds & Holbeck Building Society v. Arthur & Cole* [2002] P.N.L.R. 78, confirming the requirement of some element of conscious wrongdoing. See generally below, Ch. 28.

2. MEDICINE AND ALLIED PROFESSIONS

(a) *Consent to Treatment*

8–25 **Adults: refusal of consent.** See now *Re B* [2002] 2 All E.R. 449, where a paralysed patient exercised a clear and unclouded judgment that she wished treatment to stop, with the result that her life would end. Butler-Sloss P. stated that her wishes were paramount and ordered that the hospital should be at liberty to discontinue treatment. She also awarded damages of £100 in respect of the

---

[27e] Unreported, July 25, 2001.

treatment hitherto furnished against her wishes. In doing so, her Ladyship stated the following principles:

1. A patient was presumed to have the mental capacity to make decisions to refuse treatment.
2. If mental capacity was not in issue and the patient, having been given the relevant information and offered the available options, chose to refuse treatment, that decision had to be respected. The patient's best interests were irrelevant.
3. If there was doubt about the mental capacity of the patient, that doubt had to be resolved as soon as possible by normal medical procedures.
4. While the question of capacity was being resolved, the patient had to be cared for in accordance with the judgment of the doctors as to his best interests.
5. The question of mental capacity was separate from the nature of the decision made by the patient, however grave the consequences.
6. If disagreement still existed about competence, the patient had to be fully informed of the steps being taken and made a part of the process.
7. If the hospital was faced with an irresoluble dilemma, further steps had to be taken as a matter of priority.
8. If competence was clear but the doctors on the scene were unable to carry out the patient's wishes, other doctors had to be found who would.
9. If all appropriate steps to seek independent assistance had failed, the hospital should not hesitate to apply to the High Court or consult the Official Solicitor.

NOTE 44. See too *Re A.K. (Medical Treatment) (Consent)* [2001] 1 F.L.R. 129 (continuing to ventilate patient without consent unlawful).

The viable foetus. NOTE 53: See Scott (2000) 20 O.J.L.S. 407.   **8–28**

Mentally incapacitated patients. Although the *Bolam* test governs the question what is "good medical practice", whether treatment is in the patient's best interests is apparently a matter for the court alone to determine. It follows that *Bolam* is irrelevant here: *Re L. (S.) (Sterilisation)* [2000] 1 Lloyd's Rep. Med 339.   **8–33**

(b) *Medical negligence*

Medical negligence: the *Bolam* test. NOTE 1. *Shakoor v. Kang Situ* now reported at [2001] 1 W.L.R. 410.   **8–35**

For further discussion of whether a particular body of opinion is respectable and hence within *Bolam*, see the veterinary case of *Calver v. Westwood Veterinary Practice* [2001] Lloyd's Rep. Med. 20.   **8–37**

Failure to warn: causation. *Chester v. Afshar* [2002] EWCA Civ 724 deals with the problem of the patient who has not been warned of a risk inherent in an   **8–43**

8–43   CHAPTER 8—PROFESSIONAL LIABILITY

operation, but who would nevertheless even if properly advised have undergone the same operation, carrying the same risk, at some later date (see NOTE 33 in the text). The Court of Appeal concluded that the majority's reasoning in *Chappell v. Hart* (1998) 72 A.L.J.R. 1344 was correct, and hence that the patient could recover.

8–44   **Breach of duty: general.** Note too *L v. Robinson* [2000] 3 N.Z.L.R. 499 (improper sexual relationship with vulnerable patient makes doctor liable in negligence at common law).

8–47   **Breach of duty: diagnosis.** NOTE 56. See too the decision of the Supreme Court of Ireland in *Collins v. Mid-Western Health Board* [2000] 1 I.R. 154.

8–52   **Proving negligence.** On *res ipsa loquitur* in the medical context, see too *Gray v. Southampton & SW Hampshire HA* (2001) 57 B.M.L.R. 148.

8–57   **Antenatal injury and "wrongful life".** In Canada, as in England, it has been decided that no claim lies for "wrongful life": *Lacroix (Guardian) v. Dominique* (2001) 202 D.L.R. (4th) 121.

8–58   **Failed sterilisation.** The bar in *McFarlane*'s case on damages for the costs of raising a healthy unwanted child applies equally to other loss connected with child-rearing, such as income foregone: *Greenfield v. Irwin* [2000] 1 W.L.R. 1437. Nor, the CA has now held, can it be circumvented by attempting to reclassify unwanted pregnancy as a form of personal injury: *Greenfield v. Flather* [2001] Lloyd's Rep. Med. 143.

NOTE 24. It is now clear that *McFarlane* does not apply with full force to handicapped children. Where medical negligence gives rise to an unwanted birth, and the child is born handicapped, the mother can recover for the extra costs of raising a disabled child, though not for the ordinary costs associated with child-rearing. See *Parkinson v. St James & Seacroft University NHS Trust* [2001] 3 W.L.R. 376, CA (following *Hardman v. Amin* [2001] P.N.L.R. 303 (Henriques J.)). For these purposes, moreover, it seems to be enough that the child was in fact born handicapped. The fact that the defendant who negligently failed to prevent the birth of the child had no reason to foresee that it might be born abnormal is irrelevant to recovery: see *Groom v. Selby* [2002] Lloyd's Rep. Med. 1.

Furthermore, the Court of Appeal has now decided that what is sauce for the goose is sauce for the gander. Where the parent whose sterilisation has gone wrong is herself disabled, she is entitled to recover for the extra costs of child-rearing caused by her own disability even if the child itself is healthy: *Rees v. Darlington Memorial Hospital NHS Trust* [2002] EWCA Civ 88.

8–62   **Liability of other allied professions.** For the duty owed by the police as surrogate providers of emergency medical attention, see *Hardaker v. Newcastle HA* [2002] Lloyd's Rep. Med. 512.

NOTE 52. The decision in *X (Minors) v. Bedfordshire CC* [1995] 2 A.C. 633 has indeed been held to violate the ECHR, but only §§ 3 and 13 and not § 6: see *Z & Ors v. United Kingdom* (2002) 34 E.H.R.R. 42. The exoneration under § 6 is significant, since it may well limit the effect of *Osman v. United Kingdom* [1999] 1 F.L.R. 193 to cases where immunities are conferred on defendants *ratione personae* rather than *ratione materiae*. This seems to be confirmed by *Matthews v. Ministry of Defence* [2002] 3 All E.R. 513, holding that substantive, as against procedural, derogations from liability in tort are not within Art. 6. See too *T.P. v. United Kingdom* (2002) 34 E.H.R.R. 42, concerning *M (A Minor) v. Newham LBC*, another case decided with *X (Minors) v. Bedfordshire CC*. See below, para 12–74, and also Gearty (2002) 65 M.L.R. 87.

Health authorities and professionals not employed by them. NOTE 63. But note *Elliott v. Bickerstaff* [1999] 2 N.S.W.L.R. 214 (surgeon personally owes no non-delegable duty).   **8–64**

Causation: general. For the position where questions of causation depend on the hypothetical later actions of the same defendant, see *Smith v. NHS Litigation Authority* [2001] Lloyd's Rep. Med. 90 (assumption that defendant would have shown reasonable care, but no more).   **8–65**

Causation: loss of a chance of recovery. Damages for loss of a chance of recovery may be recoverable, despite *Hotson v. East Berkshire H.A.* [1987] A.C. 750, where the claimant's prospects of a cure depend on the hypothetical actions of a third party. See *Smith v. NHS Litigation Authority* [2001] Lloyd's Rep. Med. 90 (following *Allied Maples Group Ltd v. Simmons & Simmons* [1995] 1 W.L.R. 1602).   **8–67**

Damages. See now *Briody v. St Helens HA*, [2002] 2 W.L.R. 394 (claimant negligently rendered sterile: no damages for cost of commercial surrogacy: illegal in U.K.).   **8–69**

Also, see *Farrell v. Avon HA* [2001] Lloyd's Rep. Med. 458 (father has claim for nervous shock as primary victim on being falsely told baby dead and given wrong deceased infant to cuddle).

3. LAW

Duties to clients. NOTE 34. *Gregory v. Shepherds* now reported at [2000] P.N.L.R. 769.   **8–75**

NOTE 55. As well as *Worby v. Rosser* [2000] P.N.L.R. 140, see *Gibbons v. Nelsons* [2000] P.N.L.R. 734 (failure to warn that will had effect of exercising power of appointment: no duty to those entitled in default of exercise).   **8–78**

NOTE 56. On the relation between the claims of the estate and the would-be legatee, see also *Corbett v. Bond Pearce* [2001] P.N.L.R. 739 (will invalidly executed: solicitors settle claim by would-be legatees: no further liability for estate's costs incurred in probate litigation, since this would merely create windfall gain for those taking in default).

Extent of liability to third parties: other cases. See too *Dean v. Allin & Watts* [2001] P.N.L.R. 921; [2001] 2 Lloyd's Rep. 249 (solicitor instructed by borrower to arrange secured lending held by CA to owe duty to ensure security effective).   **8–80**

Liability under the Supreme Court Act 1981, s.51. In *Medcalf v. Mardell* [2002] 3 All E.R. 721 the HL extensively reviewed the law relating to wasted costs orders. They confirmed, as had always been assumed previously, that an   **8–83**

8–83

order under s.53 could be sought by a party against the lawyers for the other side, and that the jurisdiction was available against barristers whether or not their neglect arose out of work done in court. They also said, importantly, that where a lawyer would be prevented from defending himself properly because of his client's failure to waive privilege, there should be no order. *Medcalf* continued the earlier decision in *Brown v. Bennett (No. 2)* [2002] 1 W.L.R. 713, where Neuberger J. held in addition that the applicant must prove, on a balance of probabilities, that any costs he wishes to pass on were incurred as a result of the lawyer's improper conduct. In particular, there is no room for a partial award based on the chance that those costs would have been saved based on the analogy of *Allied Maples Group Ltd v. Simmons & Simmons* [1995] 1 W.L.R. 1602 (see p. 730).

However, an important limitation limitation was placed on s.51 by *Byrne v. Sefton Health Authority* [2002] 1 W.L.R. 775. There it was held that dilatory solicitors who had ceased to act for the claimant before the latter issued proceedings were not amenable to the wasted costs jurisdiction. They were not in the circumstances persons exercising a "right to conduct litigation" within s.51(13). Nevertheless, a person who is exercising a "right to conduct litigation" and hence is amenable to the s.51 jurisdiction presumably cannot escape liability simply because the whole or part of his improper conduct took place before proceedings were issued.

On improper conduct for purposes of wasted costs orders, see too *Medcalf v. Mardell* [2002] 3 All E.R. 721 (not improper to allege fraud on basis of privileged communications); *Snowden v. Ministry of Defence* [2001] EWCA Civ 1524 (solicitors simply failing to turn up for hearing).

See too *Harley v. McDonald* [2001] 2 W.L.R. 1749.

8–84   NOTE 85. But note now *Medcalf v. Mardell* [2001] 3 All E.R. 721 (counsel alleging fraud; wasted costs order inappropriate where counsel had credible evidence but could not use it owing to clients' refusal to waive priviledge).

8–85   **Breach of duty.** NOTE 91. See too *UCB Corporate Services Ltd v. Clyde & Co.* [2000] P.N.L.R. 841.

8–87   **Proving negligence.** *Dean v. Allin & Watts* has been upheld on appeal on this point: *Dean v. Allin & Watts* [2001] P.N.L.R. 921.

8–88   NOTE 99. See too *Patel v. Daybells* [2001] P.N.L.R. 195.

8–89   NOTE 7. See too *McIlgorm v. Bell Lamb* [2001] P.N.L.R. 642.

8–91   **Conflicts of interest.** On conflicts of interest, see too *Halewood International Ltd v. Addleshaw Booth & Co.* [2000] P.N.L.R. 788 (risk of leakage may be adequately prevented where solicitors in one firm work in separate premises).

8–93   **Solicitor acting on counsel's advice.** Other cases where solicitors have been held negligent despite having relied on counsel's advice include *Green v. Collyer-Bristow* [1999] Lloyd's Rep. P.N. 798 (conveyancer overlooking Law of Property (Miscellaneous Provisions) Act 1989); *Green v. Hancocks* [2001] P.N.L.R. 286 (elementary point on title to sue); and *Bond v. Livingstone & Co.,* [2001] P.N.L.R. 692 (simple limitation issue). Similarly, too, where counsel's misleading advice is due to the solicitors' own inadequate instructions to him: *Estill v. Cowling, Swift & Kitchen* [2000] Lloyd's Rep. P.N. 378.

Specific duties: the duty to advise. On the duty to advise on a transaction, see too *UCB Corporate Services Ltd v. Clyde & Co.* [2000] P.N.L.R. 841 (lenders' security ineffective under Statute of Frauds 1677: City solicitors who advised them on it understandably held negligent). 8–94

NOTE 37. See too *Jenmain Builders Ltd v. Steed & Steed* [2000] P.N.L.R. 616 (duty to warn purchaser client that he was in "contract race").

Specific duties: duty to provide information. The principle in *National Home Loans Corp'n plc v. Giffen Couch & Arthur* [1998] 1 W.L.R. 207 was applied by the CA in *Hilton v. Barker Booth & Eastwood* [2002] EWCA Civ 723. A solicitor acted for a party to a property deal that went disastrously wrong. Although he had previously represented the counterparty in criminal proceedings, he was held to have been under no duty to tell his client about the counterparty's record. 8–98

Specific duties: duty to take care in carrying out transaction. In processing a transaction a solicitor must follow up failure to produce relevant information: *Cottingham v. Attey Bower* [2000] P.N.L.R. 557 (vendor provides no evidence of planning consent for extension: in fact none granted: purchaser's solicitor negligent not to enquire further). 8–99

A solicitor drafting documents owes a duty to his client not only to make sure they adequately protect the client's interests, but also to draft them with sufficient precision to prevent disputes arising at all, as far as possible. See *Queen Elizabeth's School Blackburn Ltd v. Banks Wilson* [2002] P.N.L.R. 300 (imprecise restrictive covenant binding claimants' land: claimants put to expense as a result of threat of proceedings by owner of dominant tenement: expenses recoverable).

Conduct of litigation. On the measure of damages for bungled litigation, Higgins J. in the Northern Ireland High Court has held that losses flowing from the claimant's cash-flow due to failure to recover sums due to him are on principle recoverable, provided that the solicitors had reason to know of his financial circumstances: *Macmahon v. Doran & Co.* [2001] P.N.L.R. 35 (upheld on other grounds in the NI Court of Appeal: [2002] Lloyd's Rep. P.N. 93). 8–100

NOTE 81. See too *Aylwen v. Taylor Joynson Garrett* [2001] EWCA Civ 1171 (nominal damages for loss of property subject to negative equity). 8–101

Causation. The text at NOTE 88, that damages for misadvice by a solicitor are limited to the consequence of that advice being wrong, has now been upheld in two cases. *Lloyds Bank plc v. Crosse & Crosse* [2001] P.N.L.R. 34, buyers' solicitors failing to spot a troublesome restrictive covenant were liable only for the amount by which this depreciated the land concerned. Similarly where a purchaser's solicitor failed to advise that an extension had been illegally built, damages were limited to the loss due to the lack of planning consent but no more: *Cottingham v. Attey Bower* [2000] P.N.L.R. 557. However, a distinction has, it seems, to be drawn here. Where the misadvice does not go to the value of the property, and it is also the case that, had the solicitor advised properly, the lender would not have lent at all, then the solicitor is liable for the whole loss. So in the 8–102

Scottish case of *Newcastle Building Society v. Paterson Robertson & Graham*, 2001 S.C. 734, [2001] P.N.L.R. 870, solicitors who failed to advise that the borrowers owned other properties in addition to the mortgaged property and hence that the loan was a doubtful proposition were held liable for the whole loss when the borrowers defaulted. *Cf.* too *Leeds & Holbeck Building Society v. Alex Morison & Co.* 2001 S.C.L.R. 41, [2001] P.N.L.R. 346 and *Portman Building Society v. Bevan Ashford* in the text.

8–104   **Bungled litigation: measure of damages.** On damages for bungled litigation, see too *Harrison v. Bloom Camillin* [2001] P.N.L.R. 195, 222, where Neuberger J. summarised the principles in the text. He then went on to make three further points.

First, before he can recover anything for the loss of a chance of success, the claimant must prove that but for the defendant's negligence he would have persevered in taking proceedings. He must, moreover, show this on a balance of probabilities.

Secondly, in evaluating the claimant's hypothetical chances of recovery account has to be taken of the possibility that the action might have been settled.

Thirdly, a "loss of chance" claim is not ruled out even where the dispute was one of law rather than fact. Nevertheless, in such cases courts should normally decide the point there and then and make an award accordingly: only seldom will it be appropriate to speculate on the chances that the hypothetical court would have got it wrong.

In *Hunter v. Earnshaw* [2001] P.N.L.R. 982, the claimant's action for personal injury was struck out for want of prosecution owing to the negligence of his solicitors. Subsequently his condition deteriorated. Garland J. held that the measure of damages was the value of the claimant's claim at the time it was struck out (*i.e.* before the deterioration), plus the amount of any costs for which he was liable as a result of the abortive proceedings.

In many cases the damages that the claimant has lost owing to his solicitors' negligence would have been reduced by the amount of any social security benefits received. But, assuming a discount falls to be applied to the award against the solicitors, is this discount applied to the net claim (thus *de facto* reducing also the amount of social security benefits to be deducted) or to the gross claim, with the social security benefits then being deducted in full? An Australian court has plumped for the former solution: *Green v. Berry* [2001] Qd. R. 605.

NOTE 97. The possibility of 100 per cent recovery is confirmed by *Harrison v. Bloom Camillin* [2001] P.N.L.R. 195, 225.

8–105   **Remoteness of damage.** See too *Parry v. Edwards Geldard* [2001] P.N.L.R. 1032 (right of pre-emption over farmland lost because of solicitors' negligence: no liability for loss of associated milk quota, since too remote).

8–107   **Non-pecuniary loss.** A solicitor will not in the ordinary event be liable for distress suffered by his client as the result of mishandled litigation, in the absence of some indication that the litigation had as its object the client's piece of mind. Hence a client whose commercial litigation was bungled had no claim: *Johnson v. Gore Wood* [2001] 2 W.L.R. 72. Nor did a client whose matrimonial proceedings were mishandled in respect of financial provision, even though as a result he might have suffered distress from being deprived of his home: *Channon v. Lindley Johnstone (A Firm)* [2002] P.N.L.R. 884.

A solicitor whose negligence causes his client to be imprisoned for a crime he did not commit may be liable to the client for psychiatric illness suffered as a result, provided that that illness was reasonably foreseeable to a solicitor of reasonable competence in that position: *McLoughlin v. Grovers* [2002] P.N.L.R. 516.

4. SURVEYORS

Duties to clients. For the personal liability of an employed valuer, see *Merrett v. Babb* [2001] P.N.L.R. 658.   8–109

Liability to mortgagees and purchasers. In *Bank of Scotland v. Fuller Peiser* [2002] P.N.L.R. 289, surveyors provided a valuation of a hotel to a prospective purchaser. At the purchasers' request this report was made available to the purchasers' mortgage lender, who lent in reliance on it. The valuation was in fact excessive; the purchasers became insolvent, and the lenders sold the hotel at considerable loss. Lord Eassie in the Court of Session thought that the surveyors would on principle have been liable to the lenders, but in the event decided that any such liability was excluded by a statement in the report that it was prepared for the benefit of the purchaser alone, and that no liability was accepted to anybody else.   8–111

NOTE 22. But see *Ta Ho Ma Pty Ltd v. Allen* (1999) 47 N.S.W.L.R. 1 (mortgagee's claim against valuer fails since reliance unforeseeable).

NOTE 23. See too the Scotch decision in *Howes v. Crombie* [2001] P.N.L.R. 60.

Exclusion of duty. The Scots decision in *Bank of Scotland v. Fuller Peiser* [2002] P.N.L.R. 289 involved a mirror image of the situation in *Smith v. Eric S. Bush.* A valuation was provided to a purchaser containing a clause to the effect that it was for her benefit alone and that no liability would be accepted to anyone else. It was passed on to a mortgage lender, who relied on it. *Held,* by Lord Eassie, that (1) the clause was effective in its terms to prevent any duty of care arising to the lender, and (2) in the light of the lender's status as an experienced mortgage lender, this exclusion did not run foul of the Unfair Contract Terms Act 1977.   8–113

Surveyors' negligence: damages. On the effect of subsequent events on surveyors' damages, see *Devine v. Jefferys & Anor* [2001] P.N.L.R. 407 (house overvalued: buyers got into difficulties and surrendered house to mortgagees in settlement of mortgage debt: since negative equity at all times, held no loss suffered).   8–126

In *Smith v. Peter North & Partners* [2002] P.N.L.R. 274 surveyors asked to report on an equestrian property, and specifically on the cost of any repairs necessary to bring the premises up to the purchasers' standards, negligently failed to notice defects relevant to the latter instruction. Nevertheless, at the time of purchase the market value of the premises was £10,000 more than the price the purchasers paid. The Court of Appeal held that the claimants had suffered no recoverable loss, and in particular that they could not claim the expense they had

8–126   CHAPTER 8—PROFESSIONAL LIABILITY

been put to in bringing the property up to scratch. This seems, with respect, an ungenerous decision in view of the specific instructions given. *Quaere* also, whether the reasoning might fall to be reconsidered in the light of the House of Lords' decision in *Farley v. Skinner (No. 2)* [2001] 3 W.L.R. 899 (below, in this *Supplement* at para. **8–130**).

8–130   **Personal injury, inconvenience and distress.** The decision in *Farley v. Skinner (No. 2)* has been reversed by the House of Lords: see [2001] 3 W.L.R. 899, where it was held that where a surveyor is specifically instructed to report on aircraft noise, he may be liable for distress caused to a purchaser as a result of the surveyor's failure to make proper investigations. An award of £10,000, though regarded as high by Lords Steyn and Clyde, was upheld. However, it seems to have been accepted that specific instruction was necessary, Lords Steyn, Clyde, Hutton and apparently Lord Scott saying that no such damages were available in an "ordinary" surveyor's contract (see pp. 906, 915, 921, 927). It was, said Lord Steyn, sufficient to take the case out of the general rule precluding such damages if one of the objects of the contract between surveyor and client was the protection of the client from distress (see pp. 909–910).

In addition, all four of their Lordships who gave separate judgments said that distress which affected the senses, such as large amounts of noise, counted as physical inconvenience, which was recoverable in any case, provided it was not too remote. In the present case they would, it seems, have been prepared to allow the appeal on this ground as well.

It seems that *Farley* was accepted by all sides as a case turning on contractual principles. But it seems a fair inference that the same rules will be applied to al surveyors' negligence cases, whether brought in contract or tort.

See too *Hoadley v. Edwards* [2001] P.N.L.R. 964 (£5,000 for being forced to live on a virtual building site).

5. ARCHITECTS AND CONSULTING ENGINEERS

8–133   **Duties to third parties.** It seems an architect's liability in tort for physical damage caused by misdesign is limited to cases where there is no reasonable likelihood of intermediate inspection, thus approximating his position to that of a manufacturer of goods (see below, paras **9–29** *et seq.*): *Baxall Securities Ltd v. Sheard Walshaw Partnership* [2001] P.N.L.R. 257. For what counts as damages to "other premises" see *Payne v. Setchell Ltd* [2002] P.N.L.R. 146 (adjoining cottages built on a bad concrete slab are a single unit for tort purposes).

8–134   See too *Payne v. Setchell Ltd*, March 16, 2001.

See too the Scottish decision in *Howes v. Crombie* [2001] P.N.L.R. 60.

NOTE 54. Although *Birse Construction Ltd v. Haiste* regarded it as arguable that an architect involved in a project owed a duty to building contractors even though not in contractual privity with them, a New Zealand court has come to the opposite conclusion: see *Turton & Co. Ltd v. Kerslake & Partners* [2000] 3 N.Z.L.R. 406.

8–137   **Breach of duty: design and supervision.** See too, on architects' duties, *Harris v. Leech* (2000) 16 Const. L.J. 1, and *Payne v. Setchell Ltd* [2002] P.N.L.R. 146 (defective design of concrete raft).

[72]

On the temporal dimension of an architect's duty to advise, see *New Islington & Hackney HA v. Pollard Thomas & Edwards* [2001] B.L.R. 74 (architect normally *functus officio* from practical completion, and hence unlikely to be under duty to advise later re defects).

NOTE 62. See too *Bellefield Computer Services Ltd v. Turner & Sons Ltd (No. 2)*, November 9, 2001 (those involved in designing premises entitled to assume contractors will act competently and seek further instruction where necessary).

Breach of duty: negligent certification. See too *Payne v. Setchell* [2002] P.N.L.R. 146.   8–140

Liability under the Defective Premises Act 1972. For an example of liability under the Defective Premises Act 1972, see *Payne v. Setchell Ltd* [2002] P.N.L.R. 146 (though the claim there was statute-barred).   8–141

Damages. Although there may be a claim for the cost of repairs necessitated by an architect's incompetence, this will not apply where the claimant in fact has no intention of carrying out any such repairs. In such a case the "diminution in value" rule is likely to apply. See *Nordic Holdings Ltd v. Mott McDonald Ltd* (2001) 77 Con. L.R. 88.   8–142

6. FINANCE

Accountants and auditors: duties to third parties. Where auditors' reports are required in order to prevent a particular type of loss, a duty of care is likely to be owed to those suffering that loss. Thus in *Law Society v. KPMG Peat Marwick* [2000] P.N.L.R. 831 auditors to a firm of solicitors (whom the firm was bound to employ under the relevant practice rules) failed to notice that its clients were being defrauded by the partners, thus facilitating further defalcations. They were held to have owed a duty of care to the Law Society, who by long-standing arrangements had to accept liability to the defrauded victims. And in New Zealand, auditors in a similar position have been held to owe a duty to the duped clients themselves: *Price Waterhouse v. Kwan* [2000] 3 N.Z.L.R. 39.   8–145

On similar reasoning, where assets are sold at a price to be fixed by valuation the accountants performing the valuation may owe duties to either party: *Killick v. PriceWaterhouseCoopers* [2001] P.N.L.R. 1. See too *Trustees Executors & Agency Co. of NZ v. Price Waterhouse* [2000] P.N.L.R. 673 (auditors' liability to bondholders).

The duties of auditors to a group were considered by Evans-Lombe J. in *Barings plc v. Coopers & Lybrand* [2002] P.N.L.R. 321. Allegedly as a result of failings by the group auditors, Barings' Singapore subsidiaries suffered massive losses when an employee engaged in a massive illegitimate trading spree, which he persuaded the English parent company to bankroll by enormous cash injections. Evans-Lombe J. held that the subsidiaries' losses could be recovered only if (a) the claim arose from a type of transaction that was foreseeable to the auditors; (b) the auditor should have contemplated that its advice would be relied on to prevent losses arising from that type of transaction; and (c) it could be inferred that the auditor had accepted responsibility to protect the claimant from losses of that type. These factors not being shown, the action was struck out.

8–151 **Damages.** On the measure of damages available against incompetent accountants, see now the troublesome Australian decision in *Pilmer v. Duke Group Ltd* (2001) 75 A.L.J.R. 1067. Acting on bad advice from accountants, the plaintiff company took over another company, paying most of the price with shares in itself. Despite the fact that the accountants had been at fault and the target company was worthless, a majority of the High Court of Australia held that the plaintiff had suffered no loss, since the issue of shares as such had cost it nothing. *Sed quaere*. If shares could have been issued for cash but are not, has not the company suffered a loss, in the shape of an opportunity cost, in issuing them? See Nolan & Prentice (2002) 118 L.Q.R. 180.

CHAPTER 9

PRODUCT LIABILITY AND CONSUMER PROTECTION

	PARA.
■ 3. Negligence	9–08
(a) Generally	9–08
■ 4. The Consumer Protection Act 1987, Pt 1(a)	9–37

The most important developments since the last edition are the seminal decision of Burton J. in *A v. National Blood Authority* [2001] 3 All E.R. 289, on the interpretation of the concept of a "defective product" within the Consumer Protection Act 1987, and the discussion in the *Britvic* litigation (*Bacardi-Martini Beverages Ltd v. Thomas Hardy Packaging Ltd* [2002] 1 Lloyd's Rep. 62) of what amounts to damage to property other than the defective product itself. **9a**

3. NEGLIGENCE

(a) *Generally*

Liability of those undertaking quality control and certification. The chances of a successful action against certification authorities are reduced as a result of *Smith v. Secretary of State for Health*, *The Times*, March 11, 2002 (no common law duty in Secretary of State, through Committee on Safety of Medicines, to pass on warnings re dangers attaching to aspirin in certain circumstances). **9–14**

For what damage? On the damages claimable in respect of a defective product, see the Australian decision in *A.P.Q. v. Commonwealth Serum Laboratories Ltd* [1999] 3 V.R. 633 (worry caused, and medical treatment necessitated, by fact that defective serum *might* have infected plaintiff). **9–17**

"Other property": components fitted by owner. Although there is little doubt as to tortious liability where components are added to a product by the owner and then damage that product, matters are less clear where components are used to make a completely new product and as a result of one of them being defective the resulting product is also defective. The point was left open by Tomlinson J. in *Britvic Soft Drinks Ltd v. Messer U.K. Ltd*, [2002] Lloyd's Rep. 20 (carbon dioxide contaminated with benzene incorporated in fizzy drinks by manufacturer). In later litigation arising out of the same facts it was answered in the negative: *Bacardi-Martini Beverages Ltd v. Thomas Hardy Packaging Ltd* [2002] 1 Lloyd's Rep. 62. **9–20**

Failure to warn. Unsurprisingly, it has been held that there is no duty to warn of a patently obvious risk, such as being scalded by hot tea or coffee in a fast food outlet: *B (A Child) v. McDonald's Ltd* [2002] EWHC (QB) 409. **9–25**

4. THE CONSUMER PROTECTION ACT 1987, PT 1(a)

(ii) *When is a product "defective"?*

9–44 **"Defect".** The idea of what "persons generally are entitled to expect" was elucidated in a highly pro-consumer way in *A. v. National Blood Authority* [2001] 3 All E.R. 289, 334 *et seq.*, concerning transfused blood containing the hepatitis virus.

First, the concept referred to the public's legitimate expectation, not its actual expectation. Hence the fact that the public knew that there was an inevitable risk of "rogue products" was irrelevant.

Secondly, despite the reference in s.3(2) to "all the circumstances", certain matters were irrelevant, in particular (a) whether the defect could have been avoided; (b) the social benefits of the product as compared to its risks; and (c) the costs of preventing the defect.

Thirdly, a member of the public's legitimate expectation referred to the individual product that injured him, not to that product generically. Hence merely because some 1 per cent of blood products unavoidably carried the hepatitis virus, this did not mean that a recipient was not entitled to expect that the blood he got would be uncontaminated.

Fourthly, the mere fact that a product carried inherent and unavoidable risks did not of necessity mean it was not defective. It must be shown in addition that these risks were generally known to the public at large. The fact that the risk of hepatitis contamination was known in the medical world did not therefore exonerate the defendants.

In this connection the *National Blood Authority* case involved a "rogue" product—*i.e.*, one where the defect was unintentional. Nevertheless, Burton J. suggested *obiter* (see pp. 340–341) that the same reasoning applied to standard products carrying inherent dangers, such as knives or tobacco. The only reason the producer was not liable for injury caused by such things was, he said, that the risks associated with them were known to the public at large. *Sed quaere.* Suppose an inherently flammable and entirely pure proprietary chemical explodes in a factory, despite exemplary care in its production and use, and a workman is injured. It would be odd if the chemical had to be regarded as defective merely because the propensities of that chemical were unknown to the general public.

Applying the above principles, Field J. held in *B (A Child) v. McDonald's Restaurants Ltd* [2002] EWHC (QB) 490 that piping hot tea and coffee in substantial polystyrene cups were not defective products: this was how customers liked their beverages, and the risks of being scalded were well known.

See generally *Freeman* [2001] J.P.I.L. 26; Howells & Mildred (2002) 65 M.L.R. 95.

On the burden of proof of defectiveness, see *Foster v. Biosil Ltd* (2001) 59 B.M.L.R. 178.

9–45 In *A v. National Blood Authority* [2001] 3 All E.R. 289, 317 *et seq.*, Burton J. regarded the dichotomy between design and manufacturing defects as foreign to European jurisprudence, preferring instead to refer to "standard" and "non-standard" (or "rogue") products (though whether this makes much difference is open to doubt). In this connection, he held that the contaminated blood was a non-standard product. As to whether there is a difference in the concept of "defectiveness" between these two categories, see notes to para. **9.44** above.

Under the development risks defence, the question whether in the light of technical and scientific knowledge the producer could have discovered the defect refers to the defect generically. The producer will therefore be liable if the state of scientific knowledge reveals the *possibility* of the defect. The fact that the defectiveness of the particular item that injured the claimant was neither discoverable nor avoidable is irrelevant. See *A v. National Blood Authority* [2001] 3 All E.R. 289 (contaminated blood), and also *Richardson v. London Rubber Co. Ltd* [2000] Lloyd's Rep. Med. 280 (perforated condom). See too *Abouzaid v. Mothercare (U.K.) Ltd* [2000] All E.R. (D) 246, where it was pointed out that scientific knowledge was not the same as accident experience. Hence s.4(1)(e) could not protect the producer of a dangerous pushchair attachment which half-blinded a child merely because no such accident had ever happened before.

On the problem of inaccessible scientific discoveries, see *A v. National Blood Authority* [2001] 3 All E.R. 289, where Burton J. seemingly thought that such matters would be discounted only where in the form of "an unpublished document or unpublished research not available to the general public, retained within the laboratory or research department of a particular company." *Cf.* the slightly more generous view expressed by the Advocate-General in *Commission v. U.K.* [1997] 3 C.M.L.R. 923, 934.

NOTE 47. In *A v. National Blood Authority* [2001] 3 All E.R. 289 it was agreed that, following the decision in *Commission v. U.K.* [1997] 3 C.M.L.R. 923, the wording of Directive 85/374 should be applied in so far as s.4(1)(e) seemed to conflict with it.

(vi) *What damage is recoverable?*

On the nature of the damage compensable under the 1987 Act, see *Richardson v. London Rubber Co. Ltd* [2000] Lloyd's Rep. Med. 280, apparently accepting (*sed quaere*) that an unwanted pregnancy resulting from a defective condom counted as "damage" within the Act. (The action in fact failed, but for other reasons).

CHAPTER 10

OCCUPIERS' LIABILITY AND DEFECTIVE PREMISES

	PARA.
■ 2. The Occupiers' Liability Act 1957	10–02
■ 3. Liability of landlord	10–57
■ 4. Liability to trespassers	10–62
■ 5. Liability to other non-visitors on the defendant's premises	10–77

Important developments since the last edition include the enactment of the Countryside and Rights of Way Act 2000; the decision in *Darby v. National Trust* [2001] P.I.Q.R. P27, on the extent of the occupier's liability for obvious dangers; and the remarkable decision in *Tomlinson v. Congleton Borough Council, The Times*, March 22, 2002, [2002] EWCA Civ 309 on the duty to trespassers.

10a

2. THE OCCUPIERS' LIABILITY ACT 1957

Owners, lessees and licensees. A farmer who turned over a barn to her mother rent-free for the latter to run an equestrian business was nevertheless held to remain an occupier of the barn. Furthermore, although the level of actual control exercised is relevant to what will count as fault in a given occupier, the farmer was held liable for the state of a ladder giving access to the hayloft, since this was a relatively permanent aspect of the premises. See *Maddocks v. Clifton* [2001] EWCA Civ 1837.

10–08

In *Vodden v. Gayton* [2001] P.I.Q.R. P27 the owner of a field across which a fenced track ran was held to be the occupier of the track for the purposes of the Occupier's Liability Act 1984.

Other occupiers. NOTE 49. In *Prentice v. Hereward Housing Ass'n* the Court of Appeal ordered a new trial on an unrelated basis: *Prentice v. Hereward Housing Ass'n*, unrep., March 22, 2001.

10–10

Permission to enter. NOTE 66. In *Darby v. National Trust* [2001] P.I.Q.R. P27, a person who swam in an ornamental pond next to a stately home was apparently held to be a lawful visitor because the defendants did nothing to stop such activities. *Sed quaere*.

10–14

Visitors entering by right. Persons entering land pursuant to the "right to roam" granted by the Countryside and Rights of Way Act 2000 (not yet in force) are not regarded as visitors under the 1957 Act: see s.13 of the 2000 Act, amending s.2(4) of the earlier enactment. Instead they are owed a modified duty under the Occupiers' Liability Act 1984: see below, notes to **10–77**.

10–18

Private rights of way. In *Vodden v. Gayton* [2001] P.I.Q.R. P27 Toulson J. confirmed, accepting the suggestion in the text, that a user of a private right of way was owed a duty by the owner of the land under the Occupier's Liability Act 1984.

10–20

[79]

10–26 Chapter 10—Occupiers' Liability and Defective Premises

10–26 **Examples.** Not surprisingly, Field J. has declined to hold that a fast-food restaurant broke the common duty of care by serving tea and coffee piping hot—which was the only way most customers liked it. See *B (A Child) v. McDonald's Restaurants Ltd* [2002] EWHC (QB) 409.

NOTE 15. On bar-room brawls, see too *Renaissance Leisure Inc v. Frazer* (2001) 197 D.L.R. (4th) 336 (even participant in fight can claim, though subject to 40 per cent discount for contributory negligence).

10–27 No duty is owed in respect of dangers which are entirely obvious to a visitor: see *Staples v. West Dorset District Council* [1995] P.I.Q.R. P439 (holidaymaker slipping on Cobb at Lyme Regis) and *Darby v. National Trust* [2001] P.I.Q.R. P27 (foolish visitor drowned while swimming in pond outside stately home).

10–28 Where the land concerned is amenity land, an Australian court has held that this must be taken into account in fixing the level of care owed by the occupier: *Department of Natural Resources v. Harper* [2000] 1 V.R. 1 (no duty to warn about danger of falling trees in national park).

Arguably it may be more difficult to establish liability for the state of premises where the immediate cause of the claimant's injury is the deliberate act of a third party: see the Australian decision in *Modbury Triangle Shopping Centre Ltd v. Anzil* (2000) 175 A.L.R. 164 (no liability for assault in unlit car-park).

An occupier may these days be called on to make an adequate risk assessment in respect of dangers on his premises, and its absence may be evidence of negligence. See *Bailey v. Command Security Ltd*, unreported, QBD, October 25, 2001 (security guard fell off unfenced lift aperture; occupiers liable together with employers, subject to 25 per cent contributory negligence).

NOTE 25. Despite *Jolley v. Sutton LBC* [2000] 1 W.L.R. 1082, where there has been negligence in failing to warn of one danger on land but the visitor succumbs to a completely different one, the defendant may still escape on causation grounds. See *Darby v. National Trust* [2001] P.I.Q.R. P27 (National Trust not liable for death of visitor who drowned in pond merely because it had been negligent in failing to warn of danger of catching Weil's disease).

10–31 **Specific issues: liability to children.** NOTE 36. Compare *B. (a child) v. London Borough of Camden* [2001] P.I.Q.R. P143 (4-year-old burnt by very hot pipes in flat: held, in an action under s.4 of the Defective Premises Act, that the landlords were not liable. Parents in such situations could be expected to take proper precautions to protect their children).

10–32 **Visitors exercising skill in construction, maintenance, repair, etc.** On s.2(3)(b) and risks associated with the trade or calling of a visitor, see too *Eden v. West & Co* [2002] EWCA Civ 991 (joiner not saddled with risk of collapsing lintel); *Fairchild v. Glenhaven Funeral Services Ltd* [2002] 1 W.L.R. 1052 (appealed to HL on other grounds, [2002] UKHL 22) (workman injured clearing asbestos from building: occupier not liable, since entitled to assume workman's employer would take reasonable care to safeguard him from danger). But the risk must obviously be something to do with the trade or calling concerned: see *Simpson v. A1 Dairies Ltd*, unrep., January 12, 2001, [2001] EWCA Civ 13 (liability to fireman who fell into unguarded trench in farmyard hidden by surface water).

Warning of danger. Note that a claimant cannot recover for failure to warn of one type of danger if in fact he succumbs to an entirely different one: see *Darby v. National Trust* [2001] P.I.Q.R. P27 (National Trust not liable for death of visitor who drowned in pond merely because it had been negligent in failing to warn of danger of Weil's disease). **10–36**

But see now the odd case of *G. William v. W. Herts HA* [2002] ECWA Civ 1041 (employer of independent contractor held potentially liable for not ascertaining latter's insurance coverage). **10–54**

3. Liability of Landlord

Defective Premises Act 1972, s.4. See too *Sykes v. Harry* [2001] 3 W.L.R. 62 on a landlord's duty under the Defective Premises Act (defective gas fire). **10–60**

4. Liability to Trespassers

Examples. NOTE 13. See too *Scott v. Associated British Ports Ltd*, unrep., November 22, 2000 (glue-sniffing youth injured while riding on railway trucks: CA suggest a duty to fence under 1984 Act, but dismiss claim on basis of *volenti non fit injuria* under s.1(6)). **10–69**

Failing to abate the danger. See now the decision in *Tomlinson v. Congleton Borough Council, The Times*, March 22, 2002, [2002] EWCA Civ 309. An ornamental lake contained hidden dangers to which a swimmer succumbed. Notices prohibited swimming but they were, to the defendants' knowledge, flouted. The defendants were held liable by a majority of the CA (subject to a two-thirds' finding of contributory negligence) for not taking further steps costing some £10,000 to erect physical barriers to discourage swimming. The claimant would only have been barred had the risk been obvious to him so he could be said to have taken it upon himself: here that was not the case. With respect, this seems a remarkably generous decision to the claimant. **10–70**

***Volenti non fit injuria* and the 1984 Act.** NOTE 31. *Scott v. Associated British Ports Ltd* has been upheld on this point by the CA: unrep., November 22, 2000. See too *Tomlinson v. Congleton Borough Council, The Times*, March 22, 2002, [2002] EWCA Civ 309. **10–75**

5. Liability to Other Non-Visitors on the Defendant's Premises

In *Vodden v. Gayton* [2001] P.I.Q.R. P52 Toulson J. confirmed that a user of a private right of way was owed a duty of care by the owner of the underlying land under the Occupier's Liability Act 1984. The decision is problematical, however, because in that case the track concerned was also a public bridleway, and under s.1(7) of the Act no duty is supposed to be owed by virtue of it to those using the highway. Counsel for the defendants nevertheless disclaimed any reliance on s.1(7): see *ibid.* at p. 66. **10–77**

Note the effect of the Countryside and Rights of Way Act 2000 [the relevant provisions of which are, however, not yet in force].

Although persons entering land as of right under the Countryside and Rights of Way Act 2000 are not visitors of the occupier (see s.13 of that Act), they are owed a duty of care pursuant to the 1984 Act. Nevertheless, this duty is qualified in a number of ways.

First, no duty at all is owed in respect of natural features of the landscape, of anything growing on it, or of any river, stream, ditch or pond forming part of it (see the 1984 Act, ss.1(6A(a)), 1(6B), inserted by s.13 of the 2000 Act). Hence there is no duty to warn foolish visitors not to swim or pick poisonous berries. However, the duty remains in respect of (say) derelict agricultural equipment left on land which may trip up and injure the unwary walker. It should be noted, moreover, that this exemption is lost in respect of acts done with intent to cause injury or recklessly as to whether injury is caused (1984 Act, s.1(6C)).

Secondly, there is no duty in respect of walls, fences or gates, except when gates or stiles are being properly used (see the 1984 Act, ss.1(6A(b)), inserted by s.13 of the 2000 Act). Thus a child injured when climbing on a decrepit dry stone wall would have no claim. On the other hand, there is a (potentially onerous) duty to maintain, say, stiles so that they do not collapse under the pressure of hordes of ramblers.

Thirdly, regard is to be had in fixing any duty to (a) the fact that the existence of that right ought not to place an undue burden (whether financial or otherwise) on the occupier, and (b) the importance of maintaining the character of the countryside, including features of historic, traditional or archaeological interest, and (c) any code of conduct issued by the Countryside Agency.

Three further minor points are worth making. First, although the new ss.1(6A)–1(6C) of the 1984 Act refer to duties owed "by virtue of this section", it is to be hoped that they will be construed as exonerating the landowner from any liability at common law as well. Secondly, the 2000 Act says nothing about those using existing public rights of way, who under the previous law were owed no duty whatever. Presumably this rule remains, particularly since s.12(1) of the 2000 Act states that it does not increase the occupier's liability under any other enactment or rule of law in respect of the state of the land or of things done or omitted to be done on it. And lastly, presumably the occupier's duty to those exercising the "right to roam" cannot be excluded by any contract or notice.

See generally [2001] Conv. 296.

CHAPTER 11

BREACH OF STATUTORY DUTY

	PARA.
■ 1. Introduction	11–01
■ 3. Is the breach actionable?	11–09
■ 4. Damage within the ambit of the statute	11–41
■ 5. Standard of liability	11–46
■ 7. Defences	11–55

1. INTRODUCTION

The last three sentences of this paragraph were described as "regrettably, **11–02** correct" by Neuberger J. in *Todd v. Adams and Chope (t/a Trelawney Fishing Co.) (The "Maragetha Maria")* [2002] EWCA Civ 509; [2002] 2 Lloyd's Rep. 293, at [15].

3. IS THE BREACH ACTIONABLE?

NOTE 27. Add: ; nor does the duty to maintain the highway include a duty to **11–09** provide appropriate warning signs of hazards on the highway, since this does not involve repair of the physical or structural condition of the highway or render it more or less passable for ordinary traffic: *Calderdale Metropolitan Borough Council v. Gorringe* [2002] EWCA Civ 595, *The Times*, May 16, 2002.

Protection of a limited class of the public. NOTE 40. Add: Though see now **11–12** *Z v. U.K.*, [2001] 2 F.L.R. 612; [2001] 2 F.C.R. 246 (ECHR) granting compensation to the claimants in *X (Minors) v. Bedfordshire County Council* for breach of Article 3 of the European Convention for the Protection of Human Rights. The failure of a social services authority to intervene to prevent serious, long-term neglect and abuse of children amounted to inhuman and degrading treatment within the meaning of Article 3. The United Kingdom was also found to have been in breach of Article 13 of the Convention in that the applicants did not have available to them an appropriate means of determining their allegations that the authority had failed to protect them from inhuman or degrading treatment or the possibility of obtaining an appropriate award of compensation for the damage suffered as a consequence. On *Z v. UK* see Gearty (2002) 65 M.L.R. 87; Davies (2001) 117 L.Q.R. 521.

And the fact that the safety provisions in Chapter II of Part V of the Merchant Shipping Act 1995, and the Fishing Vessel (Safety Provisions) Rules 1975, S.I. 1975 No. 330, were enacted for the protection of those who go to sea in fishing vessels does not create a right of action in damages for their breach: *Todd v. Adams and Chope (t/a Trelawney Fishing Co.) (The "Maragetha Maria")* [2001] 2 Lloyd's Rep. 443; affirmed [2002] EWCA Civ 509; [2002] 2 Lloyd's Rep. 293.

11–14 **General public as a particular class.** NOTE 51. After *Keating v. Bromley London Borough Council* **add**: *Phelps v. Hillingdon London Borough Council* [2001] 2 A.C. 619, HL.

11–15 **Industrial safety legislation.** For discussion of the meaning of "work equipment" in the context of the Provision and Use of Work Equipment Regulations 1998 (S.I. 1998 No. 2306), see Goddard, C. [2000] J.P.I.L. 220; *Beck v. United Closures & Plastics Ltd*, 2001 S.L.T. 1299; *Crane v. Premier Prison Services Ltd* [2001] C.L.Y. 3298 (QBD); *Donaldson v. Brighton District Council* [2002] 4 C.L. 344.

NOTE 56. Add: For discussion of *Groves v. Lord Wimborne* and points of distinction between claims based on breach of the Factory Acts and a claim based on breach of safety regulations under the Merchant Shipping Act 1995, s.121, and the Fishing Vessel (Safety Provisions) Rules 1975, S.I. 1975 No. 330, see *Todd v. Adams and Chope (t/a Trelawney Fishing Co.) (The "Maragetha Maria")* [2002] EWCA Civ 509; [2002] 2 Lloyd's Rep. 293 at [33] to [35].

NOTE 60. Add: See further Directive 2000/54, September 18, 2000 on the protection of workers from risks related to exposure to biological agents at work: [2000] O.J. L262/21; and Directive 2000/39, June 8, 2000 on the protection of the health and safety of workers from risks related to chemical agents at work: [2000] O.J. L142/47. Directive 2001/45 of June 27, 2001 amends Council Directive 89/655 concerning minimum health and safety requirements for the use of work equipment at work: [2001] O.J. L195/46.

NOTE 61. Add: The framework Directive does not cover the impact of stress at work on the mental health of employees: *Cross v. Highlands and Islands Enterprise* [2001] I.R.L.R. 336, Court of Session, OH.

NOTE 65a. *Koonjul v. Thameslink Healthcare Services* is now reported at [2000] P.I.Q.R. P123.

Swain v. Denso Marston Ltd is now reported at [2000] P.I.Q.R. P129.

And see further on the Manual Handling Operations Regulations 1992 (S.I. 1992 No. 2793): *King v. RCO Support Services Ltd and Yorkshire Traction Company Ltd* [2001] P.I.Q.R. P206; *Fleming v. Stirling Council*, 2001 S.L.T. 123; *Postle v. Norfolk & Norwich NHS Healthcare Trust* [2000] 12 C.L. 280; *Donaldson v. Brighton District Council* [2002] 4 C.L. 344; *Skinner v. Aberdeen City Council*, 2001 Rep. L.R. 118, Court of Session, (OH); Levy, J. "Manual Handling cases—Music to the Ears" [2001] J.P.I.L. 130.

11–16 **No remedy provided by the statute.** NOTE 64. On the Workplace (Health, Safety and Welfare) Regulations 1992 see *Parker v. PFC Flooring Supplies Ltd* [2001] P.I.Q.R. P115 and *Drage v. Grassroots Ltd* [2000] 11 C.L. 298. *Parker* was affirmed at [2001] EWCA Civ 1533 on the defendant's liability in negligence, but the issue of breach of statutory duty was not addressed.

11–17 NOTE 73. *R. v. Governor of Brockhill Prison, ex parte Evans (No. 2)* is now reported at [2001] 2 A.C. 19, HL.

11–21 **Inadequate remedy.** NOTE 86. *R. v. Governor of Brockhill Prison, ex p. Evans (No. 2)* is now reported at [2001] 2 A.C. 19, HL.

11–24 **Alternative remedies.** Note that in both *TP and KM v. U.K.* [2001] 2 F.L.R. 549 and *Z. v. U.K.* [2001] 2 F.L.R. 612; [2001] 2 F.C.R. 246 (ECHR) (in which the unsuccessful claimants in *M. v. Newham London Borough Council* and *X*

(Minors) v. Bedfordshire County Council respectively claimed a breach of their human rights) the European Court of Human Rights concluded that the U.K. was in breach of Article 13 of the European Convention for the Protection of Human Rights in that there was a failure to provide an appropriate remedy for the breaches of Article 8 and Article 3, respectively, that the Court found proved. This does not, in itself, indicate that Staughton L.J.'s comments are misplaced, since his Lordship was considering the common law action for breach of statutory duty whereas the European Court of Human Rights was considering remedies for breach of the European Convention for the Protection of Human Rights. Nonetheless, it does emphasise the importance of considering the effectiveness of administrative remedies when the claimant is seeking compensation for personal injuries. See also the comments of Lord Clyde in *Phelps v. Hillingdon London Borough Council* [2001] 2 A.C. 619, 672 in the context of an action in negligence against an education authority: "even if there are alternative procedures by which some form of redress might be obtained, such as resort to judicial review, or to an ombudsman, or the adoption of such statutory procedures as are open to parents, which might achieve some correction of the situation for the future, it may only be through a claim for damages at common law that compensation for the damage done to the child may be secured for the past as well as the future."

Administrative remedies. See also *Phelps v. Hillingdon London Borough Council* [2001] 2 A.C. 619, HL, paragraph 11–31 below. **11–26**

Public law remedies. C.P.R. R53 is now C.P.R. Part 54. **11–27**

Actions against public authorities. Add: It may be that, with hindsight, some of the policy concerns expressed by Lord Browne-Wilkinson in *X (Minors) v. Bedfordshire County Council* [1995] 2 A.C. 633 come to be viewed as overstated. In *Phelps v. Hillingdon London Borough Council* [2001] 2 A.C. 619 a seven judge House of Lords held that such policy factors should not be conclusive against the possibility of a common law duty of care in negligence owed by an educational psychologist or a teacher when making an assessment of a pupil's educational needs. See further paragraph 11–33 of this *Supplement*. **11–30**

Moreover, the unsuccessful claimants in *M. v. Newham London Borough Council* and *X (Minors) v. Bedfordshire County Council* took a complaint to the European Court of Human Rights. In the case *M. v. Newham* it was held that the failure of the social services authority properly to involve the child's mother in the investigation of alleged sexual abuse of her child (with the consequence that the child was unnecessarily taken into local authority care) constituted a breach of Article 8 of the European Convention for the Protection of Human Rights, the right to respect for family life: *TP and KM v. U.K.* [2001] 2 F.L.R. 549. The local authority had refused to disclose to the mother a video of an interview with the child. If this had been done it would have been apparent to the mother that the local authority had failed to identify the abuser, and had mistakenly identified her partner as the abuser. The refusal to disclose the video denied the mother adequate involvement in the decision-making process concerning the care of her daughter, and this constituted a breach of Article 8. There was also a breach of Article 13 which guarantees a right to an effective remedy, since neither the mother nor her daughter had the possibility of obtaining an enforceable award for compensation for the damage suffered due to breach of Article 8.

11-30

In the case of *X (Minors) v. Bedfordshire County Council* the European Court of Human Rights found that the failure of the social services authority to intervene to prevent serious, long-term neglect and abuse of children constituted inhuman and degrading treatment and found the U.K. to be in breach of Article 3 of the Convention: *Z. v. U.K.* [2001] 2 F.L.R. 612; [2001] 2 F.C.R. 246 (ECHR). As in *TP and KM v. U.K.* the U.K. was also found to have been in breach of Article 13 of the Convention in that the applicants did not have available to them an appropriate means of determining their allegations that the authority had failed to protect them from inhuman or degrading treatment or the possibility of obtaining an appropriate award of compensation for the damage suffered as a consequence. In both cases the Court awarded substantial compensation. It was emphasised that the abuse in *Z. v. U.K.* was both serious and had been occurring for some considerable time. It seems likely that not all failures to intervene to protect children at risk of harm will meet the requirements of "inhuman and degrading treatment" under Article 3. See further para. 1–81. For discussion of *Z v. UK* see Gearty (2002) 65 M.L.R. 87; Davies (2001) 117 L.Q.R. 521.

Clearly, these cases are not authority for the proposition that such claims will in future give rise to an action for breach of statutory duty. Indeed, *Phelps* is clear authority that there is no private law action for breach of statutory duty based on breach of the Education Acts 1944 or 1981 in respect of the failure to provide suitable education for an individual pupil. On the other hand an action based in common law negligence, arising out of the performance of the statutory duties or a claim based on a breach of the European Convention for the Protection of Human Rights, though not necessarily coterminous with breach of a statutory provision, will go a significant to way towards filling the gap for claimants.

11-31 **Education authorities.** In *Phelps v. Hillingdon London Borough Council* [2001] 2 A.C. 619 the House of Lords held that there was no action for breach of statutory duty for a failure to identify, diagnose and treat the special educational needs of a pupil, namely the claimant's learning difficulties and/or dyslexia, in breach of the Education Acts 1944 and 1981 or the Education (Special Needs) Regulations 1983 (S.I. 1983, No. 29). Lord Slynn said, at p. 652, that although the duties were intended to benefit a particular group, mainly children with special educational needs, the Act was essentially providing a general structure for all children who fall within its provision. The general nature of the duties imposed on local authorities in the context of a national system of education and the remedies available by way of appeal and judicial review indicated that Parliament did not intend to create a statutory remedy by way of damages. Much of the Act was concerned with conferring discretionary powers or administrative duties in an area of social welfare where normally damages have not been awarded when there has been a failure to perform a statutory duty. On the other hand, their Lordships refused to strike out as disclosing no reasonable cause of action claims that an educational psychologist or teacher owed a duty of care in the tort of negligence to a pupil to exercise reasonable care when making an educational assessment of that pupil for the purpose of determining future educational provision for the child. The fact that the educational psychologist owed a duty to the education authority did not preclude a duty of care being owed to the child (a point that had been given some significance in *M. v. Newham London Borough Council* in relation to a psychiatrist's duties when interviewing a child who was suspected of being a victim of sexual abuse). Moreover, the local education authority could be vicariously liable for the negligence of an educational psychologist or teacher, notwithstanding that the breach of duty occurred in the course of the performance of a statutory duty and that a breach of the authority's duty under the Education Acts 1944 and 1981 did not give rise to a claim for breach of statutory duty at common law.

Negligence actions against public authorities. In *Phelps v. Hillingdon London Borough Council* [2001] 2 A.C. 619 the House of Lords confirmed that the fact that acts which are claimed to be negligent are carried out within the ambit of a statutory discretion is not in itself a reason why it should be held that no claim for negligence can be brought in respect of them (applying *Barrett v. Enfield London Borough Council* [2001] 2 A.C. 550). Lord Slynn commented, at p. 653, that: "it is only where what is done has involved the weighing of competing public interests or has been dictated by considerations on which Parliament could not have intended that the courts would substitute their views for the views of ministers or officials that the courts will hold that the issue is non-justiciable on the ground that the decision was made in the exercise of a statutory discretion." Moreover: "If a duty of care would exist where advice was given other than pursuant to the exercise of statutory powers, such duty of care is not excluded because the advice is given pursuant to the exercise of statutory powers. This is particularly important where other remedies laid down by the statute (*e.g.* an appeals review procedure) do not in themselves provide sufficient redress for loss which has already been caused" (*ibid.*). There may be cases, said Lord Slynn, where such liability on the part of the education authority may interfere with the performance of the local education authority's duties so that it would be wrong to recognise any liability on the part of the authority. But this was for the local authority to establish; it would not be presumed, and the circumstances where it could be established would be "exceptional". Were there any reasons of public policy why the courts should not recognise a vicarious liability on the part of a local education authority? It was important that those engaged in the provision of educational services under statute should not be hampered by the imposition of such a liability, but, Lord Slynn concluded, at p. 655, to recognise the existence of such duties was not likely to lead to that result: "The recognition of the duty of care does not of itself impose unreasonably high standards. The courts have long recognised that there is no negligence if a doctor 'exercises the ordinary skill of an ordinary competent man exercising that particular art.'"

Lord Clyde, commenting on the policy factors which, it will be recalled were influential in the decision of the House of Lords in *X (Minors) v. Bedfordshire County Council* [1995] 2 A.C. 633 to deny the existence of a claim for breach of statutory duty and for common law negligence in relation to the "child abuse cases" (see paragraph 11–30 of the main Text) said at p. 672:

> "I am not persuaded that there are sufficient grounds to exclude these claims even on grounds of public policy alone. It does not seem to me that there is any wider interest of the law which would require that no remedy in damages be available. I am not persuaded that the recognition of a liability upon employees of the education authority for damages for negligence in education would lead to a flood of claims, or even vexatious claims, which would overwhelm the school authorities, nor that it would add burdens and distractions to the already intensive life of teachers. Nor should it inspire

11-33 CHAPTER 11—BREACH OF STATUTORY DUTY

some peculiarly defensive attitude in the performance of their professional responsibilities. On the contrary it may have the healthy effect of securing that high standards are sought and secured.

Any fear of a flood of claims may be countered by the consideration that in order to get off the ground the claimant must be able to demonstrate that the standard of care fell short of that set by the *Bolam* test: *Bolam v. Friern Hospital Management Committee* [1957] 1 W.L.R. 582. That is deliberately and properly a high standard in recognition of the difficult nature of some decisions which those to whom the test applies require to make and of the room for genuine differences of view on the propriety of one course of action as against another."

NOTE 24. Add: See further *S. v. Gloucestershire County Council* [2001] Fam 313, CA.
W. v. Essex County Council is now reported at [2001] 2 A.C. 592.
Phelps v. Hillingdon London Borough Council is now reported at [2001] 2 A.C. 619.
Barrett v. Enfield London Borough Council is now reported at [2001] 2 A.C. 550.

11-34 **Other factors.** NOTE 26. *Kent v. London Ambulance Service* is now reported at [2001] Q.B. 36.

11-36 **Secondary legislation.** Add: Where the statute enables the Minister to create rules concerning the safety of a particular class of claimants through secondary legislation, but empowers the Minister to exempt certain categories of potential defendant from the rules, this will tend to indicate that there was no intention to impose civil liability for breach of those rules: *Todd v. Adams and Chope (t/a Trelawney Fishing Co.) (The "Maragetha Maria")* [2002] EWCA Civ 509; [2002] 2 Lloyd's Rep. 293 at [25] *per* Neuberger J.—no action in respect of breach of safety regulations in relation to fishing vessels under the Merchant Shipping Act 1995, s. 121, and the Fishing Vessel (Safety Provisions) Rules 1975, S.I. 1975 No. 330, because it would be strange if two identical vessels had accidents caused by the same defects but in one case there was no claim because the vessel had been exempted from the rules.

11-39 **Breach of European legislation.** NOTE 42. *R. v. Secretary of State for Transport, ex p. Factortame Ltd (No. 5)* is now reported at [2000] 1 A.C. 524.

4. DAMAGE WITHIN THE AMBIT OF THE STATUTE

11-45 **Type of damage outside scope of the Act.** Add: The Woodworking Machine Regulations 1974 (S.I. 903) reg. 13(2) imposes a duty on an employer to give a comprehensive explanation in ordinary language of the nature of the work and of the need for an employee to comply with safety instructions: *Tasci v. Pekalp of London Ltd* [2001] I.C.R. 633, CA. Thus, a failure to provide training and instruction in the safe use of a circular saw constituted a breach of the duty which contributed to the claimant's injury. The claimant was held 60 per cent contributorily negligent, since the danger in placing his hand so close to the saw was obvious, even to someone who had received no training.

The Asbestos Regulations 1931 apply to any factory or workshop where one of the specified processes involving the use of asbestos was carried on, not simply to those whose only or main business was the processing of raw asbestos or the manufacture of products from raw asbestos: *Jeromson v. Shell Tankers (UK) Ltd* [2001] EWCA Civ 100; [2001] I.C.R. 1223. Moreover, the obligation in regulation 2 to provide an exhaust was absolute unless it was not practicable, but since the danger was dust and the required precaution both known and practicable the defendants were liable for breach of the regulation.

5. THE STANDARD OF LIABILITY

Standard of care. NOTE 91. Add: Hendy, J. "Industrial Accident Claims: Reasonable Practicability" [2001] J.P.I.L. 209. **11–49**

7. DEFENCES

Defendant's breach of duty coextensive with that of the claimant. NOTE 28. **11–58** Add: *Parker v. PFC Flooring Supplies Ltd* [2001] P.I.Q.R. P115; affirmed at [2001] EWCA Civ 1533 on the question of negligence, but breach of statutory duty was not dealt with.

Chapter 12

PUBLIC AUTHORITIES

	PARA.
■ 1. Introduction	12–01
2. The Current State of Flux	12–06
(c) A Human Rights Dimension	12–08
■ 3. The Liability of Public Authorities in the Tort of Negligence at Common Law	12–19
(b) Conventional Problem Areas	12–22
(c) A Peculiarly "Public" Element	12–43
■ 4. Other Tortious Liability	12–75
(a) Constitutional Torts	12–75
(b) Euro Torts	12–80

1. Introduction

The significance of a defendant being a public authority. NOTE 1. Now Craig, *Administrative Law* (4th ed., Sweet and Maxwell, 1999) and Thompson, *Textbook on Constitutional and Administrative Law* (3rd ed., Blackstone, 1997, chapter 18). 12–01

NOTE 2. Add: Markesinis and Deakin, *Tort Law* (4th ed., Oxford, 1999) has devoted a separate section to the tortious liability of public bodies.

Categorisation. NOTE 5. Add: See *Poplar Housing and Regeneration Community Association Ltd v. Donoghue* [2001] 3 W.L.R. 183 and *R. (on the application of Heather) v. Leonard Cheshire Foundation* [2002] EWCA Civ 366 (CA). 12–02

2. The Current State of Flux

(c) A Human Rights Dimension

General relevance. NOTE 18. Add: See now the decision of the European Court of Human Rights in *Z. v. United Kingdom* [2001] 2 F.C.R. 246 and *T.P. and K.M. v. United Kingdom* [2001] 2 F.L.R. 549; see paras 1–79, 1–84, 12–09A, 12–70, 12–71 and 12–74). 12–08

Add new paragraph after paragraph 12–09:

The potential relevance of the excluded Article 13. The fact that the Human Rights Act 1998 does not include Article 13 as a directly incorporated convention right does not mean that doctrine related to that article could not similarly influence the development of English law on the tortious liability of public authorities. Article 13 provides the citizen with a right to an effective remedy, not where the applicant's civil rights and obligations are in issue, but rather where 12–09A there is an "arguable complaint" that a substantive Convention right has been violated. In *Z. v. United Kingdom*[20a] and *TP and KM v. United Kingdom*[20b] the European Court of Human Rights considered the House of Lords' restrictive approach in *X (Minors) v. Bedfordshire County Council* to the recognition of a duty of care in child abuse related negligence actions brought against a local authority.[20c] The Strasbourg court chose not to adopt the European Commission of Human Rights' earlier recommendation that their Lordships' approach in *X* amounted to a violation of the claimants' right to proper access to the courts under Article 6.[20d] They concluded, however, that, in the circumstances,[20e] there had been a violation of Article 13. In form, this particular decision of the ECHR might seem to limit its impact on the evolution of the relevant English law in future similar cases. After all, the Human Rights Act 1998 obliges an English court, as a "public authority",[20f] to decide an action before it in a manner compatible with the convention rights it incorporates, and Article 6 is incorporated whereas Article 13 is not. In substance, however, it may be that the decision exposes the potential for the residual action against the state before the Strasbourg court to act as an effective incorporator of Article 13 in appropriate cases. In a future action on similar facts before an English court, the court would be obliged to respect the ECHR's decisions in *Z* and *T.P. and K.M.*, both as a matter of conventional practice and under the court's specific obligation under section 2 of the Human Rights Act 1998 to have regard to such decisions when a question arises under the 1998 Act in connection with a convention right.[20g]

NOTE 20a. [2001] 2 F.C.R. 246; see also paras 12–70, 12–71 and 12–74. For comment see Gearty (2002) 65(1) M.L.R. 87; Davies [2001] 117 L.Q.R. 521; Lidbetter and George (2001) E.H.L.R. 599.

NOTE 20b. [2001] 2 F.L.R. 549.

NOTE 20c. [1995] 2 A.C. 633; see paras 12–45 *et seq.* and 12–60 *et seq.*

NOTE 20d. See para. 12–71.

NOTE 20e. The ECHR had decided that the child abuse out of which the negligence claims against the defendant arose was so serious that it amounted to a violation of article 3 of the Convention (the fundamental right to be protected from inhuman and degrading treatment).

NOTE 20f. See paras 12–02 and 12–17.

NOTE 20g. See also para. 12–74.

3. THE LIABILITY OF PUBLIC AUTHORITIES IN THE TORT OF NEGLIGENCE

(b) Conventional Problem Areas

(iii) Pure Omissions

(i) General Principles

12–26 **Prior creation of danger.** Add to the end of the paragraph: The Court of Appeal drew on a similar rationale in *Kane v. New Forest District Council*.[50a] The claimant had emerged from a public footpath onto a main road and was hit by a car he claimed he could not have seen given the absence of suitable sight lines at that point. He sued the local planning authority in negligence, alleging carelessness on their part in permitting the creation of an obviously unsuitable footpath. The Court of Appeal refused to strike out his action, finding, *inter alia*, that he had a realistic prospect of establishing that the defendant had, in the circumstances, actually created the source of danger.

NOTE 50a. [2002] 1 W.L.R. 312.

(iii) Public Authorities and Exceptions to the Omissions Rule

Relationship with third party causing harm. NOTE 57. Add: In *Kane v. New Forest District Council*, [2002] 1 W.L.R. 312, the Court of Appeal, distinguishing *Stovin v. Wise*, held it arguable that the local planning authority defendants had created the source of danger because they had permitted the opening of a public footpath which left its users unsighted at the point the path joined a busy main road.

12–32

Specific reliance: police and emergency services. Add: More recently, in *Cowan v. Chief Constable of Avon and Somerset*,[66a] the Court of Appeal reverted to the *Hill* position that there would often be insufficient proximity in such cases for a duty of care to be recognised. The claimant had been threatened by letter with eviction from a property which he occupied under an assured tenancy. He contacted the police, but the officers who responded to the call were unaware that, in the absence of a court order ending the tenancy, the claimant's eviction would have constituted an offence under Section 1 of the Protection from Eviction Act 1977. The officers remained at the scene only to prevent a breach of the peace. The claimant sued the police in negligence alleging that the officers owed him a duty of care to prevent the commission of a crime under Section 1 of the 1977 Act. The Court of Appeal dismissed the claim. Following *Hill*, the court held, *inter alia*,[66b] that no general duty was owed by the police to individual members of the public for their activities in the investigation and suppression of crime. In the absence of any indication of an assumption of responsibility to prevent the commission of the Section 1 offence, the police presence at the scene did not in itself create a relationship of sufficient proximity.

12–36

NOTE 66: Add: For comment, see Lewis [2000] 4 J.P.I.L. 198; Weir [2000] 4 J.P.I.L. 208.

NOTE 66a: *The Times*, December 11, 2001.

NOTE 66b: The claim was also dismissed on policy grounds (see para. 12–65 note 42).

Specific reliance: local authorities. Add: A contrasting decision more illustrative of the general difficulty establishing proximity in such cases is *Surrey County Council v. M*.[69a] M, a five year old child, had been sexually assaulted by a thirteen year old boy whose family had been housed by the council in a flat directly opposite her home. The boy had been charged in the past with serious sexual offences and had a more recent conviction for indecent assault against a child. It was alleged that the council was negligent on the basis that the boy's likely contact with M and other children meant that the assault on M was reasonably foreseeable. Adopting a line of reasoning similar to that employed by the House of Lords in *Hill*,[69b] the Court of Appeal held that the relationship between M and the council lacked the proximity required for a duty of care to be recognised, because M was within a wide category of members of the general public, rather than within an exceptional category of risk.

12–37

NOTE 68. Add: The House of Lords reversed the Court of Appeal's decision in relation to the parents' claim and allowed it to proceed to trial (*W. v. Essex County Council* [2000] 2 W.L.R. 601; see paras 12–61 and 12–73).

NOTE 69a: [2001] EWCA Civ 691.
NOTE 69b: See para. 12–36.

(iv) *Vicarious Liability*

12–42 **Narrow applicability: proximity and policy.** NOTE 82. Add: That said, it seems unlikely that a court would adopt this particular rationale to undo the limited availability of local authority vicarious liability for the default of its educational psychologists initially recognised in *X* and subsequently adopted in by the House of Lords in *Phelps* (see para. 12–42A). As Harris (2001) 117 L.Q.R. 25, at 26 has noted, their Lordships' wider purpose in *Barrett* was to emphasise that any overriding public policy "immunity" in a negligence action against a local authority should depend more on justiciability concerns than on whether the default complained of was within the ambit of discretion. On that basis, it would seem that the decisions of educational psychologists would be susceptible to judicial scrutiny, whether or not they formed part of advice given to a local authority employer to enable it to perform its statutory duties. At the same time, the emphasis on justiciability could lead a court to conclude that the direct liability route in such a case might, if anything, also be available, thereby removing the concern that its absence might be undermined by the availability of vicarious liability. The House of Lords in *Phelps* considered that their decision to allow for the availability of vicarious liability (see para. 12–42A) meant that it was unnecessary for them to use the rationale described by Harris to come to a formal decision on the availability or otherwise of direct liability on the facts (see para. 12–63, note 31). They did adopt an equivalent line of reasoning, however, as the means of disposing of the Court of Appeal's general objection to the imposition of vicarious liability on consistency grounds, while, at the same time, accepting that the local authority might, in exceptional circumstances, be able to establish that such inconsistency concerns were, indeed, valid (see para. 12–42A).

12–42A NOTE 83. Add: *Jarvis* was itself appealed and heard by the House of Lords as one of the four consolidated appeals in *Phelps* (*Phelps v. Hillingdon L.B.C.*; *Anderton v. Clwyd C.C.*; *Re G (a Minor)*; and *Jarvis v. Hampshire C.C.*).

(c) *A Peculiarly "Public" Element*

(ii) *General Factual Relevance*

12–44 **Sufficient connection to the public commitment.** Add to the end of the paragraph: In *Waters v. Commissioner of Police of the Metropolis*,[88a] the House of Lords refused to strike out a police officer's claim that her employers had negligently failed to protect her from allegedly foreseeable victimisation by fellow officers following her formal complaint that she had been raped by a colleague. Their Lordships held that the case could proceed to trial, where it could be decided predominantly on conventional principles of employer's liability. Her claim would be less likely to require the court to invoke the public policy considerations that might militate against the imposition of a duty of care than if she had alleged that her employers had been careless in the conduct of her original allegation of rape.

NOTE 88a. [2000] 1 W.L.R. 1607; see paras 12–66 and 12–68.

THE LIABILITY OF PUBLIC AUTHORITIES IN NEGLIGENCE   12–61

(iv) *Carelessness in the Performance of Statutory Powers*

(ii) Omissions and Proximity

Proximity generally. Add to the end of the paragraph: Against this, it may yet   12–51
prove significant that, in *Kent v. Griffiths*[5a] Lord Woolf M.R. seemed to draw on
a distinction between public and private bodies in connection with these particular proximity principles. His Lordship did so in rejecting the defendant's
assertion that, *inter alia*, by volunteering to act in circumstances when not
necessarily obliged at common law to do so, a public authority could benefit from
the same principles that would only expose a private volunteer to liability if he
carelessly caused additional harm.[5b] Lord Woolf concluded that, because the
ambulance service is paid from public funds, it could not be equated with the
private volunteer or benefit from the additional harm principle. This seems out of
line with decisions such as *Capital and Counties plc v. Hampshire County
Council*, *Alexandrou v. Oxford*, *O.L.L. v. Secretary of State for Transport*,[5c] where
the public body defendants were also publicly funded, but still had actions
against them determined in accordance with that additional harm principle. It
may, in that way, signal a trend for the same point to be re-considered in such
cases, effectively limiting the defendant's arguments to the non-proximity public
policy assertions that courts may now also be willing to evaluate in a more
claimant-friendly manner at a full hearing.

NOTE 5a. [2000] 2 W.L.R. 1158. See para. 12–36, *supra*, note 62.

NOTE 5b. The Court of Appeal side-stepped the defendant's other line of
argument on the inapplicability of the reliance and undertaking exception to the
omissions rule by concluding that the ambulance service defendant was under an
affirmative duty to act in the first place: See para. 12–36, *supra*, note 62.

NOTE 5c. Paras 12–52, 12–53 and 12–54 respectively.

(iii) Policy: Local Authorities

Policy and *Dorset Yacht*: the "ambit of discretion". NOTE 18. Add: In   12–58
Larner v. Solihull Metropolitan Borough Council [2001] P.I.Q.R. P17, the Court
of Appeal held that the defendant highway authority owed a duty of care to a
driver injured in an accident allegedly as a result of the defendant's failure to
comply with its statutory obligation to take appropriate road safety measures
under s.39 Road Traffic Act 1988. The allegation was that the defendant had
failed to erect warning signs sufficiently in advance of a junction it knew to be
dangerous. The Court of Appeal agreed that, in the circumstances, the defendant's conduct was so unreasonable as to be outside the ambit of even the wide
discretion afforded under s.39. Their Lordships, however, went on to find that the
defendant was not in breach of any duty of care, given the overall quality of its
systems and procedures for reviewing road safety in its area.

Policy and *X*: decision-making as a three-stage filter. Add to end of   12–61
paragraph: The House of Lords, in *W. v. Essex County Council*,[28a] and the Court
of Appeal, in *S. v. Gloucester C.C.; L. v. Tower Hamlets L.B.C.*,[28b] subsequently
confirmed an important procedural gloss on the substantive test enunciated by
Lord Browne-Wilkinson in *X*. In both cases, their Lordships expressly adopted
Lord Slynn's approach in *Barrett v. Enfield London Borough Council*[28c] that the
court's enquiry into whether the allegedly improper exercise of a discretion

12-61   CHAPTER 12—PUBLIC AUTHORITIES

involved policy considerations (stage one of Lord Browne-Wilkinson's test) should normally only be undertaken at a full trial of an action.[28d]

NOTE 28a. [2000] 2 W.L.R. 601; see para. 12–37, note 68 and para. 12–73.

NOTE 28b [2001] 2 W.L.R. 909 (also known as *D.S. v. Gloucester C.C.*; *R.L. v. Gloucester C.C.*; *R.L. v. Tower Hamlets L.B.C.*). See paras 12–62, note 30, and para. 12–73.

NOTE 28c. [1999] 3 W.L.R. 79.

NOTE 28d. See also para. 12–73.

12-62   **X applied: the excluded actions.** Add to the end of the paragraph: In *Phelps v. Hillingdon L.B.C.*[30a] the House of Lords also considered the potential for direct liability in negligence claims against a local authority concerning special needs education. Lord Slynn suggested that, while many local authority decisions in that connection would involve matters of policy (such as establishing a scheme to evaluate special needs) and would, therefore, be immune, proper examination might reveal that others did not (*e.g.* appointing an educational psychologist who was obviously not suitable for the job).[30b] His Lordship also considered that the public policy concerns raised by Lord Browne-Wilkinson in *X* (and adopted by the Court of Appeal in *Phelps*) would not necessarily justify a court concluding that it would not be fair, just and reasonable to recognise a duty in such cases. Lord Slynn suggested, *inter alia*, that the multi-disciplinary context was of less significance than in the child care cases. The direct liability question in *Phelps* was, however, not formally resolved. Lords Nicholls[30c] and Clyde[30d] preferred to leave that question open and the case was decided on vicarious liability.[30e]

See above para. 11–31.

NOTE 30a. [2000] 3 W.L.R. 776.

NOTE 30b. *ibid.*, at 795.

NOTE 30c. *ibid.*, at 805.

NOTE 30d. *ibid.*, at 813.

NOTE 30e. See para. 12–42A.

NOTE 30. Add: *H. v. Norfolk County Council* has now been overruled by the Court of Appeal's decision in *S. v. Gloucester C.C.*; *L. v. Tower Hamlets L.B.C.* [2001] 2 W.L.R. 909 (see paras 12–61 and 12–73). In *S*, the Court of Appeal confirmed that an action's potential exclusion under *X* had to be safe procedurally as well on principle. This, in turn, may also affect the courts' application of the substantive principles themselves. In common with the House of Lords in *W. v. Essex County Council* [2000] 2 W.L.R. 601 (see para. 12–37, note 68 and para. 12–73), the Court of Appeal in *S* adopted the House of Lords' concern in *Barrett v. Enfield London Borough Council* [1999] 3 W.L.R. 79 that a claimant's inability to sue a local authority in negligence should usually result from a case by case consideration of the precise nature of the criticised conduct, rather than a general defendant-centred immunity. Their Lordships applied this reasoning to the child abuse related negligence actions before them, allowing them to proceed to a full hearing, whereas, in *X*, similar actions had been dismissed at an interlocutory stage. In doing so, they suggested that it was an over-generalisation to conclude that the underlying multi-disciplinary and statutory framework meant that all local authority decisions in that connection were unsuited to review by a court at a full hearing. The criticised decisions in *S* itself involved the care of a child already in local authority care. While the court accepted that it would have to exercise caution in reviewing such decisions, they considered that such cases were distinguishable from the far more complex situation where a local authority was faced with a choice over whether or not to remove a child into care at all.

X applied: permitted actions. Add to the end of the paragraph: The parents' claim in *W* was appealed to the House of Lords, where it was allowed to proceed to a full hearing.[34a] Adopting the reasoning employed in *Barrett v. Enfield London Borough Council*,[34b] their Lordship held that, on a striking out application, it was unsafe to conclude that such a claim was unarguable.[34c] 12–63

NOTE 34a. [2000] 2 W.L.R. 601.
NOTE 34b. [1999] 3 W.L.R. 79.
NOTE 34c. See also *S. v. Gloucester C.C.; L. v. Tower Hamlets L.B.C.* [2001] 2 W.L.R. 909 (see para. 12–62, note 30 and para. 12–73).
NOTE 31. Add: See also para. 12–42, note 82, *supra*.

Policy factors in emergency service actions. NOTE 42. Add: The Court of Appeal cited similar policy reasons in *Cowan v. Chief Constable of Avon and Somerset, The Times*, December 11, 2001, in holding that, when called to prevent a breach of the peace that could have resulted from the claimant's eviction by his landlord, the police did not owe the claimant a duty of care to identify and prevent what would have been an unlawful eviction under the Protection from Eviction Act 1977. Their Lordships observed that it would not be in the public interest to impose a duty of care in such circumstances for fear that responses to urgent calls might be delayed if the police were required to analyse relevant legal information first. The claim had already been lost on proximity grounds (see para. 12–36). 12–65

(iv) Policy: The Emergency Services

Conventional policy devices in emergency service case. Add to the end of the paragraph: Similarly, in *Waters v. Commissioner of Police of the Metropolis*,[51a] the House of Lords raised, but distinguished, the policy considerations relied on in *Hill* and refused to strike out a negligence claim by a police officer against her employers following victimisation at the hands of fellow officers after she had made a formal complaint that a colleague had raped her. Their Lordships considered it significant that her claim did not call into question the police's conduct in the investigation of crime (her original allegation of rape), where the *Hill* policy factors might have served to bar her action. Rather, it centred on the police's duties to her as her employer in allegedly failing to protect her from inevitable victimisation. In such a case, the House of Lords found that the public policy issues that had held sway in *Hill* were either irrelevant,[51b] or, if applicable, less conclusive, given the presence of a significant countervailing public interest in the proper consideration of allegations of a culture of condoned victimisation in the police.[51c] 12–66

NOTE 51a. [2000] 1 W.L.R. 1607; para. 12–44.
NOTE 51b. Lords Slynn, Clyde and Millett.
NOTE 51c. Lord Hutton. See para. 12–68.

"Immunity" and conventional devices contrasted. Add to the end of the paragraph: In *Waters v. Commissioner of Police of the Metropolis*, the claimant police officer sued the police in negligence for failing to protect her from victimisation by colleagues after she had complained that a fellow officer had raped her.[58a] In the House of Lords, Lord Hutton recognised that there might be 12–68 public policy concerns militating against the recognition of a duty of care in such a case, but considered that such factors could be outweighed by a competing public interest in learning the truth about allegations of a condoned culture of retaliatory victimisation in the police.[58b]

NOTE 58a. [2000] 1 W.L.R. 1607; see para. 12-44.

NOTE 58b. Note that Lords Slynn, Clyde and Millett found that, on the facts, the public policy issues that had influenced the court in cases such as *Hill* were irrelevant (para. 12-66, note 51b).

(v) Policy and the Human Rights Dimension

12-70   ***Osman v. United Kingdom.*** Add to the end of the paragraph: The ECHR's decision to that effect in *Osman* should, however, be contrasted with its subsequent decisions in *Z. v. United Kingdom*[62a] and *T.P. and K.M. v. United Kingdom*.[62b] In those later cases, the court held that, while there had been a violation of Article 13, the House of Lords' approach to the duty of care question in *X (Minors) v. Bedfordshire County Council* did not violate Article 6. The ECHR accepted that the English courts' use of the duty of care mechanism to determine the existence of a cause of action in negligence was a valid exercise of the domestic law in which the court would not interfere.[62c]

NOTE 62a. [2001] 2 F.C.R. 246; see para. 12-08, note 18; paras 12-09A, 12-71 and 12-74.

NOTE 62b. [2001] 2 F.L.R. 549.

NOTE 62c. The ECHR expressly adopted the argument raised by Lord Browne-Wilkinson in *Barrett* (see para. 12-74).

12-71   ***Z. v. United Kingdom.*** Add to the end of the paragraph: When *Z* came to be determined by the ECHR itself, the court also found fault with the House of Lords' approach to the child abuse claims in *X*.[69a] There was, however, to be a subtle difference in the reasoning employed by the Commission and the ECHR. The ECHR held that the abuse to which the children had been subject amounted on the facts to sufficiently inhuman and degrading treatment to have violated their rights under Article 3 of the Convention. Where, however, the Commission had concluded that the children's inability to sue the local authority in the circumstances was a violation of their rights under Article 6, the ECHR disagreed. It held that English law's use of the duty of care mechanism to identify a qualifying right to sue in negligence in such cases was a matter of domestic law with which the ECHR would not interfere. Crucially, however, the ECHR held that, in the circumstances, there had been a breach of Article 13 (the right to an effective remedy) and awarded the claimants damages totalling £350,000.[69b]

NOTE 69a. [2001] 2 F.C.R. 246.

NOTE 69b. See paras 1-79—1-84, 12-09A, 12-70 and 12-74.

12-72   **Article 6 as a *procedural* right.** Add to the end of the paragraph: At the same time, it is important to emphasise that, even if the claimant manages to overcome the duty hurdle in such cases, the action may still fail on the other aspects of the conventional negligence formula, especially the question of breach.[73a] Indeed, the court has occasionally argued more generally that the difficulties of establishing breach of duty would go some way to meeting any concern that a less restrictive approach to the recognition of a duty would lead to a "flood" of claims against local authorities.[73b]

NOTE 73a. As in *Swinney* itself: *Swinney v. Chief Constable of Northumbria Police (No. 2)* (1999) 11 Admin. L.R. 811.

NOTE 73b. See, for example, *Phelps v. Hillingdon L.B.C.* [2000] 3 W.L.R. 776, at 792 (Lord Slynn), 804 (Lord Clyde), 809 (Lord Nicholls); *cf.* Harris (2001) 117 L.Q.R. 25, 27 and 28 for some compelling doubts over the reliability of the specific anti-floodgates safeguards alluded to by that their Lordships in *Phelps*.

NOTE 72. Add: See also *Waters v. Commissioner of Police of the Metropolis* [2000] 1 W.L.R. 1607, in which Lord Hutton suggested that any public policy considerations militating against the recognition of a duty of care in the claimant's action against her police employers for failing to protect her from victimisation by colleagues after she had complained that a fellow officer had raped her might be outweighed by a countervailing public interest in the court investigating the suggestion of a condoned culture of retaliatory victimisation in the police (see para. 12–66, note 51c and para. 12–68); see also *Mulcahy v. Chief Constable of the West Midlands, Independent*, July 9, 2001, CA.

Article 6 and striking out. Add to the end of the paragraph: The House of Lords (in *W. v. Essex County Council*)[78a] and the Court of Appeal (in *S. v. Gloucester County Council*)[78b] referred to *Barrett* and confirmed that the court should only strike out a negligence claim against a public authority in the clearest possible circumstances, where it could be said that there were no prospects of success. Their Lordships elaborated that a court could, in turn, only reach such a conclusion if all the material facts were before it and, if they were, where those facts were undisputed and there was no real likelihood of oral evidence altering the court's conclusions in relation to those facts. This was thought to be unusual where there was an allegation of negligence against a local authority in relation to child care or education where so much could turn on the precise nature of the local authority's criticised decision and the manner in which it had taken it. 12–73

NOTE 74. Add: see also *O v. Surrey Social Services* [2001] W.L. 1560834 Ch. D.

NOTE 75. Add: In *Bromiley v. United Kingdom*, Application no. 33747/96, November 23, 1999, The European Court of Human Rights also held that Article 6(1) would not prevent a strike-out based on lack of foreseeability or proximity, on the basis that these were general requirements that applied in all negligence actions.

NOTE 78a. [2000] 2 W.L.R. 601; see paras 12–61 and 12–62, note 30.

NOTE 78b. [2001] 2 W.L.R. 909; see para. 12–62, note 20.

Immunity as a means of avoiding Article 6? Add to the end of the paragraph: In *Z. v. United Kingdom*[79a] and *T.P. and K.M. v. United Kingdom*,[79b] the ECHR seemed to accept much of Lord Browne-Wilkinson's argument. In reviewing the House of Lords' decision in *X (Minors) v. Bedfordshire County Council*,[79c] the ECHR accepted that their Lordships decision not to allow the child abuse claims to proceed to trial did not result from any procedural bar or from the operation of any immunity which restricted access to the court. The Strasbourg court concluded that the striking out of those actions in X resulted, instead, from the proper application by the domestic court of principles of substantive law (which necessarily incorporated policy considerations) which it was not for the ECHR to rule on. The court found that the House of Lords' restrictive approach to the recognition of a duty of care in the child abuse cases in X had resulted from a 12–74 proper examination of the relevant legal principles and related policy considerations and did not, therefore, amount to a breach of article 6.[79d] At the same time, however, the ECHR in Z held that the child abuse in question amounted to a breach of the claimants' fundamental rights under Article 3 not to be subjected to inhuman or degrading treatment and that the absence of an available cause of action in relation to it violated the claimants' rights to an effective remedy under article 13. By way of compensation, the court awarded the claimants damages totalling £350,000. In *T.P. and K.M.*, the court found there to have been a violation of Article 8 and that the absence of an effective remedy similarly contravened Article 13.

NOTE 79a. [2001] 2 F.C.R. 246; see paras 1–79—1–84, 12–09A and 12–70.
NOTE 79b. [2001] 2 F.L.R. 549.
NOTE 79c. [1995] 2 A.C. 633; see paras 12–45 *et seq.* and 12–60 *et seq.*
NOTE 79d. Contrast *Osman v. United Kingdom* [1999] F.L.R. 193; see paras 1–79 and 12–70.

4. OTHER TORTIOUS LIABILITY

(a) *Constitutional Torts*

12–78   **Pure and quasi public authorities.** NOTE 86. Add: See *Poplar Housing and Regeneration Community Association Ltd v. Donoghue* [2001] 3 W.L.R. 183 and *R. (On the application of Heather) v. Leonard Cheshire Foundation* [2002] EWCA Civ 366 (CA).

(b) *Euro Torts*

(iii) *Enforcement: Damages and the Euro-Tort*

12–87   **The *Three Rivers* Case.** Replace 6th sentence ("This action failed for reasons outlined in the chapter on the liability of public officers in which that tort is examined") with the following: "This action was struck out by the Court of Appeal,[3a] but allowed to proceed by the House of Lords (Lord Hobhouse and Lord Millett dissenting)[3b] on the basis that it was arguable whether the evidence adduced by the claimants indicated negligence rather than misfeasance."

NOTE 3. Add: Now reported at [2000] 2 W.L.R. 15. For comment see Allott (2001) 60(1) C.L.J. 4. See also *Marks and Spencer plc v. Customs and Excise Commissioners* [2000] 1 C.M.L.R. 256.
NOTE 3a. [200] 2 W.L.R. 15.
NOTE 3b. [2001] 2 All E.R. 513.

CHAPTER 13

TRESPASS TO THE PERSON

	PARA.
1. Introduction	13–01
■ 2. Battery	13–05
■ 3. Assault	13–13
■ 4. False Imprisonment	13–19
(a) What constitutes false imprisonment	13–19
■ 5. Justification of trespass to the person	13–37
(b) Preventing breach of the peace, or making lawful arrest	13–40
(c) Assisting officers of the law	13–65
(d) Confinement of mentally disordered persons	13–67
(e) Parental or other authority	13–80
6. Damages	13–84

1. INTRODUCTION

Trespass: intention and negligence. NOTE 6. Add: See also *Haystead v. Chief Constable of Derbyshire* [2000] 3 All E.R. 890; [2000] 2 Cr. App. R. 339. 13–02

NOTE 9. *Revill v. Newberry* is reported at [1996] Q.B. 567.

NOTE 11. *Stubbings v. Webb* is reported at [1993] A.C. 498.

2. BATTERY

Battery. NOTE 18. *Wilson v. Pringle* is reported at [1987] Q.B. 237. 13–05

NOTE 22. Add: Striking A, which act causes injury to B is a battery of B, as where D punched W in the face causing the child in W's arms to fall, striking his head on the floor: *Haystead v. Chief Constable of Derbyshire* [2000] 3 All E.R. 890; [2000] 2 Cr. App. R. 339.

Hostile intent. NOTE 25. *Wilson v. Pringle* is reported at [1987] Q.B. 237. 13–06

How far consent a defence? NOTE 37. *R. v. Wilson* is reported at [1997] Q.B. 47. 13–08

NOTE 41. Add: *Ward v. Chief Constable of the Royal Ulster Constabulary* [2000] N.I. 543—contributory negligence applied to a claim for assault and battery.

Consent induced by fraud. NOTE 50. *R. v. Richardson* is reported at [1999] Q.B. 444. 13–10

NOTE 50. Add: *cf. R. v. Tabassum* [2000] Lloyd's Rep. Med. 404, CA—defendant guilty of indecent assault for touching the breasts of women who had consented to the procedure believing that he was medically qualified; the consent was given to the touching for medical purposes and not for any other reason, and thus there was consent to the nature of the act but not its quality, and accordingly there was no genuine consent.

13–12   **Consent or lawful excuse.** NOTE 56. *R. v. Bournewood Community and Mental Health Services NHS Trust, ex p. L* is reported at [1999] 1 A.C. 458.

3. ASSAULT

13–13   **Assault.** NOTE 61. *Thomas v. N.U.M.* is reported at [1986] Ch. 20.
NOTE 62. *R. v. Ireland* is reported at [1998] A.C. 147 and *R. v. Constanza* is reported at [1997] 2 Cr. App. R. 492.

13–15   **Criminal proceedings.** NOTE 75. *McIlkenny v. Chief Constable of the West Midlands* is reported at [1980] Q.B. 283.

13–16   **Intentional infliction of injury.** Add: In *W v. Home Office* [2001] EWCA Civ 2081; [2002] 3 W.L.R. 405 Buxton L.J. said that Wright J.'s formulation was ambiguous in two respects. First, it was not clear whether the word "calculated" required that the defendant subjectively intended to cause harm, or whether it covered acts objectively very likely to cause harm; and secondly, "infringement of the legal right to personal safety" could refer to actual physical harm or to a threat of such harm. His Lordship suggested that the headnote to the report of *Janvier v. Sweeney* [1919] 2 K.B. 316, which states "False words and threats calculated to cause, uttered with the knowledge that they are likely to cause, and actually causing physical injury to the person to whom they are uttered are actionable" best represented a general statement of the rule in *Wilkinson v. Downton*. If, however, that was not correct, then the rule must be that the defendant's act was so clearly likely to produce a result of the kind that occurred that an intention to produce it should be imputed to him, *i.e.* objective recklessness (*ibid.* at [79]). Thus, intention or recklessness merely as to severe emotional distress, from which bodily harm happens in fact to result, was not enough (*ibid.* at [80]). The outrageous nature of a defendant's conduct, producing emotional distress was not enough to impose liability. Lord Woolf C.J. agreed that for the act to be wilfully done it had "to be either one which is done with the intention of causing harm or done in circumstances where it was so likely that the harm would be incurred that an intention to produce harm has to be imputed. Certainly nothing less than recklessness would do" (*ibid.* at [44]). On the other hand, although a recognised psychiatric illness or bodily injury was required in order for damages to be recovered, his Lordship accepted that where extreme and outrageous conduct intentionally or recklessly caused severe emotional distress to the claimant the defendant should be liable for the emotional distress, *provided* that bodily harm resulted from it. Emotional distress alone was not sufficient, but if severe emotional distress caused bodily harm, and the defendant either intended this or was reckless as to the consequences then there would be liability (*ibid.* at [49]). Given that this was an intentional tort, and required intended harm, "problems as to foreseeability do not arise. If the conduct is actionable then compensation should be payable for the intended harm" (*ibid.* at [50]). The differences between Buxton L.J. and Lord Woolf C.J. are not insignificant (although Mummery L.J. agreed with the reasoning of both). Both require either subjective intention or objective recklessness as to the harm caused; and both require that the claimant sustain either physical injury or a recognised psychiatric injury. The difference lies in the nature of the "harm" that the defendant must intend. Buxton L.J. required intention or recklessness as to causing the physical or psychiatric harm itself; whereas Lord Woolf required intention or recklessness as to "severe emotional distress", provided that it is this which produces physical injury or recognised psychiatric injury. In practice this distinction will be difficult to sustain, since it is clear from the cases involving the negligent infliction of psychiatric harm that severe emotional distress may simply be part of the causal mechanism in producing psychiatric injury. It will be difficult, given modern understanding of the aetiology of certain forms of psychiatric harm, for a defendant argue that although he intended to cause (or was reckless as to causing) severe emotional distress he did not intend to cause (or was not reckless as to causing) the resulting psychiatric damage.[79a] On the facts of *W v. Home Office* (the claimants had been strip-searched when visiting a relative in prison in a manner which breached the Prison Service rules) it could not be said that there was any such intention (no matter how the intention was formulated) by the prison officers.

In *Wong v. Parkside Health NHS Trust* [2001] EWCA Civ 1721; *The Times*, December 7, 2001 the Court of Appeal emphasised that under the principle in *Wilkinson v. Downton* the damage that must result is physical harm or a recognised psychiatric illness. A "catalogue of rudeness and unfriendliness" was behaviour which was not to be expected of grown up colleagues in the workplace, but could not be regarded as "behaviour so calculated to infringe [the claimant's] legal right to personal safety that an intention to do so should be imputed to the second defendant" (*ibid.* at [17]). In order to be categorised as an act "calculated to cause physical harm" to the claimant the defendant must have intended to violate the claimant's interest in her freedom from such harm (*i.e.* physical injury or a recognised psychiatric illness). The defendant's conduct must be such that that degree of harm was so likely to result that the defendant cannot be heard to say that he did not mean it to do so. He will be taken to have meant it to do so by the combination of the likelihood of such harm being suffered as a result of his behaviour and his deliberately engaging in that behaviour (*ibid.* at [12]).

NOTE 79a. Note that Buxton L.J.'s approach not only differs from that of Lord Woolf C.J. but also from formulation of the Court of Appeal in the earlier decision of *Wong v. Parkside Health NHS Trust* [2001] EWCA Civ 1721; *The Times*, December 7, 2001.

Harassment causing injury to health. Add: In *Hunter v. Canary Wharf Ltd* [1997] A.C. 655 Lord Hoffmann accepted that there was no necessary reason to confine *Wilkinson v. Downton* to the intentional infliction of psychiatric injury (since there was no obvious policy reason to exclude from compensation the *intentional* infliction of mere distress or inconvenience). However, his Lordship considered that the Protection from Harassment Act 1997 now rendered it unnecessary to consider how a common law tort of harassment might have developed. In *Wong v. Parkside Health NHS Trust* [2001] EWCA Civ 1721; *The Times*, December 7, 2001 the Court of Appeal confirmed that the common law had not reached the point of recognising a tort of intentional harassment going beyond the tort of intentional infliction of psychiatric harm and that the 1997 Act, which confers a civil remedy for breach, had effectively precluded the development of a common law tort of harassment.

NOTE 81. Add: Note that in *W v. Home Office* [2001] EWCA Civ 2081; [2002] 3 W.L.R. 405 at [81] Buxton L.J. criticised the statement at para. 13–17 of the main text that: "It would appear that any act deliberately designed to infringe

[the] legal right to personal safety, albeit falling outside the torts of assault and battery, will now readily be classified as tortious", on the basis that *Burrows v. Azadani* [1995] 1 W.L.R. 1372 had relied on that part of *Khorasandjian v. Bush* [1993] Q.B. 727 that was disapproved in *Hunter v. Canary Wharf*; and in any event was an injunction case in which it was held that conduct could be enjoined even if it was not in itself tortious.

13–18 **Protection from Harassment Act 1997.** *R. v. Colohan*, (also reported as *R. v. C (Sean Peter)*) [2001] EWCA Crim 1251; [2001] 2 F.L.R. 757, CA—the test of whether a reasonable person would think a course of conduct amounted to harassment in s.1(2) of the Protection from Harassment Act 1997 is objective. Thus, the fact that the defendant suffers from a mental illness is irrelevant because otherwise there would be a significant gap in the protection afforded by the Act, particularly since the conduct at which the Act was aimed was likely to be conducted by those of an obsessive or otherwise unusual psychological makeup, or those suffering from an identifiable mental illness. Section 1(3)(c) also stipulates an objective test.

The remedies under the Act are available even where the harassment does not cause the claimant to fear that violence will be used. The 1997 Act does not, however, catch a single act of harassment, because there must be "a course of conduct" (s.1(1)). The harassment must occur at least twice to be actionable. A series of articles in a newspaper can constitute a course of conduct for this purpose: *Thomas v. News Group Newspapers Ltd* [2001] EWCA Civ 1233; [2002] E.M.L.R. 4.

NOTE 83. *DPP v. Mesley* should read: *DPP v. Moseley (Joanna)*, *The Times*, June 23, 1999.

Lau v. D.P.P. is now reported at [2000] 1 F.L.R. 799.

4. FALSE IMPRISONMENT

(a) *What constitutes a false imprisonment*

13–19 **Imprisonment.** NOTE 84. *R. v. Reid* is reported at [1973] Q.B. 299.

13–21 **Claimant's knowledge irrelevant.** NOTE 95. *Roberts v. Chief Constable of the Cheshire Constabulary* is reported at [1999] 1 W.L.R. 662.

NOTE 96. Add: By the same token, a claimant's mistaken belief that he has been lawfully arrested does not render lawful an otherwise unlawful arrest, and accordingly he is entitled to use reasonable force to resist the unlawful restraint: *R. v McKoy*, *The Times*, June 17, 2002, CA.

13–22 **Absence of lawful authority.** *Percy v. Hall* is reported at [1997] Q.B. 924, CA.

R. v. Governor of Brockhill Prison, ex p. Evans (No. 2) was affirmed by the House of Lords at [2001] 2 A.C. 19; see Fordham (2000) 8 Tort L. Rev. 53. Thus, a prison governor who in good faith, and in reliance on the existing law, calculates the release date of a prisoner which subsequently turns out to have been too late because the law has changed in the interim, is liable in false imprisonment for the additional days that the prisoner is detained. Liability is strict. It is irrelevant that the governor has not been negligent and has acted in good faith in accordance with the law when the release date was calculated.

NOTE 97. *R. v. Governor of Brockhill Prison, ex p. Evans* is reported at [1997] Q.B. 443.

NOTE 98. *R. v. Governor of Brockhill Prison, ex p. Evans (No. 2)* (CA) is reported at [1999] Q.B. 1043.

Defendant's intention. NOTE 1. *R. v. Bournewood Community and Mental Health Services NHS Trust, ex p. L* is reported at [1999] 1 A.C. 458.   13–23

Continuance of imprisonment. *R. v. Governor of Brockhill Prison, ex p. Evans (No. 2)* was affirmed by the House of Lords at [2001] 2 A.C. 19.   13–25

NOTE 7. *Roberts v. Chief Constable of the Cheshire Constabulary* is reported at [1999] 1 W.L.R. 662.

R. v. Governor of Brockhill Prison, ex p. Evans (No. 2) is reported at [1999] Q.B. 1043.

Imprisonment in unauthorised places or conditions. NOTE 14. *Racz v. Home Office* is reported at [1994] 2 A.C. 45.   13–27

Intolerable conditions. NOTE 19. *Racz v. Home Office* is reported at [1994] 2 A.C. 45.   13–28

Add: *Brooks v. Home Office* [1999] 2 F.L.R. 33 (QBD).

NOTE 21. Add: See *Keenan v. U.K.* (Application No. 27229/95) (2001) 10 B.H.R.C. 319—inadequate medical treatment and a lack of effective monitoring of a prisoner who was an identified suicide risk could constitute a breach of Article 3; *Price v. U.K.* (Application No. 33394/96) (2002) 11 B.H.R.C. 401—detention of a disabled prisoner in circumstances where she was likely to suffer cold, develop sores, and was unable to use the toilet or keep clean, constituted degrading treatment in contravention of Article 3.

5. JUSTIFICATION OF TRESPASS TO THE PERSON

(b) *Preventing Breach of the Peace, or making Lawful Arrest*

Reasonable force. NOTE 57. *Pollard v. Chief Constable of West Yorkshire Police* is reported at [1999] P.I.Q.R. P219.   13–41

Powers of intervention. NOTE 66. *Bibby v. Chief Constable of Essex Police* is now reported at (2000) 164 J.P. 297. In *Bibby* the Court of Appeal held that the conduct of the person to be arrested must be unreasonable, and the threat to the peace must come from the person to be arrested.   13–43

What is a breach of the peace. NOTE 76. *Ackers v. Taylor* is reported at [1974] 1 W.L.R. 405.   13–45

NOTE 79. *Percy v. D.P.P.* is reported at [1995] 1 W.L.R. 1382.

Nicol v. DPP is reported at [1996] Crim. L.R. 318 and (1996) 160 J.P. 155.

NOTE 80. Add: A breach of the peace does not necessarily involve a disturbance to members of the public: *Chief Constable of Humberside Police v. McQuade* [2001] EWCA Civ 1330; [2002] 1 W.L.R. 1347. There is a difference between public order, which is concerned with the tranquility and safety of public places, and keeping the peace, which is concerned with the prevention of

13–45   violence and damage wherever they may occur, public or private: *per* Laws L.J. at [19].

13–46   **Statutory powers.** NOTE 82. *D.P.P. v. Orum* is reported at [1989] 1 W.L.R. 88.
NOTE 83. *Rukira v. D.P.P* should read *Rukwira v. D.P.P.*

13–47   NOTE 85. *D.P.P. v. Orum* is reported at [1989] 1 W.L.R. 88.

13–50   **Statutory powers of summary arrest.** NOTE 99. *Gapper v. Chief Constable of the Avon and Somerset Constabulary* is now reported at [2000] 1 Q.B. 29.

13–52   **Arrestable offences under the Police and Criminal Evidence Act 1984.** Add: The Criminal Justice and Police Act 2001, s.71 adds to the list of arrestable offences: kerb crawling (under s.1 of the Sexual Offences Act 1985); and failing to stop and report an accident causing personal injury (under s.170(4) of the Road Traffic Act 1988).
An arrestable offence is a domestic offence, not an extradition offence committed in another jurisdiction: *R. (on the application of Rottman) v. Commissioner of Police for the Metropolis* [2002] UKHL 20; [2002] 2 All E.R. 865, at [66].

13–53   **Reasonable cause for suspicion.** Add: *Hough v. Chief Constable of Staffordshire* [2001] EWCA Civ 39, *The Times*, February 14, 2001—an entry in the police national computer is sufficient objective justification for an arrest, where the police officer believed that H might be armed with a gun. The fact that the entry was false was irrelevant. A police officer is entitled to base the grounds for his suspicion on information received from a police informant or from a member of the public. If the situation was not urgent, the police officer may have to make additional enquiries before he would be treated as having reasonable grounds for suspicion
NOTE 14. *O'Hara v. Chief Constable of the Royal Ulster Constabulary* is reported at [1997] A.C. 286.

13–54   **Acting on reasonable suspicion.** NOTE 16. Add: Similarly, a default warrant issued by magistrates in respect of unpaid fines can be executed at the discretion of the police, but that discretion has to be exercised reasonably, applying *Wednesbury* grounds: *Henderson v. Chief Constable of Cleveland* [2001] EWCA Civ 335, [2001] 1 W.L.R. 1103. Thus, it could be lawful for the police to delay the execution of the warrant until the conclusion of a criminal investigation.

13–56   **The grounds for arrest.** NOTE 26. The arrest is not unlawful simply because the reason for the arrest is given by a police officer who did not carry out the arrest: *Dhesi v. Chief Constable of West Midlands Police*, *The Times*, May 9, 2000, CA.
NOTE 28. *R. v. Chalkley* is reported at [1998] Q.B. 848.

13–57   **A reasonable explanation.** NOTE 33. Add: Where a person has been informed of the reason for his arrest, and the lawfulness of the arrest is established, his subjective belief that he had not committed an offence is irrelevant. An attempt to resist arrest constitutes an offence contrary to the Offences against the Person

Act 1861, s.38, and would constitute a battery in tort: *R. v. Lee* [2001] 1 Cr. App. R. 293, CA.

Constables and private persons. Add: Once at the police station the Police and Criminal Evidence Act 1984, s.40 provides a procedure for review of a prisoner's continued detention. A failure to comply with that procedure renders the detention unlawful: *Roberts v. Chief Constable of the Cheshire Constabulary* is reported at [1999] 1 W.L.R. 662. **13–61**

Restraints on persons in custody. NOTE 52. *Lindley v. Rutter* is reported at [1981] Q.B. 128. **13–62**

NOTE 54. *Secretary of State for the Home Department v. Robb* is reported at [1995] Fam. 127. **13–63**
Re T. (Adult: Refusal of Medical Treatment) is reported at [1993] Fam. 95.
NOTE 54. Add: *cf.* however, the position where the prisoner lacks the relevant mental capacity: *R. v. Collins and Ashworth Hospital Authority, ex p. Brady* [2000] Lloyd's Rep. Med. 355. Moreover, *quaere* whether there are circumstances in which state or public interests should prevail over a self-determined hunger strike so as to enable intervention: *per* Kay J. at [72]–[73]. Kay J. noted the incongruity of a law that imposes a common law duty to take reasonable care to prevent a prisoner committing suicide or harming himself (on which see *Reeves v. Commissioner of Police for the Metropolis* [2000] 1 A.C. 360; though note that this duty is not owed where there is no foreseeable risk of suicide by the prisoner: *Orange v. Chief Constable of West Yorkshire Police* [2001] EWCA Civ 611; [2001] 3 W.L.R. 736, CA) and a rule by which the prison authorities have no power to intervene to prevent a prisoner from starving himself to death. Thus, his Lordship observed, at [71], that: "It would be somewhat odd if there is a duty to prevent suicide by an act (for example, the use of a knife left in a cell) but not even a power to intervene to prevent self-destruction by starvation. I can see no moral justification for the law indulging its fascination with the difference between acts and omissions in a context such as this and no logical need for it to do so."

(c) *Assisting Officers of the Law*

Assisting officers of the law. NOTE 59. *Morris v. Beardmore* is reported at [1981] A.C. 446. **13–65**
Davidson v. Chief Constable of South Wales should read *Davidson v. Chief Constable of North Wales*.

(d) *Confinement of Mentally Disordered Persons*

NOTE 66a. Delete the text and substitute: The draft Mental Health Bill 2002 will make major changes to the Mental Health Act 1983, though the draft Bill is still at the consultation stage (see *www.doh.gov.uk/mentalhealth/draftbill2002*). If implemented, the major change for patients other than offenders is that a new Mental Health Tribunal will authorise all compulsory treatment beyond 28 days and that patients may be subject to community based orders rather than detention in hospital. There are also proposals to allow for the appointment of a nominated person to act on behalf of patients who are not formally detained but who are **13–67** being treated without their consent because they lack the capacity to consent to treatment, and to give them the right to challenge admission and treatment before a Mental Health Tribunal.

Note 67. *R. v. Bournewood Community and Mental Health Services NHS Trust, ex p. L* is reported at [1999] 1 A.C. 458.

13–69 **Mental disorder.** Note 73. *St George's Healthcare NHS Trust v. S* is reported at [1999] Fam. 26.

Note 74. Note that in *R. v. Canons Park Mental Health Review Tribunal, ex p. A.* [1995] Q.B. 60 the Court of Appeal reversed the decision of the Divisional Court, holding that the discharge criteria contained in s.72 of the Mental Health Act 1983 were not a "mirror image" of the compulsory admission criteria in s.3. Thus, the fact that the patient's condition was not treatable did not mean that she was bound to be discharged under s.72(1)(b). Moreover, the question of what constituted medical treatment should not be construed narrowly. The fact that the patient was unwilling to co-operate in the only form of treatment that was likely to alleviate or prevent a deterioration in her condition (in this case, group therapy) did not mean that she failed to satisfy the treatability test, since Parliament cannot have intended that a patient should be deemed to be untreatable merely because she refused to co-operate with suitable treatment. However, in *R. v. London South and South West Region Mental Health Review Tribunal, ex p. Moyle* [2000] Lloyd's Rep. Med. 143, Latham J. held that the reasoning of the majority in the *Canons Park* case could not stand with the decision of the House of Lords in the Scottish case *Reid v. Secretary of State for Scotland* [1999] 2 A.C. 512, HL. Accordingly, the criteria for discharge are meant to be matching or mirror images of the admission criteria. It is submitted that this approach is consistent with that of the Court of Appeal in *R. (on the application of H) v. Mental Health Review Tribunal for North and East London Region* [2001] EWCA Civ 415, [2002] Q.B. 1 (see para. 13–70 of this *Supplement*), since it is unlikely that the Court of Appeal decision in *Canons Park* would withstand a challenge under Article 5 of the European Convention for the Protection of Human Rights. If the criteria for an initial compulsory detention are no longer satisfied, it is difficult to see how continued detention can be justified.

Note 76. *R. v. Hallstrom, ex p. W. (No. 2)* is reported at [1986] Q.B. 1090.

R. v. BHB Community Healthcare NHS Trust, ex p. Barker is reported at [1999] Lloyd's Rep. Med. 101; [1999] 1 F.L.R. 106; (1999) 47 B.M.L.R. 112.

Note that there is now provision for supervised discharge and after-care: see para. 13–76.

13–70 **Procedural safeguards.** Note 77. *T. v. T.* is reported as *Re T* at [1988] Fam. 52.

Note 78. *W. v. L. (Mental Health Patient)* is reported at [1974] Q.B. 711.

Whitbread v. Kingston and District NHS Trust is reported at (1998) 39 B.M.L.R. 94.

Note 79. *Re S-C (mental patient: habeas corpus)* is reported at [1996] Q.B. 599.

Add: In *R. (on the application of H) v. Mental Health Review Tribunal for North and East London Region* [2001] EWCA Civ 415, [2002] Q.B. 1 the Court of Appeal held that s.73 of the Mental Health Act 1983 was incompatible with Article 5 of the European Convention for the Protection of Human Rights because the burden of proof rested on a restricted patient, detained in a secure hospital following his conviction for manslaughter, to show that he no longer suffered from a mental disorder which warranted his detention. The 1983 Act infringed a person's right to liberty under Article 5 because it failed to require a tribunal to discharge a patient where it could not be shown that he was suffering from a mental disorder which warranted detention. *cf. R. v. Mental Health Review Tribunal, ex p. Hall* [1999] 4 All E.R. 883, where the Court of Appeal held that the failure of the local social services and health authorities to make the necessary arrangements to comply with the conditions attached to a conditional discharge imposed by a mental health review tribunal, with the result that the patient remained detained, did not render the tribunal's decision unlawful; nor was it a breach of Article 5(1) of the European Convention for the Protection of Human Rights. Moreover, s.117 of the Mental Health Act 1983 does not impose an absolute obligation on a health authority to provide aftercare services when a detained patient is conditionally discharged, and this does not contravene Article 5 if as a consequence the discharge cannot be put into effect: *R. v. Camden and Islington Health Authority* [2001] Lloyd's Rep. Med. 152, CA.

NOTE 82. Add: Unreasonable delay in hearing an application to a mental health review tribunal by a detained patient can constitute a breach of Article 5(4) of the European Convention on Human Rights which requires the lawfulness of a person's detention to be considered speedily by a court: *R. (on the application of C) v. The Mental Health Review Tribunal, London and South West Region* [2001] EWCA Civ 1110; [2002] 1 W.L.R. 176; *R. (on the application of K) v. Mental Health Review Tribunal* [2002] EWHC 639 (Admin); (2002) 152 N.L.J. 672.

Consent to treatment. NOTE 87. *B. v. Croydon Health Authority* is reported at [1995] Fam. 133.

St George's Healthcare NHS Trust v. S is reported at [1999] Fam. 26

After *B. v. Croydon Health Authority* **Add:** See also *R. v. Collins and Ashworth Hospital Authority, ex p. Brady* [2000] Lloyd's Rep. Med. 355.

NOTE 88. *T. v. T.* is reported as *Re T* at [1988] Fam. 52.

Safeguards. The "second opinion" doctor must form his own independent opinion on the existence of the statutory criteria—he should not simply review the responsible medical officer's decision that the criteria are satisfied. At the very least he must act in good faith and with reasonable care in forming his judgment: *R. (on the application of W) v. Broadmoor Hospital* [2001] EWCA Civ 1545; [2002] 1 W.L.R. 419 at [71] *per* Hale L.J.

Protection against civil or criminal proceedings. NOTE 3. Add: On judicial review of a decision involving the forcible treatment of a detained patient, the test to be applied in determining the lawfulness of the decision is no longer *Wednesbury* unreasonableness, nor even the so-called super-*Wednesbury* test adopted in *R. v Ministry of Defence, ex parte Smith* [1996] Q.B. 517 applied to cases involving human rights. Rather there must be an assessment of the substantive merits of the decision, involving the finding of primary facts following oral evidence (if necessary): *R. (on the application of W) v. Broadmoor Hospital* [2001] EWCA Civ 1545; [2002] 1 W.L.R. 419.

Re Waldron is reported at [1986] Q.B. 824.

NOTE 5. Add: It is arguable that a private law action brought under s.7 of the Human Rights Act 1998 would also require leave under s.139(2) of the Mental Health Act 1983: *R. (on the application of W) v. Broadmoor Hospital* [2001]

13–78

EWCA Civ 1545; [2002] 1 W.L.R. 419 *per* Brooke L.J. at [54] and Hale L.J. at [61]. Note, however, that s.139(4) provides that s.139 does not apply to proceedings against the Secretary of State, a health authority or a NHS Trust. It is clear that s.139(2) does not apply (and therefore leave is not required for an action against these defendants) and the traditional view has also been that, irrespective of the substantive defence provided to a doctor by s.139(1), the hospital employing that doctor would be vicariously liable for his actions (*e.g.* in the tort of battery) even if the doctor was not liable because he acted in good faith and with reasonable care: see *ibid.* at [24] *per* Simon Brown L.J. and [58] *per* Hale L.J. However, Hale L.J. went on to suggest that a health authority or NHS Trust could only be held vicariously liable for those actions for which the doctors would themselves be liable, which would indirectly confer the benefit of s.139(1) on the employers. Brooke L.J. went further (at [42] and [43]) and suggested, provisionally, that a hospital authority may not be vicariously liable at all for the actions a responsible medical officer (RMO) in making treatment decisions under ss.57 or 58 of the Act, since the Act vests the duty to carry out the specified functions in the RMO personally. It was not the hospital, through the agency of one of its medical staff, in whom was vested the power to direct treatment without consent, but the RMO himself.

Note that if the draft Mental Health Bill 2002 is enacted this may reverse the burden of proof under s.139; in other words it will be a defence for the person complained against to demonstrate that he acted in good faith and with reasonable care.

Winch v. Jones is reported at [1986] Q.B. 296.

(e) *Parental or other authority*

13–81 **Discipline and control.** See *R. v. H (Reasonable Chastisement)*, [2001] 2 F.L.R. 431, CA—factors which go to whether the chastisement is reasonable include: (i) the nature and context of the defendant's behaviour; (ii) the duration of that behaviour; (iii) the physical and mental consequences in respect of the child; (iv) the age and personal characteristics of the child; (v) the reasons given by the defendant for administering the punishment.

6. DAMAGES

13–84 **Damages in trespass.** NOTE 36. *Thompson v. Commissioner of Police for the Metropolis* is reported at [1998] Q.B. 498.

13–85 NOTE 37. *Holgate v. Chief Constable of Lancashire* should read *Holden v. Chief Constable of Lancashire* and is reported at [1987] Q.B. 380.

NOTE 39. *Barbara v. Home Office* is reported at (1984) 134 New L.J. 888

NOTE 41. *Thompson v. Commissioner of Police for the Metropolis* is reported at [1998] Q.B. 498.

In *Kuddus v. Chief Constable of Leicestershire Constabulary* [2001] UKHL 29; [2001] 3 All E.R. 193 the House of Lords held that the so-called "cause of action" test established by the Court of Appeal in *AB v. South West Water Services Ltd* [1993] Q.B. 507, whereby exemplary damages could only be awarded where the claim gave rise to a cause of action that before 1964 had been accepted as grounding a claim for exemplary damages, was not good law. The question was the nature of the conduct and whether it fitted into Lord Devlin's categories in *Rookes v. Barnard* [1964] A.C. 1129, not the basis of the cause of action. Their Lordships expressed differing views on the question of whether exemplary damages were appropriate where the claim was based on the defendant's vicarious liability, but this point had not been argued and was left open.

Compensation by the criminal courts. NOTE 44. *R. v. Chappell* is reported at (1985) 80 Cr. App. R. 31, and (1984) 6 Cr. App. R. (S.) 214. **13–86**

NOTE 47. *R. v. Thomson Holidays Ltd* is reported at [1974] Q.B. 592.

NOTE 48. *R. v. Vivian* is reported at [1979] 1 W.L.R. 291.

NOTE 49. Delete the text and substitute: See the Criminal Injuries Compensation Act 1995; Miers [2001] J.P.I.L. 371.

CHAPTER 14

WRONGFUL INTERFERENCE WITH GOODS

	PARA.
1. General	14–01
■ 2. Modes of conversion	14–08
(a) Conversion by taking or receiving property	14–11
(b) Conversion by transfer	14–18
(d) Conversion by keeping	14–25
(f) Conversion by denial of right	14–36
3. Subject-matter of conversion	14–38
■ 4. Person entitled to sue	14–46
(a) Generally	14–46
(b) Title by mere possession	14–52
■ 9. Damages	14–99
(a) General rule: value of the goods	14–99
(b) Damages beyond value of goods: special damages	14–113
(c) Nature of claimant's interest	14–118
(d) Return of chattel	14–127
14. Replevin	14–146

Significant developments since the previous edition have been the confirmation in *Costello v. Chief Constable of Derbyshire* [2001] 1 W.L.R. 1437 that, for the purposes of the law of conversion, even a thief's title is good as against anyone who cannot show a better one, and the extensive discussion by the CA and HL in *Kuwait Airways v. Iraq Airways Co.* [2001] 1 Lloyd's Rep. 161; [2002] 2 W.L.R. 1353 of the measure of damages in conversion. **14a**

1. GENERAL

Wrongful interference with goods. On the nature of remedies for wrongful interference with goods, see too Birks (2000) 11 K.C.L.J. 1–10. **14–01**

2. MODES OF CONVERSION

Forms of conversion. Mance J.'s decision in *Kuwait Airways v. Iraq Airways Co.* has been largely upheld in the CA on this point ([2001] 1 Lloyd's Rep. 161, 229 *et seq.*), and subsequently in the HL (see [2002] 2 W.L.R. 1353). **14–09**

Mance J.'s decision in *Kuwait Airways v. Iraq Airways Co.* has been largely upheld in the CA on this point (see [2001] 1 Lloyd's Rep. 161). The HL did not discuss the point (see [2002] 2 W.L.R. 1353). **14–10**

(a) *Conversion by Taking or Receiving Property*

Mance J.'s decision in *Kuwait Airways v. Iraq Airways Co.* has been upheld in the CA on this point (see [2001] 1 Lloyd's Rep. 161, 178), and subsequently in the HL (see [2002] UKHL 19, §§ 37 *et seq.*). **14–12**

[113]

14–14   CHAPTER 14—WRONGFUL INTERFERENCE WITH GOODS

14–14   **Taking and using goods.** Mance J.'s decision in *Kuwait Airways v. Iraq Airways Co.* has been upheld in the CA (see [2001] 1 Lloyd's Rep. 161), and subsequently in the HL (see [2002] 2 W.L.R. 1353, 1365 *et seq.*).

(b) *Conversion by Transfer*

14–18   **Transfer of some right over the property.** Where a chattel is on the defendant's land and he expels the true owner and then allows a third party to remove it, this is conversion: see *Smith (Administrator of Cosslett (Contractors) Ltd v. Bridgend CC* [2001] 3 W.L.R. 1347, esp. at pp. 1358, 1366.

(d) *Conversion by keeping*

14–32   **Other evidence of unlawful keeping.** Mance J.'s decision in *Kuwait Airways v. Iraq Airways Co.* has been upheld in the CA: see [2001] 1 Lloyd's Rep. 161), and subsequently in the HL (see [2002] 2 W.L.R. 1353, 1365 *et seq., per* Lord Nicholls).

(f) *Conversion by denial of right*

14–36   Mance J.'s decision in *Kuwait Airways v. Iraq Airways Co.* has been upheld in the CA (see [2001] 1 Lloyd's Rep. 161) and subsequently in the HL—see [2002] 2 W.L.R. 1353, 1365 *et seq., per* Lord Nicholls.

3. SUBJECT-MATTER OF CONVERSION

14–41   **Negotiable instruments and securities.** NOTE 55. *Smith v. Lloyds TSB plc* has been affirmed in the CA: [2000] 2 All E.R. Comm 293. See too Hare [2001] C.L.J. 35.

4. PERSON ENTITLED TO SUE

(a) *Generally*

14–46   **Claimant must have possession or immediate right to possession.** On who has the right to sue in relation to a converted cheque, see *Surrey Asset Finance Ltd v. National Westminster Bank plc, The Times,* November 30, 2000. Until the cheque has been delivered to the payee the immediate right to possession remains in the drawer: once delivery has been effected (as was held to be the case here), the right is in the payee, and the drawer cannot sue.

14–48   **Claimant's right must exist at time of conversion.** Note too *Smith (Administrator of Cosslett (Contractors) Ltd v. Bridgend CC* [2001] 3 W.L.R. 1347. The defendants refused to allow an insolvent contractor onto their land to retrieve certain plant, and subsequently allowed a third party to take the plant away under a purported contract of sale. At the time of the refusal the claimant contractor had no right to immediate possession. At the time when the plant was disposed of, it had, owing to the intervention of an administrator and the effect of s.395 of the Companies Act 1985. The defendants were held liable in conversion.

Right to immediate possession: transferees. NOTE 97. On the nature of a lessee's interest (in the context of a finance lease), see *On Demand Information plc (in Administrative Receivership) v. Michael Gerson (Finance) plc* [2001] 1 W.L.R. 155, 171, where Robert Walker L.J. said: "Contractual rights which entitle the hirer to indefinite possession of chattels so long as the hire payments are duly made, and which qualify and limit the owner's general property in the chattels, cannot aptly be described as purely contractual rights."(The decision was later reversed in the HL, but on unrelated grounds: *On Demand Information plc (in Administrative Receivership) v. Michael Gerson (Finance) plc* [2002] 2 W.L.R. 919.)

14–50

(b) *Title by mere possession*

It now seems that the maxim *ex turpi causa* will not bar proceedings for conversion of stolen property: the principle that no-one should be deprived of his property except by law trumps any distaste felt by the court at indemnifying the dishonest. See *Costello v. Chief Constable of Derbyshire*, [2001] 1 W.L.R. 1437 (police detain stolen car but cannot show who true owner is: liable in conversion to thief for full value). The decision in *Costello* was later approved by the Privy Council in *Jaroo v. Att-Gen of Trinidad* [2002] 2 W.L.R. 705, where indeed the protection of a mere possessory title was held covered by a constitutional guarantee of the sanctity of property. See too Fox [2002] C.L.J. 27; *Verrecchia v. Met. Police Comm'r*, unreported, March 15, 2001.

14–53

NOTE 144. See now C.P.R. Part 19, 5A.

14–90

9. DAMAGES

(a) *General Rule: Value of the Goods*

The victim of a conversion is entitled to recover the value of the property converted without reference to what might have happened after the conversion. So in *Kuwait Airways v. Iraq Airways Co.* [2002] 2 W.L.R. 1353, where aircraft were stolen by Iraqi forces from Kuwait and then destroyed in the ensuing hostilities, the House of Lords held that the owners were entitled to recover their value without reference to the question whether they would have been destroyed anyway even if they had not been converted. The reason was that conversion was a wrong to possession, and the claimant was entitled to be put into the position he would have been in had he retained the possession to which he was entitled.

14–99

Decline in value after conversion. On cases like *Brandeis Goldschmidt Ltd v. Western Transport Ltd* [1981] Q.B. 564 and the use of arbitrary measures of damages, see now Lord Nicholls's statement in *Kuwait Airways v. Iraq Airways Co.* [2002] 2 W.L.R. 1353, 1372:

14–103

"The aim of the law, in respect of the wrongful interference with goods, is to provide a just remedy. Despite its proprietary base, this tort does not stand apart and command awards of damages measured by some special and artificial standard of its own.

14-103 CHAPTER 14—WRONGFUL INTERFERENCE WITH GOODS

The fundamental object of an award of damages in respect of this tort, as with all wrongs, is to award just compensation for loss suffered. Normally ('prima facie') the measure of damages is the market value of the goods at the time the defendant expropriated them. This is the general rule, because generally this measure represents the amount of the basic loss suffered by the plaintiff owner. He has been dispossessed of his goods by the defendant.

Depending on the circumstances some other measure, yielding a higher or lower amount, may be appropriate. The plaintiff may have suffered additional damage consequential on the loss of his goods."

In *Solloway v. McLaughlin* [1938] A.C. 247 and *BBMB Finance v. Eda Holdings Ltd* [1990] 1 W.L.R. 409, brokers converted securities, sold them and subsequently repurchased them when they had gone down in value before re-crediting their clients' account. The brokers pocketed the difference. In both cases the Privy Council held the clients entitled to that difference by way of damages. Lord Nicholls in *Kuwait Airways v. Iraq Airways Co.* [2002] 2 W.L.R. 1353, 1376–1377 thought such cases better explained as involving damages based on the profit made by the defendant under the principle in *Att-Gen v. Blake* [2001] 1 A.C. 268, 278–280.

14-104 **How is the value assessed?** On the valuation of a chattel in a highly volatile market, see *Kuwait Airways v. Iraq Airways Co.* [2001] 1 Lloyd's Rep. 161, 262–263. There the CA held that aircraft wrongfully abstracted by the Iraqi army on its invasion of Kuwait fell to be valued on the "current market price" principle, taking into account a "base value" and then adjusting it according to the strength of the market for aircraft at the relevant time.

Nor is it relevant to a claim in conversion that the owner of the goods has not yet paid for them: *Center Optical (Hong Kong) Ltd v. Jardine Transport Services (China) Ltd* [2001] 2 Lloyd's Rep. 678 (High Court of Hong Kong).

14-109 **Presumption of value against wrongdoer.** *Colbeck v. Diamanta (UK) Ltd* [2002] EWHC 616 vindicates the scepticism expressed in the text about the presumption that, where the converter cannot produce the goods, they are deemed to be "of the highest possible value". Diamonds were entrusted to a Hatton Garden dealer who could not produce them on demand. Their weight was known, but their value depended on their cut and colour, on which there was no clear information. Field J. declined to award damages on the assumption that the diamonds had been "finest quality" (the highest grade). As he put it, "the presumption against the wrongdoer must be consistent with the rest of the facts, and in my judgment to presume that the diamonds were of the finest quality is not consistent with the rest of the facts of this case."

14-111 **Particular forms of property: securities and documents.** NOTE 36. See too *Smith v. Lloyds TSB plc* [2000] 2 All E.R. Comm 293 (altered cheque unenforceable under Bills of Exchange Act 1882: no substantial damages for conversion); Hare [2001] C.L.J. 35.

(b) *Damages Beyond Value of Goods: Special Damages*

14-114 **Consequential damage if not too remote.** For the rule of remoteness as regards wrongful interference, see now Lord Nicholls in *Kuwait Airways Corp'n v. Iraqi Airways Co.* [2002] 2 W.L.R. 1353, 1378 *et seq*. There his Lordship divided converters into knowing wrongdoers and others. The former were liable only for foreseeable losses: the latter for al losses naturally resulting from the conversion.

(c) *Nature of claimant's interest*

The claimant with limited interest. NOTE 76. See too *Chartered Trust plc v. King*, unrep., February 23, 2001. **14–122**

(d) *Return of Chattel*

The result in *Hunter BNZ Finance v. ANZ Banking Group* [1990] V.R. 41 is now open to some question. In *Sanwa Australia Finance Ltd v. Finchill Pty Ltd* [2001] N.S.W.C.A. 466 financiers provided a cheque to would-be suppliers under a bogus leasing transaction with A. The suppliers converted the cheque by endorsing it to A without supplying the goods: A paid a few instalments to the financiers to allay suspicion, and then became insolvent. In an action for conversion against the suppliers, the financiers' damages were reduced by the amount of the instalments received. **14–129**

14. REPLEVIN

Replevin only in case of trespass. NOTE 90. Note that when the Private Security Industry Act 2001 comes into force, it will be an offence to wheel-clamp cars without a licence: see s.3(2)(j). **14–147**

Chapter 15

DECEIT

	PARA.
1. Introduction	15–01
4. Representation must be intended to be acted upon by claimant	15–27
5. Claimant must have been influenced by misrepresentation	15–32
6. Damage	15–39
7. Statutory liability under Misrepresentation Act 1967, s.2(1)	15–44

1. Introduction

Definition. Fn. 3: *P. v. B.* (Paternity: Damages for Deceit) [2001] 1 F.L.R. 1041, Stanley Burnton J. Actionable deceit could arise between cohabitees but would only be commenced when the relationship had already broken down. **15–01**

Fraud and misrepresentation generally. Bar Council guidance (following the case of *Medcalf v. Mardell*, [2001] C.P.L.R. 140; [2001] Lloyd's Rep. P.N. 146) is that counsel should not plead any allegation of fraud without clear instructions and reasonably credible admissible evidence establishing a prima facie case of fraud. This was endorsed by the Court of Appeal in *Cornwall Gardens Pte Ltd v. Garrard & Co Ltd* [2001] E.W.C.A. Civ. 699 (noted in *The Times*, June 19, 2001). However the House of Lords in *Medcalf v. Mardell* (wasted costs order) [2002] UKHL 27, [2002] 3 W.L.R. 172 set aside the wasted costs order, applying a less stringent test *viz*. Whether the barristers had material of any kind before them which justified the making of the allegation. In *Biggs v. Sotnicks (a firm)* [2002] EWCA Civ 272, [2002] Lloyd's Rep. P.N. 331 the Court of Appeal discussed the correct interpretation of section 32(1) of the Limitation Act 1980. The CA followed the classic statement of what s.32(1) requires, contained in the judgment of Millett L.J. in *Paragon Finance plc v. Thakerar & Co.* [1999] 1 All E.R. 400, 418. He asserted: "[the plaintiffs] must establish that they could not have discovered the fraud without exceptional measures which they could not reasonably have been expected to take". The CA rejected the proposed amendment of this by Crane J. in *UCB Home Loans v. Carr* [2000] Lloyd's P.N.L.R. 754, 757, where he suggested that the word "exceptional" should be omitted from the passage cited. **15–02**

4. Representation must be Intended to be Acted upon by Claimants

Fraud and illegal transactions. Fn. 18: The "pragmatic" approach of Bingham L.J. in *Saunders v. Edwards* [1987] 1 W.L.R. 116 followed by Collins J. in *Daido Asia Japan Co Ltd v. Rothen*, unreported, [2002] B.C.C. 589. **15–03**

Misstatement of opinion. *Barings plc v. Coopers v. Lybrand (No. 5)* [2002] EWHC 461, [2002] Lloyd's Rep. P.N. 395. **15–10**

15–10

As between the two parties, the claimants' employee was better equipped with information or the means of information than the defendants. So the employee was representing not only that he had an honest belief but that he had reasonable grounds for the belief he had expressed. *Brown v. Raphael* [1958] Ch. 1636, CA, applied. State of mind necessary for an action of deceit. See 15–17, *Jaffray v. Society of Lloyd's* [2002] EWCA Civ 1101.

15–18 **Knowledge of untruth.** *Barings plc v. Coopers v. Lybrand (No. 5)* [2002] EWHC 461, [2002] Lloyd's Rep. P.N. 395.

Though motive is irrelevant to liability in deceit, it may be a relevant consideration when trying to decide whether a person made a statement which he must have known to be false.

15–25 **Principal's liability for statements by agent.** *Noel v. Poland* [2001] 2 B.C.L.R. 645; [2002] Lloyd's Rep. I.R. 30, Toulson J. Toulson J. criticised the decision of the CA in *Standard Chartered Bank v. Pakistan National Shipping Corp (No. 2)* [2000] 1 Lloyd's Rep. 218 that a director who deliberately presented fraudulent documents on behalf of a company was not personally liable in deceit. Toulson J.'s criticism reflects the views of Collins J. in *Daido Asia Japan Ltd v. Rothen*, [2002] B.C.C. 589 (where Collins J. "got round" the CA decision in *Standard Chartered Bank* by finding that the company director had authorised, directed and procured the deceit). The CA in *Standard Chartered Bank* had cited *Williams v. Natural Life Health Foods Ltd* [1998] 1 W.L.R., a decision on negligent misstatement, to hold that even for deceit there must be an assumption of responsibility by the director such as to create a special relationship between the claimant and the director before the director could be personally liable. However as Toulson J. pointed out there was no logic in treating claims for deceit against company directors any differently from claims in deceit against any other agent of the company. An agent who committed a tort on behalf of a principal was personally liable. Earlier authorities that established this were not cited in *Standard Chartered Bank*. There is also adverse criticism of *Standard Chartered Bank* by Watts 116 L.Q.R. (2000) 525.

15–27 **Representation must be intended to be acted on by claimant.** *Bradford Building Society v. Borders* [1941] 2 All E.R. 205 applied in *Goose v. Wilson Sandford & Co (No. 2)* [2001] Lloyd's Rep. P.N. 189, CA.

5. Claimant must have been Influenced by the Misrepresentation

15–35 **The defence of contributory negligence and deceit.** Fn. 37: The subsequent decision of the Court of Appeal in *Standard Chartered Bank v. Pakistan National Shipping Corp* [2000] 1 Lloyd's Rep. 218 which decided that there is no defence of contributory deceit now reported: *Standard Chartered Bank v. Pakistan National Shipping Corp No. 4 (Reduction of Damages)* [2001] Q.B. 167. *Barings plc v. Coopers v. Lybrand (No. 5)* [2002] EWHC 461 [2002] Lloyd's Rep. P.N. 395: *Standard Chartered Bank v. Pakistan National Shipping Corporation (No. 4)* [2001] Q.B. 167 discussed.

6. Damage

Measure of Damages. *Standard Chartered Bank v. Pakistan National Shipping Corporation (Assessment of Damages)* [2001] E.W.C.A. Civ. 55, [2001] 1 All E.R. (Comm) 822, CA. Market value not applied as the claimant was "locked into" the goods in question. The "date of transaction" rule not applied in *Flack v. Pattinson*, unreported, December 19, 2001, Geoffrey Vos Q.C., sitting as a Deputy High Court Judge. Here deceit led to the purchase of an historic racing car. The misrepresentation continued to operate and caused the claimant to retain the car while he attempted to discover whether the statements which induced the sale were true. Subsequently he was locked into retaining the car until it was auctioned. *Smith New Court Securities Ltd v. Scrimgeour Vickers (Asset Management) Ltd* [1997] A.C. 254, applied.   **15–40**

Consequential losses. *KBC Bank v. Industrial Steels (U.K.) Ltd* [2001] 1 Lloyd's Rep. 370, David Steel J. The defendant was liable in deceit to the claimant when it presented false documents to the claimant causing it to pay the defendant the price of goods under a letter of credit. The damages recovered included the cost of litigation brought by the claimant against third parties (the banks who had issued the letters of credit) at a time when the defendant was still alleging that its documents were genuine and compliant. The fact that the claimant had negligently failed to notice that the documents were non-compliant was irrelevant.   **15–42**

Fraud and exemplary damages. Fn. 69: The Court of Appeal decision in *Kuddus v. Chief Constable of Leicestershire* (denying exemplary damages in the tort of misfeasance in public office, based on the view that Lord Devlin's speech in *Rookes v. Barnard* did not extend the range of torts in which awards of exemplary damages could be made and following the CA decision in *AB v. South West Water Services* [1993] Q.B. 507) was overturned by the House of Lords, [2001] UKHL 29, [2001] 3 All E.R. 193. This therefore reopens the question whether exemplary damages may be awarded for the tort of deceit as within Lord Devlin's category of "conduct calculated to make a profit".   **15–43**

7. Statutory Liability under Misrepresentation Act 1967, s.2(1)

Measure of Damages. *Royscot v. Rogerson* [1991] 2 Q.B. 297 applied in *Spice Girls v. Aprilla World Service BV (Damages)* [2001] E.M.L.R. 8, Arden J.   **15–45**

CHAPTER 16

MALICIOUS PROSECUTION

	PARA.
2. Kinds of damage caused	16–02
6. Vexatious use of process	16–50

2. KINDS OF DAMAGE CAUSED

Nature of damage thereby caused. NOTE 6. *Savill v. Roberts* should be cited **16–02** as (1698) 12 Mod. 208.

NOTE 7. Add: For analysis and criticism of *Gregory* see Cane (2000) 116 **16–03** L.Q.R. 346.

NOTE 9. Add: *Sallows v. Griffiths* [2001] F.S.R. 15, CA.

6. VEXATIOUS USE OF PROCESS

Vexatious litigants. NOTE 16. Add: See also *Att.-Gen. v. Barker (Civil Pro-* **16–51** *ceedings Order)* [2000] 1 F.L.R. 759; *Att.-Gen. v. Covey, Att.-Gen. v. Matthews, The Times*, March 2, 2001, CA.

No civil action for perjury. NOTE 24. Note that, on appeal, the House of **16–53** Lords overruled the Court of Appeal on this point, preferring to limit the absolute immunity to statements of evidence that the witness would be giving at the trial: *Docker v. Chief Constable of the West Midlands Police* [2001] 1 A.C. 435.

CHAPTER 17

PUBLIC OFFICERS

	PARA.
8. Misfeasance in public office	17–133
(b) Scope of the tort: public office	17–136
(d) The mental element: misfeasance	17–144
(e) Quantum	17–146

8. Misfeasance in Public Office

(b) *Scope of the Tort: Public Office*

Police officers. NOTE 53. Add: Subsequently, in *Docker v. Chief Constable of the West Midlands Police* [2001] 1 A.C. 435, the House of Lords limited the available immunity to oral evidence given at trial and to written statements of evidence that the witness would actually be giving at trial (see also para. 16–53, note 24). **17–137**

Social workers. NOTE 72. Add: Claims in misfeasance in public office were rejected by the Court of Appeal in *Jarvis v. Hampshire County Council* [2000] E.L.R. 36 and not appealed when *Jarvis* went to the House of Lords as one of the four appeals heard as *Phelps v. Hillingdon LBC* [2000] 3 W.L.R. 776 (see para. 12–42A). **17–141**

(d) *The Mental Element: Misfeasance*

Knowledge of consequences. Add to the end of the paragraph: Subsequently, the House of Lords first affirmed the Court of Appeal's decision and reasoning on the scope of the tort,[80a] and then (by a majority) refused to strike out the claimant's action, preferring to leave it to the trial judge to determine whether the evidence indicated negligence rather than misfeasance.[80b] Also, in *Thomas v. Chief Constable of Cleveland*,[80c] the Court of Appeal confirmed that the effect of *Three Rivers* was that "bad faith" as described by the Court of Appeal in that case was an essential ingredient pervasive to both the "targeted malice" and "knowing/reckless unlawful conduct" alternatives for establishing the mental element required by the tort. **17–145**

NOTE 80a. *Three Rivers District Council v. Bank of England (No. 3)* [2000] 2 W.L.R. 1220; Allott (2001) 60(1) C.L.J. 4; Dzakpasu (2002) 17(2) J.I.B.L. 41; see also *Greville v. Sprake* [2001] EWCA Civ 234, CA.

NOTE 80b. *Three Rivers District Council v. Bank of England (No. 3) (Summary Judgment)* [2001] 2 All E.R. 513; see Blyth and Cavalli (2001) 3(5) J.I.F.M. 199.

NOTE 80c. [2001] EWCA Civ 1552.

NOTE 80. Add: Affirmed by the Court of Appeal in *Hall v. Bank of England* [2000] Lloyd's Rep. Bank 186.

(e) *Quantum*

17–146 **Compensatory.** Add to the end of the paragraph: On appeal, the House of Lords reversed the decision of the Court of Appeal. Their Lordships held that the fact that misfeasance in public office was not a tort for which exemplary damages had been awarded before did not preclude the plaintiff's claim for exemplary damages, which was, therefore, arguable and ought to proceed to trial.[83a]

NOTE 83a. *Kuddus v. Chief Constable of Leicestershire* [2001] 2 W.L.R. 1289, HL.

CHAPTER 18

TRESPASS TO LAND AND DISPOSSESSION

		PARA.
1.	The nature of trespass	18–01
2.	Who may sue for trespass	18–10
6.	Justification of Trespass	18–49
■ 7.	Measure of damages	18–65
	(a) General	18–65
■ 9.	Statutes of Limitation	18–83

Since the publication of the 18th edition, there have been three main cases of note in the context of trespass to land: (i) *British Waterways Board v. Severn Trent Water Ltd* [2002] Ch. 25 (on the boundary between trespass and nuisance), and (ii) *Davies v. Ilieff* 2000 WL 33201551 (on the damages payable in the context of wrongful occupation of the claimant's home), and (iii) *Nelson v. Nicholson, The Independent*, January 22, 2001 (on the entitlement to an injunction).

18a

In *British Waterways Board v. Severn Trent Water Ltd* the Court of Appeal held that fouling a canal or river constitutes a trespass to land in respect of which the owner of the watercourse is entitled to sue. Earlier authority had established that the fouling of land adjacent to a watercourse does not amount to trespass, for want of directness. But in the instant case, where the respondent had continued to discharge water from its sewers into the appellant's canal after the licence to do so had been terminated, the Court of Appeal granted a declaration to the effect that there was no implied power under the Water Industry Act 1991 to discharge sewage into the canal.

In *Davies v. Ilieff* the defendant bought and registered in her own name a house in London in 1979. She lived there together with her mother, the claimant, for three years before marrying and moving to Italy. In 1998, after a serious failure on the part of the mother to make building alterations to the premises, the defendant entered the premises, changed the locks and removed the personal possessions of the claimant and her new husband. She placed them in the claimant's car, pushed it into a nearby street and left it there, unlocked. In this factually complex case, the claimant sought, *inter alia*, damages in respect of her daughter's trespass to her home. Sitting as a judge of the Chancery Division, Mr B. Livesey Q.C. held that the defendant had wrongly evicted her mother without adequate notice and was therefore liable in respect of the alleged trespass. In view of the fact that the claimant had been due three month's notice, but received none, the question that arose was one as to the appropriate measure of damages. Mr Livesey, mindful of the decision in *Invergui Investments Ltd v. Hackett* [1995] 3 All E.R. 841, took as his starting point the ordinary letting value of the property for the three month period, which was £3,250. But he then distinguished that case on the basis that, whereas the house in this case was the actual home of the claimant, the premises in *Invergui Investments* had been commercial premises. He thus concluded that in addition to the three month letting value, the claimant

18a CHAPTER 18—TRESPASS TO LAND AND DISPOSSESSION

was "entitled to general damages in addition, to reflect the insult of the trespass". He added a figure of £1,500.

In *Nelson v. Nicholson* the claimants, Mr and Mrs Nelson, had recently resolved a boundary dispute between themselves and their neighbours, the Nicholsons. In resolving the boundary dispute, it transpired that the defendants had planted a leylandii hedge on the claimants' land. They conceded that this constituted a trespass. The claimants sought a mandatory injunction to compel the defendants to remove the leylandii hedge as they could not do themselves under the terms of a restrictive covenant which prevented them from removing any fence, hedge, tree or shrubs within thirty feet of the boundary between the two plots of land. In response, the defendants proposed an undertaking whereby they would keep the hedge trimmed to a height no greater than seven feet. The claimants sought to insist on the injunction as such an undertaking would not bind the defendants' successors. In the event, even though the hedge was neither a present nor prospective inconvenience to the claimants, a unanimous Court of Appeal held that a mandatory injunction requiring the defendants to remove the hedge was the appropriate remedy. The fact that the restrictive covenant prevented the claimants resorting to self-help meant that the only effective remedy was injunctive relief of this kind.

1. THE NATURE OF TRESPASS

18–08 **Trespass distinguished from nuisance.** Add to end of paragraph:
In *British Waterways Board v. Severn Trent Water Ltd.* (NOTE 44a) the Court of Appeal made it clear that an action may be brought by the riparian right owner in respect of the direct fouling of a river, notwithstanding that an action would not lie in respect of the fouling of adjoining land. The difference in approach rests with the fact that, in the case of fouling a river or other watercourse, the crucial requirement of directness would be satisfied.
NOTE 44a: [2002] Ch. 25.

18–09 **Trespass lies without damage.** Add to end of paragraph:
And, where a potential threat is posed by something growing on the claimant's land which was planted there by the defendant, the claimant may seek a mandatory injunction to have the defendant remove it. (NOTE 49a)
NOTE 49a: *Nelson v. Nicholson, The Independent*, January 22, 2001.

2. WHO MAY SUE FOR TRESPASS

18–17 **Self-help by rightful owner.** NOTE 89. Add: On the other hand, in cases where self-help would entail an act by the claimant that is prohibited by a restrictive covenant, the appropriate remedy is a mandatory injunction requiring the defendant to take the necessary remedial action: *Nelson v. Nicholson, The Independent*, January 22, 2001.

6. JUSTIFICATION OF TRESPASS

18–35 **Justification of trespass.** Add to end of paragraph:
In relation to justification of an entry by easement, the Court of Appeal clarified in *Hanina v. Morland* (NOTE 78a) that if the right claimed was one as to

exclusive and unrestricted possession it could not be an easement within section 62 of the Law of Property Act 1925. Aldous L.J. identified that the normal idea of an easement amounts to a right held by the owner of the dominant tenement over a servient tenement. He therefore held there to be no easement in this case where the defendant's claim in respect of the use of the claimant's flat rooftop was tantamount to a right of unrestricted, exclusive possession. But in light of the fact that the user had been without damage to the roof, nominal damages only were awarded.

NOTE 78a: (2000) 97(47) L.S. Gaz. 41.

Modern statutes. Add to end of paragraph: 18–37

In *British Waterways Board v. Severn Trent Water Ltd* (NOTE 88a) it was recognised that a statute may authorise certain acts that would otherwise constitute a trespass in a similar manner to the way in which statutory authority provides a defence in nuisance. Indeed, at first instance it was held that BWB had the implied statutory power to discharge water from its sewers into the respondent's canal. By section 159 of the Water Industry Act 1991 the appellant had the power to "lay a relevant pipe ... in any land which is not in, under or over a street". It was thus held at first instance that such a power must carry with it the implied authority to discharge the contents of such a pipe. In the Court of Appeal, however, that decision was reversed. Peter Gibson L.J. held that no such incidental power of discharge should be implied and that discharge into the canal required a licence from STW. The crux of his decision was that, in the absence of such a licence "the water now discharged into the canal of BWB could, albeit at some expense, be re-routed to be discharged elsewhere".

NOTE 88a: [2002] Ch. 25.

Justification under easements of other descriptions. NOTE 42. Add: Exclusive possession is fatal to the existence of an easement: *Hanina v. Morland* (2000) 97(47) L.S. Gaz 41. 18–49

NOTE 48. Add: and *Martin v. Childs* [2002] EWCA Civ 283.

Effect of revocation. NOTE 66. Insert before other cases listed in the NOTE: *British Waterways Board v. Severn Trent Water Ltd* [2002] Ch. 25. 18–53

7. MEASURE OF DAMAGES

(a) *General*

NOTE 28. Replace with: Such damages are likely to be nominal only: see *Hanina v. Morland* (2000) 97(47) L.S. Gaz 41; *Nelson v. Nicholson, The Independent*, January 22, 2001; *BRB (Residuary) Ltd v. Cully* 2001 W.L. 1476357. Injunctions may also be obtained in such cases: *Patel v. W.H. Smith (Eziot) Ltd* [1987] 1 W.L.R. 853, CA. 18–65

(i) Trespass productive of benefit to the defendant without damage to the claimant. Add to end of paragraph: 18–66

On the other hand, where the premises concerned are the claimant's home rather than merely commercial residential premises, the court may add to the ordinary letting value a sum by way of general damages intended to reflect the

18–66

insult of the trespass. This was the approach adopted in *Davies v. Ilieff* (NOTE 31a).
   NOTE 31a: 2000 W.L. 33201551.

9. STATUTES OF LIMITATION

18–83   **When right of action accrues.** NOTE 13: Replace final sentence with: See also *Lambeth L.B.C. v. Blackburn* (2001) 33 H.L.R. 74 making it clear that a squatter who changes the locks on the premises in which he is squatting may reasonably be taken to have formed the intention to exclude the world at large, including the true owner.

CHAPTER 19

NUISANCE

	PARA.
■ 1. The nature of nuisance	19–01
2. Nuisance and the standard of duty	19–29
■ 3. Who can sue for nuisance	19–42
■ 4. Who can be sued for nuisance?	19–49
■ 5. Defences to an action of nuisance?	19–63
(b) Act of a trespasser	19–64
■ 6. Nuisance to water rights	19–78
■ 10. Obstruction of highway	19–106
11. Prescriptive right to commit nuisance	19–124
■ 12. Authorisation by statute	19–126

19a In *Delaware Mansions Ltd v. Westminster City Council* the law relating to liability for damage caused by encroaching tree-roots was comprehensively reviewed by the House of Lords. In *Marcic v. Thames Water Utilities Ltd* the Court of Appeal significantly extended the common law liability in nuisance of statutory sewerage authorities for damage caused by flooding. In two decisions, *Palmer v. Bowman* and *Byebrook Barn Centre v. Kent County Council*, the same court considered the rights and duties of occupiers in relation to naturally occurring water. In *Pemberton v. Southwark London Borough Council* the Court of Appeal also decided an important point on the right to sue for nuisance after *Hunter v. Canary Wharf*. In *McKenna v. British Aluminium Ltd*, however, the High Court held that the common law's restrictive insistence upon the need for a proprietary interest in the land affected, to bring a claim for nuisance, might itself need to be reappraised after the Human Rights Act 1998. The considerable potential significance of that legislation in this area is also highlighted by the reasoning at first instance in *Marcic v. Thames Water Utilities Ltd*, in which the High Court invoked the European Convention for the Protection of Human Rights and Fundamental Freedoms in order to impose liability upon the defendants.

1. THE NATURE OF NUISANCE

19–04 Add to footnote 16: See also *Jan de Nul (U.K.) v. NV Royal Belge* [2000] 2 Lloyd's Rep. 700.

19–08 In *Anglian Water Services v. Crawshaw Robbins & Co.* [2001] B.L.R. 173 Stanley Burnton J. held that "the negligent interruption of a supply of gas by a third party is not actionable as a private nuisance" (para. 143). The defendants damaged gas pipes during the installation of new water mains and, as a result, householders in the area were deprived for several days of gas for cooking and heating. His Lordship's primary ground of decision, citing the dicta from *Hunter v. Canary Wharf* referred to in the text, was that "nuisance requires something coming on to the land of the claimant" (para. 136, italics supplied).

19–10 **Interference with enjoyment.** In *Anglian Water Services v. Crawshaw Robbins & Co.* (see 19–08 above) Stanley Burnton J. doubted whether "an inability to cook" as a result of loss of the gas supply would, by itself, constitute "such an interference with the use and enjoyment of land as to support an action in nuisance" (para. 124). Substitute portable appliances would sometimes be available, and it was therefore "possible to regard the interruption of the supply of gas as an interference with the use of gas appliances rather than with the use of land" (para. 142).

19–21 **The duty.** In *Byebrook Barn Centre v. Kent County Council, The Times*, January 5, 2001, the Court of Appeal applied *Leakey v. National Trust* to hold a highway authority liable for flooding caused when a naturally occurring stream overflowed as it passed through a culvert owned by the defendant highway authority. The authority was aware that the culvert had become inadequate to carry the stream, but had failed to take remedial measures.

19–22 **Nuisance primarily a wrong to occupiers of land.** It is possible that the restrictive requirement of a legally protected interest in the land, as a prerequisite for a successful nuisance claim, might need to be reconsidered in the light of the Human Rights Act 1998. In *McKenna v. British Aluminium Ltd, The Times*, April 25, 2002, the claimants sought damages for emissions emanating from the defendant's property. The defendant applied to strike out the claims on the ground that the claimants did not have a proprietary interest in the land affected. Neuberger J. dismissed the application, holding that it was arguable that this aspect of the common law might require modification in the light of the 1998 Act. In his dissenting speech in *Hunter v. Canary Wharf Ltd* itself, which was decided before the Act, Lord Cooke of Thorndon had emphasised that Article 8 of the European Convention for the Protection of Human Rights and Fundamental Freedoms confers a right to respect for a person's "home" (see [1997] 2 All E.R. 426 at 458–49). Moreover, in *Marcic v. Thames Water Utilities Ltd* [2002] 2 All E.R. 55 affirming [2001] 3 All E.R. 698 the Court of Appeal upheld a decision of Judge Richard Havery Q.C. to the effect that Article 8, which has been directly applicable since the 1998 Act came into force, had been contravened when the defendants had failed to prevent the claimant's home from being flooded. Although the claimant in this case owned his own home, so that the proprietary interest requirement was not in issue, the decision necessarily reinforces the potential of the 1998 Act to bring that requirement into question: i.e. as a technical limitation on liability which is difficult to reconcile with the broad wording of the Convention. More generally, the importance of Article 8 in situations broadly similar to those encompassed by the law of nuisance, is highlighted by the decision of the European Court of Human Rights in *Hatton v. United Kingdom* [2002] 1 F.C.R. 732. In this case damages were awarded to residents near Heathrow airport in respect of noise caused by night-time flying.

19–23 **Continuing nuisances.** In *Delaware Mansions Ltd v. Westminster City Council* [2001] 4 All E.R. 737 the House of Lords upheld the decision of the Court of Appeal referred to in the text. The judgment of Lord Cooke of Thorndon includes a comprehensive review of the authorities on damage caused by encroaching tree-roots. In confirming the liability of the respondents for damage caused by their tree, Lord Cooke said:

"I think that the answer to the issue falls to be found by applying the concepts of reasonableness between neighbours (real or figurative) and reasonable foreseeability which underlie much modern tort law and, more particularly, the law of nuisance . . . In the end, in my opinion, the law can be summed up in the proposition that, where there is a continuing nuisance of which the defendant knew or ought to have known, reasonable remedial expenditure may be recovered by the owner who has had to incur it" ([2001] 4 All E.R. 737 at 747 and 750, paragraphs 29 and 38 of the judgment).

Damages. Add to NOTE 39: See also *Jan de Nul (U.K.) v. NV Royal Belge* [2000] 2 Lloyd's Rep. 700 at 716. **19–27**

2. NUISANCE AND THE STANDARD OF DUTY

Intermediate positions. The equivalent paragraph in the 17th edition of this work was referred to by the Court of Appeal in *Marcic v. Thames Water Utilities Ltd* [2002] 2 All E.R. 55 at 79 (paras 85–86), in which the Court quoted with approval the proposition that "in relation to private nuisance there seems no reason why the maxim *res ipsa loquitur* should not apply in appropriate cases to require the defendant to show that he was not at fault and was not negligent" (see 17th edn, page 904, para. 18–28). **19–32**

Cambridge Water. In *Jan de Nul (U.K.) v. NV Royal Belge* [2000] 2 Lloyd's Rep. 700 Moore-Bick J. held, applying the reasoning of Lord Goff in the *Cambridge Water* case, that liability could arise in nuisance for the foreseeable siltation of neighbouring properties, even where those responsible "had taken all reasonable precautions to avoid such damage": see *Jan de Nul (U.K.) v. NV Royal Belge* [2000] 2 Lloyd's Rep. 700 at 713. **19–36**

Add to NOTE 61: See also *Hamilton v. Papakura District Council, The Times*, March 5, 2002 (PC).

3. WHO CAN SUE FOR NUISANCE?

Occupiers and residents. In *Pemberton v. Southwark London Borough Council* [2000] 1 W.L.R. 1672 the Court of Appeal held that a former secure tenant of the defendant Council, who had become instead a "tolerated trespasser" as a result of the provisions of Part IV of the Housing Act 1985, nevertheless had an interest in the premises sufficient to bring an action in private nuisance. The claimant's secure tenancy had been terminated by an order for possession, but the execution of that order had been suspended by the court on condition that she paid rent arrears to the defendants. She subsequently brought an action against the defendants in nuisance in respect of cockroach infestation during her continued occupation of the premises. The defendants contended that, her tenancy having ceased, she was not entitled to sue in nuisance. The Court adopted the terminology of "tolerated trespasser", which had been coined by Lord Browne-Wilkinson in *Burrows v. Brent London Borough Council* (see [1996] 1 W.L.R. 1448 at 1455) to describe the status of someone remaining in possession under the same circumstances as the claimant, and held that that status was sufficient to ground a nuisance action. The defendants, relying upon a passage in the speech of Lord Hoffmann in *Hunter v. Canary Wharf Ltd* (see [1997] A.C. 655 at 703), **19–42**

19-42 CHAPTER 19—NUISANCE

contended that trespassers could only sue in nuisance if their occupation was such as would eventually be capable of defeating the owner's title by adverse possession. This argument was, however, rejected. Sir Christopher Slade said:

> "... during the period between the termination of the secure tenancy and either its revival or the execution of the order for possession (which I will call the 'limbo period') the occupation of the tenant derives not so much from any agreement between the parties as from the 1985 Act itself... Since the 'tolerated trespasser' has the right to exclusive possession of the relevant property during the 'limbo period', there is in my judgment nothing to prevent his pursuing a cause of action against his landlords or anyone else during that period, in accordance with the principles laid down in *Hunter v. Canary Wharf Ltd*, provided that he can establish the other essential ingredients of the tort... Lord Hoffmann was clearly not directing his mind to the rights of a person having the peculiar status of a 'tolerated trespasser' to sue in nuisance—a status quite different in law from that of an ordinary trespasser" ([2000] 1 W.L.R. 1672 at 1685–1686).

The House of Lords has dismissed a petition for leave to appeal from this decision: see [2001] 1 W.L.R. 538.

In *Jan de Nul (U.K.) v. NV Royal Belge* [2000] 2 Lloyd's Rep. 700, Moore-Bick J. held that licences to moor boats on a river did not confer a right to sue in private nuisance: see [2000] 2 Lloyd's Rep. 700 at 719.

It is possible that the basis of the decision in *Hunter v. Canary Wharf Ltd* itself, to the effect that a legally protected interest interest in the property affected is necessary to support a claim in private nuisance, may need to be reconsidered in the light of the subsequent coming into force of the Human Rights Act 1998. In *McKenna v. British Aluminium Ltd, The Times*, April 25, 2002, Neuberger J. refused to strike out a nuisance action by claimants who had no proprietary interest, holding that it was arguable that the requirement for such an interest might be incompatible with European Convention for the Protection of Human Rights and Fundamental Freedoms. See, further, 19–22, above.

NOTE 80. For *Delaware Mansions Ltd v. Westminster City Council, The Times*, August 25, 1999, CA substitute *Delaware Mansions Ltd v. Westminster City Council* [2001] 4 All E.R. 737, HL.

19-48 **Public nuisances** Add to NOTE 8, after *Stoke-on-Trent City Council v. B & Q Retail*: *Nottingham City Council v. Z* [2002] 1 W.L.R. 607.

4. WHO CAN BE SUED FOR NUISANCE

19-52 The situations in which vicarious liability can arise for nuisances caused by independent contractors were reviewed by Judge Anthony Thornton Q.C. in *Johnson v. BJW Property Developments Ltd*, January 30, 2002 (LEXIS) (Queen's Bench Division, Technology and Construction Court). Liability was imposed where the defendant's contractor had negligently modified a fireplace in a party wall, resulting eventually in extensive fire damage to the claimant's adjoining premises.

19-54 **Continuance of nuisance.** In *Marcic v. Thames Water Utilities Ltd* [2002] 2 All E.R. 55 the Court of Appeal held that a water company can be liable, on the principle of continuance of nuisance, for flooding caused by its sewers becoming overloaded. Lord Phillips M.R., delivering the judgment of the Court said:

"The sewers form part of a system which Thames are operating as a commercial venture in order to make profits for their shareholders. Thames are in no more favourable position than a landowner on whose property a hazard accumulates by the act of a trespasser or of nature. At all material times Thames had, or should have had, knowledge of the hazard. If the principles identified in *Goldman v. Hargrave* and *Leakey's* case are applied, these facts placed Thames under a duty to Mr Marcic to take such steps as, in all the circumstances, were reasonable to prevent the discharge of surface and foul water onto Mr Marcic's property" ([2002] 2 All E.R. 55 at 78, para. 83).

5. DEFENCES TO AN ACTION FOR NUISANCE

(b) Act of a Trespasser

Continuance. Add to NOTE 79: See also *Marcic v. Thames Water Utilities Ltd* [2002] 2 All E.R. 55.   19–65

6. NUISANCE TO WATER RIGHTS

Rights and duties of riparian owner. The reference in NOTE 45 to *Radstock Co-operative and Industrial Society v. Norton-Radstock UDC* should now be read in the light of the decision of the Court of Appeal in *Byebrook Barn Centre v. Kent County Council, The Times,* January 5, 2001. The Court considered that the proposition that natural changes cannot make an installation into a nuisance, if it was not one when originally constructed, was inconsistent with the development of the law relating to naturally occurring nuisances in cases such as *Leakey v. Natural Trust* [1980] Q.B. 485.   19–82

Sewage. In *British Waterways Board v. Severn Trent Water Ltd* [2001] 3 All E.R. 673 the Court of Appeal rejected a contention, which had found favour in the court below, that section 159 of the Water Industry Act 1991 conferred an implied power on sewerage undertakers to discharge water into watercourses without the consent of the owner. Water companies could acquire compulsorily, by statute, the power to make such discharges, but only on payment of compensation.   19–84

Percolation downhill. In *Palmer v. Bowman* [2000] 1 W.L.R. 842 the Court of Appeal held that since the drainage of naturally occurring water from higher to lower land, in undefined channels, is itself a process of nature, it follows that no easement is required to justify such drainage. Accordingly no such easement can exist and claimants, who sought to establish such an easement by lost modern grant, failed. In holding that the occupier of lower land cannot complain of such natural discharges of water, the Court of Appeal followed the reasoning of Piers Ashworth Q.C., sitting as a deputy judge of the High Court, in *Home Brewery plc v. William Davis & Co. (Loughborough) Ltd* [1987] Q.B. 339. On the facts of *Palmer v. Bowman,* however, it was unnecessary for the Court of Appeal to decide whether the actual decision in the *Home Brewery* case, to the effect that the occupier of the higher land nevertheless cannot complain if the lower occupier impedes the natural flow by making reasonable use of his own land, was correct. The court emphasised that it expressed no view on that question (see per   19–86

19–86   CHAPTER 19—NUISANCE

Rattee J., with whom Aldous and Auld L.JJ. agreed, in [2000] 1 W.L.R. 842 at 855).

7. WITHDRAWAL OF SUPPORT

19–95   **Support for buildings.** This paragraph, and particularly the quotation from Lord Denning M.R. in *Phipps v. Pears*, must now be read in the light of the decision of the Court of Appeal in *Rees v. Skerrett* [2001] 1 W.L.R. 1541. The defendant's property was demolished, leaving the wall of the claimant's adjoining terraced house exposed. The court held that damage attributable to the suction effect of wind, to which the claimant's property had not formerly been subjected, was within the scope of the right of support. Moreover, in the light of the principle established in *Leakey v. National Trust*, one owner may now owe a common law duty to take reasonable steps to protect the neighbouring property from foreseeable weather damage caused by demolition of his own property.

10. OBSTRUCTION OF HIGHWAY

19–106   **What is sufficient special damage.** In *Jan de Nul (U.K.) v. NV Royal Belge* [2000] 2 Lloyd's Rep. 700 Moore-Bick J. held (citing the previous edition of this work) that a claimant able to show direct and substantial injury suffered by the public at large may recover general damages in public nuisance, and is not required to prove specific loss. He also held that interference with the public right to fish in tidal waters could constitute a public nuisance.

Add at the beginning of NOTE 55: For the law governing situations in which obstruction of the highway can constitute a public nuisance see *East Hertfordshire District Council v. Isobel Hospice Trading Ltd* [2001] J.P.L. 597 (Mr J. Beatson Q.C. sitting as a Deputy Judge of the High Court.

19–111   **Creation of dangers in highway.** In *Wandsworth London Borough Council v. Railtrack plc*, The Times, August 2, 2001 the Court of Appeal held that pigeon-droppings on the highway created a hazard to pedestrians and constituted a public nuisance. The defendants, owners of a bridge under which the pigeons roosted, were held liable since they had knowledge of the nuisance and had failed to take reasonable steps to abate it.

19–122   **Standard of care.** Add to NOTE 41: But there is no blanket immunity for authorities which, in the exercise of their planning functions, actually *cause* a dangerous situation to be created: *Kane v. New Forest District Council* [2002] 1 W.L.R. 312, CA (dangerous footpath).

11. PRESCRIPTIVE RIGHT TO COMMIT NUISANCE

19–124   **Prescriptive right to commit nuisance.** In *Palmer v. Bowman* [2000] 1 W.L.R. 842 the Court of Appeal held that no easement can be acquired for the drainage of naturally occurring water from higher to lower land in undefined channels, since such drainage is itself a natural process for which no easement is necessary.

12. Authorisation by Statute

Add to Note 70: See also *Marcic v. Thames Water Utilities Ltd* [2002] 2 All E.R. 55 at 79 (para. 86). **19–127**

Some support for the "suggested new principle", referred to in the text, may be derived from the approach of the Court of Appeal in *Marcic v. Thames Water Utilities Ltd* in which the Court observed that sewerage undertakers should not assume "that their liability to pay compensation for damage done by discharge from an overloaded sewer is dependent upon whether or not there are measures which they should reasonably have taken to prevent the discharge": see [2002] 2 All E.R. 55 at 86 (para. 119). **19–129**

Statutory powers saving liability for nuisance. If a nuisance caused by overloaded sewers can only be abated by the sewerage undertaker using its own statutory powers to acquire land, in order to expand its sewage treatment facilities, the undertaker may be under a common law duty to exercise those powers. In *Marcic v. Thames Water Utilities Ltd* [2002] 2 All E.R. 55 at 79–81 (paras 90–95) the Court of Appeal rejected as "absurd" (para. 95) the contention that no regard should be had to the defendants' statutory powers in determining whether they had acted reasonably. **19–134**

CHAPTER 20

RYLANDS V. FLETCHER LIABILITY

	PARA.
■ 1. The rule of strict liability	20–01
■ 3. Water	20–29
■ 4. Fire	20–46
■ 5. Gas	20–63

In a decision of considerable potential significance the High Court held, in **20a** *McKenna v. British Aluminium Ltd*, that it was arguable that the Human Rights Act 1998 had had the effect of enabling claimants without any proprietary interest in the land affected to sue under the rule in *Rylands v. Fletcher*.

No less than three decisions of the Court of Appeal, *Stockport Metropolitan Borough Council v. British Gas Plc*, *Palmer v. Bowman*, and *Byebrook Barn Centre v. Kent County Council*, considered the rights and duties of neighbouring occupiers with respect to escaping or percolating water. In *Marcic v. Thames Water Utilities Ltd* the same court imposed liability on a statutory water undertaker for damage caused by flooding. In *Ribee v. Norrie* the Court of Appeal also reached a significant decision on the liability of an occupier for the escape of fire.

1. The Rule of Strict Liability

Effect of *Cambridge Water*. In *Stockport Metropolitan Borough Council v.* **20–12** *British Gas Plc* [2001] All E.R. (D) 190 a service pipe, owned and controlled by the defendant Council, supplied water to a block of flats. The internal cross-section of the pipe was "between 16 and 36 times as great as the internal area of an ordinary domestic supply pipe leading to an average single house". When the pipe fractured, allowing water to escape and cause damage, the Court of Appeal declined to hold the defendants liable under the rule in *Rylands v. Fletcher*. Schiemann L.J., delivering the judgment of the Court, quoted from the speech of Lord Goff in *Cambridge Water* and concluded, in effect, that the pipe was not a "non-natural user" of land: "There was nothing . . . to suggest that the pipe was in any way unusual in its dimensions when seen in the context of the supply of water to a tower block of a type of which there must be hundreds if not thousands of examples round the country" (*per* Schiemann L.J., *ibid.*).

To whom liability is owed. In *McKenna v. British Aluminium Ltd*, *The Times*, **20–14** April 25, 2002 Neuberger J. accepted that, prior to the implementation of the Human Rights Act 1998, only those with an interest in the land affected could sue under the rule in *Rylands v. Fletcher*, on the basis that the rule is an extension of the law of nuisance. He refused, however, to strike out a claim under the rule brought by claimants without such an interest, holding that it was arguable that a more expansive view of those entitled to claim should now be taken. Article 8 of the European Convention for the Protection of Human Rights and Fundamental Freedoms, and Article 1 of the First Protocol respectively, refer in broad

[139]

20–14   CHAPTER 20—RYLANDS V. FLETCHER LIABILITY

terms to protection of a person's "home" and "possessions". (See also 19–22 and 19–42, above.)

20–15   **Economic loss.** This paragraph was referred to by Stanley Burnton J. in *Anglian Water Services Ltd v. Crawshaw Robins & Co. Ltd* [2001] B.L.R. 173 at 149 (para. 149 of the judgment) confirming the irrecoverability of non-physical loss in claims under the rule in *Rylands v. Fletcher.*

20–17   **Remoteness of damage.** In *Hamilton v. Papakura District Council, The Times,* March 5, 2002, the need to establish foreseeability of the relevant damage in claims under the rule in *Rylands v. Fletcher* was emphasised by the Judicial Committee of the Privy Council. The Board refused to impose liability upon a water-supplier for damage to the claimant's ultra-sensitive crops allegedly caused by the presence in the water of small quantities of herbicide.

3. WATER

20–29   **Liability in respect of water.** In *Palmer v. Bowman* [2000] 1 W.L.R. 842 the Court of Appeal confirmed that there is no liability upon the occupier of higher land for the natural flow or percolation of naturally occurring water on to lower land.

20–30   **Barriers.** In *Palmer v. Bowman* [2000] 1 All E.R. 22 the Court of Appeal chose to express no view on the correctness of the decision in *Home Brewery plc v. William Davis & Co. (Loughborough) Ltd* that the occupier of higher land cannot complain if the occupier of lower land pens back naturally percolating water, provided that in so doing "reasonable" use is made of the lower land (see *per* Rattee J., with whom Auld and Aldous L.JJ. agreed, in [2000] 1 W.L.R. 842 at 845).

20–33   **Accumulating water.** In *Stockport Metropolitan Borough Council v. British Gas Plc* [2001] All E.R. (D) 190 the Court of Appeal held that accumulating water in a large service pipe (up to 36 times greater in size than an ordinary domestic water pipe) did *not* give rise to liability under the rule.

20–34   In *Stockport Metropolitan Borough Council v. British Gas Plc* (see above) escaping water poured into a disused railway embankment which, along with the pipe from which the water originally escaped, was owned by the defendants. The embankment eventually collapsed causing damage to the claimants. The Court of Appeal rejected a submission that *Rylands v. Fletcher* liability could be imposed upon the defendant Council for artificially accumulating water in the embankment after it had escaped from the pipe. Schiemann L.J., delivering the judgment of Court, observed that the "whole basis of strict liability is the deliberate accumulation of water in the place from which it escaped". On the assumption (see above) that there was no liability under the principle for the initial escape of the water from the pipe in which it had been carried, the Court held that it followed that there could be no such liability for what occurred subsequently.

20–36   **Strict liability by statute.** Section 209(1) of the Water Industry Act was considered by Stanley Burnton J. in *Anglian Water Services Ltd v. Crawshaw*

Robins & Co. Ltd [2001] B.L.R. 173. He held that the section should be interpreted "on the basis that its object is to render a water undertaker liable notwithstanding the absence of negligence" (see [2001] B.L.R. 173 at 199, para. 149 of the judgment). His Lordship also held, however, that the words "loss or damage" in the section should not be extended beyond those heads of damage normally recoverable in negligence. In consequence the phrase would be confined to "loss of property or damage to property" (*ibid.*). In the case itself an escape of water had been responsible for interrupting the domestic supply of gas to residents in the vicinity, but Stanley Burnton J. held that this interruption was not within the section since the "purely non-physical is excluded from recovery" (*ibid.*).

Statutory provisions. The proposition in the text that flooding caused by an "omission to enlarge the capacity of the sewer" will not give rise to liability "if the sewage authority has taken the sewers over from some predecessor" must now be regarded as subject to major qualification in the light of the decision of the Court of Appeal in *Marcic v. Thames Water Utilities Ltd* [2002] 2 All E.R. 55. In this case the court held that a statutory sewerage undertaker was obliged to take reasonable steps to prevent flood water from spreading from its sewers, notwithstanding that the water had originated elsewhere. The undertaker, which was a profitable commercial concern, was in no better position than an owner upon whose land a naturally occurring condition, or one brought about by the acts of trespassers, causes a nuisance to neighbouring occupiers. Such owners have to take such steps as might be reasonable and practicable to abate the nuisance. Moreover, in deciding whether the undertaker had acted reasonably the court was entitled to take into account any statutory powers which could have been invoked to facilitate the construction of more effective sewage works. **20–38**

Diversion of natural stream. Add to footnote 77: See also *Byebrook Barn Centre v. Kent County Council*, *The Times*, January 5, 2001, CA. **20–39**

4. FIRE

Danger from fire. The state of the law relating to liability for fire damage, under the rule in *Rylands v. Fletcher* and also in negligence and nuisance, was fully reviewed by Judge Anthony Thornton Q.C. (Queen's Bench Division, Technology and Construction Court) in *Johnson v. BJW Property Developments Ltd*, January 30, 2002 (LEXIS). **20–46**

Dangerous operations involving the creation of fire. In *Johnson v. BJW Property Developments Ltd*, January 30, 2002 (LEXIS) the defendant's independent contractor negligently removed fire protection from a domestic fireplace while installing a replacement surround. As a result fire eventually spread to the claimant's adjoining premises causing severe damage. Judge Anthony Thornton Q.C. (Queen's Bench Division, Technology and Construction Court) held that the defendant was vicariously liable for the negligence of its contractor. **20–55**

Liability of occupier. This paragraph should now be read in the light of the decision of the Court of Appeal *Ribee v. Norrie*, *The Times*, November 22, 2000. The Court held that a tenant is not a "stranger", and that the landlord will be **20–60**

20–60 liable for fires negligently caused by his tenants unless the latter's behaviour was wholly outside the terms of the tenancy. One of the defendant's tenants negligently dropped a cigarette, causing a fire which spread to the premises of the claimant. The Court of Appeal, reversing the court below, held that this was sufficient to impose liability on the defendant. The Court emphasised that the defendant, who did not live on the premises, had done nothing to discourage smoking by his tenants, which was clearly foreseeable. Nevertheless, in so far as the defendant could not be said to have "authorised" the fire, this decision may have extended the scope of a landlord's liability somewhat beyond that suggested by previous authority.

5. Gas

20–65 **Nuisance.** The nature of nuisance liability in respect of the supply of gas was considered, in somewhat unusual circumstances, in *Anglian Water Services Ltd v. Crawshaw Robins & Co. Ltd* [2001] B.L.R. 173. Instead of an escape of gas, the case was concerned with a situation in which the defendant third parties *disrupted* the supply of gas to domestic premises. Stanley Burnton J. declined to impose liability for the inconvenience resulting from loss of cooking and heating facilities. He said:

> "My conclusion is that the negligent interruption of a supply of gas by a third party is not actionable as a private nuisance. It does not involve an invasion of any substance or form of energy on to the claimant's land. It is not one of the exceptional cases of liability in nuisance without such an invasion. A home owner or tenant does not have a property right in the supply of gas. His or her protection lies in his or her rights against the gas supplier". (See [2001] B.L.R. 173 at 198, para. 143 of the judgment).

CHAPTER 21

ANIMALS

	PARA.
■ 2. The Animals Act 1971	21–03
(a) Strict liability for animals under section 2	21–03

2. THE ANIMALS ACT 1971

(a) Strict Liability for Animals under section 2

Liability for animals of a non-dangerous species. In *Flack v. Hudson* [2001] **21–04**
2 W.L.R. 982, CA the claimant's wife was riding the defendant's horse (she and the defendant both being "keepers" for the purposes of the Act) when the horse took fright at the noise of a tractor and threw her, causing injuries from which she died. The Court of Appeal upheld the judgment for the claimant on the ground that the owner was or should have been aware of the horse's tendency to take fright when confronted by farm machinery.

In *Gloster v. Chief Constable of Greater Manchester* [2000] P.I.Q.R. 114 a police officer, failed to establish that the police authority was liable under section 2(2) for the injury he suffered when bitten by a police dog.

In *Mirhavedy v. Henley* [2002] 2 W.L.R. 566 the claimant motorist suffered personal injuries when the car he was driving collided with the defendants' horse which had panicked and escaped with several others from its field. It was not clear what had frightened the horses in this way. The claimant sued in negligence and under section 2 of the Animals Act 1971. The claim in negligence failed as the field where the animals were kept was adequately and securely fenced, and at first instance the Animals Act claim also failed as the judge held that, although the characteristics of the horses were within section 2(2)(b), being normal for that species in particular circumstances, the action failed on causation as the characteristic in question—to bolt in this way when frightened—was not the cause of the damage.

The Court of Appeal upheld the ruling on negligence, but overruled the decision on Animals Act liability. In doing so, the Court looked critically and thoroughly at section 2(2) of the Act and the existing authorities. Hale L.J. gave the judgment of the court, and having summarized the cases and the difficulty of interpreting the section stated that the test laid down by Lord Browne-Wilkinson in *Pepper v. Hart* [1993] A.C. 593 was satisfied and that the Court would, therefore, adopt the unusual course of examining the relevant parliamentary material and the law reform proposals which led to the bill being passed, bearing in mind the limitations laid down by Lord Browne Wilkinson in *Melluish v. BMI (No. 3) Ltd* [1996] A.C. 454, 481, as to which preparatory materials are appropriate.

Having reviewed the relevant material, the court concluded that the characteristics exhibited by the defendant's horses were within the section and that, contrary to the decision of the Court below, causation was satisfied, since it was the horses' characteristic in the unusual circumstances of being frightened and bolting into the road which caused the damage to the claimant. The court was strongly influenced by the evident intention of Parliament, based on the report of the Law Commission, that owners of animals of a non-dangerous species should be strictly liable for damage caused by them.

In *Clarke v. Barber* [2002] 5 C.L. 70, the court held that liability under section 2(2), being strict and hence not "breach of duty", was not subject to the three year limitation period under the Limitation Act 1980.

21–05 **Interpretation of section 2(2).** Hale L.J. in *Mirhavedy v. Henley* provides a penetrating and comprehensive review of the difficulties of interpreting section 2(2), justifying reference to preparatory materials to discover Parliamentary intentions.

21–06 **Characteristics of the animal.** The Court held in *Flack v. Hudson* that the horse's propensity to be frightened of farm machinery was a "characteristic" within section 2(2) and rendered the defendant liable even though there had not previously been an analogous incident to that which caused the death of the claimant's wife.

See also *Whitehead v. Alexander* [2000] C.L.Y. 205 where the claimant failed to establish that a severe horse bite was a characteristic not normally found in other horses.

In *Mirhavedy v. Henley* [2002] 2 W.L.R. 566 the Court of Appeal held that the characteristic of the defendant's horse to bolt when frightened so that it escaped from a properly fenced field was a "characteristic" within the second limb of section 2(2)(b) of the Animals Act namely "characteristics of the animal which are not normally found in animals of the same species or are not normally to be found except at particular times or in particular circumstances".

21–07 **Knowledge of the animal's propensities.** See *Flack v. Hudson* (above para. 21–04).

21–08 **The "keeper" of an animal.** In *Flack v. Hudson* counsel for the defendant argued that since both she and the rider, the claimant's wife had both been "keepers" for the purposes of the Act, the latter was precluded from suing since one "keeper" could not sue another of the same animal. The Court of Appeal rejected this argument on the ground that such an intention would have to be clearly stated in the Act if Parliament had intended such a conclusion.

In *Mirhavedy v. Henley* [2002] 2 W.L.R. 566 Hale L.J. in the Court of Appeal addressed the question whether the defendant owners of the horse which caused the claimant's injuries had the required "knowledge" and concluded that section 2(2)(c) merely requires knowledge of the "characteristics" and not both of the characteristics and also of the circumstances which gave rise to them. Clearly the Court of Appeal was influenced by the consideration that, in the words of Hale L.J. " . . . if the rationale for the strict liability is the greater vigilance needed and the greater opportunity to insure brought by that knowledge then those can be employed whether or not the particular circumstances are known to exist at the time".

CHAPTER 22

DEFAMATION

	PARA.
■ 1. Generally	22–01
■ 2. What is defamatory?	22–19
■ 3. Construction of language used	22–34
5. Unintentional defamation	22–60
6. Publication	22–61
■ 7. Defences	22–76
(2) Justification	22–78
(3) Privilege	22–91
(4) Reports	22–142
(5) Fair comment and criticism	22–158
■ 8. Malice	22–183
■ 10. Damages	22–203
(1) In general	22–203
(3) Mitigation of damages	22–217

1. GENERALLY

Action of defamation. In *Berezovsky v. Michaels* [2000] 2 All E.R. 986 the claimants were Russian businessmen who alleged that they had been libelled by an article published in an American magazine, circulated primarily in the USA but also to a limited extent in England and in Russia. The Court of Appeal, overruling the judgment at first instance that England was a *forum non conveniens*, held that the action could appropriately be brought in the English courts and this decision was upheld by the House of Lords. However in *Multigroup Bulgaria Ltd v. Oxford Analytical* (unreported) February 1, 2001, Eady J. refused to allow the claimant holding company to sue in libel on the ground that it had not shown sufficient reputation within the jurisdiction of the English courts. **22–01**

The problems which arise where a publication has occurred in several different jurisdictions and the English courts must decide issues under the English law of defamation were discussed by Eady J. in *Lukowiak v. Unidad Editorial S.A.*, *The Times*, July 23, 2001.

Since the Human Rights Act 1998 the influence of the jurisprudence of the European Court of Human Rights has been frequently acknowledged by the English courts. Cases such as *Bladet Tomso v. Norway* (1999) 6 B.H.R.C. 599, ECHR, *De Haes v. Belgium* (1997) 25 E.H.R.R. 445, and *Thorgeirson v. Iceland* 14 E.H.R.R. 843 have been cited, especially in cases involving actions against journalists and newspapers. Recent cases, since *Reynolds*, especially the litigation between *Loutchansky v. Times Newspapers* (see below) have demonstrated the readiness of the English courts to recognize the importance of the freedom of the press in reporting matters of genuine public interest (see below).

Trial by jury. In the case of *Grobbelaar v. News Group Newspapers* [2001] 2 All E.R. 437, CA, the claimant, a prominent professional football goalkeeper, had been unsuccessfully prosecuted for taking bribes to fix the outcome of matches. **22–02**

22-02

He subsequently brought a libel action against the defendants in respect of material published in their newspaper, based on interviews which they had had with him, to the effect that he had taken bribes and had been corrupt in influencing the outcome of matches. The defendants produced considerable evidence by way of justification but the jury gave a verdict in the claimant's favour. The Court of Appeal, acting in accordance with its rarely used power under section 69 of the Supreme Court Act, overruled the jury's verdict, on the ground that no reasonable jury could have reached such a conclusion.

In *Safeway Stores v. Tate* [2001] 2 W.L.R. 1377 the defendant had made allegations of fraud against the claimants. Summary judgment was granted to the claimants under rule 24 of the CPR 1998 and the defendant appealed against that order. On the date fixed for the hearing no jury had yet been empanelled. The Court of Appeal allowed the appeal on the ground that the right to trial by jury under section 69(1) of the Supreme Court Act 1981 was so important to a claimant in a libel case that it could only be overridden by a subsequent Act of Parliament and not by rules of court. However in *Alexander v. Arts Council of Wales* [2001] 1 W.L.R. 1840, the Court of Appeal upheld the decision of the judge at first instance to remove a case from the jury. A sued the defendants for slander and libel in respect of comments made by them at a press briefing. In reaching the decision of the Court of Appeal Lord Woolf confirmed that it was open to the judge to determine that the evidence relied on by the claimant could not possibly have given rise to a finding by a jury of malice, even if the statements were held to be defamatory. It was therefore proper not to allow the claimant to have his case put before a jury. It seems therefore that if there is a material issue of fact in a defamation case, section 69 of the Supreme Court Act 1981 entitles a party to trial by jury but the judge may first decide whether or not there is such an issue and in its absence no right to trial by jury can be asserted. The case does not conflict with *Safeway Stores v. Tate* where there was an issue to be tried.

Deference to a libel jury was shown by the Court of Appeal in *Kiam v. MGN* [2002] 2 All E.R. 219, where the Court dismissed the defendants' appeal against the amount of damages awarded for libel. Although the award exceeded the amount suggested by the trial judge, the Court held (Sedley L.J. dissenting) that it would not interfere with the jury's award unless it substantially exceeded the highest amount which a reasonable jury could have awarded.

22-03 **Complexity of defamation.** In *McVicar v. United Kingdom* (2002) N.L.J. 579, the applicant argued that, in view of the complexities of defamation law and procedure, the fact that he was unable to obtain legal aid for his defamation action violated his right under Article 6. The ECHR rejected this claim.

22-05 **The Defamation Act 1996.** The new summary procedure for disposal of defamation actions under sections 8 and 9 of the Defamation Act 1996 was applied in *James Gilbert Ltd v. MGN* [2000] E.M.L.R. 680, QBD. The defendants had alleged that JG were engaged in unethical business practices, including using an Indian sub-contractor which employed child labour, and breaking a promise to investigate the issue. JG sought summary disposal of the action under section 8 of the 1996 Defamation Act and this was duly granted. In allowing the application the court looked at the question whether the proposed defence (of qualified privilege) had a real chance of success. In deciding whether to grant summary disposal the court would take into account the seriousness and nature of the issue, whether it was of public concern, what source had been used by the defendants, whether they had sought the claimant's comments, whether the article had contained the gist of the claimant's version and the circumstances of the publication including its timing.

In *Burstein v. Times Newspapers* [2001] 1 W.L.R. 579 May L.J. in the Court of Appeal held that the judge at first instance had been correct in deciding that the claimant's action for libel should be summarily disposed of under section 8 of the 1996 Act; this was in accordance with the "broad discretion" accorded to judges under the 1996 Act.

In *Loutchansky v. Times Newspapers Ltd*, [2001] 3 W.L.R. 404, the Court of Appeal upheld the judgment of Gray J. at first instance that the issue of damages for defamation could be dealt with by section 8 by summary disposal separate from the issue of liability.

In *Lukowiak v. Unidad Editorial S.A., The Times*, July 23, 2001, the claimant, a British soldier, sued an Argentinian newspaper company for libelling him in an article reporting statements made in Argentina that he was being investigated as a war criminal. The statements followed the publication of a book by him which described his killing an Argentine soldier. Eady J. refused to give summary judgment since, although there was no realistic possibility of a defence of justification succeeding, other live issues remained, such as the issue of malice and the question as to whether there had been actionable publication via the website.

See also *Milne v. Telegraph Group* [2001] E.M.L.R. 30 where summary procedure under section 8 was exercised.

The Civil Procedure Rules 1998. In *GKR Karate v. Yorkshire Post* the Court of Appeal, in upholding the decision that qualified privilege and malice should be tried as preliminary issues, affirmed the significance of the CPR in strengthening the judge's discretion in improving the conduct of litigation.

22–06

In *Alexander v. Arts Council of Wales* the Lord Chief Justice confirmed that Part 24 CPR which provides for summary disposal of tort claims applies to defamation actions, but that it does not give a right to summary judgment in a defamation case where there are issues fit to be placed before a jury, as in *Safeway Stores v. Tate*.

In *Daniels v. Griffiths* [2001] EWCA Civ 1376 and in *Swain v. Hillman* [2001] 1 All E.R. 91 the Court of Appeal considered the grounds on which Part 24 summary judgment will be appropriate (if the case has "no real prospect of success").

For the relationship between summary procedure under rule 24 of the CPR 1998 (applicable to defamation and other tort actions) and the summary procedure specifically applicable to defamation under sections 8 and 9 of the 1996 Act, see Gatley, Chapter 29, p. 713, suggesting that the threshold of likelihood of success may be different in the two cases.

A new pre-action protocol was introduced in November 2000.

The impact of new means of communication. In *Totalise PLC v. Motley Fool, The Times*, March 15, 2001, [2002] 1 W.L.R. 1233, Totalise, an internet service provider, applied under the Contempt of Court Act for an order requiring two website operators, M and T, to disclose the source of defamatory material which had been posted anonymously on their websites. The application was granted since the court held that the disclosure was necessary in the interests of

22–07

[147]

22-07 CHAPTER 22—DEFAMATION

justice. There was a prima facie case against "Zeddust", the author of the offending material which had a potentially vast audience.

In *Loutchansky v. Times Newspapers (No. 2)* [2002] 2 W.L.R. 640 the appellants' counsel argued that the rule of the common law, which establishes that every publication of a libel gives rise to an action for defamation, should be changed by the court so as to accord with the realities of internet communication. The Court of Appeal refused to change the law, confirming the "single publication" rule laid down in the case of *Duke of Brunswick and Luneberg v. Harmer*, (1849) 14 Q.B. 185.

22-08 **Conflict between free speech and reputation.** In *Kerry O'Shea v. MGN* [2001] All E.R. (D) 65, the Court of Appeal discussed this conflict (see below para. **22-12**). See also the discussion of the New Zealand Court of Appeal in *Lange v. Atkinson (No. 2)* [2000] 3 N.Z.L.R. 385, CA NZ.

The conflict between free speech and reputation continues at the heart of defamation litigation, especially where publication in the media is concerned. (See especially *Loutchansky v. Times (No. 2)* [2002] 2 W.L.R. 640, *Al-Fagih v. HH Saudi Research and Marketing (UK) Ltd*, [2001] EWCA Civ 1634, *Lukowiak v. Unidad Editorial SA, The Times*, July 23, 2001).

22-09 **The Human Rights Act 1998.** In several earlier cases the English courts have based their decisions rather on common law and general principles than on the Human Rights Act (*e.g.* in *McCartan, Turkington & Breen v. Times Newspapers* [2000] 3 W.L.R. 1670).

However they are increasingly referring expressly to the European Convention and to decisions of the European Court of Human Rights, especially in relation to Article 10 (see below) 22–12 but also to Articles 6 and 8 (see below).

See A. Lester, European Convention on Human Rights and Media Law, Y.C. & M.L. 5 2000, pp. 381–390.

22-10 **Article 6.** In *McVicar v. United Kingdom* (App. No. 46311/99) ECHR N.L.J. Law Reports Vol. 152 p. 579 (May 7, 2002) the applicant, a journalist, had been sued and held liable for defamatory reports written by him relating to an athlete. He had been obliged to represent himself in the High Court action, since legal aid is unavailable for defamation actions in English law. He applied to the European Court of Human Rights on the ground that the fact that legal aid was not available to him amounted to a breach of Article 6, since he was thereby deprived of a right to a fair trial. The ECIIR dismissed his claim.

22-11 **Article 8.** In *Reavey v. Century Newspapers* [2001] N.I. 187, O, a journalist, wrote an article in the defendants' newspaper, stating , on the basis of a leaked police report, that the claimant's brothers, who had been murdered by loyalist terrorists, were IRA members and were responsible for terrorist acts. O also alleged that the claimant, R, was an IRA member. R sought disclosure of the report and the name of the person who supplied it, relying on Article 8 (respect for family life). The Court refused, holding that R's right under Article 8 could not prevail over the freedom of expression of the defendants under Article 10.

22-12 **Article 10.** In *Kerry O'Shea v. MGN* [2001] All E.R. (D) 65, the Court of Appeal held that it would be a breach of Article 10 and an unwarranted application of strict liability for unintentional defamation to find the defendants

[148]

liable for libel where they had published a pornographic advertisement incorporating a photograph of a woman and the claimant complained that it was so like her that her acquaintances believed it was in fact her in the advertisement.

In *Loutchansky v. Times* and in *Al Fagih v. HH Saudi Research and Marketing* and *Lukowiak v. Unidad Editorial S.A*, the Court of Appeal discussed the importance of Article 10, especially in the context of newspaper reporting.

See also *Bladet Tromso v. Norway* (App. No. 21980/93) 6 B.H.R.C. 599.

NOTE 28. Add: I. Loveland, "Libel law and freedom of political expression in the U.K." E.H.R.L.R. 2000 pp. 476–492.

2. WHAT IS DEFAMATORY?

Falsehood and Malice. See *Loutchansky v. Times (No. 2)* on the question of falsehood and malice in newspaper reports. 22–14

NOTE 44. Add: *Best v. Charter Medical of England Ltd* [2001] EWCA Civ 1588.

Defamatory nature. In *Hannah v. Scottish Daily Record* 2000 S.L.T. 673 (OH) the defendants had published an article describing H's drunken disorderly behaviour in a "nightclub brothel" in Marbella. They were able to justify the fact that he had been guilty of disorderly conduct but the court accepted that the use of the term "brothel" implied that he had engaged in sexual misconduct and this was not justified. 22–20

In another Scottish case, *McCue v. Scottish Daily Record Mail Ltd (No. 4)* 2000 Rep. L.R. 133 (OH), M was licensee of a public house and connected with other premises mentioned in a newspaper report as being the place where drug dealing and other criminal activities took place. He sued the newspapers on the ground that the report implied that he was involved in serious crime but the court held that he was being unduly sensitive and there were no grounds for that implication.

See also *Skrine & Co v. Euromoney Publications plc.* [2001] EWCA Civ 1479; [2002] E.M.L.R. 15.

3. CONSTRUCTION OF LANGUAGE USED

Defamatory matter published as hearsay. The rule on repetition was discussed in *Al-Fagih v. HH Saudi Research and Marketing* and in *Lukowiak v. Unidad Editorial*, in both of which the allegations made by the defendants consisted of "reportage" of allegations made by others and merely reported by the newspaper in question. The rule established in *Stern v. Piper* and *Shah v. Standard Chartered Bank* was confirmed, although the Court acknowledged the special difficulties connected with the duty of a free press to report disputes on matters of public interest. Eady J. in Lukowiak also considered the effect of the 2001 Strasbourg decision in *Thoma v. Luxembourg* where it was held that "a general requirement for journalists systematically to distance themselves from the content of a quotation that might insult or provoke others or damage their reputation was not reconcilable with the press's role . . . " and would be an infringement of Article 10. However in the event he decided the issue of the reported allegations in the overall context of qualified privilege. In *Al-Fagih* the 22–39

[149]

22-39   CHAPTER 22—DEFAMATION

Court of Appeal confirmed that the question of reported allegations in the defendant's newspaper was to be viewed overall in the light of the defence of qualified privilege as stated in *Reynolds*. In the recent case of *Chase v. Newsgroup* [2002] EWHC 1101 Eady J. rejected the invitation of counsel to depart from the decisions in *Stern* and *Shah*, asserting that the rule contained in those cases is a limit "prescribed by law" within Article 10.

22-44   See *Cornelius v. De Taranto* [2002] E.M.L.R. 6 CA.

22-49   **"Lucas-Box meanings"**. Add: *Cook v. News Group*, December 18, 2000.
Lukowiak v. Unidad Editorial S.A., The Times, July 23, 2001.
Windsor v. Boycott [2001] EWCA Civ 1321.
Chase v. Newsgroup [2002] EWHC 1101.
Carlton v. Newsgroup [2002] E.M.L.R. 16 CA.

5. UNINTENTIONAL DEFAMATION

22-60   **Unintentional defamation.** In *Kerry O'Shea v. MGN* [2001] E.M.L.R. 40, the claimant sued the defendants in respect of a pornographic advertisement for an internet service provider published in five consecutive issues of their newspaper. The advertisement contained a picture of a woman who was "the look alike or spit and image" of the claimant but who was in fact a "glamour model". The claimant adduced evidence to the effect that family members and a friend had reasonably understood the photograph to be of her and had therefore believed that she was involved in the website in question. Morland J., stated that he was unable to conclude "that a jury could not have reasonably decided that the defamation referred to the claimant" and he had then to consider whether this case of "unintentional defamation" was an impermissible restriction of freedom of expression under Article 10. Clearly the "strict liability" incurred by an unintentional defamer is such a restriction; the question then arises "is it necessary for the protection of others?" (here the claimant). Quoting Lord Keith of Kinkel in *Derbyshire C.C. v. Times Newspapers*, the learned judge described the meaning of "necessary" here as required by "a pressing social need" and bearing in mind that the restriction(s) "should be no more than is proportionate to the legitimate aim of the society to which they belong". Photographs are an essential adjunct of journalistic articles and it would be an unwarranted burden on an editor to be expected to check if a picture of one person resembled someone else who would be defamed by the publication. If such a publication were made maliciously, the tort of malicious falsehood would provide a remedy but, in the present circumstances, to extend the strict liability for unintentional defamation to the publication of a "look alike" picture which accidentally defames someone would be a breach of Article 10 of the European Convention.

6. PUBLICATION

22-67   **Publication by agent.** In *Regan v. Taylor*, N.L.J.R., March 9, 2000, Vol. 150, p. 392, the defendant was a solicitor representing a police officer in several libel actions. In an interview he described the magazine "Scallywag", of which the claimant was editor, in deeply unfavourable terms, without having any specific authority from his client. He claimed that his statement was covered by qualified privilege and the Court of Appeal upheld the decision of the court at first instance to enter summary judgment for him since there was no reasonable prospect of this defence being rebutted.

7. DEFENCES

(2) Justification

Justification. Justification was discussed by the Court of Appeal in *Grobbelaar v. News Group Newspapers* [2001] 2 All E.R. 437, CA. See also the discussion of justification and its relationship to qualified privilege in pleading in the Court of Appeal in *GKR Karate v. Yorkshire Post*. 22–78

See also *Chase v. Newsgroup* [2002] EWHC 1101.

Repetition of a Defamatory Statement. The question of "reportage" of allegations or rumours (see 22–39 above) is especially significant in relation to the defence of justification. The decision of the Court of Appeal in *Shah v. Standard Bank* was discussed by that Court in *Al-Fagih v. HH Saudi Research* and at first instance in *Lukowiak v. Unidad Editorial S.A.* and in *Chase v. Newsgroup*, [2002] EWHC 1101. 22–79

Breach of confidence. The law of breach of confidence will inevitably on occasions come into conflict with freedom of expression under Article 10. Sometimes the disclosure of a confidence will be deemed to be a breach of Article 8 (respect for family life), as in *Douglas v. Hello! Ltd* [2001] 2 All E.R. 289. In the case of *Campbell v. MGN* [2002] EWHC 499 the claimant, a well known fashion model, succeeded in her claim that for a newspaper to publish a photograph of her leaving a meeting of Narcotics Anonymous was a breach of confidence though the photograph had been taken by a news photographer in public. 22–90

In *Cornelius v. de Taranto* [2002] E.M.L.R. 6 CA the Court of Appeal held that although the claimant had consented to the defendant's referral of her to a consultant psychiatrist, she had not consented to the disclosure of his report (which was allegedly defamatory), to her GP, the consultant and her solicitors which was therefore a breach of confidence.

(3) Privilege

(a) *Absolute Privilege*

In the New Zealand case of *Buchanan v. Jennings*, [2001] N.Z.L.R. 71, the defendant MP, during a debate in Parliament, criticised the New Zealand Wool Board's sponsorship of a rugby team's tour of the U.K. for excessive expenditure and suggested that the plaintiff, a senior member of the Board, had engineered the sponsorship for personal reasons. His remarks were reported in the media. Some weeks later the defendant was interviewed by a newspaper and the subsequent article both reported the original comments and stated that the defendant stood by what he had said. When sued he pleaded absolute privilege since he had not actually repeated the allegation outside Parliament. The New 22–99

Zealand Court of Appeal held that he was not entitled to the defence since he knew that the article was likely to report his comments and in it he had said that he did not resile from his allegation.

22–100 **Section 13 of the Defamation Act 1996.** The section was discussed by the House of Lords in *Hamilton v. Al Fayed* [2000] 2 All E.R. 224.

22–101 **Actions by MPs.** The House of Lords in *Hamilton v. Al Fayed* [2000] 2 All E.R. 224 affirmed the judgment of the Court of Appeal. Section 13 had been waived by the respondent and the action would not encroach in any other way on Parliamentary privilege.

22–103 **Official communications.** In *Mahon v. Rahn* [2000] 4 All E.R. 41 the claimants sued the defendant bankers for a report which they had provided to the TSA in the course of their investigations into fraud. The defendants had also sent the report to the SFO which had initiated an unsuccessful prosecution against the claimants for fraud. After their acquittal the claimants sued the defendants but it was held that the report was covered by absolute privilege.

22–106 **Privilege against production.** In *Reavey v. Century Newspapers*, [2001] N.I. 187, R sought disclosure of a report which had formed the basis of an article in the defendants' newspaper alleging that his murdered brothers and he himself were IRA members. Disclosure was refused, the Court holding that the freedom of the press under Article 10 to report such matters prevailed over R's right to respect for family life under Article 8.

(b) *Qualified privilege*

22–110 For summaries of the historical development of qualified privilege see *Loutchansky v. Times Newspapers* [2001] E.M.L.R. 898 *per* Gray J. and Lord Phillips M.R. in *Loutchansky (No. 2)* [2002] 2 W.L.R. 640.

22–113 In *Loutchansky v. Times Newspapers (No. 2)* the Court of Appeal considerd the issue of malice in relation to qualified privilege, especially in cases of press reporting, as in *Reynolds*. The emphasis in such cases is to be on the duty-interest test laid down in *Reynolds*, but the ultimate test is that of responsible journalism and the standard of duty should not be too stringent or too low. Lord Phillips concluded that where the *Reynolds* test of qualified privilege is satisfied, there is little scope for a finding of malice. The tests of whether the publication was reckless or made for a dominant motive of injuring the claimant would be dealt with by Lord Nicholls' ten tests in *Reynolds*.

In *Al Fagih v. HH Saudi Research and Marketing* the Court of Appeal refused to rule that a failure to verify allegations reported in a newspaper, where these were important in the interests of the paper's readership, amounted to malice so as to defeat the defence of qualified privilege.

22–121 **Grounds of qualified privilege.** Since *Reynolds v. Times Newspapers* there has been a tendency to expand the defence of qualified privilege in cases of publication to the public at large in newspapers of material of legitimate public interest. In *Loutchansky v. Times Newspapers (No. 2)* the Court of Appeal accepted and developed the defence of qualified privilege as applied to the press applying the test of responsible journalism. See below para. **22–122**.

In *Baldwin v. Rusbridger, The Times,* July 23, 2001, the defendant editor whose newspaper had been successfully sued for libel, wrote an article criticizing the legal system in a manner defamatory of the claimant. The court held that he could not claim qualified privilege for this statement which amounted to "trial by media".

Reynolds v. Times Newspapers. A number of cases have raised the question whether the broader category of information legitimately disseminated to the public extended to other sorts of information especially as the House of Lords in *Reynolds* had rejected a generic category of "political information" appropriate for the protection of qualified privilege. In *GKR Karate v. Yorkshire Post* [2000] 2 All E.R. 931 the claimants sued the defendant newspaper for libel in an article in which it was suggested that the claimants were selling karate classes taught by unqualified instructors for large sums of money. In pleading qualified privilege the defendants asserted that the public had a right to know about unscrupulous practices of the sort which they alleged and that it was therefore in line with *Reynolds* to raise the defence in respect of the articles as a preliminary issue. Popplewell J. decided that the questions of qualified privilege and malice could be heard as preliminary issues despite the claimants' objection that without a full hearing the test of qualified privilege laid down in *Reynolds* could not be properly applied, nor could the question of malice be properly examined. Counsel for the claimants argued further that the issue of qualified privilege should not be heard in this way, before the question of justification should be decided at trial, to the claimants' disadvantage. However the decision was upheld by the Court of Appeal which considered, in the words of May L.J., that to decide these matters as preliminary issues was "fair, sensible and economic".

22–122

It was held in *McIntyre v. Chief Constable of Kent* [2002] All E.R. (D) 338 that there is no rule of practice to the effect that courts should direct issues of qualified privilege to be heard in advance of the main trial of a defamation action.

In *Grobbelaar v. News Group Newspapers* [2001] 2 All E.R. 437, CA the Court of Appeal discussed the principle of qualified privilege as a defence to publishing material of public interest.

In *Lange v. Atkinson (No. 2)* 2000 3 N.Z.L.R. 385, CA (NZ) the New Zealand Court of Appeal discussed the ruling in *Reynolds v. Times Newspapers* in considering whether qualified privilege applied to statements made about a prominent politician. The Court held that, in all the circumstances, including the different culture and traditions of New Zealand society, it would take a broader approach to political matters and accept the legitimacy of comment on political affairs in a more generic sense than the House of Lords in *Reynolds.*

See *Goddard v. Day* 194 D.L.R. (4th) 559 2001 for a discussion of a Canadian approach to this issue.

In *McCartan and Turkington v. Times Newspapers (Northern Ireland)* [2002] 3 W.L.R. 1670 the defence of qualified privilege was applied to a report of a press conference held in Northern Ireland in connection with the campaign to clear Private Lee Clegg of the conviction for shooting dead a "joy rider". The claimants were Legg's erstwhile solicitors who sued the newspaper for libel contained in the report, some of which was read out at the meeting. The Northern Ireland Court of Appeal upheld the judgment that the press conference was not a "public meeting" for the purpose of the statutory defence under the Defamation

Act (Northern Ireland) 1955 but the House of Lords overruled this judgment on the ground that "public meeting" must be interpreted "in the light of the law of freedom of expression as it exists today". The defence therefore succeeded without their Lordships relying on the Human Rights Act, section 3.

The ten factors stated by Lord Nicholls in Reynolds as being necessary to qualified privilege in similar cases have been further discussed in several cases involving press reports relating to matters of public interest. In the litigation between *Loutchansky v. Times Newspapers* the claimant, a Russian businessman, sued the defendants for libelling him in reports, stating that he had been engaged in international criminal activities. The defendants raised the defence of qualified privilege on the grounds that the allegations were so serious that the public were entitled to know about them. In *Loutchansky v. Times Newspapers* [2001] 3 W.L.R. 404 they sought to amend their defence to include facts of which they had not been aware at the time of publication but which supported their contention that the public should be informed of the complaints. The Court of Appeal dismissed their appeal stating that defendants could only rely for purposes of qualified privilege on matters of which they knew at the time of publication and they could not go trawling for relevant matters afterwards. The right to freedom of expression would not be unduly restricted if the defendants were prevented from raising facts found at a later stage after the articles had been published.

In *Loutchansky v. Times Newspapers (No. 2)* [2002] 2 W.L.R. 640 the Court of Appeal considered the question of the liability of newspapers in the light of *Reynolds* and held that where there was the necessary duty in the press and a corresponding legitimate public interest in being informed of the material in question then, subject to the *Reynolds* tests, the defence of qualified privilege will apply, subject only to the requirement that the defendants must have fulfilled the test of responsible journalism; such a standard should not be set too high or too low. Lord Phillips said "Once *Reynolds* privilege is recognized, as it should be, as a different jurisprudential creature from the traditional form of privilege from which it sprang, the particular nature of the 'interest' and 'duty' which underlie it can more easily be understood." He accepted that a responsible journalist might equally decide to publish or not to publish an item and disapproved the test of whether to publish suggested by Gray J. in the court below, namely that publication would be in accordance with a duty to publish if the journalist would be open to criticism if he did not publish it. This is too limiting. The cases stress that there is no privilege to publish an untruth but it could on occasions be in the public interest to publish an article, true or false.

See also *Al Fagih v. HH Saudi Research and Marketing* [2001] EWCA Civ 1634, where the defendant newspaper published an account of allegations which had been made about the claimant in the course of a political dispute in the expatriate Saudi community. At first instance Smith J. held that the allegations could not be covered by qualified privilege but the Court of Appeal overruled that decision.

22–139 **Public interest.** *Loutchansky v. Times Newspapers (No. 2)* [2002] 2 W.L.R. 640. In *Al Fagih* the test of "public interest" was fulfilled where the defendant newspaper, which was published in the UK but was read almost exclusively by the expatriate Saudi community, published a report of a bitter dispute between two Saudi politicians belonging to a political committee.

See also *GKR Karate v. Yorkshire Post*.

(4) Reports

(d) *Of other proceedings and meetings*

Reports of other proceedings and matters. In *McCartan Turkington & Breen v. Times Newspapers* [2001] 3 W.L.R. 1670, the claimants raised, *inter alia*, the argument that the defendants' article had quoted from a press release which had not actually been read aloud at the press conference. The House of Lords refused to rule that this therefore fell outside the protection of qualified privilege—it could be regarded as common practice and part of the "proceedings" of the meeting.

22–152

Statements covered by qualified privilege under the Defamation Act 1996. See *McCartan Turkington & Breen v. Times Newspapers* [2000] 3 W.L.R. 1670 (decided under the Defamation Act (Northern Ireland) 1955, section 7, corresponding to section 7 of the 1952 Defamation Act. Reports of public meetings are now covered by section 15 and para. 12, Sch. 1 of the Defamation Act 1996.

22–153

Statements privileged subject to explanation or contradiction. See *McCartan Turkington & Breen v. Times Newspapers* [2000] 3 W.L.R. 1670.

22–156

(5) Fair comment and criticism

(a) *What is meant by comment*

Defence of fair comment. In *Burstein v. Times Newspapers* [2001] 1 W.L.R. 579 the defendants appealed against a decision of a judge of first instance to permit summary disposal of the claimant's libel action, where the defendants wished to raise the defence of fair comment and to rely on facts pleaded in that defence to claim a reduction of damages. The Court of Appeal dismissed their appeal.

22–159

In *Branson v. Bower* [2001] EWCA 791, the claimant sued the defendant journalist for libel in respect of an article critical of the claimant's motives in bidding for the National Lottery. The defendant sought summary judgment under Part 24, CPR but this was refused. While recognising that there is jurisdiction in defamation cases, the court must bear in mind the provisions of the Supreme Court Act Section 69, which provides for a qualified right to jury trial. Eady J. quoted with approval the test stated by the Court of Appeal in *Alexander v. Arts Council of Wales* [2001] 1 W.L.R. 1840, to the effect that in deciding whether to grant summary judgment in defamation, the court should apply a test analogous to that used in criminal trials as in *R. v. Galbraith* [1981] 1 W.L.R. 1039.

Eady J. confirmed that the remarks published by the defendant were comment rather than fact and that the defendant should not be required to justify them (since it is in accordance with English common law and with the decisions of the European Court of Human Rights that opinions on matters of public interest need not be justified.) This ruling was accepted by the Court of Appeal [2001] E.M.L.R. 800.

In *Cheng v. Tse Wai Chun* [2000] 3 H.K.L.R.D. 418 in the Court of Final Appeal of Hong Kong Lord Nicholls outlined the history and principles of the defence of fair comment. Eady J. in *Branson v. Bower* acknowledged that Cheng is merely of persuasive authority but recognized its importance. (He also applied it in the case of *Sugar v. Associated Newspapers* (unreported) February 6, 2001). In accordance with the views expressed by Lord Nicholls, he rejected the suggestion that there may be a different test where the words complained of attribute corrupt or dishonourable motives to the claimant, since this would be unduly burdensome and confusing. He concluded that the only two requirements of the defence of fair comment are that the defendant should have expressed the opinions honestly and that he should have done so on facts accurately stated. He also rejected the notion that in order to raise the defence, a defendant should have taken due care; to introduce negligence into fair comment would be undesirable.

22–162 **Province of judge and jury.** See *Branson v. Bower* [2001] EWCA 791, [2002] 2 W.L.R. 452 at pp. 457–8.

22–164 **Opinion honestly held.** It was confirmed in *Branson v. Bower* that for where fair comment is pleaded "the touchstone is always honesty and it should not be watered down by considering issues such as fairness or moderation". (*per* Eady J. at p. 456. Also p. 459.).

22–165 **Fact and comment.** See *Branson v. Bower* [2001] EWCA 791, [2002] 2 W.L.R. 452.

22–168 **Statement to be treated as comment.** In *Branson v. Bower* [2002] 2 W.L.R. 452 the Court of Appeal upheld the judge's ruling that the defendants comments on the claimant's motives in bidding for the lottery were comment and not fact.

22–171 **Fair and honest criticism.** In *Branson v. Bower* [2001] EWCA 791, Eady J. held that there is no separate category of fair comment where the statement complained of imputes corrupt or dishonourable motives.

8. MALICE

22–183 **Meaning of malice.** In *GKR Karate v. Yorkshire Post* the Court of Appeal upheld the decision of a judge at first instance to allow the issue of malice to be decided as a preliminary issue. For a discussion of malice see *Alexander v. Arts Council of Wales* [2001].

In *Branson v. Bower* the court approved the Court of Appeal's comments in *Alexander v. Arts Council of Wales* and held that a claimant should only be prevented from having his case as to malice heard by a jury if malice could not realistically be proved by a jury.

10. DAMAGES

(1) In General

22–207 **Aggravation.** Aggravated damages were awarded in *Kiam v. MGN* [2002] 2 All E.R. 219.

In *Thornberry v. Coleman* [2001] EWCA Civ 1858 the claimant in a slander action failed in her appeal against an award of a single sum by way of damages when there had been two slanders by the defendant and she claimed that she was entitled to aggravated damages, especially as the defendant had in effect repeated the allegation.

Exemplary or punitive damages. In *Kuddus v. Chief Constable of Leicestershire* [2001] 2 W.L.R. 1289, the Court of Appeal discussed the principles of exemplary damages, ruling that the power to award exemplary damages was not limited to cases where the cause of action had been recognised before 1964 as giving grounds for such damages. 22–211

(3) Mitigation of Damages

Bad reputation of claimant. NOTE 35. And see *Carlton Communications v. News Group; Cook v. News Group*, [2001] EWCA Civ. 1644; [2002] E.M.L.R. 16 CA. 22–222

Excessive Damages 22–227

In *Kiam v. MGN* [2002] 2 All E.R. 219, the claimant sued for libel, arising from the publication by the defendants in their newspaper of an article which seriously damaged his reputation as a businessman. There were aggravating features in the defendants' conduct and the trial judge directed the jury that they could take these into account in awarding damages. He suggested an amount up to £80,000 as a possible sum, but in the event the jury awarded the claimant £105,000. The Court of Appeal (Sedley L.J. dissenting) refused to overrule this award as excessive under Section 8 of the Courts and Legal Services Act, on the ground that it was not so excessive that no reasonable jury could have awarded the amount in question.

Costs 22–229

In *Hamilton v. Al Fayed* (costs), *The Times*, July 25, 2001, the Court of Appeal refused to make an order for costs against the persons who had provided financial contributions to Neil Hamilton's legal expenses in his action against Mohamed Al Fayed. The action had stood a reasonable likelihood of success and the court refused to penalize those who had provided funding to enable Mr. Hamilton to sue when he had not got the necessary financial means and legal aid was not available.

CHAPTER 23

MALICIOUS FALSEHOOD

	PARA.
■ 2. Essentials of the action	23–09
(b) Malice	23–11
(c) Damage	23–17
3. Rival traders	23–19

2. ESSENTIALS OF THE ACTION

Essentials of the action. Bar Council guidance that counsel should not plead any allegation of fraud without clear instructions and reasonably credible admissible evidence (see above) also applied to an allegation of malicious falsehood: *Cornwall Gardens Pte Ltd v. Garrard & Co Ltd* [2001] E.W.C.A. Civ. 699 (noted in *The Times*, June 19, 2001). However, now note the House of Lords' decision in *Medcalf v. Mardell* [2002] UKHL 27, [2002] 3 W.L.R. 172. This is discussed in 15–02, above.

23–09

(b) *Malice*

The requirement of malice and free speech. *Ferguson v. Associated Newspapers Ltd*, unreported, December 3, 2001, Gray J. "Malice, even where it is put as an absence of honest belief rather than knowledge of falsity, remains an allegation which is not to be made lightly."

23–11

(c) *Damage*

Where no proof of special damage required. *Ferguson v. Associated Newspapers Ltd*, unreported, December 3, 2001, Gray J. The concept of "calculated to cause damage" in section 3 of the Defamation Act 1952 should be given the meaning of "likely" or "probable" to cause damage rather than something which might well happen or something which is a possibility. The justification for this approach was in part Article 10 European Convention Human Rights which requires that any restriction on freedom of expression must be strictly justified as necessary in a democratic society.

23–17

Where proof of special damage required. *Khodaparast v. Shad* [2000] All E.R. 545, CA followed in *Smith v. Stemler* [2001] C.L.Y. 2309 with damages awarded for injury to feelings (£15,000) as well as economic loss (derogatory reference leading to summary dismissal).

23–18

3. RIVAL TRADERS

Comparative advertising. *Jupiter Unit Trust Managers Ltd v. Johnson Fry Asset Managers plc*, unreported, April 19, 2000. Morland J. noted that where

23–19

[159]

23–19

damages are sought in respect of a single example of "knocking" comparative advertising it may be difficult to attribute any substantial damage to that particular piece of comparative advertising especially in the context of a continuing market war between two trade rivals. In *DSG Retail Ltd v. Comet Group Plc* [2002] EWHC 116, Owen J. held inaccurate price comparisons to be actionable as more than "mere puffs".

In *British Airways Plc v. Ryanair Ltd* [2001] E.T.M.R. 24, Jacob J. refused to accept that mere "vulgar abuse" in a comparative advertisement amounted to malicious falsehood.

23–20 *Jupiter Unit Trust Managers Ltd v. Johnson Fry Asset Managers plc*, unreported, April 19, 2000, Morland J. When considering comparative advertising in relation to a claim for malicious falsehood the court should consider whether the defendant in "puffing" his own product has overstepped the permissible limit of denigration or disparagement of his rival's product so that the reasonable man would take the defendant's claims seriously. *De Beers Abrasive Products v. International General Electric* [1975] 1 W.L.R. 972 applied.

Sallows v. Griffiths [2001] F.S.R. 15 (p. 188). The claimant was unable to show that the falsehoods in the circumstances in which they were made were calculated to cause him damage in his office, profession or business, other than the loss resulting from his consequential wrongful dismissal, for which he had been compensated.

23–22 **Trade Marks Act 1994.** In *British Airways Plc v. Ryanair Ltd* [2001] E.T.M.R. 24 Jacob J. reiterated his view, first expressed in *Cable & Wireless plc v. BT* [1998] F.S.R. 383, that in a comparative advertising case the addition of a malicious falsehood claim to a claim of infringement of a registered trade mark added little.

NOTE 3: *Emaco v. Dyson Appliances Ltd* now reported [1999] E.T.M.R. 903.

CHAPTER 24

ECONOMIC TORTS

		PARA.
■	1. General	24–01
■	2. Procuring a breach of contract	24–15
	3. Intimidation	24–65
	4. Unlawful interference	24–88
	5. Conspiracy	24–116
■	6. Trade disputes	24–138

1. GENERAL

The core economic torts. NOTE 1. Add: D. Howarth and J. O'Sullivan (eds), Hepple, Howarth and Matthews *Tort: Cases and Materials* (5th ed., 2000) Chap. 15; H. Carty, *An Analysis of the Economic Torts* (2001). **24–01**

Inducing breach of contract. NOTE 23. Add: *cf.* Mustill L.J. in *Unilever v. Gillette* [1989] R.P.C. and Chadwick L.J. in *MCA Records Inc v. Charly Records Ltd* [2002] F.S.R 401, who both left this point open. **24–03**

NOTE 33. Add: And see the doubt about the force of the decision raised by Laddie J. in *Michaels v. Taylor Woodrow Developments Ltd* [2001] Ch. 493, 513. **24–06**

The Framework. NOTE 67. Add: See now the convincing discussion of unlawful means by Laddie J. in *Michaels v. Taylor Woodrow Developments Ltd* [2001] Ch. 493, 502–516; see below paras 24–94 note 39 and 24–127 note 7. **24–11**

NOTE 68. Add: But see the criticism of the first two of these decisions in *Michaels v. Taylor Woodrow Developments Ltd* [2001] 2 W.L.R. 224, 243–5.

NOTE 72. Add: [2001] 1 W.L.R 127, HL. **24–12**

NOTE 14. Add: On conspiracy and joint tortfeasors, *Kuwait Oil Tanker SAK v. Al Bader* [2000] 2 All E.R. Comm. 271, CA. See too below para. 24–127 note 12. **24–14**

NOTE 75. Add: Contrast the more extensive views on the ambit of vicarious liability in *Moores v. Bude-Stratton Town Council* [2001] I.C.R. 271, EAT and *Lister v. Hesley Hall Ltd* [2002] 1 A.C. 215 HL.

NOTE 77. Add: On conspiracy and joint tortfeasors see *Kuwait Oil Tanker SAK v. Al Bader* [2000] 2 All E.R. Comm. 271 CA. See too below para. 24–127 note 12.

2. PROCURING A BREACH OF CONTRACT

Recklessness. NOTE 15. Add: See too, Jacob J., *Oren v. Red Box Toy Factory Ltd* [1999] F.S.R. 785, agreeing with Peter Gibson L.J. **24–20**

24–21 **Inferred intention.** NOTE 18. Add: *In Gainers Inc v. Pocklingtons Holiday Inc.* (2001) 194 D.L.R 109 it was said that there would be no liability if the defendant acted under a *bona fide* belief that contractual rights would not be infringed, but in order to be *bona fide* some reasonable basis for the belief had to exist.

24–27 **Collective agreements.** NOTE 57. Add: *Henry v. London General Transport Services* [2001] I.R.L.R. 132 (effect of custom and practice on incorporation of terms into employment contracts).

24–28 **An obligation to recognise.** NOTE 63. Add: See now, Wedderburn (1999) 28 I.L.J. 1, 33–42; B. Simpson (2000) 29 I.L.J. 193; S. Moore, S. Wood, P. Davies (2000) 29 I.L.J. 406; R. Rideout (2002) 31 I.L.J. 1, 13–31.

24–37 **Procuring breach of equitable obligations.** NOTE 26. Add: On equitable compensation for breach of fiduciary duty: *Cia. de Seguros Imperio v. Heath (REBX) Ltd* [2001] 1 W.L.R. 112, CA.

NOTE 29. Add: V. Sims (2001) 30 I.L.J. 101; *Symbian Ltd v. Christiansen* [2001] I.R.L.R. 77 (duty of fidelity). But for Commonwealth discussions of fiduciary duty and the contract of employment, see R. McCallum and A. Stewart "Employee Loyalty in Australia" (1999) 20 Comp. Lab. Law and Policy Jo. 155, 160, and "Employee Duty of Loyalty—a Canadian Perspective" J. Oakley *ibid.* 185, 190–4.

24–39 **Trust, fiduciary duties and accessory liability.** NOTE 43. Amend reference to *Bank of Credit and Commerce International SA v. Ali to* [2002] 1 A.C. 251, HL Add: *BCCI v. Akindele* [2000] 3 W.L.R. 000, CA; *Walker v. Stones* [2001] 2 W.L.R. 623, CA; *Trusor AB v. Smallbone (No.2)* [2001] 1 W.L.R 1177; R. Nolan (2000) 59 C.L.J. 447 (knowing receipt); *Caslo Computer Ltd v. Sago, The Times,* February 2, 2001 (knowing assistance).

24–41 **Breach of confidence.** NOTE 53. Add: see now *Douglas v. Hello! Ltd* [2001] Q.B. 967, CA; *Venables v. News Group Newspapers* [2001] 2 W.L.R. 1038.

24–44 **Companies as employers.** NOTE 76. Add: See too *AGDA Systems Intl. Ltd v. Valcom Ltd* (1999) 168 D.L.R (4th) 351 (Ont CA); *Ontario Ltd v. Magna International Inc.* (2001) 200 D.L.R (4th) 521 (Ont CA); *Kay Aviation b v. v. Rofe* (2002) 202 D.L.R (4th) 683 (Pr.Ed. Is. Sup.Ct. App. Div.).

24–49 **Inconsistent translations.** NOTE 10. Add: See too *Harry Winton Investments Ltd. v. CIBC Development Corp.* (2001) 199 D.L.R (4th) 709 (Ont CA).

(c) *Indirect procurement*

24–56 **Unlawful means.** NOTE 47. Add: On unlawful means, see *Michaels v. Taylor Woodrow Developments Ltd* [2001] Ch. 493; below paras 24–94, 24–105, 24–106, 24–127.

24–61 **Interim injunction.** NOTE 84. Add: On contempt of court and breach of confidence: *Ashworth Hospital Authority v. MGN Ltd* [2001] 1 W.L.R. 515, CA. On third parties and contempt of court: *Att.-Gen. v. Punch Ltd* [2001] Q.B. 1028, CA.

Justification. NOTE 5. Add: see too *Gainers Inc. v Pockington Holdings Inc.* (2001) 194 D.L.R. (4th) 109 (Alberta CA). 24–63

3. INTIMIDATION

Harassment. NOTE 33. Add: An employer may be liable for unreasonably failing to protect an employee from fellow employees' harassment: *Waters v. Commissioner of Police of the Metropolis* [2000] 1 W.L.R. 1607, HL. 24–67

NOTE 36. Add: *I. v. DPP* [2001] 2 W.L.R. 765, HL (threat of violence implied from conduct); *Thomas v. News Group Newspapers, The Times*, July 25, 2001, CA (press articles calculated to incite racial hatred can be harassment).

NOTE 24. Add: In *Michaels v. Taylor Woodrow Development Ltd* [2001] Ch. 493, 513, Laddie J. decided that in *Associates British Ports v. T.G.W.U.* [1989] I W.L.R. 939. the Court of Appeal were not "determining this issue" as to liability, as it was in interlocutory decision "considering only whether it was arguable". 24–78

Breach of contract. NOTE 31. Add: C. MacMillan (2000) 63 M.L.R 721. 24–80

"Two party" and "three-party" intimidation. NOTE 76. Add: R. Bigwood, "Economic Duress by (Threatened) Breach of Contract" (2001) 117 L.Q.R 376. 24–85

4. UNLAWFUL INTERFERENCE

Unlawful Means. NOTE 17. Add: See now *Michaels v. Taylor Woodrow Developments Ltd* [2001] Ch. 493, 510. 24–91

Common Principles? NOTE 40. Add: In *Michaels v Taylor Woodrow Developments Ltd* [2001] Ch. 493, 503, Laddie J. while acknowledging the possibility of inconsistency between different economic torts on this issue concluded that they should be assumed to be the same: "to the extent that a means is treated as unlawful for one economic tort, so to the same extent it should be treated as unlawful for the others." 24–94

Breach of confidence. NOTE 78. Add: In an exceptional case, breach of contract involving breach of confidence akin to breach of a fiduciary obligation can give rise to the remedy of an account of profits: *Att.-Gen. v. Blake* [2001] 1 A.C 268, HL. And see G. Philipson and H. Fenwick, "Breach of Confidence as a Privacy Remedy in the Human Rights Act" (2000) 63 M.L.R. 660. 24–97

NOTE 14. Add: On the distinction between aiding and inducing, see *Anyanwu v. South Bank Student Union* [2001] 1 W.L.R. 638, HL. 24–102

Three difficulties. NOTE 41. Add: The *Williams* decision must now be regarded as doubtful after the analysis of Laddie J. in *Michaels v. Taylor Woodrow Developments Ltd* [2001] Ch. 493, 513–5; if Dillon L.J. were right: "A lone driver acting for one retailer, who assists his employer to take business from 24–105

24–105   its competitor by driving faster than the speed limit, would be liable for unlawfully interfering with the competitor's business," 515. The dictum of Dillon L.J. that anything illegal under any statute is unlawful means was not the judgement of the court: *ibid*.

24–106   **The "Dock Strike" Case.** NOTE 42. Add: In *Michales v. Taylor Woodrow Developments Ltd* [2001] Ch. 493, 513. Laddie J. decided that as this was only a interlocutory decision the Court of Appeal "were not determining this issue but considering only whether it was arguable".

5. CONSPIRACY

24–118   **The combination.** NOTE 25. Add: For an apparent evasion of the rule that a union may not be "treated" as a corporate body in TULRCA 1992, s.10(2) see *London Underground Ltd v. RMT* [2001] I.C.R. 647, 662.

24–126   **Breach of statute.** NOTE 92. Add: But see *Australian Workers' Union v. BHP Iron-Ore Pty Ltd* [2001] F.C.A. 3 noted in D. Noakes and A. Cardell-Ree (2001) 14 Aus. J. Lab. L. 89.

24–127   **Other forms of unlawful means.** NOTE 7. Add : See too *Michaels v. Taylor Woodrow Developments Ltd* [2001] Ch. 593, 516, "Where a wrongful act consists of breach of the provisions of a statute . . . it will only support an action for conspiracy by unlawful means if it is determined that the intention of the legislature was that such causes of action should be available to enforce the provisions of the legislation" per Laddie J. summarising the conclusions of his convincingly reasoned analysis of the torts of conspiracy and unlawful interference with business with also included the view that what amounted to unlawful means was the same in both torts, see above para 24–94.

NOTE 9. Add: on joint or concurrent tortfeasors and separate tortfeasors see *Rahman v. Arearose Ltd* [2000] 3 W.L.R. 1184 CA.

NOTE 11. Add: D. Fox (2001) 60 C.L.J. 33: *R v. Secretary of State for Transport, ex p. Factortame* [2001] 1 W.L.R. 942.

NOTE 12. Amend reference to: *Kuwait Oil Tankers SAK v. Al Bader* [2000] 2 All E.R Comm. 271 CA.

Add: In *Michaels v. Taylor Woodrow Developments Ltd* [2001] Ch. 593, 516, Laddie J. acknowledged that it is possible to sue for wrongful means conspiracy where some but not all of the conspirators would be liable individually for the wrongful act. In this respect the tort of conspiracy "dovetails with, or overlaps, the law of joint tortfeasance." But the courts could suppress the pleading of conspiracy where the same allegation could be expressed in terms of joint tortfeasance.

24–129   NOTE 25. Add: See too the doubts of Laddie J. about the binding force of the Court of Appeal decision in the "dock strike case" in *Michaels v. Taylor Woodrow Developments Ltd* [2001] Ch. 493, 513.

24–132   NOTE 47. Add: But see now *Hall v. Woslston Hall Leisure Ltd* [2001] 1 W.L.R. 225, CA.

6. TRADE DISPUTES

Trade disputes and the economic torts. NOTE 93. Add: on third parties and contempt of court: *Att.-Gen. v. Punch Ltd* [2001] Q.B. 1028, CA.
 Amend text to NOTE 96 to: Simple conspiracy, attending at or near a place of work for the purpose merely of peaceful communication of information or peaceful persuasion (picketing), "interference" with trade, business or employment and inducing a breach of a contract of employment.

24–139

Restriction of immunities. NOTE 17. Amend to See TULRCA 1992, s.235A, inserted by TURER Act 1993, s.22; see *P v. NAS/UWT* [2001] I.C.R. 1241, CA; below, para. 24–181.

24–141

Judicial analysis. Line 16. Insert NOTE 24a after "grounds".
 Amend NOTE 24 to: See below, para. 24–189; *American Cyanmid Co. v. Ethicon Ltd* [1975] A.C. 396, HL; and on the balance of convenience *Associated British Ports v. T.G.W.U* [1989] 1 W.L.R. 939 at 957, 962 and 968 CA insisting that the judge must consider the "public interest": reversed on other grounds *ibid.*, HL; see above, para. 24–106.
 Add NOTE 24a. Technically the words of s.20 are based on the doctrine *qui facit per alium facit per se* (see s.20(1) " . . . taken to have been done by the union") rather than vicarious liability, but nothing seems to turn upon this.
 NOTE 34. Amend references to TULRCA 1992, s.235A(b) to TULRCA 1992, s.235A(6).

24–142

Trade disputes and procuring breach of contract. NOTE 51. Amend McCarthy, *Legal Interventions in Collective Bargaining* to McCarthy (ed.) *Legal Interventions in Industrial Relations: Gains and Losses* (1992), Chap. 4.

24–144

Breach of contract. Amend subsections (1) and (2) merely anticipated the decision of the House of Lords in 1983: that which is by statute not "actionable" is not unlawful[82] to subparagraphs (a) and (b) merely anticipated the decision of the House of Lords in 1983: that which is by statute not "actionable" is not unlawful.[82]

24–167

Trade disputes and ballots. NOTE 10. Amend to: For example the ERA 1999, Sched. 3, para 6, inserting TULRCA s.229(2A) and amending TULRCA s.246, defines the legal character of overtime bans and call-out bans as action short of a strike for the purpose of ballot papers (reversing *Connex S.E. Ltd v. R.M.T.* [1999] I.R.L.R. 249, CA).
 NOTE 12. Add on the 2000 revision of the *Code of Practice* see Simpson (2001) 30 I.L.J. 194.

24–171

Entitlement to vote. NOTE 21. Add: In s.232B(2) the reference to s.230(2A) is an error for s.230(2B): *P v. NAS/UWT* [2001] I.C.R. 1241, 1258 CA.
 NOTE 23. Amend to TULRCA 1992 s.227(1). In *P v. NAS/UWT* [2001] I.C.R 1241 Waller L.J. endorsed the reasoning of Millet L.J. in *London Underground Ltd v. R.M.T* [1996] I.C.R 170, 178 to the effect that the words "at the time of the ballot" in that section mean the time when the ballot papers were sent out. In *P v. NAS/UWT* [2001] I.C.R. 1241 CA it was held that although section 232B does not expressly apply to a small accidental failure to comply with section 232A

24–173

24–173 (which was inserted in 1999 in place of the former section 227(2)), there was no such failure where a failure to comply with section 227(1) was accidental and unlikely to affect the result of the ballot. Contrast *Midland Mainline Ltd v. RMT* [2001] I.R.L.R 813 CA where the Schiemann L.J. said that there would be a failure to comply with section 227(1) where members who had not been balloted or called on to take industrial action were "induced to take industrial action by their own feelings that this is appropriate" or "in the knowledge that many of their colleagues will expect them to take industrial action, will do so", a conclusion "any reasonably worldly-wise judge would reach . . . independently of any evidence" *ibid.* 816.

24–175 **Separate workplace ballots.** NOTE 32. Amend to TULRCA 1992, s.226C; the Code of Practice 2000 states that where 50 or fewer members are entitled to vote, the union may want to consider whether the appointment of a scrutineer would still be of benefit in enabling the union, to demonstrate compliance until the statutory requirements more easily (para. 13).

24–176 **Voting and calling action.** NOTE 45. Amend to "If you take part in a strike or other industrial action, you may be in breach of your contract of employment. However, if you are dismissed for taking part in strike or other industrial action which is called officially, the dismissal will be unfair if it takes place fewer than eight weeks after you started taking part in the action, and depending on the circumstances may be unfair if takes place later": s.229(4). The second sentence was added by the Employment Relations Act 1999 Sched. 3, para. 6. The union may comment on this statement, but only in a separate document. On accompanying documents being equated with the paper, see *Blue Circle v. T.G.W.U*, unreported, July 7, 1989, *per* Alliot J. (union therefore limited to 24 hours strike specifically mentioned); convincingly criticised by Simpson in (1989) 18 I.L.J. 234.

24–177 **Ballot papers and questions.** NOTE 52. Amend reference to TULRCA 1992, s.292(2A) to TULRCA 1992, s.229(2A).

24–178 **Ballot papers and notices.** NOTE 65. Add: The information, under ss.226A (3A) and 234A (5A), is limited to information in the union's possession, but this was given a wide judicial interpretation in the remarkable Court of Appeal decision in *London Underground Ltd v. RMT* [2001] I.C.R. 647, 663: "I would say that information was possessed by the defendant union if it was possessed by any official of the union who, in accordance with the union's rules and normal operating procedures, was concerned with maintaining records kept for the union's purposes." See Wedderburn "Underground Labour Injunctions" (2001) 30 I.L.J. 206.

On obligatory information as to the "category" of workers involved: *Sefton MB v. UNISON and Flanagan* July 2, 2001, Sachs J., and *Westminster City Council v. UNISON* [2001] I.C.R. 1046 CA *per* Buxton L.J." a very broad word and not to be either exclusively or narrowly defined. It means no more than a reference to the general type of workers" at 1063.

NOTE 66. Amend to See ss.226 (3A) (b), 234A(5A)(b)

24.181 **Impeding supplies.** NOTE 88. Add: See the unsuccessful application in *P v. NAS/UWT* [2001] I.C.R 1241, CA.

Contemplation or furtherance of a trade dispute. NOTE 57. Add: On the "likelihood" test for injunctions and the impact of the Human Rights Act 1998, see *Imutran Ltd v. Uncaged Campaigns Ltd* [2001] 2 All E.R. 385 (freedom of expression).   **24–190**

(c) *The content*

NOTE 97. Add: See too *P v. NAS/UWT* [2001] I.C.R 1241, CA (dispute as to reasonableness of employer's instructions to teach pupil in classroom).   **24.197**

NOTE 99. Add: In *P v. NAS/UWT* [2001] ICR 1241, CA Waller L.J. was "less certain" than the trial judge that a dispute over the head teacher's instruction to teach an allegedly disruptive pupil did not relate to "the physical conditions in which the teachers were required to work".

NOTE 5. Add: See too *Westminster City Council v. UNISON* [2001] I.C.R. 1046 CA, where although the union "made no bones about their opposition to the privatisation of the assessment and advice unit, on no view was the threat of the strike used to further that opposition . . . " The judge . . . appears to assume that the workers . . . must have been swayed by [the unions] political or policy arguments about the theory of privatisation when he had specific evidence given at some length that that was not the case *per* Buxton L.J. at 1062–3. The uncontroverted evidence was that the dispute was solely about the identity of the employer and was, therefore a trade dispute.   **24–198**

NOTE 6. Add: In January 2002, the European Court of Human Rights rejected the union's complaint that this decision was incompatible with Article 11 of the European Convention on Human Rights as inadmissible.

CHAPTER 25

STATUTORY INTELLECTUAL PROPERTY RIGHTS

	PARA.
2. Copyright and related rights	25–03
■ 3. Infringement of copyright	25–18
■ 8. Design rights	25–45
■ 10. Registered trade marks	25–65
■ 11. Patents	25–79

2. Copyright and Related Rights

Literary and dramatic works. NOTE 28. Add: On the scope of protection of a typographical arrangement see: *Newspaper Licensing Agency Ltd v. Marks & Spencer plc* [2001] 3 W.L.R. 290.   **25–07**

NOTE 29. Add: As an author allows each part of a text to move on from one stage to the next he creates a new work in which copyright subsists. Earlier drafts can be separate copyright works: *Sweeney v. Macmillan Publishers Ltd* [2002] R.P.C. 35.

Database rights. Add to text: In *British Horseracing Board Ltd v. William Hill Organisation Ltd*, the Court of Appeal referred certain questions on the scope of database right to the European Court of Justice (unreported judgment of CA, dated July 31, 2001 on appeal from a decision of Laddie J. reported at [2001] R.P.C. 612).   **25–08**

Musical and artistic works. Add to text: In the case of a photograph there can be sufficient originality for copyright to subsist in the selection of the position of the objects photographed, the angle and the lighting: *AntiquesPortfolio.Com plc v. Rodney Fitch & Co. Ltd* [2001] F.S.R. 345.   **25–09**

NOTE 42. Add: In *Vermaat and Powell v. Boncrest Ltd* [2001] F.S.R. 43, it was held that the author of a work of artistic craftsmanship had to be both a craftsman and an artist and that the patchwork in question, while pleasing to the eye, was not sufficiently artistic to qualify as such.

3. Infringement of Copyright

Importation of infringing copies. NOTE 72. Add: "Authorise" can include commissioning another to produce an article to a particular design: *Pensher Security Doors Co. Ltd v. Sunderland CC* [2000] R.P.C. 249.   **25–19**

NOTE 74. Add: The reference to *Monsoon v. India Imports* is [1993] F.S.R. 486. See also on secondary infringement: *Pensher Security Dors Co. Ltd v. Sunderland C.C.* [2000] R.P.C. 249.

Causal derivation and substantial similarity—copying a substantial part.   **25–21**
NOTE 89. Add: As to copyright in architectural drawings and the right to use the

25–21 common stock of architectural ideas, see: *Jones v. London Borough of Tower Hamlets* [2001] R.P.C. 407 *cf. Cala Homes (South) Ltd v. Alfred McAlpine Homes East Ltd* [1995] F.S.R. 818.

25–22 **Causal derivation and substantial similarity—copying a substantial part.** The House of Lords allowed an appeal by the claimant in *Designers Guild Ltd v. Russell Williams (Textiles) Ltd* [2001] F.S.R. 113, restoring the judge's finding of infringement. Copied features must be a substantial part of the copyright work but not necessarily of the defendant's work. The question to be asked is whether the defendant's work incorporate a substantial part of the skill and labour expended by the designer of the claimant's work.

25–26 **Exceptions to infringement—fair dealing.** Add to text: As to public interest defences to copyright infringement see: *Ashdown v. Telegraph Group Ltd* Judgment of the Court of Appeal, unreported on appeal from [2001] E.M.L.R. 20; *Hyde Park Residence Ltd v. Yelland* [2000] 3 W.L.R. 215; [2000] E.M.L.R. 363 C.A. and *Imutran v. Uncaged Campaigns Ltd* [2001] E.M.L.R. 21 (V-C).

25–31 **Damages or account of profits.** Add to NOTE 51: In *Nottinghamshire Healthcare National Health Service Trust v. News Group Newspapers Ltd* [2002] E.M.L.R. 33, Pumfrey J. surveyed the law on additional damages. He awarded compensatory damages of £450 and additional damages to bring the total sum to £10,000 in respect of the flagrant reproduction in a newspaper of a confidential medical photograph of a patient in a secure medical unit.

Add to text: A person who has not committed acts of infringement himself but who has procured and intended those acts be done by another or has joined with an infringer in concerted action to secure that those acts were done may be liable as a joint tortfeasor: *MCA Records Inc. v. Charley Records Ltd* [2002] F.S.R. 401 (CA).

8. DESIGN RIGHTS

25–48 **Meaning of "design", "commonplace" etc.** Add to text: In *Scholes Windows Ltd v. Magnet Ltd* [2002] F.S.R. 172, the Court of Appeal upheld a finding that the design field in question was windows and not U-PVC windows in finding a design commonplace in the wider field.

25–51 **Design right infringement—remedies.** NOTE 44. Add: As to the requirement of knowledge for secondary infringement see: *A Fulton Co. Ltd v. Grant Barnett & Co. Ltd* [2001] R.P.C. 16 (proceedings maintainable without commencing a new claim even though knowledge only acquired following claim). Where the defendant's design is sufficiently similar to the claimant's design, the burden of proof can shift to the defendant to prove that there was no copying.

10. REGISTERED TRADE MARKS

25–68 **Registration of trade marks and applications for registration of trade marks.** NOTE 92. Add: On the requirement of distinctiveness, see *BACH and BACH Flower Remedies Trade Marks* [2000] R.P.C. 513 (CA).

Licensing and assignment of registered trade marks. Add to text: The courts will generally uphold, in the face of a restraint of trade or competition law attack, a *bona fide* agreement seeking to settle global trade mark disputes by restricting the parties' use of trade marks in specified ways: see *WWF-World Wide Fund for Nature v. World Wrestling Federation Entertainment Inc.* [2002] F.S.R. 530 (CA).

Infringement of registered trade marks. Add to text: The courts will generally uphold, in the face of a restraint of trade or competition law attack, a bona fide agreement seeking to settle global trade mark disputes by restricting the parties' use of trade marks in specified ways: see *WWF-World Wide Fund for Nature v. World Wrestling Federation Entertainment Inc.* [2002] F.S.R. 530 (CA).

25–73

NOTE 19. Add: In *Arsenal Football Club plc v. Reed* [2001] E.T.M.R. 77, the High Court referred to the European Court of Justice the question whether the cause of action for infringement required the defendant's use to be use as a trade mark. The defendant had used the sign "Arsenal" on clothing intending to indicate allegiance to the team, not the trade origin of the clothing. The Advocate-General has now delivered his opinion in that case and the judgment of the ECJ is awaited. As to use not constituting trade mark use see also: *Rugby Football Union v. Cotton Traders Ltd* [2002] E.T.M.R. 76—no infringement by use of English team rose emblem on rugby shirts. See also for circumstances in which use of a trade mark in a descriptive sense may not infringe: *Holterhoff v. Freiesleben* Case C–2/00 [2002] E.T.M.R. 917 (ECJ). As to infringement by use on a foreign web-site, see *Euromarket Designs Inc. v. Peters and Crate & Barrel Ltd* [2001] F.S.R. 288 and *800 Flowers Trade Mark* [2002] F.S.R. 191 (CA).

NOTE 20. Add: The ECJ gave guidance as to how identity between two marks should be assessed for the purposes of section 10(1) of the Act in *SA Societe LTJ v. SA Sadas* Case C–291/00 [2002] E.T.M.R. 441.

NOTE 22. Add: See also on the effect of s.10(3) *Pfizer Ltd v. Eurofood Link (U.K.) Ltd* [2000] E.T.M.R. 896; [2001] F.S.R. 17 (VIAGRA registered for anti-impotence tablets could prevent use of VIAGRENE for aphrodisiac drink under s.10(2) or s.10(3) as an alternative); *General Motors Corporation v. Yplon* [2000] R.P.C. 572.

Limitations on the effect of a registered trade mark. NOTE 25. Add: The provisions of s.10(6) are independent of the provisions of the Comparative Advertising Directive. Vulgar abuse making use of a trade mark, is protected by s.10(6) and is not actionable: *British Airways plc v. Ryanair Ltd* [2001] F.S.R. 541 ("Expensive BA _____ DS" with price comparison: claim failed). Section 10(6) falls to be interpreted narrowly and restricted to cases in which the use of the mark is not on the proprietor's own goods: *Levi Strauss & Co. v. Tesco Stores Ltd.* Judgment of Pumfrey J., July 31, 2002 [2000] EWHC 1556 (Ch). Where a competitor uses a trade mark proprietor's product numbers, that may constitute comparative advertising, but the competitor will only be liable for trade mark infringement, if the effect of the reference to them is to create in the mind of the persons at whom the advertising is directed an association between the manufacturer whose products are identified and the competing supplier: *Toshiba Europe GmbH v. Katun Germany GmbH* Case C–112/99 [2002] F.S.R. 618 (ECJ).

25–74

NOTE 26. Add: However honest a defendant's subjective intentions were, any use of his own name which amounted to passing off would not be in accordance with honest practices in industrial or commercial matters and the "own name" defence would not apply in such circumstances: *Asprey and Garrard Ltd v. WRA (Guns) Ltd* [2002] F.S.R. 487. In *Scandecor Development AB v. Scandecor Marketing AB*, referred to in the main text, the House of Lords [2002] F.S.R. 7 referred questions to the ECJ concerning the scope of the own name defence but the case settled before an answer was given. In *Re Nichols TM*, July 23, 2002 [2002] EWHC 1424 (Ch) Jacob J. referred questions to the ECJ including whether the own name defence extends to corporate entities and the meaning of honest practices in industrial or commercial matters in that context.

NOTE 28. Add: See: *Boehringer Ingelheim KG v. Swingward Ltd* Case C–143/00 [2002] E.T.M.R. 898 for further guidance on the circumstances in which altering the packaging of the products will be permissible.

The ECJ has given a restrictive interpretation of the concept of consent in its judgment in *Zino Davidoff SA v. A&G Imports Ltd* Joined Cases C–414/99 to C–416/99 [2002] E.T.M.R. 9 holding that consent to goods being placed on the market in the EEA could not be inferred from the fact that the proprietor has not communicated the opposition to marketing, that no warning was given or that no contractual reservations were made at the time of sale. The effect of the ECJ's judgment is that only express consent to subsequent marketing in the EEA is likely to suffice to exhaust the proprietor's registered trade mark rights.

25–75 **Proceedings for trade mark infringement and remedies.** NOTE 31. Add: On the approach to summary assessment of damages in a case in which there was user of a trade mark on a web-site, resulting in some benefit to the claimant see *Roadtech Computer Systems Limited v. Mandata Limited* [2000] E.T.M.R. 970 (Damages assessed at £15,000).

25–76 **Criminal offences and customs powers.** Add to text: Repeated dealing in counterfeit goods is regarded as a serious offence meriting a substantial custodial sentence: *R. v. Burns* [2001] F.S.R. 423 (12 months imprisonment). See also: *R. v. Keane* [2001] F.S.R. 63 on the requirements for the offence of selling goods with a sign likely to be mistaken for a trade mark.

25–78 **Action for groundless threats of trade mark infringement proceedings.** NOTE 40: Add: "Veiled and muffled" threat held actionable in *L'Oreal (U.K.) Ltd v. Johnson & Johnson* [2000] F.S.R. 686.

11. PATENTS

25–82 **Application for a patent—priority date.** NOTE 45. Add: The English court will sometimes stay proceedings concerning a European Patent (U.K.), pending the determination of opposition proceedings in the EPO. For principles, see: *General Hospital Corp's European Patent (U.K.)* [2000] F.S.R. 633 (CA). See also: *Uniliver plc v. Frisa N.V.* [2002] F.S.R. 708.

25–85 **The specification—description and claims.** Add to text: The *Catnic* principles have received further consideration in *Wheatley (Davina) v. Drillsafe Ltd* [2001] R.P.C. 133 and *Cartonneries de Thulin S.A. v. CTP White Knight Ltd*

[2001] R.P.C. 107. In *Rohm and Haas Co. v. Collag Ltd* [2002] F.S.R. 28 the Court of Appeal gave guidance as to the limited circumstances in which patent prosecution history could be used as an aid to construction.

Other grounds upon which a patent may be revoked. NOTE 63. Add: For a helpful review of the contemporary approach to obviousness see *DSM NV's Patent* [2001] R.P.C. 675 and *Dyson Appliances Ltd v. Hoover Ltd* [2001] R.P.C. 26. **25–87**

Amendment. NOTE 81. Add: *Kimberly Clark Worldwide Inc. v. Procter & Gamble Limited (No. 2)* is now reported at [2001] F.S.R. 22 and [2000] R.P.C. 422 (CA). Amendment will be refused if there has been culpable delay: *Instance v. CCL Label Inc.* [2002] F.S.R. 27. **25–89**

Infringement. Add to text: It is not an infringement of patent to repair an existing patented product but it is an infringement to make a new one under the guise of repair: *United Wire Ltd v. Screen Repair Services (Scotland) Ltd* [2001] F.S.R. 365 (HL). **25–90**

Action for infringement, relief and remedies. NOTE 14. Add: See *Coflexip S.A. v. Stolt Comex Seaway MS Ltd* [2001] R.P.C. 182 for guidance as to the appropriate scope of an injunction in a patent case. **25–95**

Compulsory licences, licences of right and Crown use. Add to text: The provisions concerning the circumstances in which a compulsory licence may be granted have been substantially altered by the effect of the TRIPS agreement as they apply to patents of WTO member country proprietors. Reference should now be made to Patents Act 1977, s.48A which sets out the more limited grounds upon which a compulsory licence may be made in respct of such patents. **25–98**

Action to restrain unjustified threats of infringement proceedings. Add to text: In *Unilever plc v. The Procter & Gamble Company* [2000] F.S.R. 344 the Court of Appeal held that a threat made in the context of a without prejudice meeting discussing settlement of worldwide litigation was not an admissible basis for a threats action. See also: *Kooltrade Ltd v. XTS Ltd* [2001] F.S.R. 158 on whether a threat is entitled to without prejudice privilege. **25–100**

NOTE 38: A threat "veiled and muffled by protestations of a continuing state of indecision" as to whether proceedings would be commenced is potentially actionable: *L'Oreal (U.K.) Ltd v. Johnson & Johnson* [2000] F.S.R. 686.

CHAPTER 26

PASSING OFF

General principles. *Irvine v. Talksport Ltd* [2002] EWHC 367; [2002] 2 All E.R. 414. The defendants' advertising brochure included a photograph of the claimant, the famous Formula One driver. This photograph had been manipulated to remove the mobile phone Irvine actually had in his hand and replace it with the image of a portable radio to which the words "Talk Radio" had been added. Talk Radio was the name then used by the defendant company. Laddie J. held that there was an implicit representation of endorsement and that this false representation of endorsement rendered the defendant liable in passing off. He stressed the evolving nature of this action, noting that old cases "do not illustrate more recent developments".

26–01

Misrepresentation. NOTE 38: In *Reality Group Ltd v. Chance* [2002] F.S.R. 13 Patten J. refused to strike out the claim that the defendants' application to register the name "Reality" as a Community Trade Mark was in itself passing off. Patten J. drew an analogy with the registration of domain names, referring to *British Telecommunications plc v. One in a Million Ltd* [1999] F.S.R. 1.

26–08

Misrepresentations actionable as passing off. *Arsenal FC plc v. Reed, The Times,* [2001] 2 C.M.L.R. 23, Laddie J. The defendant for a considerable period of time had sold unofficial Arsenal memorabilia and souvenirs, bearing the words "Arsenal" and "The Gunners" and the football club's crest and cannon device. Arsenal FC alleged that this was passing off on the basis that the public would believe that the products in question were associated, connected with or licensed by Arsenal FC. Laddie J. (noting that there was no direct evidence of confusion) held that the use of the words and signs carried no message of trade origin and it was clear that some customers bought the merchandise simply to show allegiance to the club.

26–09

Primark Stores Ltd v. Lollypop Clothing Ltd [2001] F.S.R. 37, John Martin Q.C., sitting as a Deputy High Court Judge. Jeans bearing the claimant's registered trademarks were supplied by the defendant to retailers. The defendant contended that it was arguable that the jeans he so supplied were "genuine" jeans supplied to him by the claimant's supplier and that therefore there was no deception. Held these items were not actually the claimant's jeans until they had been "adopted" as such by the claimant. There was no evidence that the claimant had dealt with the goods in any way which implied that he had taken responsibility for them. *Vokes v. Evans* (1932) 49 R.P.C. applied. *Irvine v. Talksport Ltd* [2002] EWHC 367; [2002] 2 All E.R. 414. False representations of endorsement amounted to passing off: *McCulloch v. Lewis A May* [1947] 5 R.P.C. 58 rejected; *Henderson v. Radio Corporation Pty Ltd* [1969] R.P.C. 218 (a decision of the High Court of New South Wales sitting in its appellate jurisdiction) preferred. "If someone acquires a valuable reputation or goodwill the law of passing off will protect it from unlicensed use by other parties". However Laddie J. was keen to contrast the approach to be taken in endorsement cases (where the celebrity encourages the public to buy the product) from merchandising cases (where the celebrity image is used to enhance the attractiveness of the product to the public).

26–11 **Goodwill.** *MedGen Inc v. Passion for Life Products Ltd* [2001] F.S.R. 30 (p. 496), Kevin Garnett Q.C., sitting as a Deputy High Court Judge : the goodwill in the trade name belonged to the exclusive U.K. distributor of the product, not the U.S. manufacturer of the product. The distributor alone was thought of as the source in the U.K. *Sutherland v. V2 Music Ltd* [2002] E.M.L.R. 2, residual goodwill existed and could be protected, *Ad-Lib Club v. Granville* [1972] R.P.C. 673 followed. In *Teleworks Ltd v. Telework Group plc* [2002] R.P.C. 27 Christopher Floyd Q.C., sitting as a Deputy High Court judge stressed that the reputation had to be proved at the date when the defendant started the activities complained of. He found the concept of "future goodwill" unhelpful, noting "it is wrong in principle to form a view as to what the goodwill might be in the future and to consider the question of misrepresentation against a background of that enhanced goodwill".

26–12 **Traders.** In *Burge v. Haycock* [2002] R.P.C. 28, the chief executive of the pressure group the "Countryside Alliance" was awarded an interim injunction to restrain the defendant from falsely describing himself as a Countryside Alliance candidate in a local election. As the cases on charitable and professional bodies showed, a claimant could succeed in the tort of passing off even though not carrying a commercial activity. The Countryside Alliance has a goodwill in its name.

NOTE 81: *Kean v. McGivan* [1982] F.S.R. 119, distinguished by the Court of Appeal in *Burge v. Haycock* [2002] R.P.C. 28 as *ex tempore* and a decision on its own facts.

In *Irvine v. Talksport Ltd* [2002] EWHC 367; [2002] 2 All E.R. 414, Laddie J. stressed the "substantial reputation" of the claimant Formula One driver: "Mr Irvine has a property right in his goodwill which he can protect from unlicensed appropriation consisting of a false claim or suggestion of endorsement of a third party's goods or business". (p. 436)

26–14 **Damage.** *Irvine v. Talksport Ltd* [2002] EWHC 367; [2002] 2 All E.R. 414. Laddie J. noted that damage included not only harm to reputation but any dilution of the goodwill: "the law will not allow others to so use goodwill as to reduce, blur or diminish its exclusivity" (p. 426). He did, however, go on to stress that there is still a need to demonstrate a misrepresentation.

26–16 **Honest concurrent use and use of own name.** *Dawnday & Co. Ltd v. Cantor Fitzgerald Int* [2000] R.P.C. 669, CA. The licence given to the defendant to use the claimant's name during a joint venture was revoked when the defendant was no longer part of that venture.

26–18 **Proof of deception and confusion.** In *BP Amoco v. John Kelly Ltd* [2002] F.S.R. 5, CA Northern Ireland, the court accepted that where the parties used the same colour for the get-up of their petrol stations there might be customer confusion at the point of entering the petrol station. However at the time of sale a normally observant person would be aware of the defendants' use of its own logo and so no deception was likely. The court cited Lord Jauncey in the Jif

Lemon case, *Reckitt & Colman Products Ltd v. Borden Inc* [1990] R.P.C. 341, p. 417 "mere confusion which does not lead to a sale is not sufficient".

Instruments of deception. NOTE 10: The wider view of what constitutes an instrument of deception was applied by Bernard Livesey Q.C., sitting as a Deputy High Court judge in *EasyJet Airline Co. Ltd v. Dainty* [2002] F.S.R. 6.

26–19

CHAPTER 27

BREACH OF CONFIDENCE

	PARA.
1. General Principles	27–01
2. Information in respect of which an action for breach of confidence may arise	27–05
3. Where an obligation of confidence arises	27–08
4. Misuse	27–22
5. Parties	27–28
6. Defences	27–32
7. Remedies	27–44

1. GENERAL PRINCIPLES

The duty of confidence. NOTE 1. Add: Toulson and Phipps, *Confidentiality* (1996) is a particularly helpful work referred to with approval in *Susan Thomas v. Elizabeth Pearce* [2000] F.S.R. 718.   27–01

NOTE 5. Add: That TRIPS is not directly effective has been confirmed by the E.C.J. in *Parfums Christian Dior v. Evora* Case C–53/96 [1998] E.C.R. I–3603 and see also: *VOF Schieving-Nijstad v. Robert Groenveld* Case C–89/99 Opinion of Advocate General Jacobs [2001] E.T.M.R. 630.

Requirements for liability. TEXT. Add: The Court of Appeal has considered the question of whether detriment to the claimant is an essential ingredient of the cause of action (*R. v. Department of Health, ex p. Source Informatics Ltd* [2001] F.S.R. 74). However, that case did not turn on the question and it was suggested that it was possible to take a broad approach, applying the test of whether the confidant's conscience is troubled by disclosure (p. 86).   27–02

NOTE 8. Add: In *Cadbury Schweppes Inc. v. FBI Foods Ltd* [2000] F.S.R. 491, the Supreme Court of Canada articulated out a broad basis in equity for granting relief for breach of confidence, holding that there was sufficient detriment to the confider that the information was given to somebody he would rather it was not given to, even if the disclosure could not result in any positive harm.

NOTE 11. Add: *A. v. B (Copyright: Diary pages)* [2000] E.M.L.R. 1007.

NOTE 15. Add: As to the balance, see *Venables v. News Group Newspapers Ltd* [2001] 2 W.L.R. 1038, in which a worldwide injunction was granted preventing disclosure of information about the claimants, the child murderers of James Bulger but principally on the basis of their rights to life, such being in danger. Thus the confidentiality was preserved as an aid to a different, more fundamental right. See also *Ashworth Security Hospital v. MGN Ltd* [2001] F.S.R. 559 (extracts of diary of Ian Brady, the moors murderer, obtained from secure hospital's medical database and reported in the press).

Relationship with right to privacy. TEXT. Add: On an application for interlocutory relief, in a case involving unauthorised photographs of a celebrity wedding, the Court of Appeal indicated a cautious willingness to expand the law   27–03 of confidence, in the light of the Human Rights Act 1998, to create an effective right to privacy: *Douglas v. Hello! Ltd* [2001] 2 W.L.R. 992. Sedley L.J. suggested that a right of privacy as such may now exist saying that there was a powerfully arguable case that the claimants had "a right of privacy which English law will today recognise, and where appropriate, protect ... grounded in the equitable doctrine of breach of confidence, which accords recognition to the fact that the law has to protect not only those whose trust has been abused but those who find themselves subject to an unwanted intrusion into their personal lives".

Since *Douglas v. Hello! Ltd* [2001] 2 W.L.R. 992 there have been several cases where well-known persons have sought to keep the press from publishing matters concerning their private lives. Relief is more readily granted in respect of photographic representations and detailed accounts of private matters than of the bare facts. Further, the courts have in the main granted relief on the basis of breach of confidence rather than a free standing right of privacy (albeit as interpreted and applied in the light of Human Rights Act considerations).

The leading case, to which primary reference should now be made, is *A v. B plc* [2002] E.M.L.R. 371, [2002] EWCA Civ 337, where a footballer unsuccessfully sought to restrain a newspaper from publishing details of his extra marital affairs. The Court of Appeal gave general guidance with a view to rendering it unnecessary to cite extensive further authority.

The Court of Appeal recognised that a public figure was entitled to have his or her privacy protected in appropriate circumstances, but said that such a person must expect and accept that his or her actions will be more closely scrutinised by the media. If a person has courted public attention he or she may have less ground to object subsequent media intrusion.

As to the basis of the action for protecting privacy, the court said that "In the great majority of situations, if not all situations, where the protection of privacy is justified, relating to events after the Human Rights Act came into force, an action for breach of confidence now will, where this is appropriate, provide the necessary protection ... A duty of confidence will arise whenever the party subject to the duty is in a situation where he either knows or ought to know that the other person can reasonably expect his privacy to be protected ... The range of situations in which protection can be provided is therefore extensive. Obviously, the necessary relationship can be expressly created. More often its existence will have to be inferred from the facts. Whether duty of confidence does exist will depend on all the circumstances of the relationship between the parties at the time of the threatened or actual breach of the alleged duty of confidence."

The Court of Appeal sought to discourage extended argument concerning (a) the existence of a new cause of action in tort which protects privacy (b) whether there was an interest capable of being the subject of a claim to privacy—in most cases this would be obvious (c) whether there was a sufficient public interest in publication—if the public interest was involved, this would also be obvious. The court concluded by saying that in situations where the balance may not point clearly in either direction, interim relief should be refused.

On the facts, it was held that the extra-marital relationships of the sort in which A had engaged were not the categories of relationships which the court should be astute to protect when the other parties to them did not wish them to be confidential. It was unlikely that a permanent injunction would be granted and an interlocutory injunction would be an unjustified interference with the freedom of the press. See below as to the court's approach to the public interest.

Other examples: The following examples illustrate the kinds of case in which the courts have recently been prepared to intervene to restrain disclosure of certain private information:

- *Theakston v. MGN Ltd* [2002] E.M.L.R. 398. Details of sexual activity with prostitutes by well-known presenter of television programme for young people. *Held*: Injunction refused to restrain publication of story but granted to restrain publication of photographs. The claimant had courted publicity. He was also a presenter for youth and his assertion that publication might jeopardise his job pointed in favour of rather than against the public interest in publication. It was unlikely that a final injunction would be granted at trial. The court observed that it was impossible to invest with the protection of confidentiality all acts of physical intimacy regardless of circumstances. The court also referred to the "particularly intrusive" nature of photographs and the "high willingness" to prevent publication of them relying, *inter alia*, upon *Holden v. Express Newspapers* (an unreported decision of Eady J., June 7, 2001, in which the court had prevented publication of topless photographs of an actress in an hotel garden).

- *Campbell v. MGN* [2002] E.M.L.R. 617. A newspaper sought to publish photographs and details of a well-known model's attendance at narcotics anonymous meetings which had been obtained by covert photography. *Held*: Damages of £3,500 (including aggravated damages of £1000 in respect of a subsequent article "trashing her as a person") for breach of confidence and breach of s.13 of the Data Protection Act 1998 in respect of the publication of the photographs. The public interest was held to justify publishing the fact that the model had been misleadingly denying her drug addiction.

- *H v. Associated Newspapers Ltd*; *H v. N (a health authority)* [2002] E.M.L.R. 425. Healthcare worker disclosing HIV positive status confidentially to his employer, the health authority and seeking to restrain health authority from obtaining details of his private patients. Newspaper wishing to publish story and obtain information from which identity of healthcare worker might be identified. *Held*: an injunction would be granted to prevent indirect identification of the worker but not to prevent naming the speciality with which H was concerned.

2. INFORMATION IN RESPECT OF WHICH AN ACTION FOR BREACH OF CONFIDENCE MAY ARISE

The quality of confidence. NOTE 33. Add: *Mars v. Techknowledge* [2000] E.C.D.R. 99 (reverse engineering of a freely available product did not constitute a breach of confidence). 27–05

Need for identification of the confidential information. NOTE 40. Add: *Triomed (Proprietary) Limited v. Beecham Group Plc* [2001] F.S.R. 583, *SBJ Stephenson Ltd v. Mandy* [2000] F.S.R. 286. 27–07

27–07   CHAPTER 27—BREACH OF CONFIDENCE

NOTE 41. Add: *The Gadget Shop Ltd v. The Bug.Com Ltd* [2001] F.S.R. 383.

3. WHERE AN OBLIGATION OF CONFIDENCE ARISES

27–08   NOTE 45. Add: *Thomas (Susan) v. Pearce (Elizabeth) and another* [2000] F.S.R. 718. The first defendant was an ex-employee of the claimant who gave their client list to her new employer (the second defendant). The question that arose in this case was whether another employee of the second defendant owed a duty of confidence. Held: the correct test was whether that employee had acted honestly. More was required than careless, naïve or stupid behaviour. There had to be an awareness that the information was confidential, or a willingness to turn a blind eye.

In *A v. B plc* [2002] E.M.L.R. 21 the Court of Appeal said: "A duty of confidence will arise whenever the party subject to the duty is in a situation where he either knows or ought to know that the other person can reasonably expect his privacy to be protected . . . The range of situations in which protection can be provided is therefore extensive. Obviously, the necessary relationship can be expressly created. More often its existence will have to be inferred from the facts. Whether duty of confidence does exist will depend on all the circumstances of the relationship between the parties at the time of the threatened or actual breach of the alleged duty of confidence."

An obligation of confidence can be imposed after the information has been communicated provided that the information has not in the meantime been published and provided that the obligation of confidence is asserted and drawn to the attention of the person to whom the information is confided: *Surface Technology plc v. Young* [2002] F.S.R. 387. As to communication in circumstances giving rise to an obligation of confidence see also: *WB v. H Bauer Publishing Ltd* [2002] E.M.L.R. 145.

27–09   **By specific contractual provision.** NOTE 46. Add: *A. T. Poeton (Gloucester Plating) Ltd v. Horton (Michael Ikem)* [2001] F.S.R. 169 (A relevant factor in determining the extent to which the employer had impressed upon the employee the confidentiality of information was whether the employer's claim to confidentiality was much wider than was justified); *SBJ Stephenson Ltd v. Mandy* [2000] F.S.R. 286 (Clauses as to confidentiality would be binding only if they identified to the reader what information they would legitimately protect). An obligation of confidence can survive repudiation of the contract: *Campbell v. Frisbee* [2002] E.M.L.R. 656.

27–11   **Commercial relationships.** NOTE 52. Add: *Cadbury Schweppes Inc v. FBI Foods Ltd* (Supreme Court of Canada) [2000] F.S.R. 491 (Recipe for tomato juice and clam broth drink, although the information in this case was described by the court as "nothing very special").

NOTE 53. Add: *R. v. Department of Health, ex p. Source Informatics Ltd* now reported at [2001] F.S.R. 74.

27–12   **Rights against employees, directors and partners.** NOTE 69. Add: *Cadbury Schweppes Inc. v. FBI Foods Ltd* (Supreme Court of Canada) [2000] F.S.R. 491.

NOTE 72. Add: *SBJ Stephenson Ltd v. Mandy* [2000] F.S.R. 286 (Distinction between information deliberately learned and innocently carried in the employee's head could not be definite as a matter of principle on whether information protectable post employment).

Rights against employees, directors and partners. NOTE 74. Add: *A. T. Poeton (Gloucester Plating) Ltd v. Horton (Michael Ikem)* [2001] F.S.R. 169.   27–14

Professional advisors. NOTE 88. Add. A duty of confidence is owed in respect of a medico-legal report commissioned by the claimant from the defendant: *Cornelius v. De Taranto* [2002] E.M.L.R. 113 (CA).   27–16
TEXT. Add: *"This applies, for instance, to lawyers, bankers, accountants, doctors,* **hospitals**[88a]*, possibly clergymen, and even photographers."*
Add NOTE 88a: *Ashworth Security Hospital v. MGN Ltd* [2001] F.S.R. 559.

Family and personal relationships. NOTE 92. Add: *A v. B (Copyright: Diary pages)* [2000] E.M.L.R. 1007 (whether copied diary pages could be used in evidence in divorce proceedings).   27–17
By statutory provision. As to the application of the Data Protection Act 1998 see *Campbell v. MGN* [2002] E.M.L.R. 617 where the court awarded damages under s.13 of the Act in respect of the publication of photographs of a well-known model's attendance at narcotics anonymous meetings which had been obtained by covert photography. The case contains a helpful exposition of the law as it applies to "privacy" cases.   27–19

Other situations giving rise to an obligation of confidence. NOTE 7. Add: *Douglas v. Hello! Ltd* [2001] 2 W.L.R. 992. See also *R. (on the application of Ford) v. Press Complaints Commission* [2002] E.M.L.R. 95 where it was held that the Press Complaints Commission was entitled to consider that there was no reasonable expectation of privacy on the public beach where the applicant was photographed. Compare with *Theakston v. MGN Ltd* [2002] E.M.L.R. 398 and the reference there to the highly intrusive nature of photographs.   27–21
NOTE 9. Add: *R. v. Department of Health, ex p. Source Informatics Ltd* [2001] F.S.R. 74.

4. MISUSE

Involuntary or accidental use. NOTE 13. Add: *cf.* with the situation in which the confidant does not know the information is confidential *Thomas (Susan) v. Pearce (Elizabeth) and another* [2000] F.S.R. 718.   27–23

5. PARTIES

The claimant. TEXT. Add: The issue is not always clear-cut. For example a patient's medical records may give rise to a right of confidence owed to the hospital that compiles those records as well to the patient.[22A]   27–28
Add NOTE 22a: *Ashworth Security Hospital v. MGN Ltd* [2001] F.S.R. 559.
NOTE 27. Add: On assignment of confidential information, see *Buchanan v. Alba Diagnostics Ltd* [2000] R.P.C. 367 (Ct. of Session).

6. DEFENCES

27-36 **Disclosure of matters of real public concern.** Add to text: In *A v. B plc* [2002] E.M.L.R. 371, the Court of Appeal gave general guidance as to the circumstances in which considerations of public interest were likely to affect the grant or refusal of an interim injunction, saying: " ... even where there is no public interest in a particular publication interference with freedom of expression has to be justified. However, the existence of a public interest in publication strengthens the case for not granting an injunction. Again, in the majority of situations whether the public interest is involved or not will be obvious. In the grey area cases the public interest, if it exists, is unlikely to be decisive ... In the borderline case the application will usually be capable of being resolved without deciding whether there is a public interest in publication."

NOTE 46. Add: *Venables v. News Group Newspapers Ltd* [2001] 2 W.L.R. 1038.

27-37 Add to text: Confidential information concerning welfare of research laboratory animals proposed to be disclosed through the press and by publication of a book. *Held*: injunction granted with proviso permitting disclosure to relevant regulatory authorities: *Imutran Ltd v. Uncaged Campaigns Ltd* [2001] E.M.L.R. 563. This case reviewed the application of the principles in *Douglas v. Hello! Ltd supra* and *Hyde Park Residence Ltd v. Yelland* [2000] E.M.L.R. 363.

NOTE 50, Add: see also *H v. Associated Newspapers Ltd*; *H v. N (a health authority)* [2002] E.M.L.R. 425.

NOTE 57, Add: see also *Campbell v. Frisbee* [2002] E.M.L.R. 656: no public interest in publication by former employee of well-known model's alleged private sexual relations.

NOTE 59. Add: *cf. Douglas v. Hello! Ltd* [2001] 2 W.L.R. 992

27-43 **Freedom of expression and the effect of the Human Rights Act 1998.** Add text: In *Douglas v. Hello!* [2001] 2 W.L.R. 992, Brooke L.J. said that where there was a very strong likelihood that the claimant would establish that an Article 10(2) justification would succeed at trial, this represented a powerful reason why the court should exercise its discretion to grant an interim injunction to restrain publication, following *NWL Ltd v. Woods* [1979] I.C.R. 867. Sedley L.J., said that since the case affected the Convention right of freedom of expression, s.12 of the Human Rights Act required the court to have regard to Article 10. This could not consistently with s.3 and Article 17 have given the Article 10(1) right of free expression a presumptive priority over other rights. In fact the court was required to consider Article 10(2) along with 10(1). There was therefore a conflict between the right to privacy and the right to free expression which should be determined principally by considerations of proportionality. In *Venables v. News Group Newspapers Ltd* [2001] 2 W.L.R. 1038, the President of the Family Division, said that the exceptions in Article 10(2) were to be construed narrowly, and that the onus lay on those seeking restriction of publication to show that they were in accordance with the law, necessary in a democratic society to satisfy one of the strong and pressing social needs identified in Article 10(2), and proportionate to the legitimate aim pursued.

See on the impact of the Human Rights Act, s.12(3): *A v. B plc* [2002] E.M.L.R. 371 where the Court of Appeal gave general guidance on the approach stating that frequently what is required is not a technical approach to the law but a balancing of the facts. If the balance does not point clearly in either direction interim relief should be refused. See also: *Imutran Ltd v. Uncaged Campaigns Ltd* [2001] E.M.L.R. 21.

The Court will also have regard to the interests of a person who albeit not a journalist has information of a journalistic nature to impart: *Theakston v. MGN Ltd* [2002] E.M.L.R. 398.

7. REMEDIES

Injunction. NOTE 74. Add: *Sun Valley Foods Ltd v. John Philip Vincent* [2000] F.S.R. 825, *Triomed (Proprietary) Limited v. Beecham Group Plc* [2001] F.S.R. 583. **27–44**

NOTE 76. Add: In *Cadbury Schweppes Inc v. FBI Foods Ltd* [2000] F.S.R. 491, the Supreme Court of Canada refused final injunctive relief relying on the claimant's delay, the defendant's change of positioning the interim, the nature of the information and the ability to provide a remedy in damages. A permanent injunction would have inflicted damage on the defendant's business disproportionate to the legitimate interests of the claimant. The claimant was award loss of profits. The assessment should be tailored to give a broadly equitable result, without mathematical exactitude and taking a flexible and imaginative approach.

Damages or account of profits. TEXT. Add: The market value of the information is not the appropriate measure of damages, unless the confider is in the business of selling information (*Cadbury Schweppes Inc. v. FBI Foods Ltd* (Supreme Court of Canada) [2000] F.S.R. 491). **27–45**

TEXT. Add: In some circumstances, damages for injury to a claimant's feelings as a result of a breach of confidence may be awarded: *Cornelius v. de Taranto* [2001] E.M.L.R. 329.

The "springboard doctrine". TEXT. Add: It is not sufficient for the claimants merely to allege that the applicant has obtained a "springboard", since an important part of their case was to show the correct duration of such relief (*Triomed (Proprietary) Limited v. Beecham Group Plc* [2001] F.S.R. 583). It is also insufficient to show unlawful use of the information; the claimants must establish that the defendants have thereby gained an unfair competitive advantage which was continuing, and would continue in the future, at the date of the hearing (*Sun Valley Foods Ltd v. John Philip Vincent* [2000] F.S.R. 825). **27–46**

NOTE 96. Add: *Triomed (Proprietary) Limited v. Beecham Group Plc* [2001] F.S.R. 583.

CHAPTER 28

BREACH OF FIDUCIARY DUTY

	PARA.
1. Introduction	28–01
■ 2. The fiduciary principle	28–05
■ 3. Typical fiduciary duties	28–11
■ 6. Claim to equitable compensation for non-disclosure	28–21

1. Introduction

A broad definition. NOTE 3. Now Goff and Jones, *The Law of Restitution* (6th ed., 2002).   **28–01**

Developments in legal practice and theory. NOTE 10. Add: Simpson (ed.), *Professional Negligence and Liability* (LLP, 2000), paras 9.97–9.98, 1.36–1.37, 1.38 and 1.39.   **28–04**

NOTE 11. See now Cooke and Oughton, *The Common Law of Obligations* (3rd ed., Butterworths, 2000).

2. The Fiduciary Principle

Fiduciary obligation as determinant of fiduciary status. NOTE 13. Add: There have also been attempts to use a plea of breach of fiduciary duty to circumvent the Limitation Act 1980. These have met with little success. In *Compagnhia de Sequros Imperio v. Heath (R.E.B.X.) Ltd* [2001] 1 W.L.R. 112 the Court of Appeal held that the provisions of the Act relating to claims in contract and tort would apply by analogy to claims for breach of fiduciary duty, even if dishonesty were established.   **28–05**

Imposed by law. Add to the end of the paragraph: This is well illustrated by the Court of Appeal's decision in *Longstaff v. Birtles*.[31a] The claimants had sought advice from the defendant solicitors concerning the prospective purchase of a small hotel business. The transaction fell through and the solicitor-client relationship between the parties ended. Subsequently, the defendants suggested to the claimants that they might wish to purchase a partnership share in an existing small hotel business in which the defendants were partners. The defendants entered the partnership, which proved unsuccessful and was eventually dissolved. The claimants sued, alleging professional liability at common law through the defendants' failure to insist that they obtain independent legal advice before entering into the partnership. The trial judge dismissed the action, on the basis that, as the retainer had by that time ended, the defendants did not owe common law duties in contract and tort at the material time. Before the Court of Appeal, the claimants amended their pleadings to allege breach of fiduciary duty. The Court of Appeal allowed the appeal, holding that the defendants' failure to   **28–09**

[187]

28–09 CHAPTER 28—BREACH OF FIDUCIARY DUTY

insist that the claimants took independent legal advice prior to becoming involved with them in their business constituted a clear conflict of interest and, consequently, a breach of fiduciary duty. The Court of Appeal emphasised that there was a relationship of trust and confidence between the parties and that that relationship did not cease on the termination of the retainer in respect of the intended purchase of the first hotel business.

NOTE 31a. [2002] 1 W.L.R. 470.

3. TYPICAL FIDUCIARY DUTIES

28–12 **Personal gain.** NOTE 38. Add: Note *Fyffes Group Ltd v. Templeman* [2000] 2 Lloyd's Rep. 643, in which the court confirmed the potential for an action for equitable compensation against the briber in such circumstances (see para. 28–23, NOTE 67c, below).

6. CLAIM TO EQUITABLE COMPENSATION FOR NON-DISCLOSURE

28–23 *Bristol & West Building Society v. Mothew.* Add to the end of the paragraph: Subsequently, in *Nationwide Building Society v. Richard Grosse & Co.*,[67a] Blackburne J. held that the defendant solicitors had committed such a breach of their fiduciary duty to lender clients (the claimants) in a property transaction in which they acted also for the borrower. The claimants sued for losses sustained when it transpired that the mortgaged property had had its value inflated because, in a back to back transaction, it had been sold to the borrower on the same day it had been purchased by a company in which the borrower had shares. Blackburne J. accepted evidence that the defendants either knew that the borrower's conduct was suspect or recklessly failed to recognise that it might be. He concluded that they had, therefore, consciously preferred the interests of one client above the other and that they were, as a result, in breach of fiduciary duty to that client. Similarly, in *Leeds and Holbeck Building Society v. Arthur and Cole*,[67b] the court confirmed that, in order to establish the disloyalty and infidelity required to meet the "bad faith" requirement for there to be a breach of fiduciary duty in circumstances in which a solicitor was instructed by two parties to a transaction, the aggrieved party did not have to establish dishonesty. It was sufficient to show that the errant solicitor had consciously and intentionally preferred the interests of one client to another.[67c]

NOTE 67a. [1999] Lloyd's Rep. P.N. 348.

28–25 **Causation.** NOTE 67b. [2002] P.N.L.R. 4 (citing *Nationwide Building Society v. Balmer Radmore* [1999] Lloyd's Rep. P.N. 241).

NOTE 67c. *Cf.* Developments in the law relating to the imposition of liability, as constructive trustee, for assisting in breach of trust, which appear to have confirmed that the "bad faith" required in that context does equate to subjective dishonesty: *Royal Brunei Airlines Sdn. Bhd v. Tan* [1995] 2 A.C. 378; *Twinsectra Ltd v. Yardley* [2002] 2 W.L.R. 802. There is a similar basis of liability for assisting in breach of fiduciary duty, where subjective dishonesty is also required. Where, therefore, a fiduciary has (in breach of fiduciary duty: *Attorney-General for Hong Kong v. Reid* [1994] 1 A.C. 324, para. 28–12, *supra*) received a bribe, such a cause of action would allow the principal to claim compensation from the briber: *Consul Development Pty Ltd v. D.P.C. Estates Pty Ltd* [1975] 132 C.L.R. 373, confirmed and applied in *Fyffes Group Ltd v. Templeman* [2000] 2 Lloyd's Rep. 643; for comment on *Fyffes*, see Mitchell [2001] 117 L.Q.R. 207 and Handley [2001] 117 L.Q.R. 536.

NOTE 75. Add: *cf. Collins v. Brebner* [2000] Lloyd's Rep. P.N. 587, CA, in which a claimant who established a fraudulent breach of *trust* was still obliged to prove causation.

Loss after decline in market value. NOTE 76. Add: Note that the Australian High Court has expressly declined to follow the *South Australia* decision: *Kenny & Good Pty Ltd v. M.G.I.C.A. (1992) Ltd* [2000] Lloyd's Rep. P.N. 25.

Chapter 29

DAMAGES

	PARA.
■ 2. General Principles	29–02
■ 3. Damages for personal injuries	29–16
4. Death: Survival of causes of action	29–64
■ 5. Death as a cause of action	29–72
■ 6. Destruction of or damage to goods	29–108
■ 7. Recovery of costs of action	29–115
■ 8. Equitable damages	29–117
■ 9. Exemplary damages	29–121
■ 10. Restitutionary damages	29–133
■ 11. Appeals on quantum of damages	29–135

2. General Principles

Mitigation. Note 52. Add: Coote, "Damages, *The Liesbosch* and Impecuniosity" [2001] C.L.J. 511. **29–08**

(f) Certainty. Note 75. Add: In *Sharif v. Garrett & Co.* [2002] 3 All E.R. 195, **29–12** CA the claimant brought an action against a firm of solicitors seeking damages for the loss of a claim which had been struck out because a fair trial was no longer possible, due to the solicitors' delay. It was held that in those circumstances the judge should not seek to try the original issue himself in assessing the chance of success.

3. Damages for Personal Injuries

Medical and other expenses. Add after the second sentence: Where the **29–19—** claimant has been deprived of her womb because of the defendant's negligence **29–20** and therefore cannot have children, the costs of surrogacy are not recoverable, at least if the child would not be genetically linked to the claimant (ie where neither the baby nor the pregnancy would be hers): *Briody v. St Helens and Knowsley Health Authority* [2002] 2 W.L.R. 394, CA.

Note 16. Add after the second sentence: *Lowe v. Guise* [2002] 3 All E.R. 454, CA (recovery for the fact that the injury prevented the claimant carrying out as many hours of gratuitous care for his disabled brother as previously, the difference being made up by his mother).

Discount rate. Exercising his powers under section 1(1) of the Damages Act **29–28** 1996, the Lord Chancellor set a discount rate of 2.5 per cent as from June 28, 2001: see the Damages (Personal Injury) Order 2001, S.I. 2001 No. 2301. For the Lord Chancellor's reasons in setting that discount rate, see www.lcd.gov.uk/civil/discount.htm.

Although, by section 1(2) of the 1996 Act, a court may apply a different rate from that set if it is "more appropriate in the case in question", in *Warriner v. Warriner* [2002] 1 W.L.R. 1703 the Court of Appeal held that regard should be

29–28 CHAPTER 29—DAMAGES

had to the reasons given by the Lord Chancellor for setting the 2.5 per cent rate and that a departure should be made only if the case fell outside the categories considered by him. It was said that, in the interests of certainty, a departure from the rate set would therefore probably be rare. In the instant case, there was nothing unusual justifying a lower rate than 2.5 per cent.

29–31 **Effect of claimant's liability to tax.** NOTE 78. Add at the end of second sentence: Maugham and Peacock, "Taxing Damages Awards" (2000) 150 N.L.J. 1153.

29–34 **Receipts of social security benefits.** NOTE 95. Add after the reference to s.8: The compensation payable (and hence the amount from which there can be a deduction) includes interest awarded on the damages: *Griffiths v. British Coal Corporation* [2001] 1 W.L.R. 1493, CA.

29–53 **Damages for wrongful birth.** At the end of the third sentence, insert: In *Parkinson v. St James and Seacroft University Hospital NHS Trust* [2001] W.L.R. 376, a mother gave birth to a disabled boy following a negligent sterilisation operation. The Court of Appeal awarded her damages for the costs of providing for the child's special needs and care, attributable to his disability, but not the ordinary costs of his upbringing. *McFarlane v. Tayside Health Board* was distinguished because the child in that case was healthy; *Emeh v. Kensington Area Health Authority* [1958] Q.B. 1012 was regarded as impliedly overruled by *McFarlane* to the extent that *Emeh* had compensated all economic loss (including ordinary maintenance costs) consequent on having the disabled child. See also *Rand v. East Dorset Health Authority* (2000) 56 B.M.L.R. 39; *Hardman v. Amin* [2000] Lloyd's Med. Rep. 498; *Lee v. Taunton and Somerset NHS Trust* [2001] 1 F.L.R. 419.

Parkinson was followed in *Groom v. Selby* [2002] P.I.Q.R. P18, CA. See also Quick, "Damages for Wrongful Conception", (2002) Tort L.R. 5. In *Rees v. Darlington Memorial Hospital NHS Trust* [2002] 2 W.L.R. 1483 a sterilisation operation was negligently carried out on a mother disabled by severe visual impairment, who subsequently gave birth to a healthy child. The Court of Appeal, by a majority, applied the approach in *Parkinson* to hold that damages could be awarded for such of the upbringing costs as were attributable to *the mother's* disability. See Mahendra, "Left holding the baby—Act III", (2002) 152 N.L.J. 409.

NOTE 94. Add: In *Greenwich v. Irwin* [2001] 1 W.L.R. 1279, the Court of Appeal applied *McFarlane* to dismiss a claim for loss of earnings by a mother in giving up work to look after a healthy child born as a result of the defendant's negligence; and dismissed an argument that *McFarlane* infringed a mother's rights under Article 8 of the ECHR.

29–61 **Structured settlements.** NOTE 33. Add: For the impact of structured settlements on a claimant's entitlement to social security benefits, see Lewis, "Structured Settlements and State Benefits" (2001) 151 N.L.J. 1066.

4. DEATH: SURVIVAL OF CAUSES OF ACTION

29–65 **Statute.** Insert a NOTE 38a at the end of the first sentence:
[38a] Claims for compensation for discrimination contrary to the Race Relations

Act 1976, the Sex Discrimination Act 1975, or the Disability Discrimination Act 1995, are causes of action within section 1(1) of the Law Reform (Miscellaneous Provisions) Act 1934 and therefore survive for the benefit of the victim's estate: *Harris v. Lewisham and Guy's Mental Health Trust* [2000] 3 All E.R. 769, CA.

5. Death as a Cause of Action

Action under the Fatal Accidents Act. Note 85. Add: "Action" under s.2(3) of the 1976 Act is, by Human Rights Act 1998 ss.3(1) and 6(1), to be interpreted as "served process", so that the existence of a previous unserved writ does not bar a new claim brought within the limitation period: *Cachia v. Faluyi* [2001] 1 W.L.R. 1966, CA. — 29–73

Dependants. Note 99. Add: For an argument that the restrictive nature of the present list is contrary to the Human Rights Act 1998, see Davis, Gumbel and Witcomb, "A question of dependency" (2001) 151 N.L.J. 997. — 29–74

Multipliers. Note 77. Add: In *White v. ESAB Group (UK) Ltd* [2002] P.I.Q.R. Q6 Nelson J. would have preferred to calculate the multiplier from the date of trial rather than the date of death. However, he held that he was precluded from doing so by *Cookson v. Knowles* and *Graham v. Dodds*. The decision in *Corbett* was not applicable, since there were "no new facts of any significance". — 29–90

Pecuniary gains. Add after the second sentence: In *H v. S*, *The Times*, July 3, 2002, CA the approach in *Hunt v. Severs* was applied in such a case. Infant children were, following the death of their mother, receiving care from their father, who was not the tortfeasor and had not previously provided them with any care or support. It was held that this was a benefit to be disregarded under section 4, and that damages could only be awarded if they would be used to reimburse the voluntary carer for his services. This was to be done by means of a trust, which the court could act to enforce; *Bordin v. St Mary's NHS Trust* [2000] Lloyd's L.R. (Med.) 287 was disapproved. — 29–96

6. Destruction of or Damage to Goods

Damage to goods. Note 69. Add: Nor is it relevant that the claimant has no legal liability to pay the repair costs because they are covered by a consumer credit agreement that is unenforceable against the claimant: *Burdis v. Livsey* [2002] EWCA 510. — 29–110

7. Recovery of Costs of Action

Add: In *Union Discount Co Ltd v. Zoller* [2002] 1 W.L.R. 1517, CA the defendants brought an action in New York in breach of a contractual provision that all claims should be brought in England. The foreign court struck out the action in view of that provision. It made no adjudication as to costs; its rules did — 29–115 not provide for the recovery of costs except in exceptional circumstances. *Berry v. British Transport Commission* was applied to hold the claimants entitled to claim as damages, by an action for breach of contract, the costs incurred by them in the New York proceedings.

8. EQUITABLE DAMAGES

29–117—
29–119
Jurisdiction to award damages. See, generally, the interesting decision on equitable damages at first instance in *Marcic v. Thames Water Utilities Ltd (No. 2)* [2002] 2 W.L.R. 1000 (rvsd in part, without affecting equitable damages, by the Court of Appeal which held that the defendant was also liable in the (common law) tort of nuisance: [2002] 2 W.L.R. 1000). The claimant owned property that was regularly subject to flooding. In an action against the defendant, a sewerage undertaker, the claimant sought damages and a mandatory injunction ordering the defendant to implement a scheme to stop the flooding. Judge Richard Havery Q.C. held that the defendant was not liable in the (common law) tort of nuisance but was liable for the wrong of infringing the claimant's convention rights under Article 8 of the Human Rights Act 1988. However, he refused a mandatory injunction on the ground that this would require supervision by the court. As regards damages, he held that these should be awarded for both past and future wrongs. The claimant was therefore entitled to the difference between the value his property would have had if rendered non-susceptible to wrongful flooding minus its actual value. As regards the damages for future flooding caused by the future wrongs, these were being awarded in substitution for the mandatory injunction. The judge was satisfied that the defendant would commit the future wrongs because they intended not to carry out works necessary to remedy the nuisance. Pressed with the argument that he should follow the common law and refuse equitable damages for the future wrongs, Judge Havery Q.C. said, at 1008, "The common law would not afford the claimant just satisfaction. He would have to bring onerous proceedings from time to time to enforce his rights. Nor would he be able to recover any diminution in the value of his property caused by the prospect of future wrongs." In awarding equitable damages for future wrongs, he also rejected a novel argument that this would be contrary to the jurisprudence on the European Convention on Human Rights.

9. EXEMPLARY DAMAGES

29–121
Distinguished from aggravated damages. NOTE 33. Add after the reference to *Deane v. Ealing L.B.C.* [1993] I.C.R. 329: *Gbaja-Biamila v. DHL International (U.K.) Ltd* [2000] I.C.R. 730.

NOTE 41. Add: For the logical view that there can be no separate award of aggravated damages over and above a general award for injury to feelings, see *McConnell v. Police Authority for Northern Ireland* [1997] I.R.L.R. 625, 629; *Gbaja-Biamila v. DHL International (U.K.) Ltd* [2000] I.C.R. 730.

29–128
No exemplary damages prior to *Rookes v. Barnard*. In *Kuddus v. Chief Constable of Leicestershire* [2001] 2 W.L.R. 1789 the House of Lords has overruled *A.B. v. South West Water Services Ltd* [1983] Q.B. 507 so that there is no longer a requirement that the tort be one for which exemplary damages had

been awarded prior to 1964 (the so-called "cause of action" test). On the facts of the case this meant that, if the other requirements for the award of exemplary damages were satisfied, exemplary damages could be awarded for the tort of misfeasance in public office.

10. Restitutionary Damages

NOTE 89. Add: Edelman, *Gain-Based Damages* (2002).   **29–133**

11. Appeals on Quantum of Damages

Appeals from jury. NOTE 6. Add: In *Kiam v. MGN Ltd* [2002] 2 All E.R. 219, CA it was held (by a majority) that the "proper award" is "the highest award which the jury could reasonably have thought necessary", and that the jury's award should not be disturbed unless it substantially exceeds that sum. The bracket suggested by the judge was £40,000 to £80,000 and the jury awarded £105,000; this was not "out of all proportion to what could sensibly have been thought appropriate" given the deference to be shown to jury awards in defamation cases. Guidance on the use of brackets was also given.   **29–135**

CHAPTER 30

INJUNCTIONS

		PARA.
■	5. Interim injunctions	30–17
	6. Injunctions and declarations against the Crown	30–50

5. Interim Injunctions

Public Interest. Add: In *R. v. Secretary of State for Health, ex p. Imperial Tobacco Ltd* [2001] 1 All E.R. 50 the House of Lords left unresolved the question whether domestic law or community law applies to determine whether an interim injunction should be granted restraining the Secretary of State from making regulations to implement an allegedly invalid directive.   **30–21**

Freedom of speech. By s.12(4) of the Human Rights Act 1998, a court shall not grant an interim injunction restraining publication before trial (where this might affect the exercise of the Convention right to freedom of expression) "unless the court is satisfied that the applicant is likely to establish that publication shall not be allowed". In applying this test to grant interim injunctions for breach of confidence and breach of copyright, Sir Andrew Morritt V.-C. in *Imutran Ltd v. Uncaged Campaigns Ltd* [2001] 2 All E.R. 385 recognised that it imposed a slightly higher standard than that formulated in the *American Cyanamid* case.   **30–22**

Prerequisites. NOTE 91. Insert before last sentence: See also *Rowland v. Gulfpac Ltd* [1999] 1 Lloyd's Rep. Bank 86; *Papamichael v. National Westminster Bank plc* [2002] 1 Lloyd's Rep. 332.   **30–39**

Prerequisites. NOTE 96. Add: In *C Inc. plc v. L* (2001) 151 N.L.J. 535 it was held that a freezing injunction can be ordered in respect of assets owned by a third party (C) where A (the claimant) has a substantive right against B (the defendant) and B has a right against C which it can satisfy out of C's assets. In so doing, Aikens J. relied upon the decision of the High Court of Australia in *Cardile v. LED Builders Pty Ltd* [1999] H.C.A. 18.   **30–40**

NOTE 97. Add after fourth sentence: In *Yukong Line Ltd v. Rendsburg Investments Corporation* [2001] 2 Lloyd's Rep 113, CA it was held that a freezing injunction may still be granted where the defendant's assets cannot be specifically identified in the hands of the third party; and that in such circumstances the order may cover the general assets of the third party up to the amount of the defendant's assets apparently held.

Prerequisites. NOTE 13. Add after third sentence: A third party bank is entitled to an unfettered variation to realise and dispose of assets covered by the freezing order, in which it has a security interest, provided it is acting in good faith in the   **30–42**

ordinary course of its business: *Gangway Ltd v. Caledonian Park Investments (Jersey) Ltd* [2001] 2 Lloyd's Rep. 715.

30–43 **Effect on third party.** NOTE 18. Add: In *Bank of China v. NBM* [2002] 1 Lloyd's Rep. 506, the Court of Appeal upheld David Steel J.'s decision that that further proviso (the *Baltic* proviso) should be included in a world-wide freezing order unless inappropriate, rather than only included if appropriate.

30–44 **Ancillary relief.** NOTE 19. Add: A disclosure order is prima facie the normal provision where a freezing injunction is granted: *Motorola Credit Corporation v. Uzan, The Times,* July 10, 2002, CA.

NOTE 22. Add to the second sentence: *Den Norske Bank A.S.A. v. Antonators* [1999] Q.B. 271, CA.

30–46 **Claimant disclosure.** NOTE 30. Add: *Memory Corporation Plc v. Sidhu (No. 2)* [2001] 1 W.L.R. 1443, CA.

6. INJUNCTIONS AND DECLARATIONS AGAINST THE CROWN

30–50 **Injunctions and declarations against the Crown.** NOTE 38. Add: For the suggested use of an interim declaration under CPR, r. 25.1(1)(b) to resolve a bank's dilemma in not wishing to pay money out to a customer suspected of fraud, see *Bank of Scotland v. A Ltd* [2001] 1 W.L.R. 751, CA.

Chapter 32

DISCHARGE OF TORTS

	PARA.
■ 6. Res Judicata	32–24

6. Res Judicata

Principle of *res judicata*. NOTE 10. Add: *Friend v. Civil Aviation Authority* **32–24** [2001] 4 All E.R. 385, CA; Handley, "A Closer Look at *Henderson v. Henderson*" (2002) 118 L.Q.R. 397.

NOTE 12. Add: *Johnson v. Gore Wood & Co.* [2001] 2 W.L.R. 72, HL; *Steliou v. Compton* [2002] 2 All E.R. 737.

CHAPTER 33

LIMITATION

	PARA.
■ 1. Introduction	33–01
■ 2. Limitation of actions for damages for personal injuries and death	33–29
3. Limitation of actions for latent damage (other than personal injury) in the tort of negligence	33–55

1. Introduction

Periods of limitation. Add to the end of the first paragraph: By section 2 of the Limitation Act 1980 the general limitation period for an action founded on tort is six years from the date on which the cause of action accrued.[6a]   **33–01**

[6a] A claim for damages for breach of EC law is an action for a tort within section 2 of the 1980 Act: *R. v. Secretary of State for Transport, ex p. Factortame (No. 7), The Times*, January 10, 2001.

NOTE 1. Add: Law Commission Report, *Limitation of Actions*, Law Com. No. 270 (2001).

NOTE 10. Add to the list of cases: *Lloyds Bank plc v. Rogers* [1999] 3 E.G.L.R. 83, CA; *Stewart v. Engel* [2000] 1 W.L.R. 2268, CA; *Shade v. Compton Partnership* [2000] P.N.L.R. 218, CA; *Savings and Investment Bank Ltd v. Fincken, The Times*, November 15, 2002, CA; *Goode v. Martin* [2002] 1 W.L.R. 1828, CA; *Horne-Roberts v. SmithKline Beecham plc* [2002] 1 W.L.R. 1662, CA (on which it was held that section 35 applies to allow additions even after the expiry of the 10-year long-stop period in section 11A(3)).

Limitation and the court's power to strike out an action for want of prosecution. NOTE 30. Add: *Clark v. University of Lincolnshire and Humberside* [2001] 1 W.L.R. 1988, CA.   **33–04**

Parties in existence. Add: The effect of a direction under Companies Act 1985, section 651(1) that the dissolution of a company was void is that the company is treated as continuing to exist, and thus accrual of a cause of action occurs at the time at which it would have happened had there been no dissolution: *Smith v. White Knight Laundry Ltd* [2001] 3 All E.R. 862, CA.   **33–16**

Fraud, mistake and deliberate concealment: Limitation Act 1980, s.32. In *Brocklesby v. Armitage and Guest* [2001] 1 All E.R. 172, CA (applied by Laddie J. in *Liverpool Roman Catholic Archdiocese Trustees Incorporated v. Goldberg* [2001] 1 All E.R. 182), the Court of Appeal held that, for the purposes of section 32(1)(b), provided the defendant acted deliberately in committing the breach of duty, it did not matter that he did not know that, as a matter of law, he was committing a breach. In Morritt L.J.'s words, at 181, "[I]t is not necessary for the purpose of extending the limitation period pursuant to s. 32(1)(b) to the 1980 Act   **33–25**

to demonstrate that the fact relevant to the claimant's right of action has been deliberately concealed in any sense greater than that the commission of the act was deliberate in the sense of being intentional and that that act or omission, as the case may be, did involve a breach of duty whether or not the actor appreciated that legal consequence." So, for example in the *Goldberg* case, a defendant who (allegedly) negligently gave legal advice could be said to have deliberately concealed a fact relevant to the claimant's rights of action because the advice was given intentionally. For criticism see Nasir, "Deliberate Concealment and the Limitation Act" (2000) 150 N.L.J. 1526; Turner, "Rewriting Limitation" (2001) 151 N.L.J. 574. In *Cave v. Robinson Jarvis & Rolf* [2001] Lloyd's Rep. P.N. 290, the Court of Appeal considered itself bound to follow *Brocklesby*, albeit that Jonathan Parker L.J. said that he was "uneasy" about that decision.

On appeal to the House of Lords (*Cave v. Robinson Jarvis & Rolf* [2002] 2 W.L.R. 1107), the interpretation of section 32 adopted in *Brocklesby v. Armitage and Guest* [2001] 1 All E.R. 172 was rejected. It was held that section 32(2) operates only where the defendant knew he was committing, or intended to commit, a breach of duty; inadvertent want of care is insufficient. *Liverpool Roman Catholic Archdiocese Trustees Incorporated v. Goldberg* [2001] 1 All E.R. 182 was overruled and *Brocklesby* disapproved (Lord Scott emphasised that the result could be supported on an alternative ground given by Morritt L.J.).

2. LIMITATION OF ACTIONS FOR DAMAGES FOR PERSONAL INJURIES AND DEATH

33–30 **General.** NOTE 42. Add: See also *McDonnell v. Congregation of Christian Brothers Trustees* [2001] P.I.Q.R. P28.

33–33 **The knowledge of the claimant.** NOTE 57. Add: See also *Sniezek v. Bundy (Letchworth) Ltd* [2000] P.I.Q.R. P213, CA.

The discretion of the Court. Add: That is, there is no rule of law that the faults of the claimant's solicitor are to be attributed to the claimant.

NOTE 4. Insert at the start: *Das v. Ganju* [1999] Lloyd's Rep. Med. 198, CA; *Corbin v. Penfold Metallising Co. Ltd* [2000] Lloyd's Rep. Med. 247, CA; *Steeds v. Peverel Management Services Ltd, The Times*, May 16, 2001.

33–47 Amend the final sentence to read: However, under section 33(3)(f) the legal advice received (*e.g.* that, incorrectly, there is no cause of action) is to be taken into account in considering whether to exercise the discretion to disapply the limitation period.[6]

33–48 NOTE 11. Amend reference to *Long v. Tolchard & Sons Ltd* [2001] P.I.Q.R. P18, CA.

3. LIMITATION OF ACTIONS FOR LATENT DAMAGE (OTHER THAN PERSONAL INJURY) IN THE TORT OF NEGLIGENCE

33–58 **The Latent Damage Act 1986, ss.1–2.** NOTE 61. Add to the list of cases: *Oakes v. Hopcroft* (2000) 56 B.M.L.R. 136, CA.